Middle East Dilemma

Middle East Dilemma

THE POLITICS AND ECONOMICS OF ARAB INTEGRATION

Michael C. Hudson

Editor

Published in Association with the Center for the Contemporary Arab Studies, Georgetown Universtiy

Columbia University Press

NEW YORK

Columbia University Press

Publishers Since 1893

New York

Copyright © 1999 by The Center for Contemporary Arab
Studies, Georgetown University

Middle East dillema : the politics and economics of Arab
integration / Michael C. Hudson, editor.

p. cm.

Includes bibliographical references and index.

ISBN 0–231–11138–X (cloth), — ISBN 0–231–11139–8 (pbk.)

1. Arab countries—Economic integration. I. Hudson,
Michael C.

DS39.M53 1998   98–9823052

320.956'09'048—DC21   CIP

Library of Congress Cataloging-in-Publication Data

CIP

Casebound editions of Columbia University Press books are
printed on permanent and durable acid-free paper.
Printed in the United States of America

c 10 9 8 7 6 5 4 3 2 1

p 10 9 8 7 6 5 4 3 2 1

Contents

III Economic Integration

List of Tables and Figures

List of Figures

List of Tables

List of Contributors

The Contributors

Bahgat Korany is Professor of Political Science at the University of Montréal.

Paul Noble is Professor of Political Science at McGill University in Montréal.

Bassam Tibi is Georgia Augusta Professor of International Relations and Director at the University of Göttingen, Germany, and Robert Bosch Fellow at Harvard University, Weatherhead Center for International Affairs.

Mustapha Kamil Al-Sayyid is Professor of Political Science at Cairo University and the American University in Cairo.

Frauke Heard-Bey is a Senior Researcher at the Center for Research and Documentation, Abu Dhabi, United Arab Emirates.

Abdul Khaleq Abdulla is Associate Professor of Political Science at the University of the Emirates, Al-Ain, Abu Dhabi, United Arab Emirates.

I. William Zartman is the Jacob Blaustein Professor of International Organizations and Conflict Resolution, and Director of the African Studies and Conflict Management Programs at the Paul H. Nitze School of Advanced International Studies, Johns Hopkins University.

Robert D. Burrowes is Adjunct Professor at the Henry M. Jackson School of International Studies and Political Science, University of Washington, Seattle.

Roger Owen is the A.J. Meyer Professor of Middle East History in the History Department at Harvard University and Director of the Harvard Center for Middle Eastern Studies.

Yusif A. Sayigh is a former Professor of Economics at the American University of Beirut and an independent science consultant based in Beirut.

Antoine B. Zahlan is a former Professor of Physics at the American University of Beirut and an independent consultant based in London.

Nemat Shafik is Director for Private Sector and Finance, the Middle East and North Africa Region, of the World Bank in Washington.

Atif A. Kubursi is Professor of Economics at McMaster University in Hamilton, Ontario, Canada.

Michael C. Hudson is Professor of International Relations and the Seif Ghobash Professor of Arab Studies at Georgetown University.

Preface and Acknowledgments

This project took shape in the aftermath of one of the most disintegrative events in modern Arab history—the Gulf crisis and war of 1990–91. The faculty executive committee of the Georgetown University Center for Contemporary Arab Studies decided to organize a symposium in April 1992 to reflect not just on the immediate consequences of the war but on these other trends as well. The situation in the region continued to change dramatically. Of particular importance, the Arab-Israeli "peace process" began to unfold, with its own significant implications for Arab unity, security, coordination, and cooperation. We therefore decided to ask many of the symposium participants to revise their papers in light of these new developments and to commission some new ones. What we have tried to provide is a new assessment of Arab regional integration in its broadest sense. The assembled scholars bring to bear a variety of theoretical perspectives from political science, international relations, history, and economics. We have sought to analyze not only the Arab region as a whole, with attention to economic as well as security aspects, but also to investigate through case studies a number of subregional integrative experiments. We hope that we have exposed some of the complexities of contemporary Arab regional relationships—nearly a century after the Arab national movement began to take shape.

The views expressed are those of the individual authors and do not necessarily reflect the views of the Center for Contemporary Arab Studies. No particular rigor has been exercised in the transliteration of Arabic names and terms: familiar proper names (e.g., Nasser, not Abd al-Nasir) are rendered in conventional fashion, and terms generally conform to a simplified version of the system used in the *International Journal of Middle East Studies.*

As will be clear from the chapters to follow, the editor and several contributors owe an intellectual debt to the late Karl W. Deutsch for his work on national and regional integration. As his former student, I would like to dedicate this book to his memory.

The editor gratefully acknowledges the assistance of Maggy Zanger, publications director at the Center for Contemporary Arab Studies, for her many contributions; she was assisted by Martha Wenger and Blanca Madani; Dr. Ibrahim Ibrahim and Dr. Michael Simpson, co-chairs of the 1992 symposium; Vera Hudson, Vivian A. Auld, and Steve Johnson-Leva for technical assistance; my student research assistant Nadia Ziyadeh; the external evaluators engaged by the Center for Contemporary Arab Studies; and the two anonymous readers of the entire manuscript for Columbia University Press, whose comments were particularly valuable.

Michael C. Hudson
June 1998

Middle East Dilemma

Michael C. Hudson

Arab integration? One does not have to be an Orientalist of the kind that Edward Said so deftly deconstructed to wonder whether this is an oxymoron. So pervasive today is the image of Arab *disintegration* that we tend to forget that the dream of Arab nationalists has always been of the far more robust term, *unity*. But decades of bitter experience, often maliciously exaggerated by hostile commentators, has turned even dedicated Arab nationalists into cynics, and the quest for unity to many has become a bad joke. How many times have we heard that famous aphorism about the Holy Roman Empire adapted to the "United Arab Republic" (between Egypt and Syria from 1958 to 1961), to wit, that it was neither united, nor Arab, nor a republic.

The quest for Arab unity has been a dominant theme of Arab politics in the twentieth century. Recent developments, however, have rendered this dream more elusive than ever, as the Arab world's external dependence and internal fragmentation have increased. The weakening and eventual collapse of the Soviet Union as the patron of Arab nationalist regimes and the growing penetration of Israel and the United States into domestic Arab arenas clearly have dealt major setbacks to the pan-Arab project. Israel's humiliation of Gamal Abdel Nasser in the 1967 war was a body blow to Arabism. More recently the hollowness of Arab unity was devastatingly exposed when a U.S.-led international coalition that included several Arab states crushed Iraq, following Saddam Hussein's ill-conceived effort to swallow Kuwait. On the internal level as well the fragmentation of political culture in many parts of the Arab world has tarnished the ideological claims of Arab nationalists concerning the viability—even the reality—of an Arab *umma*, or community, from the Atlantic to the Gulf. Yet at the same time, new possibilities for subregional and functional integration have arisen. Despite the manifest failure of Arab nationalist ideologies and structures to unify a "nation" now divided into some twenty sovereign states (some more sovereign than others), there have been repeated efforts, subregional in scope, to achieve a measure of integration or at least coordination. Some have failed outright, such as the UAR; others, such as the Gulf Cooperation Council, the United Arab Emirates, the Arab Maghrib Union, and unified Yemen have endured, albeit with varying degrees of success. Economic development and social modernization have created a "logic of integration." For example, the explosive growth of oil revenues generated a vast movement of labor and remittances across borders. The Egyptian political sociologist Saad Eddin Ibrahim observed that the volume of transnational social transactions in the 1970s and 1980s reached unprecedented levels (Ibrahim 1982, 154–59) even as—ironically—the ideological and structural manifestations of *'uruba* (pan-Arabism) were decaying.

It is clear, therefore, that any serious assessment of the state of integration or disintegration in the Arab world today must take account of multiple, complex, and even contradictory trends. Only by doing so can one begin to unravel what I once called "the integration puzzle in Arab politics": despite failure after failure on the political level, the ideal of unity is still there (Hudson 1979, 81 ff). Indeed, the recent global and regional upheavals have if anything underlined the costs of disunity. The inability to mobilize the considerable collective human and material resources of a "nation" of more than 200 million people accounts in part for the powerlessness which Arab intellectuals like Edward Said (1996) see as the fundamental problem facing the Arabs today: "Whereas Israel can roll its tanks across borders, its air force can bomb civilians at will, its propagandists can fill the Western media with their lies about self-defense and the war against terrorism, the Arabs for their part can only bleat out squeaks of anger."

It is not our intention in this book to argue the political case for or against Arab unity. Instead, our interest is twofold: primarily, to assess as carefully as possible the state of regional integration and cooperation in the Arab world in light of the major developments of the past decades; and secondarily, to explain why integration in general, let alone unity, has proven so elusive a goal. I propose to begin by raising some conceptual and theoretical questions. How do we define integration, and what does international relations theory tell us about integration processes and the behavior of states in a complex, uncertain, and insecure environment? Integration theorists, structural realists, and liberal institutionalists offer different approaches. Then, turning from theory to behavior, I review the historical trajectory of the Arab unity movement, first in its ideological aspect through a summary of Arab nationalist thought and political activity, second in its formal institutional aspect through a discussion of the League of Arab States, and third with some comments on the meaning of the second Gulf war for Arab integration. I conclude with some provisional thoughts on why unity (defined as fusion) has failed but why other forms of integration may eventually succeed.

Theoretical Issues

What do we mean by "integration" in general and Arab integration in particular? Like most social concepts, this term has numerous definitions which are context-dependent. Within a given society and political order, such as the United States, we may speak of "racial integration" as a process through which a culturally distinctive subcommunity becomes accepted as a part of the larger community—subject on an equal basis to its various institutional rules and accessible to its rights. While a given minority does not necessarily lose its distinctive cultural character—the "melting pot" metaphor is perhaps misleading (Glazer and Moynihan, 1970)—it does partake, on a nondiscriminatory basis, of the rights and obligations of the citizenry, or the nation. Were the Arab world in fact a single society and political order the "integration problematic" would most likely center on *gemeinschaft* questions of Arab "identity" and on the problems of ethnic and sectarian discrimination. The research agenda would be similar in many ways to the study of racial integration in the U.S., with a focus on the legal system and on the nature of social divisions (see Horowitz 1985). To what extent are Kurds, Berbers, blacks, Christians, Jews, and non-Arabic-speakers integrated, or integratable, into this putative single "Arab nation"? This is undoubtedly one of the most fundamental problems in the politics of each of the twenty-two members of the League of Arab states. But, while it is ultimately germane to our concerns, inasmuch as the nature of "imagined communities" (Anderson 1983, 1991) within sovereign boundaries affect a state's external policies, this is not the kind of integration that we are primarily addressing in this book.

The integration that we are concerned with is rooted in a different context: not one society or political order, but many. Our research question is the same as the Arab nationalists' ideological quest: what are the factors promoting—and inhibiting, if not actually preventing—integration of some kind between these twenty-two separate states? *E pluribus unum*: is it possible? is it likely? Most readers of the chapters that follow will answer "no"—a single, fused, unified political order is, at best, highly improbable and extremely unlikely. Indeed, it is so unlikely that it makes an uninteresting research subject. But to define integration in such purist terms runs the risk of our missing, or misunderstanding, one of the main factors contributing to the chronic tension and instability in the Middle East region. However elusive ideal integration (i.e., unity through fusion) may be for the Arabs, the *impulse to integrate* has roiled regional politics ever since the beginnings of the modern Middle East state system after World War I. And it continues to do so, even though (as Malik Mufti 1996, recently has demonstrated) most fusion-style integration efforts have failed. These failures in turn may well have eroded the widespread but uninstitutionalized popular enthusiasm for unity that drove Arab ruling elites (sometimes against their better judgment (as Mufti, 87–98, argues) into fusionist projects. Yet if the domestic, *gemeinschaft*, "sociological" drives toward unity have flagged, the externally driven, rationalistic imperatives for Arab unity have never been stronger. In the Arab *mashriq* (east), Israel is the military and economic hegemon; to the north and farther east Turkey and Iran pose their own agendas. In the Arab *maghrib* (west) and all along the southern Mediterranean the divided Arab countries face the growing economic leverage of an increasingly unified European community. And overarching the entire Arab world, east and west, is the world's only global power, the United States, pursuing policies that many (if not most) Arabs regard as hostile to their national, cultural, and material aspirations. Divisions create vulnerabilities which generate the contempt and ridicule so regularly heaped upon the Arabs at the dawn of the twenty-first century.

If integration defined as fusion is unrealizable, are there forms of integration short of that ideal that constitute a more attainable goal? The discipline of international relations has much to say on this point, providing us with a spectrum of inter-state relationships ranging from the austere images of realist theory—with its focus on the balance of power, insecurity, survival, and (the inevitability of) war—to the "softer" formulations of integration theorists, "regime" theorists, interdependency theorists, liberal institutionalists, and constructivists (see, among others, Waltz 1979, Haas 1964, Krasner 1983, Keohane and Nye 1975, and Lapid and Kratochwil 1996). I shall return to some of these applications at the end of this chapter to see if they throw any new light on the current *disintegrated* condition of the Arab regional system. Suffice it to point out here that the discipline provides us with some helpful varieties of "integration," some of which would seem to have considerable relevance to the Arab world.

If the Arab state "system" (and I use the term advisedly) is far from ready for fusion into a single unified nation-state, it is also quite far removed from a "pure" balance-of-power (or balance-of-threat) system (neorealists such as Walt 1987, to the contrary notwithstanding), characterized by states relating to each other essentially through the dark calculus of the security dilemma. Somewhere in the middle are relationships that may be characterized (at particular times and in particular places) by *coordination* of security and economic policies, indicative of a certain interdependency in policymaking; or by *cooperation*, in which governments, without encroaching on their sovereignty, engage in common pursuits, through treaties or alliances of varying duration.

Four decades ago the distinguished political scientist Karl W. Deutsch and a group of colleagues undertook an imaginative historical-comparative study of integration experiments in the North Atlantic area (Deutsch, et al, 1957). While their analysis focused on a region different in so many ways from the one under consideration here, their typology, I believe, can be fruitfully applied to the Arab world. Its two key components were *integration* and *amalgamation*. By integration was meant ". . . the attainment, within a territory, of a 'sense of community' and of institutions and practices strong enough and widespread enough to assure, for a 'long' time, dependable expectations of 'peaceful change' among its population" (Deutsch, 5). An "integrated" group of people within a given territory were said to form a "security-community." By amalgamation was meant "the formal merger of two or more previously independent units into a single larger unit, with some type of common government after amalgamation" (Deutsch, p. 6). The "common government" could be either unitary or federal. Dichotomizing these two variables yielded a four-fold typology (see Figure 1–1).

The "amalgamated security community" (Cell 2) encompasses the Arab nationalists' dream. The current reality, of course, is quite different. There is no amalgamation in this agglomeration of twenty-two independent states—the Arab League, as we shall see, protects rather than erodes these sovereignties. For the same reason, Cell 4 ("amalgamated, but not a security-community") is also ruled out as a valid characterization of the region. Whether there is integration, with its attendant "sense of community," is a much more complicated question, and we immediately see the shortcomings of dichotomized variables and of "snapshot" as opposed to "trend" conceptualizations. Arguably, the myriad processes of societal interaction that have burgeoned across the region over the past several decades constitute a powerful (but under-studied) engine of regional integration. Driven by economic growth and the development of communications and transportation infrastructure, there may be a great deal more sociocultural integration than the naive Arab nationalists of the 1940s and 1950s ever imagined. So argues Saad Eddin Ibrahim (1982, 156): "the Arab world is more closely linked socioeconomically at present than at any time in its modern history." The problem is that interdependence does not lead directly to the growth of political community; and there are obviously many competing com-

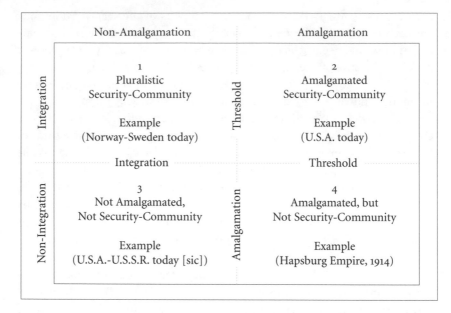

	Non-Amalgamation		Amalgamation
	1		2
Integration	Pluralistic Security-Community	Threshold	Amalgamated Security-Community
	Example (Norway-Sweden today)		Example (U.S.A. today)
	Integration		Threshold
	3		4
Non-Integration	Not Amalgamated, Not Security-Community	Amalgamation	Amalgamated, but Not Security-Community
	Example (U.S.A.-U.S.S.R. today [sic])		Example (Hapsburg Empire, 1914)

FIGURE 1.1   Deutsch's Typology of Political Communities

munal and public identities and loyalties across this far-flung region stretching from the Atlantic to the Gulf.

But the Arab region as a whole does not fit comfortably into Cell 3 ("not amalgamated, not a security-community") either: there are too many cultural and even structural commonalities to challenge the austere classical realist paradigm of states as atoms (albeit rational and security-conscious!) bouncing about in a medium of "anarchy." Cell 3 captures neither the warmth nor the heat of interstate relations in this complex, interpenetrated environment of ill-formed states and semi-realized community(ies). In the Arab world proximity and familiarity breed many things—not just contempt, but also common aspirations and almost paranoic rivalries. Can we then safely classify the Arab region in the only remaining Cell—1—the "pluralistic security-community," i.e., one that is "integrated" while maintaining the legal independence of separate governments? It would take a Procrustean effort to do so, considering that Deutsch and his colleagues suggest the relationship between Norway and Sweden or between the U.S. and Canada as examples (from the North Atlantic area) of the type. Anyone who has had the trying experience of crossing borders in the Arab world will not be reminded of such cases. Yet the differences may not be as vast as they first appear to be. Many Arab countries allow citizens from specified other Arab countries to enter without the need of a passport or visa—

an identity card will do. The collective self-defense articles in the Arab League charter in theory indicate a "security community," although in practice these mechanisms have languished. The Arab League is no NATO, although it was intended to serve as such in the confrontation with Israel. One might observe, perhaps optimistically, that the Arab region is a potential pluralistic security-community, or a half-formed one. The difficulty, in terms of Deutsch's concept, is that while there may indeed be "a sense of community," it is not buttressed by sufficiently strong institutions or practices (on either the domestic or regional levels) to assure over the long haul "dependable expectations of peaceful change." It is in this respect that the Arab world differs so markedly from the European community, as Tibi rightly argues in chapter 4 below.

It is worth noting, however, that the integration/amalgamation condition in certain parts of the Arab region is (at times, at least) more positive than for the Arab world as a whole. "Outbreaks of integration" (though almost never at the amalgamated security-community level) have occurred, some of them recently. The unification of the two Yemen states in 1990 (discussed below by Burrowes), though precarious, is a rare example of a fusion (Type 2) kind of integration. One might conceivably place the United Arab Emirates federation of 1971 (see Heard-Bey, chapter 6 below) in this category as well, although the seven emirates that federated had not been previously independent of British domination. The one Arab subregion that can make a reasonably robust claim to "pluralistic security-community" (Type 1) status, is the Gulf Cooperation Council, described by Abdalla in Ch. 7; despite its manifest weaknesses, especially in promoting collective security, the GCC has displayed a certain institutional durability underpinned by quite distinctive sociocultural integration. Other dyadic relationships have at times taken on Type 1 characteristics: for example, Egypt-Sudan, Egypt-Libya, Saudi Arabia-Yemen, Syria-Lebanon, and Jordan-Palestine. In all these cases, one observes to some degree what Keohane and Nye call "policy interdependence"—"the extent to which decisions taken by actors in one part of a system affect (intentionally or unintentionally) other actors' policy decisions elsewhere in the system" (Keohane and Nye 1975, p. 371). *Wahda* (unity) in the traditional sense may be a chimera, but *takamal* (integration), *tansiq* (coordination), and *ta'awun* (cooperation) are not as scarce as the daily newspaper headlines might lead one to expect.

Decline of the Arab Unity Project

July 14, 1958—Jubilant crowds of young men are surging through the Hamidiyyah *suk* in Damascus. One of them explains breathlessly to an

American student standing nearby that the Western puppet monarchy in neighboring Iraq has just been overthrown. Another obstacle to Arab unity has given way. Soon, he exults, Iraq will be added to the newly minted union between Syria and Egypt (just five months old), and it won't be long before the traitor King in Jordan will go the way of his slaughtered cousins in Baghdad. And to the west in Lebanon it is only a matter of time before the (Arab) nationalists triumph in their civil war against the pro-Western regime in Beirut. Anyone introduced to Arab politics at that particular moment, as I was, carries a lasting image of nationalist enthusiasm that seemed destined to erase "artificial" borders and unify a national community too long and wrongly divided. But today Arab unity appears to have been consigned to the dustbin of history, and even unity's poor relations—integration, coordination, and cooperation (as Bassam Tibi describes them in chapter 4 below)—seem at best fragile, limited, and cosmetic.

Arab nationalism has had two faces. One is overtly "political"—a movement replete with ideology, leaders, and parties. The other is "structural"—a number of formal institutions, of which the Arab League and the periodic summit meetings of Arab heads of state are preeminent—to organize the existing sovereign Arab governments for regional integration, collective security, and a unified position in global politics.

The Political Dimension

As a political movement, Arab nationalism's ascendency coincided with the farthest extension and then the decline of European imperialism. Among its historical precursors (in the eyes of nationalist writers) were the development of a modern state in Egypt by Muhammad Ali, the rise of Wahhabism in Arabia, the Syrian and Lebanese literary *nahda* (renaissance), the Islamic modernist movement of Muhammad Abdu in Egypt, various pan-Arab conferences (1913, 1937, 1939), the Arab Revolt of 1915, and the Palestinian revolt of 1936–39 (Cecil Hourani, quoted in Salman 1986, p. 118). Primarily centered in the *mashriq*, the idea of Arab unity resonated most deeply after Britain and France filled the vacuum left by the defunct Ottoman Turkish empire after World War I. By the end of World War II, with the gradual retreat of Britain and France as imperialist powers, the idea had taken on concrete political form.

The rise of the Ba'th (Arab Socialist Renaissance Party) in Syria, the Arab Nationalists' Movement in Lebanon, and Nasserism in Egypt signaled the spread of the idea beyond the salon and the coffee house to the "street." If the Ba'th and the ANM sought to mobilize the masses through semi-clandestine cells, Nasser used the mass media to project a heroic image of himself as the spearhead of Arab unity. For the Arabs, the trauma of the establishment of Israel lent further impetus to the unity project. The year 1958 perhaps marks its apogee. In February of that year Egypt and Syria formed the United Arab Republic and a few weeks later the Kingdom of Yemen joined them to create the United Arab States. Scarcely was the ink dry on the UAR Unification Proclamation when Jordan and Iraq, each ruled by branches of the Hashemite family, created their own "Arab Union." In a book entitled *Arab Unity: Hope and Fulfillment* the Palestinian writer Fayez Sayegh saw the events of "the fateful month" of February 1958 as a dramatic step forward.

> For the first time in centuries, Arab forces have now appeared on the stage of Arab life ready and able to remake Arab history . . . No longer is Arab society content with reciting a script written by someone else . . . At long last, the Arabs have now emerged, in their own homeland, as the makers of their own history. . . . (Sayegh 1958, xiv–xv).

Unfortunately for Arab nationalists, the course was soon to turn downhill. Three years later the UAR split apart (see Al-Sayyid, chapter 5 below). Even though the Ba'th was able to seize power in Syria and Iraq in the 1960s, the two leaderships fell quickly into bitter rivalry—an ironic twist on their ideology of unity. Ba'thists fell out with Nasserists. Nasser and Nasserism were weakened by Egypt's imbroglio in trying to sustain the republican revolution in Yemen, and then by Egypt's catastrophic defeat at the hands of Israel in the 1967 Six-Day War. Monarchies (like Jordan and Saudi Arabia) that the unionists had labeled as reactionary, tribal, Western-dominated puppet regimes successfully resisted the unity wave. And by the mid-1970s it was becoming clear that the Soviet Union's will and ability to back the Arab nationalist camp was declining. With the Ba'th increasingly parochial, the ANM transformed into a left-wing Palestinian nationalist organization, and the deceased Nasser replaced by the pro-American, "Egypt first" leader Anwar Sadat, the unity project was but a shadow of its former self.

Egypt's defection from the ranks of Arab solidarity at Camp David was followed just over a decade later by the Iraqi invasion of Kuwait and "Desert Storm," in which some Arab regimes joined the Western coalition against Iraq to the evident outrage of other regimes and a sizeable part of Arab public opinion. Then, after the United States cajoled the key Arab parties and Israel into a "comprehensive" conference at Madrid, inaugurating what would become known as "the peace process," the Arab parties who had solemnly pledged to pursue a common strategy soon fell apart. At Oslo the Palestinians defected, enticed by the possibility of a separate deal with Israel, and the Jordanians hastily followed suit. Syria was left on its own to negotiate with Israel. Once again the Arabs were divided. As hostile sentiment mounted across the Arab world at what some saw as a new era of foreign (U.S. and Israeli) domination, most of the old Arab nationalist constituency looked with disgust on the failed vehicles of their unity aspirations: neither the ideological programs nor the organizational capacities of the Ba'thists, the Arab Nationalists, or the Nasserists had come close to achieving the goal of Arab unity. And so some began turning to Islamist symbols, leaders, and parties.

The Structural Dimension

The "structural" dimension of the contemporary Arab unity project has been embodied primarily in the League of Arab States and the "institution" of Arab summit meetings. But fusion-style unity is not the kind of integration that these structures were intended to promote. To be sure, the Alexandria Protocol of October 1944, which paved the way for the Arab League Pact several months later, envisaged consolidating the ties that bind the Arab countries and enhancing coordination and cooperation, but it also called for protecting the independence and sovereignty of the member states (text in Hurewitz 1979, 2, 732–34). The Arab League Pact of March 1945 further emphasized state sovereignty. According to one student, "whereas the Protocol had emphasized Arab unity and envisaged ultimate surrender of sovereignty, the Pact stressed the independence and sovereignty of member states" (Salman 1986, p. 115).

Created by the then seven sovereign Arab states (Syria, Trans-Jordan, Iraq, Saudi Arabia, Lebanon, Egypt, and Yemen), the Arab League was intended to strengthen relations between the Arab states "upon a basis of respect for the independence and sovereignty of these states" (text in Macdonald 1965, 319–26). It was supposed to promote cooperation in economic and financial affairs, communications, cultural affairs, nationality, passports and extradition matters, social affairs, and health problems. Articles 5 and 6 of the Charter prohibited any resort to force for resolving disputes among member-states, and attacked member-states were given the right to appeal to the League Council to take measures—by unanimous decision (excluding the aggressor member-state)—to repulse the aggression. In 1950 the Arab League member-states signed a "joint defense and economic cooperation treaty" providing for collective security measures including a Joint Defense Council and a Permanent Military Commission (text in Macdonald, 327–33).

By 1974, as other Arab countries became independent of European control, membership in the League had risen to twenty-two, including Somalia and Mauritania as well as Palestine (despite its non-state status). With the unification of the Yemen Arab Republic and the People's Democratic Republic of Yemen in 1993, Arab League membership dropped by one, but with the improbable addition of the Federal Islamic Republic of the Comoro Islands (between Mozambique and Madagascar) the same year it remains at twenty-two. Today the Arab League also is an umbrella organization for seventeen specialized agencies, dealing with functions such as maritime transport, civil aviation, economic and social development, educational, cultural, and scientific affairs, monetary policy, broadcasting, and telecommunications. There are also fifteen permanent committees for matters concerning (among other things) oil, human rights, and women (Salafy 1989, 4–15). But the League itself is a very small organization: it has only around 400 employees in its secretariat and offices around the world, and 200–300 local employees in the Cairo headquarters (Khaled Abdalla 1997). By comparison, the main organs of the European Union (in Brussels alone) employ over 20,000 people—quite a challenge for those who propose the EU as a model for future Arab institutional integration.

While the League's specialized agencies and permanent committees have contributed to functional integration within the Arab world, the League itself has largely failed on the political level. Its efforts to foster economic integration have been generally ineffectual, and its military and collective security functions never materialized. It has been more successful in organizing a common Arab stand on international issues than it has been in regulating inter-Arab disputes. By far the most important of the former has been the question of Palestine and Israel. The League grew up, as it were, with the Palestine problem, and for many years it helped organize a solid consensus opposing Israel's establishment and subsequent expansion. It organized and maintained the Arab Boycott Office and promoted the cause of the Palestinian refugees.

But, on the negative side of the ledger, it never succeeded in organizing any effective collective defense or deterrent against Israel, let alone a negotiated solution. And it was incapable of preventing Egypt's defection from the common Arab stand after the Camp David negotiations in 1978 and the Egypt-Israel peace treaty in 1979. Subsequently, it played no role in the U.S.-sponsored "peace process" that began at Madrid in 1991 and led eventually to bilateral Palestinian-Israeli and Jordanian-Israeli agreements and the development of contacts between Israel and several other Arab states. On the inter-Arab stage, the League was even more ineffectual. Arab League mediation was attempted in a number of crises, such as the Lebanese civil war of 1958, the Jordan-Palestinian crisis of 1970, the conflicts between North and South Yemen, and the early stage of the 1975–1989 Lebanese civil war (Hudson 1995, 130–34, 137–39). But in none of these cases was the mediation decisive in resolving the conflict. And in the greatest modern crisis in inter-Arab relations—the Iraqi invasion of Kuwait in 1990—the League was even less in evidence than it had been during the Iraq-Kuwait crisis at the time of Kuwait's independence in 1962.

Such impotence should hardly be surprising; the League lacks the legal and political authority to override the sovereign autonomy of the member-states. The Secretary-General's powers are essentially managerial: he is appointed only at the level of Ambassador by a two-thirds vote of the League Council, and his only specifically designated authority is drafting the budget (Articles 13–14). Most important, the preamble of the League Charter makes it clear that the sovereignty and independence of the member-states is inviolable. Indeed, from the beginning, Lebanon and other small states insisted on the rule of unanimous decision, reflecting their apprehension at the possibility of being dominated, if not eventually swallowed, by larger states. These apprehensions proved to have some foundation, inasmuch as the largest one, Egypt, was consistently the driving force in the League, supplying its secretary-general, its site, and much of its bureaucracy over the ensuing half century years, with the exception of the post-Camp David period of Egyptian isolation. During the Nasser period in particular, many members saw the League as an instrument of Egyptian expansionism rather than as a neutral and evenhanded instrument for inter-Arab conflict resolution. The price of unanimity has been paralysis and irrelevance. Commenting on the League's fiftieth anniversary ceremony in March 1995, a former Arab League official, Clovis Maksoud, observed sadly that only one Arab head of state—President Mubarak of Egypt—bothered to attend (Maksoud 1995, 589). On this occasion the League Council, recognizing the organization's enfeebled condition, proposed a "pact for security and Arab cooperation" that would have created an Arab court of justice, greater powers for the secretary-general, and the creation of an "Arab peace-keeping force." The June 1996 Arab summit meeting in Cairo gave general approval and instructed the Arab League secretariat to develop the plan, but a year later the plan was still awaiting approval from the member governments.

Other than the Arab League, the main institutional approach to Arab integration has been the periodic summit meetings of Arab heads of state. The first Arab summit, convened by Nasser, was held in Cairo in January 1964 to discuss Israel's plans to divert Jordan River waters; it also created the Palestine Liberation Organization. As of June 1996, there had been nineteen Arab summit meetings. Summitry had at least one advantage over the Arab League structure: the real powers were represented. But summit meetings, in general, could not erase the balance-of-power and ideological cleavages inherent in the Arab state system. While certain summits may have been useful to display a common (but often short-lived) unity in response to a particular crisis, such as the Khartoum summit of 1967 in which the Arab states articulated their rejection of Israel's conquests in the Six-Day War, they also frequently highlighted inter-Arab divisions. Immediately following Iraq's invasion of Kuwait in August 1990, a hastily called summit in Cairo exposed the most bitter quarrel since the establishment of the Arab League, instead of healing it: just twelve of the twenty-one members voted for a resolution to condemn Iraq and to send troops to join the U.S.-led international coalition to liberate Kuwait. The others either rejected the resolution, abstained, expressed reservations, or were absent. So intense were the passions that members of the Iraqi delegation reportedly threw plates of food at the Kuwaitis, and the Kuwaiti foreign minister collapsed (Kifner 1990, 6). As Ghassan Salamé has observed, poor personal relations between Arab heads of state, who sometimes vilify each other in public, can seriously hinder the success of a summit (Salamé 1988, 274).

Instead of healing inter-Arab conflicts, summit meetings are more likely to be infected by them. It was impossible for the Arab heads of state to convene a summit between 1990 and 1996—a period of enormous change in the regional system. The very factors necessitating a meeting made it impossible to hold one: the damage from the Iraq-Kuwait crisis and the breakthroughs in the Arab-Israeli peace process—from Madrid to Oslo and beyond. It was only the election of a hard-line government in Israel that enabled Arab leaders to assemble once again in Cairo in June 1996 to voice a "unified" stand reminiscent of the Nasserite era. Instead of shaping a more coherent Arab order, the institution of the "Arab summit meeting" thus far has mainly reflected the security dilemmas, rivalries, and personal animosities characteristic of what a classical international relations theorist might describe as a quasi-anarchic "self-help" system (Waltz 1979, ch. 6), in which the "selfish" rationalism of state actors generally prevails over "collective rationality" despite the latter's promise of greater benefits for each and all.

Lessons of the Second Gulf War

The Gulf crisis of 1990–91, in the eyes of many analysts, marks the final collapse of the Arab unity project. Apart from occasional raids and border skirmishes, inter-Arab warfare in the post-World War I era has been almost nonexistent. But in August 1990 Iraq launched a massive invasion of Kuwait, and the U.S.-led international coalition (including Arab members), which drove the Iraqis out and imposed on them punishing sanctions of long duration, was said by many observers at the time to have marked—once and for all—the end of

Arabism. Certainly it was a historic setback for Arab integration, let alone unity. The regime in Baghdad, which had issued an "Arab National Charter" in 1980 proclaiming nonaggression as the governing principle of inter-Arab relations, tried its hand at forced "amalgamation" of its wealthy, diminutive, and difficult neighbor. The crisis and war that followed could hardly be said to be characteristic of a "pluralistic security-community," let alone an amalgamated one. The Arab regional system seemed rather to be playing by neorealist, balance-of-power rules. Both Iraq and the anti-Iraq coalition were driven by their respective conceptions of "vital national interest." Iraq of course asserted an "Arab unity" justification in terms of advancing the larger Arab struggle against Israel, but this certainly was not its primary driving force. In making the claim, however, Baghdad was seeking—and to a significant degree it succeeded in generating—widespread popular support across the Arab world.

But once the United States had demonstrated its determination to roll back the Iraqi invasion that support was not sufficient to prevent the formation of an Arab anti-Iraq coalition. The American intervention was crucial. Counterfactual speculation is always risky, but had Washington adopted a less decisive course (and it came close to doing so), one can imagine an outcome that would not have been so detrimental to a certain conception, at least, of Arab integration. An Arab-driven diplomatic process, instead of being nipped in the bud by American diplomacy, probably would have led to a negotiated solution between Iraq and Kuwait. Arab public opinion largely favored such a process, although Arab ruling elites must have feared the ramifications of a possible complete absorption of Kuwait. But there were no sufficiently capable Arab collective security institutions in place to challenge the Iraqi aggression militarily. Intervention by either Iran or Israel would have strengthened the Iraqi claim to be leading an all-Arab struggle. In the event, "Arab unity" was undoubtedly a casualty of the second Gulf War, but the primary lesson was that an exogenous agent—the United States—had both the determination and the capability to freeze the system of multiple sovereignties and to create a less unstable balance of power in the Gulf region. Had Iraq succeeded, its widespread popular support across the region probably would have increased further; it very likely would have become the hegemon of the Arab Mashriq, supported by Jordan, the Palestinians, and unified Yemen—able to bend Saudi Arabia and the other GCC states into "policy coordination" of various kinds, and to present Syria with a difficult diplomatic situation. Without active American and European backing, would a counter-coalition of Syria and Egypt (even with the problematic support of Iran and Israel) have had the ability and the will to roll back Iraq? Probably not, especially if Saddam Hussein had had the political sense to propose a compromise leaving Kuwait intact but diminished. The military triumph of "Desert Storm" has led most analysts to discount (once again) the Arab integrative impulse; but had Saddam Hussein's gambit unfolded differently, we might now be trying to explain the emergence of Iraq as the Prussia of a unifiable Arab east. That said, there is no gainsaying the fact that the actual turn of events was a historic setback for Arab integration by any definition.

Why the Unity Project Failed

Even ardent Arab nationalists who believe that unity is still attainable would probably agree that the "Arab unity project" thus far has been a disappointment, to put it mildly. How can we explain this failure? Possible answers are numerous and complex; many are suggested explicitly or implicitly in the chapters to follow. But the historical record just sketched suggests that the obstacles to unity fall into four categories: indigenous sociopolitical factors; unsupportive economic interests; the structure of the Arab/Middle East state system; and exogenous strategic, economic, and cultural patterns.

The indigenous obstacles refer to conditions in the domestic or intra-state arena—what international relations theorists sometimes call the "second-image" level of analysis (Waltz 1959, chs. 4–5). These include the low levels of political legitimacy accruing to Arab regimes and even to Arab states. Certainly legitimacy is a difficult concept to measure, and it varies considerably among different regimes at different times; nevertheless, the patterns of protest, instability, and governmental repression in most Arab countries over several decades lends plausibility to the generalization. Greater regime legitimacy might have given regime leaders the security, confidence, and capability to take the risks and accept the costs of more integrative policies. A related matter is the general lack of democracy in Arab regimes. Related as well is the reckless or parochial leadership often displayed by Arab kings and presidents. Beneath the rhetoric of Arab brotherhood heard at Arab summits has been mutual suspicion, ideological conflict, and, sometimes, personal animosity that tends to divide rather than unite. How can heads of state agree to cooperation involving some degree of mutual dependency (even shared sovereignty), especially in the military field, when their *mukhabarats* are busily trying to subvert one another?

On the level of political elites, it is hardly surprising that the "ruling circles" with a vested interest in maintaining their influence within individual states would be less than supportive of unification or integration projects that might diminish their privileged positions. On the popular level too there are problems arising from the low levels of education: the enthusiasm of the "masses" for various unity ideologies has been too easily manipulated and too susceptible to dissipation to provide a constant anchor in public opinion for integration. Finally, one might argue that the Arab nationalists have failed to produce a sufficiently compelling philosophy (let alone ideology) of unity. An American analyst perhaps will be pardoned for observing that there is no Arab equivalent of *The Federalist Papers*—a closely reasoned document that appeals to pragmatic interests and universal moral principles more than to emotion-laden sentiments about imagined past glories.

The second category of obstacles revolves around economic structures and relations. As several of the chapters in part III of this book point out, the general lack of complementarity in the economies of the Arab countries provided no strong incentives for economic integration. This accounts for the extremely low level of inter-Arab trade—around five percent. To be sure, on a broader level it has been argued that the distribution of factors of production should be conducive to regional development. The Gulf Cooperation Council countries have capital; Egypt, Yemen, and the Levant have manpower; and the Sudan has land. In fact, however, only labor has flowed freely across the region; and as Nemat Shafik writes in chapter 13, the Middle East remains one of the least integrated regions of the world in terms of capital and trade flows. There are other economic problems as well. Until recently many of the economies were state-driven rather than market-driven, and in the Arab (nationalist) socialist regimes the prevailing ideologies favored central planning, a large public sector, inappropriate emphasis on heavy industry, and an autarkic rather than integrative orientation. National pride and insecurity thwarted attempts at regional economic planning, as Yusif Sayigh notes in chapter 11. But even now, as Arab economies slowly liberalize, it does not appear that emerging economic interest groups, such as chambers of commerce, are as interested in regional cooperation as they are in deepening bilateral commercial and investment relationships with the major industrialized economies. Moreover, technological dependency on the West continues to deepen (as A. B. Zahlan points out in chapter 12), a condition that impedes regional economic development.

The third set of obstacles involves the structure of the Middle East and Arab state system. This system, as Korany shows in the following chapter, generates serious impediments to integrative political activity. As noted above, the dynamics of a "self-help" international system (according to structural-realist theory) are driven by the quest of states for security; and in a turbulent region like the Middle East that quest can take on paranoic proportions. The Arab unity project, at least in its early ideological form, assumed that the established Arab states and their rulers would simply give way to the higher stage of unity. However persuasive the arguments about the illegitimacy of "lines in the sand" drawn by European diplomats might be, it did not necessarily follow that these lines could easily be erased-especially after the passage of time and the growth of "chauvinistic" interests. Defective as they may have been, the state-actors in the Middle East have so far proved more durable than their transnational movement competitors, be they the Muslim Brothers, Communists, or Ba'thists.

Furthermore, since the death of Nasser and the subsequent decline of Egypt's regional influence, there has been no "center" in the Arab political system around which smaller states might have opted to "bandwagon"—in Stephen Walt's term (Walt 1987, ch. 2). Indeed, even in Nasser's heyday, some small Arab states took advantage of the United States' influence to "balance" against the Egyptian leader. But with the emergence of a more polycentric system in the 1970s, the security of individual states was enhanced by the absence of a potential regional hegemon: unification on the Prussian model was no longer a plausible scenario. Despite (or even because of) this development, Arab integrationists might have still hoped that the Arab League model of integration based on sovereign state-actors might finally become a reality. But insecurities, animosities, and suspicions have remained powerful disincentives to cooperation, as the second Gulf War amply illustrated. Furthermore, some Arab states in the 1980s and 1990s have begun seeking good relationships with non-Arab regional powers like Israel, Iran, and Turkey, raising the question whether an "Arab state system" really exists any longer.

Fourth, and in my view most important, are the obstacles that arise out of the global environment in which the Arab world finds itself ever more firmly embedded. External penetration is nowhere more important than in the economic realm. As Roger Owen explains in Chapter 10, the Arab world was incorporated into the world market in the nineteenth century and split into separate pieces. Except for certain brief periods since then, Western finance, investment, trade, and aid factors have constrained independent Arab decisionmaking in both domestic and external policy. Studies by dependency theorists such as Samir Amin (1982) and Abbas Alnasrawi (1991) have revealed the profound political implications of Arab economic dependency.

The global system also strongly penetrates and divides the Arab world in strategic terms. From the 1950s to the 1980s the rivalry between the United States and the Soviet Union was mirrored in what Malcolm Kerr (1971) dubbed "the Arab Cold War." Since the collapse of the Soviet Union the United States has been left as "the only remaining superpower" and finds itself playing a hegemonic role in the region analogous to that of Britain from the mid-nineteenth to the mid-twentieth century. To be sure, for purposes of its own Britain found it expedient to encourage limited types of Arab federation: it supported the idea of the Arab League; and it sought to build smaller federations in the Gulf and south Arabia. But the United States has generally been leery of Arab integration.

Although Washington favored the establishment of the Arab Gulf Cooperation Council in 1981 as a response to the Islamic revolutionary regime in Iran (as Abdul Khaleq Abdulla describes in chapter 7) and the Soviet invasion of Afghanistan, the American government today is working to create a new *Middle East* regional order in which Israel will play a leading role. Washington, remaining wary of any kind of pan-Arab groupings that might conceivably threaten Israel or Saudi Arabia and its small Gulf neighbors, prefers to emphasize bilateral relationships.

Inasmuch as the new American hegemon deploys formidable global as well as regional influence, it poses a significant problem for Arab integrationists. U.S. policy successfully divided the Arabs in the second Gulf War and thwarted "an Arab solution" that sought to preempt a U.S.-led international military intervention. Having won that war, the U.S. government, in Abdalla's opinion, has played a "unilateralist, imperialist, and militarist" role vis-à-vis the Arab GCC states (Abdulla 1996, 4). By declaring no fewer than four Arab states-Iraq, Syria, Sudan, and Libya (along with non-Arab Iran)-as "rogues" or "supporters of terrorism," the Clinton Administration tries to separate "the good guys from the bad guys." While it offers mild support for coordination among the small and vulnerable "good guys" of the Gulf, its general preference is for small separate units over large amalgamated ones, both among the "good guys" but especially among the "rogues."

Finally, the cultural aspect of global penetration of the Arab world needs to be noted. Much of the Arab nationalist resistance to Western domination was fueled by the desire to protect indigenous cultural values and heritage from the objectionable aspects of a powerful alien culture. Today the struggle between Islamist movements across the Arab world and relatively secularized and Westernized ruling elites reflects the same concern. For Arabs the problem of coping with the Western cultural onslaught was (and still is) complicated by the desire to embrace some parts of it while rejecting other parts. The conflict is captured in the title of a recent book, *Jihad vs. McWorld*, by Benjamin Barber (1995). Global forces, including new communications and information technologies, are creating what some see as a "consumer culture," characterized by materialism and pragmatism. But the producers and protectors of indigenous culture are fighting back, sometimes utilizing the same technologies of their adversaries. While the long-term consequences of such a struggle could be integrative, the immediate effects in the Arab world have been divisive. Broadly speaking, the major political cleavage of the late twentieth century pits those who would unite or integrate the Arabs within the framework of an indigenous culture, steeped in Islam, against certain leaders, ruling elites, and (upper) social strata convinced that integration into a European-Mediterranean and/or

American-Israeli regional state system is the proper future course. This cleavage cuts across geographical boundaries and national (state) sociopolitical arenas, further complicating the possibilities for integration.

Unity Downsized: Toward a Status Report on Arab Integration

As the papers in this volume make clear, the historical Arab unity project is but a shadow of its former self, whether one views it from political or structural standpoints. Fundamental changes in the global political and economic order, as well as profound social and cultural trends inside the Arab world, have created an environment vastly more complex than that perceived by the fathers of Arab nationalist ideologies or the architects of a regional order anchored by an Arab League. But the papers also show that the impulse for integration of some kind, at some level is very much alive. The idea of unity by fusion has largely given way, as Bassam Tibi notes in chapter 4, to goals of cooperation or coordination within a state-system framework. The idea of subregional integration, as exemplified by the Gulf Cooperation Council and the Arab Maghrib Union, has gained ground over the older notion of a pan-Arab community from the Atlantic to the Gulf. Many analysts feel that essentially apolitical functional integration through specialized transnational nongovernmental organizations—from sports leagues to women's organizations—is about the best that can be expected. And there are those who expect that the revolution in information technologies—direct satellite television, cellular telephony, and the Internet—may intensify the sense of Arab community to such an extent that there will be political consequences. In an article describing the "sad torpor" that pervades the Arab League, *The Economist* (1991) concluded: "In the meantime, another institution may be more effective at maintaining the dream of Arab unity. For millions of listeners the BBC's Arabic service continues to provide a sense of something worth belonging to."

In Part I, "The Changing Arab Regional System," we begin our inventory with three papers that consider the present state of integration across the Arab world as a whole and how it has been affected by changing global conditions. Bahgat Korany (chapter 2) brings a structural-realist approach to the subject and rightly reminds us of the continuing relevance of the balance of power in understanding Arab world dynamics. He concludes, however, that what the Arabs have displayed since the end of the second Gulf War is a "balance of weakness." While he considers the possibilities of a new and stable arrangement based on "interdependence" he warns that attempts to bypass "the Arab core" of the Middle East could lead to new friction. Paul Noble (chapter 3), in a comprehensive survey of the regional scene, presents a sympathetic yet deeply skeptical analysis of the prospects for Arab cooperation. Of the multiple challenges buffeting the Arab countries, the most serious ones are internal—notably what he sees as the erosion of intersocietal relations. Bassam Tibi, in chapter 4, "From Pan-Arabism to the Community of Sovereign Arab States," traces the decline of the Arab "imagined community" and the rise, however shaky, of the Arab state system. He calls unequivocally for a community of states "based on mutual respect" and recommends a close study of the European integration experiment. He also insists that the Arab should no longer be defined as an ethnic category but instead "as a citizen of a democratic state." Again, the European experience offers a model in terms of the democratic behavior of states in a regional system and the democratic contestation of interests within states and between them.

With the decline of the pan-Arab project, the focus of integrative activity has shifted to the subregional level. Here the record of success has been mixed. Part II, Experiments in Political Integration, offers five case studies which explore in detail the forces behind these projects and the obstacles that they have faced. It is appropriate to be begin with Mustafa Kamil Al-Sayyid's analysis (chapter 5) of the short-lived (1958–1961) "United Arab Republic" of Egypt and Syria because it was a product of the larger Arab unity impulse. Its progenitors thought of it as a stepping stone to a larger unification process, not as a subregional end in itself. Al-Sayyid shows how regional and international considerations interacted with specific domestic pressure groups and public opinion first to establish and later to bring down the UAR.

In sharp and instructive contrast, the process of unification of the seven Gulf shaykhdoms that became the United Arab Emirates, was long, leisurely, traditional, and incremental. In chapter 6 Frauke Heard-Bey cites good leadership, an attitude of tolerance, and the unhurried practice of traditional etiquette and protocol as important factors in explaining what is arguably one of the only integrative success stories in the Arab world, and certainly the most long-lived—a quarter-century. Can such a strategy lead to a more inclusive political community in the Gulf area? Chapter 7, by Abdul Khaleq Abdulla analyzes the Gulf Cooperation Council, in which the UAE is one of the six member-states. While the "cultural glue" that holds the GCC together is similar, the circumstances are more difficult, the scope much larger, and the results, so far, less impressive. Abdulla notes the remarkable haste with which the GCC was established, shortly after and largely in response to the Iranian revolution. He details the conflicting ideas that Saudi Arabia, Kuwait, and Oman held about its functions and shows how considerations of local sovereignty remain powerful obstacles to effective military integration, in particular. According to the author, the GCC's detachment from social realities and lack of popular base seem not to have adversely affected its durability. Although it has fallen far short of its goals, the GCC is often cited as the most successful of the subregional integration experiments.

North Africa (the Maghrib), according to I. William Zartman (chapter 8), displays a tangible regional identity despite the unevenness of state formation among its constituent parts (Algeria, Morocco, Tunisia, Libya, and Mauritania) and recurrent quarrels among them. His chapter traces "the ups and downs" of efforts since the 1960s to promote integration among them, culminating in the establishment of the Arab Maghrib Union in 1989. But integration has never advanced beyond the diplomatic level: economic integration is still minuscule and the prospects for political integration "have been met with understandable incredulity from the Maghribis themselves." The post-independence impetus for regional cooperation based on the nationalist struggles has given way in the 1990s to a European focus under the "Mediterannean" rubric. Maghribis, however, are not blind to the advantages of a common stand in negotiating with the European Community.

The final subregional case is the most recent one: the unification of North and South Yemen in 1990. Like the Arab Gulf states and perhaps the Maghrib the two Yemens possessed a distinctive and common political subculture. Yemeni nationalists and progressives on both side of the old British-drawn border had long called for unification. In chapter 9 Robert D. Burrowes narrates the chain of events that led two authoritarian single-party regimes unexpectedly to submerge their deeply rooted mutual suspicions in a fusion of two states that had periodically gone to war against each other. The surprise was compounded by a decision to move toward multiparty democracy as a way of organizing politics in the unified country. As of 1998, Yemen's unification had lasted twice as long as the UAR and had the distinction of being the only viable example in the Arab world of full (fusion) unity. That said, the union did have an unsteady beginning and could not avoid a brief but bloody civil war in 1994 to become—perhaps—cemented. The immediate cost, however, was a shrinkage of the democratic space, and one must wonder, recalling Tibi's essay, whether in the long run fruitful integration is possible without an open democratic political order.

The emergence and occasional modest success of Arab subregional groupings should not obscure the fact that the Arab homeland is littered with similar failed projects. One thinks, for example, of the aborted Federation of Arab Republics (Egypt, Syria, and Libya, 1971–73), and the Arab Cooperation Council (Iraq, Jordan, Egypt, and North Yemen, 1989–90). It is not obvious from our case studies and examples such as these that subregional unification is in itself a successful strategy of integration: the results clearly are mixed. Nor is there any compelling evidence that they comprise an intermediate step on the road to eventual full Arab unification. Advocates of pan-Arabism are doubtful: at a seminar in 1996 an Arab League ambassador (Armazani 1996) insisted that if the Arab League did not exist it would have to be invented, and that the proof of this was that subregional groupings like the GCC and the AMU had failed.

Economic integration is the focus of Part III. We begin in chapter 10 with Roger Owen's analysis of inter-Arab economic relations in the twentieth century. Owen reviews the historical explanations for the low level of Arab economic integration, which emphasize the distorting effects of the colonial period and global economic forces. He questions some of these arguments and along the way draws our attention to a now largely forgotten period of intraregional trade growth during World War II when the United States and Britain organized the Middle East Supply Center. He reviews the efforts to organize an Arab common market and the negative effects on integration of import-substitution industrialization development strategies. Today Arab economic policymakers need to consider the merits and demerits of two externally driven rival approaches to regional development: the Euro-Mediterranean free trade area plan and the American-Israeli plan for a region-wide free trade area growing out of the Arab-Israeli "peace process."

Yusif A. Sayigh, who has played a leading role over the years advising Arab governments on economic policy, was involved in efforts to harness new Arab oil wealth in the 1970s and 1980s for sustainable, integrated regional development. While there was considerable progress in the 1970s, the 1980s, he writes in chapter 11, yielded only a "poor harvest." His paper is at once an authoritative history and a blunt critique of the Joint Arab Economic Action project. Among other things, he discusses the effects of subregional groupings on Arab region-wide planning, particularly the problems of cooperation between the GCC and countries in the Mashriq and the Maghrib. Economic factors alone, he writes, cannot account for the disappointing record of the 1980s.

The next two papers examine the impact on integration of key economic sectors. Antoine B. Zahlan examines technology as a disintegrative factor (chapter 12). He observes that the Arab-Islamic world until the sixteenth century was unified by "a unique system of trade and transport." This system was gradually fragmented by European penetration, beginning with the Portuguese. European industrialization and colonization accelerated the breakdown. Even the recent achievement of political independence has not been accompanied by socioeconomic or technological integration. Although the Arabs today have the potential for indigenous technological capacity, they devote relatively small percentages of their resources (compared to other world regions) toward developing it and remain almost totally dependent for technology and technology training on the industrialized societies.

The economic factor that has made the most positive contribution to regional integration is labor. According to Nemat Shafik (chapter 13), labor mobility and its associated capital flows has been the most important mechanism through which the benefits of the oil windfall have been spread to the poorer states of the region. She reviews the history of efforts to promote Arab economic integration and then examines recent trade and capital flows before turning to labor. Unlike other parts of the world in which trade in goods drives regional integration, in the Arab world the "engine" has been labor flows and associated remittances. This is due in part to "extreme differences in factor endowments across the region" and also to outward-oriented trading policies, as well as various political factors. After examining the pros and cons, she concludes guardedly that labor migration is probably a stepping stone toward regional integration rather than a substitute for it, but that it may not be the most desirable one.

The final paper in this section, by Atif A. Kubursi (chapter 14), takes a critical look at the prospects for Arab economic integration after the Oslo accords in the Arab-Israeli "peace process." Noting recent assessments of the Arabs' political deficiencies and their "abysmal" economic growth, he asks whether peace with Israel will bring prosperity or domination of the Arab economic future? After analyzing the uneven record of Arab past economic cooperation efforts and a discussion of regional cooperation projects in other parts of the world (notably the European Community and the Association of Southeast Asian Nations), he turns his attention to the "new Middle East" envisioned by Israeli and American politicians. If the Israeli-Palestinian relationship is representative of this new order, then (in his opinion) it places the Arabs at a significant disadvantage. Suggesting that there is an "Arab disease" analogous to the "Dutch disease" well-known to development economists, Kubursi sees the heavy dependence on oil rents as a structural weakness from which many other serious problems flow. This dependency "has reduced Arab incentives to diversify their economies, develop alternative manufacturing capacities, promote export-oriented industries, encourage domestic savings, and anchor income on solid productivity grounds." For Israel, he concludes, the "peace dividend" will be massive while for Palestinians and Arabs they are precarious and illusive.

Arab Integration: The Next Phase

In 1988 the Center for Arab Unity Studies in Beirut, a leading think tank, published a massive study on "The Future of the Arab Nation," the product of around 100 intellectuals and researchers and some six years of work (CAUS

1991). It proposed three prospective scenarios: the "scenario of division" (basically a continuation of present parochial country-based patterns); the "scenario
of coordination and cooperation" (which envisioned gradual reforms, limited
cooperation, and subregional organizations for the Arabian peninsula, the
Fertile Crescent, the Nile Valley, and North Africa); and the "scenario of Arab
federal unity" (an admittedly "radical transformation" involving "a federal state
comprising most of the principal Arab countries . . . impl[ying] a single foreign
policy, a single army, a single currency, and a single education system, as the
minimum"). This scenario assumed that pluralism and respect for diversity
would be present at all levels (CAUS 1991, 391). While the authors were cautious
about making predictions, they did imply that the scenario of division probably would not last because country political systems were failing to deal with
growing economic and political problems. External pressures were mainly
responible for holding these divisions in place. They held out some optimism
for the second scenario but admitted that the third was a long way off, although
they discerned that "the first steps" were being taken toward a "new project for
Arab revival." The writers called upon "alternative elites" from "the heart of the
modern middle class" to learn from the mistakes of the eras of liberalism
(which neglected social problems and the nationalist cause) and socialist
nationalism (which neglected democracy, human rights, and the "cultural
[Islamic?] heritage"). These elites would face the task of formulating "a com-
posite outlook that harmonizes all the popular demands that have been conceived in the collective mind and conscience of the Arab nation during the last
100 years" (CAUS, 1991 490). It should be noted that the project began at a favorable moment—with high oil prices and ambitious development hopes (see
Sayigh, Ch. 11 below)—but ended with collapsed oil prices, costly years of Iraq-
Iran warfare, and the Palestinian *intifada*. And worse was just to come: the collapse of the Soviet Union and the second Gulf War. With all its methodological
drawbacks and perhaps naive recommendations, the CAUS report is significant
both for what it is—one of a number of serious intellectual efforts to explicate
complex realities instead of retreating toward ideological slogans—and for
what it says—especially its focus on the groups and institutions of civil society
and its attention to pluralistic and federal mechanisms for ensuring equity,
legitimacy, and diversity in the development of all-Arab coordination and
cooperation—or even federal (or confederal) unity. But viewed a decade later,
the report seems to understate the problems (or blame them excessively on
exogenous forces). Certainly its tone is brighter than that of most of the studies
in this book.

Generally, the studies presented here paint a gloomy picture of the prospects
for Arab integration. Indeed, they might seem to suggest that there are far more

factors promoting—even "over-determining" a permanent condition of Arab *disintegration*. At the minimum, they raise many tough questions for proponents of integration. Is the idea of an Arab political and economic community in the broadest sense any longer viable, in light of the rise of a global economy and an external political order that penetrate "the Arab world" in so many ways? Is regional coordination or cooperation forever hostage to domestic authoritarianism and instability? Are the lessons of previous integration experiments so dismal as to erode future integration impulses, or is it possible that Arab politicians might learn from past experiences? Does integration by various definitions (unification, coordination, etc.) make any sense any more, and if so to whom? Is Arabism dead, after all?

If by Arabism we mean the fusionist romanticism of the Ba'th, or the Prussian model of Nasserist Egypt or Saddam Hussein's Iraq, then we should summon the coroner, not the paramedics. But if we are imagining an Arabism based on cooperation and coordination, with respect for existing (but diminished) sovereignties, then I think we should call for the obstetrician. Arabism of this kind, I believe, has a future.

The prevailing pessimism is derived to some extent from neorealist international relations theory. To the extent that the Arab Middle East and North Africa fit the classical model of insecure states trying to survive in an anarchic environment, there is no reason to expect much in the way of structured cooperation. But Walt's (1987) elegant exposition of a neorealist interpretation is unsatisfactory because it does not comprehend the sociological and cultural elements that make the Arab state system uniquely porous. The neorealist paradigm has been significantly challenged, however, by institutionalist and constructivist approaches (Keohane 1989, Lapid and Kratochwil 1996) which seek to bring political structures, culture, and domestic politics into the explanatory equation. Barnett (1993, 1995), for example, goes so far as to posit that pan-Arabism is an "informal institution" of the Arab state system. But, he argues, its integrative momentum is stymied by role conflicts within Arab elites, torn by commitments (mainly interest-driven) to new and shaky "sovereignties," and sentiment toward the greater Arab nation. Telhami (1994) writes that "one important commodity of competition in Arab politics has not been military power (which explains why Walt abandoned that scheme), but instruments of legitimacy. . . . [L]egitimacy, posited in ways that are compatible with a minimalist neo-realist paradigm, can help explain not only individual foreign policy decisions, but also patterns of interstate relations in the Middle East that were not sufficiently accounted for by the distribution of power alone." Gause (1993) also criticizes Walt for underestimating "what is unique to the international relations of the Middle East—the challenge that transnational ideological identifications pose for the state system inherited from European colonialism." Brynen (1993) argues persuasively for "closely integrating the contemporary approaches of scholars of Middle East domestic politics into foreign policy analysis."

We must tread carefully here for several reasons. First, as Korany (chapter 2) reminds us, the neorealist perspective clearly retains a great deal of validity even if it fails to tell the whole story, particularly as Arab states have grown (bureaucratically, at least) and aged. Second, we certainly need to avoid lurching back to the naive cultural essentialism that drove Arab unity efforts (and some analyses) at least through the 1960s. Third, while what Waltz (1959) once called the "second-image" model (in which "domestic" state and societal level dynamics shape "external" behavior) may have special relevance to the Arab state system, those dynamics do not all point in the direction of regional integration—an important point discussed by Noble in chapter 3. The paradoxical (not to say self-contradictory) behavior of domestic elites over Arab unity has been well-described in the work of Kerr (1971), Seale (1965) and Mufti (1996) and is also illustrated in our case studies in Part II, especially Al-Sayyid's on the UAR and Abdalla's on the GCC: they want it but they also fear it; they exploit it for tactical purposes (outbidding an opponent), but it is almost nobody's first priority. Fourth, we need to exercise similar caution in ascertaining what Gourevitch (1978) has called "second-image reversed" effects (in which domestic outcomes are significantly shaped by exogenous forces): the political economy of "globalization" may promote integrative economic liberalization in the Arab world, but it also encourages vertical "north-south" bilateralism. If Washington, the global hegemon, prefers a "New Middle East" (with Israel in a leading role), it can exert powerful effects on the ruling elites of twenty-two weak and divided Arab League member-states.

That said, one can still argue that prospects for phased cooperative, sovereignty-based integration are not as bleak as a cursory reading of the following chapters might imply. Why? First, as just noted, institutionalist, constructivist, and reflective international relations theory offers a perspective that is less deterministic than neorealist "billiard-ball" or economistic approaches and more amenable to the possibilities of human agency, institution-building, and culture. In the second place, we are talking about a kind of integration very different from the fusionist unity project whose dismal history I sketched in the preceding pages. The four obstacles to that kind of unity that I identified—indigenous sociopolitical factors, mercantilist economic orientations, the structure of the state system, and exogenous patterns—are not necessarily (or not entirely) inimical to this more modestly defined integration.

(1) Sociopolitical trends at the domestic level are perhaps the most impor-

tant. The spread of mass media and information technologies; the physical mobility of labor, professional elites, and tourists; intraregion development assistance; and mass education are among the factors constructing a more widely and deeply imagined Arab community. Also on the indigenous level is the complex transformation of the Arab state. Most observers now believe that it is "there to stay." Some stress its growth and capabilities, a development that may be generating sufficient confidence within ruling elites to consider "policy coordination" or even modest shared sovereignty with neighbors. Others contend that it is actually getting weaker relative to other social formations, such as the liberalizing economy, which implies the rise as well of civil society and a middle class with an interest in regional cooperation. Since the 1980s there has been some indication that Arab states have been developing more open and elaborate forms of political participation, raising the possibility of of more representative and less capricious governments—capable of integrative "policy coordination" with their neighbors. The evidence for such a trend is, to say the least, mixed, and perhaps not as persuasive as it was a decade ago (see Hudson 1987, 1991, 1994, and Norton 1995), but it cannot be dismissed (see *Civil Society*, passim).

(2) The slow but inexorable liberalization of statist economic systems is creating a climate in which intraregion enterprise is becoming easier and a "common market" project is once again being broached. During the "easy" phase of the Arab-Israeli "peace process," (1993–95) when optimism was high, many Arab analysts forecasted and endorsed the emergence of a new regional order (Peres's "New Middle East") that would transform the region "from geopolitics to geoeconomics" (Said Aly 1996): the Arab states, the Palestinians, Israel, and (eventually) Iran and Iraq would cooperate together in trade, development, water issues, arms control, and a range of other areas. But with the Arab-Israeli peace process (with all its inequities) virtually comatose since early 1996 the question of an Arab regional economy as opposed to a "new Middle East" is again on the agenda (Kubursi, chapter 14). Should the "peace process" miraculously produce a mutually legitimate political agreement, it would make "geoeconomic" sense for Israel to be included, perhaps as an "associate member" in Arab regional economic arrangements. Generally, to the extent that globalization fosters a more integrated world economy—and society—the Arabs may have some new opportunities and incentives for regional cooperation.

(3) If the Arab state *system* has (for neorealist reasons) been a deterrent to fusionist integration, it may be less inhospitable to coordination or even broader alliances that do not threaten country sovereignty. Rationality, not just common culture, suggests that for a weak and divided Arab world collective security and economic development require some degree of integration. This is

all the more true to the extent that the powerful non-Arab neighbors—Israel especially—remain hostile not just to state interests but Arab national concerns as well. Arab solidarity also takes on greater value in the negotiation of economic relationships with the European Union, the U.S., and other regional blocs. Inter-Arab relations are not just confined to state-driven security issues: indeed, while states' sovereignty is eroded by issues that transcend borders, there is reason to think that transnational sociocultural linkages are multiplying (as Saad Eddin Ibrahim argued) and that through functional NGOs, the ideas of Arab identity and community are being reimagined and deepened. This process needs empirical investigation.

(4) It must be said, however, that exogenous conditions are generally as inhospitable to Arab sovereignty-based integration as they were to unionist integration. While the disappearance of the Soviet Union has brought an end to "the Arab cold war" the emergence of the U.S. as the only remaining superpower constitutes a formidable obstacle. Inasmuch as U.S. policies today are formulated in coordination with Israel, Washington can only oppose any collective Arab institution-building. And it has the means to do so inasmuch as it wields significant military-security and economic instruments. Europe offers a more sympathetic political attitude but lacks the power to be played as a counterweight to the U.S.; moreover, European protectionist attitudes also pose problems. By the same token, however, these very problems would seem to call for an institutionalized, collective Arab regional response. Should the Arabs' relations with the outside world—especially the U.S.—continue to worsen, we cannot exclude the possibility of a kind of xenophobic "defensive integration" gaining ground. In such a case some Arab regimes will find the "rationality" of their privileged relations with Washington colliding with a transnational, culturally driven movement to resist Western encroachment—a revival of nativist anti-imperialism.

What all this means, I believe, is not that a new phase in Arab integration—sovereignty based cooperation with pluralist institutional underpinnings—is about to dawn but only that such a thing is more possible than most observers think. There is also a distinct possibility, however, of a very different scenario that we might call "praetorian-based radicalism." If socioeconomic conditions across the region continue to worsen, and if the main region-wide threat to stability—the Arab-Israeli conflict—continues to fester, then domestic tensions that feed radical ideological projects could lead to an era of both intra- and inter-Arab turmoil reminiscent of the 1950s and 1960s—only this time the coloration will be Islamist-nationalist instead of secular-national-unionist.

The scenario that emerges will depend on a multiplicity of developments at different levels—domestic, regional, global—and in different domains—economic, political, social. My guess is that the next phase will be shaped most decisively by domestic political factors. To the extent that there is a trend toward civil society, pluralist institutions, and liberalization, then the possibilities for an interest-based integrative process buttressed (along the European model) by multilayered linkages, elaborate but effective structures, and legitimate decisonmaking procedures are brighter than with an array of authoritarian, "fierce," but not very capable states and regimes. These Arab states will be more capable of cooperative integration with their neighbors (through enhanced legitimacy) if they also undertake decentralization at home, in order to give distinctive ethnic, sectarian and regional subcommunities a sense of security and well-being in the national political order. Finally, if we may assume (as I do) that intellectuals and decisionmakers in the Arab world are learning from the extensive integrative and unionist activity of the past century, then there is a rich body of experiences (not all of them negative—cf. Heard-Bey, chapter 6, and Burrowes, chapter 9) from which to draw lessons for the future.

References

"Arab Unity's Paling Symbol." *The Economist*, December 7, 1991.

Abdalla, Abdul Khaleq. "The US-GCC Relationship: The Current Phase." Unpublished paper, Washington, April 1996.

Abdallah, Amb. Khaled [Arab League representative to the U.S.]. Personal communication, September 4, 1997.

Alnasrawi, Abbas. *Arab Nationalism, Oil, and the Political Economy of Dependency*. New York: Greenwood Press, 1991.

Amin, Samir. *The Arab Economy Today*. London: Zed Books, 1982.

Anderson, Benedict. *Imagined Communities*. London: Verso, 1983, 1991.

Antonius, George. *The Arab Awakening*. London: Hamish Hamilton, 1938, 1961.

Armazani, Ghayth [Ambassador of the Arab League to Great Britain]. "The Arab League and the New Middle East," seminar presented at the Center for Contemporary Arab Studies, Georgetown University, April 9, 1996.

Barber, Benjamin R. *Jihad vs. McWorld*. New York: Times Books, 1995.

Barnett, Michael N. "Institutions, Roles, and Disorder: The Case of the Arab States System." *International Studies Quarterly* 37 (1993), 271–96.

Barnett, Michael N. "Sovereignty, Nationalism, and Regional Order in the Arab States System." *International Organization* 49:3 (Summer 1995), 479–510.

Bechtold, Peter K. "New Attempts at Arab Cooperation: The Federation of Arab Republics, 1971-?" *Middle East Journal*, 27:2 (Spring 1973), 152–72.

Brynen, Rex. "Between Parsimony and Parochialism: Comparative Politics, International Relations, and the Study of Middle East Foreign Policy." paper delivered at the American Political Science Association annual meeting, Washington, 1993.

Cantori, Louis J. And Steven L. Spiegel. *The International Politics of Regions: A Comparative Approach*. Englewood Cliffs, NJ: Prentice Hall, 1970.

Center for Arab Unity Studies (CAUS). *The Future of the Arab Nation: Challenges and Options*. London: Routledge, 1991.

Cleveland, William L. *The Making of an Arab Nationalist: Ottomanism and Arabism in the Life and Thought of Sati' Al-Husri*. Princeton, NJ: Princeton University Press, 1971.

Deutsch, Karl W. et al. *Political Community and the North Atlantic Area*. Princeton, NJ: Princeton University Press, 1957.

Gause, F. Gregory, III. "Systemic Approaches and Middle East International Relations." paper delivered at the annual meeting of the American Political Science Association, Washington, DC, September 1993.

Glazer, Nathan and Daniel P. Moynihan. *Beyond the Melting Pot: The Negroes, Puerto Ricans, Jews, Italians, and Irish of New York City*. Cambridge: MIT. Press, 1970.

Gomaa, Ahmed M. *The Foundation of the League of Arab States*. London: Longman, 1977.

Gourevitch, Peter. "The Second Image Reversed: The International Sources of Domestic Politics." *International Organization* 32, 4 (Autumn 1978).

Haas, Ernst B. *Beyond the Nation-State*. Stanford, CA: Stanford University Press, 1964.

Haim, Sylvia G., ed. *Arab Nationalism: An Anthology*. Berkeley: University of California Press, 1962.

Horowitz, Donald. *Ethnic Groups in Conflict*. Berkeley: University of California Press, 1985.

Hourani, Albert. *Arabic Thought in the Liberal Age*. London: Oxford University Press, 1962.

Hudson, Michael C. "The Integration Puzzle in Arab Politics." In Michael C. Hudson, ed. *The Arab Future: Critical Issues*. Washington, DC: Georgetown University Center for Contemporary Arab Studies, 1979, 181–94.

Hudson, Michael C. "Democratization and the Problem of Legitimacy in Middle East Politics." *Middle East Studies Association Bulletin*, 22, 2 (1987), 157–72.

Hudson, Michael C. "After the Gulf War: Prospects for Democratization in the Arab States." *Middle East Journal* 45, 3 (Summer 1991), 407–26.

Hudson, Michael C. "The Domestic Context and Perspectives [on Intervention] in Lebanon." In Milton J. Esman and Shibley Telhami, eds. *International Organizations and Ethnic Conflict*. Ithaca, NY: Cornell University Press, 1995, 126–47.

Hudson, Michael C. "Obstacles to Democratization in the Middle East." *Contention* 5, 1 (Fall 1995), 81–106.

Hurewitz, J.C., ed. *The Middle East and North Africa in World Politics: A Documentary Record*. Volume 2. "British-French Supremacy, 1914–1945." New Haven: Yale University Press, 1979.

Ibrahim, Saad Eddin. *The New Arab Social Order*. Boulder, CO: Westview Press, 1982.

Keohane, Robert O. *International Institutions and State Power: Essays in International Relations Theory*. Boulder, CO: Westview Press, 1989.

Keohane, Robert O. and Joseph S. Nye, Jr. "International Interdependence and Integration." Ch. 5 in Fred I. Greenstein and Nelson W. Polsby, eds. *Handbook of Political Science*, vol. 8. "International Politics." Reading, MA: Addison-Wesley, 1975.

Kerr, Malcolm H. *The Arab Cold War*. 3rd ed. New York: Oxford University Press, 1971.

Khalidi, Rashid, Lisa Anderson, Muhammad Muslih, and Reeva S. Simon, eds. *The Origins of Arab Nationalism*. New York: Columbia University Press, 1991.

Kifner, John. "Arabs Send Troops to Help Saudis." *New York Times*, August 11, 1990.

Krasner, Stephen D., ed. *International Regimes*. Ithaca, NY: Cornell University Press, 1983.

Lapid, Yosef and Friedrich V. Kratochwil, eds. *The Return of Culture and Identity in International Relations Theory*. Boulder, CO: Lynne Rienner Publishers, 1996.

Macdonald, Robert W. *The League of Arab States: A Study in the Dynamics of Regional Organization*. Princeton, NJ: Princeton University Press, 1965.

Maksoud, Clovis. "Diminished Sovereignty, Enhanced Sovereignty: United Nations-Arab League Relations at 50." *Middle East Journal* 49:4 (Autumn 1995), 582–94.

Mufti, Malik. *Sovereign Creations: Pan-Arabism and Political Order in Syria and Iraq*. Ithaca: Cornell University Press, 1996.

Norton, Augustus Richard, ed. *Civil Society in the Middle East* (2 vols). Leiden: E.J. Brill, 1995, 1996.

Nusseibeh, Hazem Zaki. *The Ideas of Arab Nationalism*. Ithaca, NY: Cornell University Press, 1956.

Said, Edward W. *Orientalism*. New York: Vintage Books, 1979.

Said, Edward W. "Arab Powerlessness." *Al-Ahram Weekly* (Cairo). April 25, 1996.

Said Ali, Abdel Monem. "From Geopolitics to Geoeconomics: Collective Security in the Middle East and North Africa." In Josef Janning and Dirk Rumberg, eds. *Peace and Stability in the Middle East and North Africa*. Gutersloh: Bertelsmann Foundation Publishers, 1996, 17–38.

Salafy, Ali. *The League of Arab States: Role and Objectives*. Washington, DC: Arab Information Center, 1989.

Salamé, Ghassan. "Integration in the Arab World: The Institutional Framework." In Giacomo Luciani and Ghassan Salamé, eds. *The Politics of Arab Integration*. London: Croom-Helm, 1988.

Salman, Munir A. "The Arab League: A Critical Assessment of the Political Efficacy of a Regional Organization." Ph.D. dissertation, Northern Arizona University, 1986.

Sayegh, Fayez A. *Arab Unity: Hope and Fulfillment*. New York: Devin-Adair, 1958.

Seale, Patrick. *The Struggle for Syria*. London: Oxford University Press, 1965; and New Haven, CT: Yale University Press, 1986.

Taylor, Alan R. *The Arab Balance of Power*. Syracuse, NY: Syracuse University Press, 1982.

Telhami, Shibley. "Power and Legitimacy in Arab Alliances." paper delivered at the annual meeting of The American Political Science Association, New York, 1994.

Tibi, Bassam. *Arab Nationalism: A Critical Enquiry*. Translated by Marion Farouk Sluglett and Peter Sluglett. New York: St. Martin's Press, 1971.

Walt, Stephen M. *The Origins of Alliances*. Ithaca, NY: Cornell University Press, 1987.

Waltz, Kenneth N. *Man, the State, and War*. New York: Columbia University Press, 1959.

Waltz, Kenneth N. *Theory of International Politics*. Reading, MA: Addison-Wesley, 1979.

Zeine, Zeine N. *The Struggle for Arab Independence*. Beirut: Khayat's, 1960.

The Arab World and the New Balance of Power in the New Middle East

chapter 2

Bahgat Korany

In the international tinderbox that is the Middle East, the 1990–91 Gulf War is usually treated as a watershed. Ever since, a growing industry of writing on the "New Middle East" has acquired increasing relevance. The enlarged and ongoing Arab-Israeli peace process added visibility to the "newness" concept.

Despite much critique by many of the validity of the concept of "balance of power," it still captures, in summary form, world and regional structures. It also determines—in reality or in perception—the behavior of different actors. As the Middle East specialist of the Clinton administration, Martin Indyk, put it in discussing the post-Gulf War context: "the administration's approach (to the region) . . . starts from the balance of power." (Indyk, et. al. 1994, 1–26). Consequently, it is important to show the nature of this balance, its evolution, and the meaning in concrete terms of its newness.

The first section of this paper looks at the ambiguities surrounding the balance of power concept, some of the problems in its practice, and, finally, presents the definition used here. The next two sections move to application to show how regional dynamics—with their Arab/non-Arab distinction—could be grouped through the balance of power conceptual lens. Section three specifically deals with the evolution of the balance from a pattern of attempted (Egyptian) hegemony to a pattern of power diffusion after the rise of "petro-powers." Power-diffusion could favor partnership, as during the 1973 October war where military action and oil embargo decisions were coordinated, or during the second Gulf War. But this latter partnership was not transformed into an international regime because it lacked transparency, predictability, and the necessary *longue durée*. This handicap was even more apparent in the formation of passing coalitions (with the exception of the Gulf Cooperation Council). Section four concentrates on the present post-Gulf War context, characterized by an Arab balance of weakness. Then the question is raised in section five as to whether, in the new context of peace-building around the Arab-Israeli core conflict, we should now envisage a different conceptual lens from the balance of power, i.e., interdependence, and thus talk of a balance of benefits. Given the oscillation of current regional politics between warfare and welfare, this final part shows how it is necessary to use simultaneously the two conceptual lenses to better decode the present Middle East complexity.

Defining the Balance of Power

In 1836, Richard Cobden, in talking about Russia, condemned balance of power as a fallacy, a mistake, an incomprehensible concept: asserting the theory was "mere chimera—a creation of the politician's brain—a phantasme, without definite form or tangible existence—a mere conjunction of syllables, forming words which convey sound without meaning" (Cobden 1867, Moul 1989).

About 117 years later, a prominent specialist of international relations, Ernest Haas (1953), found that the concept indeed has meaning, or rather more than one—in fact too many. He counted at least eight distinct meanings ranging from any distribution of power, to parity in distribution, to dominance. He attributed the ambiguity of the concept to the fact that people use the same words but intend different meanings.

The confusion is logical since there is no standard unit of power comparable to pound weights or pound sterling. The heated debate about whether there is a U.S. decline of power or not (Kennedy 1987, Nye 1990) reflects this ambiguity in power measurements.

In addition to these problems in the measurement of power of states, we have other basic issues in the theory that are shrouded in ambiguity: e.g., the role of the balancer: is it an eternal bystander like Britain in the nineteenth century or an active third party in conflict-resolution like the United States during the Camp David Accords? Another ambiguity is whether the balance of terror that characterized the Cold War period is also a balance of power, and whether wealth necessarily means strength (e.g., the oil-producing Gulf countries).

To put a temporary end to this conceptual discussion and concentrate on regional dynamics themselves, we can agree that power among states is not uniquely military and that it is always relative, never absolute. In fact, such an understanding of power is crucial in saving the balance of power concept and making it useful in discussing present structures and processes in the Middle East.

The Evolving Regional Balance of Power: the Arab/Non-Arab Dichotomy

For most of this century, the basic structure of regional relations has traditionally been dominated and shaped by the distinction between Arab and non-Arab. The revolt of the "Arab Provinces" against Ottoman rule on the eve of World War I and the evolution of the Arab national movement generally, was based on this Arab/non-Arab distinction. It was, however, the 1948 establishment of the state of Israel that made this distinction politically acute and, indeed, bloody. Typically, Heikal put this conditioning frame of reference in clear-cut terms, and it is worth quoting him in detail on this continuous struggle for predominance:

> The advocates of the two systems have spared no effort, using all the means at their disposal, both overt and covert, to advance their cause.
>
> 1. *The Middle Eastern System.* First advocated by Britain, France, the United States, and Turkey, the real architect of the system was, in fact, the United States, backed by Great Britain. This system saw the Middle East in geographical terms, as a vulnerable land mass lying close to the Soviet Union. Wholly preoccupied with the Soviet threat, the architects of the system held that the countries of the area must organize themselves against this threat by joining in an alliance with others who were concerned for the region's security. This alliance would have to coordinate its defense with other countries exposed to the "red Peril" in Europe and Asia. A Middle Eastern alliance would be the final link in a chain of alliances (including NATO and SEATO) encircling the southern frontiers of the Soviet Union. In the logic of this system, the Arab countries were expected to join in an alliance with Turkey, Iran, Pakistan, even Israel—that is, the Middle Eastern countries directly concerned with the region—as well as with the United States, Britain, and France, the international parties concerned with the region's security as well as being the major participants in NATO and SEATO.
>
> 2. *The Arab System.* Based on a different outlook toward the region, this system saw the Middle East not as a hinterland lying between Europe and Asia—a simple geographical expansion—but as one nation having common interests and security priorities distinct from those of the West. According to this logic, the countries of the area, which enjoyed unity of language, religion, history and culture should—indeed could—create their own system to counter any threat from whatever source. And the main threat, as the advo-

cates of this system saw it, came from Israel, not only because it cut across the African-Asian land bridge but also because, with its seizure of the Auja area demilitarized under the Rhodes armistice agreement, it was clear that it harbored expansionist aims. At the same time, while admittedly the Soviet Union did represent a threat, it was felt that there was not immediate or direct danger from that source. Many people in the area, including Gamal Abdel Nasser, held that the lack of common borders between the Arab nation and the Soviet Union would deter the Soviets from undertaking any military act against it. And in any case, Nasser felt that the answer to communist infiltration did not lie in joining Western-sponsored alliances with their imperialist overtones, but rather in promoting internal economic and social development and in affirming the spirit of nationalism and independence.

If the advocates of the Arab system required any proof of the validity of their theory, this was amply provided by the 1956 Suez War, an operation launched by two discredited colonial powers, Britain and France, in retaliation for Egypt's nationalization of the Suez Canal. Although it is hard to see how this particular settling of accounts could have concerned it in any way, Israel nonetheless joined the ill-fated attack, in a spirit compared by Moshe Dayan in his book on the 1956 campaign to that of a cyclist peddling uphill who grabs the back of a passing truck that happens to be going in the same direction (Heikal 1978a, 720).

Much more than the Suez Crisis, it was the 1954–55 debate over the Baghdad Pact that shaped the structure of regional relations, not only with the big powers but also among Arab countries as well as with their neighbors (Korany 1976, 198–300).

The Baghdad Pact project started formally with the Turko-Pakistani Treaty on April 4, 1953, followed by Anglo-Saxon attempts to incorporate Iraq and Iran into the new "anti-communist" organization destined to stretch from the Bosphorus to the Indus. Britain was enthusiastic in welcoming this arrangement because it offered Britain a new treaty instead of the existing Anglo-Iraqi one which was to expire by 1957. Thus, on February 24, 1955, Turkey and Iraq signed their mutual assistance pact, Britain joined on April 5, 1955, followed in September by Pakistan and in November by Iran.

Nasser reacted violently to Iraq's "defection." This issue dominated policies in the Arab interstate society for almost the entire year. Nasser's arguments were diffused through the widely heard Cairo Radio, which gave them added weight. He also contacted Arab nationalists throughout the region, explaining that Iraq had violated the solidarity of the League in committing itself to outside obligations. He threatened to withdraw from the League, a move that would have brought about its demise. Nasser's line of attack was simple. He emphasized

Pan-Arabism against "imperialism and Zionism" and said that the Baghdad Pact was not aimed at the "real" enemy of the Arabs—Israel—but was instead an alliance with those who had created and still supported this "imperialist base" against the Arabs, i.e., the Western states.

Not only was the pact unrelated to the Arabs' defense against their "real" enemies, according to Nasser, but it was an imperialist formula permitting imperialist forces into the Arab world through the backdoor. The appeal of this argument to ex-colonial people was strengthened when "material evidence" was cited to "prove" its truth. According to the agreement governing British accession to the Turko-Iraqi pact, "the airfields in Iraq occupied by Great Britain in accordance with the 1932 treaty were to pass under Iraqi sovereignty; but the existing facilities of overflying, landing and servicing British aircraft in Iraq were to be maintained and British military personnel would remain in Iraq, under British command, for this purpose, and would enjoy appropriate amenities. Furthermore, the installations on the airfields retained for British use were to remain British property" (Barraclough and Wall 1960, 28).

Consequently, as a British analyst summarized the new agreement, "The effects of the new agreement were therefore juridical rather than practical; in other words, although sovereignty and legal ownership passed to Iraq, effective use by Great Britain remained largely undisturbed" (Ibid.).

Thus, Nasser insisted, as far as the relationship between the Arabs and the Western powers and their "regional stooges" was concerned, Iraq's step meant a return to the old treaty relationships which brought the newly independent state back into the "imperialist sphere of influence." Instead, an alternative Arab strategy could achieve the Arab nationalist aim of independence by materializing Arab solidarity on the basis of the 1950 Arab League Collective Security Pact. In practice, as Salah Salem, expressed it, efforts have to be focused on arranging and organizing the "Arab house," consolidating Arab military and economic capabilities, and coordinating Arab efforts and plans. At this stage, no commitments should be concluded with foreign states. This is why Arab states should not participate in the Turko-Pakistani alliance or any other defense arrangements outside the "Arab homeland." This "unification of an Arab policy," as Turkish newspapers expressed it, would put an end to the dispersion of Arab capabilities and the "wasting of energy" through disunity. Moreover, a "unified Arab stand" would make of the Arab states a "weighty" interlocutor, and give them an elevated status in the international system. And Nasser emphasized why such an "Arab strategy" would appeal to the "masses" *psychologically*: "The Arabs have been colonized for a long time and they are always afraid of falling back again under Western domination." This is why "defense of the area . . . has to spring from the area itself," otherwise the Arabs would not feel that "they are defending their own families, their own children, their own property . . . [but] British or American interest." (Nasser 1960)

Consequently, if the Western powers were really interested in having independent states that would provide Middle East defense against "communist danger," Nasser thought, they should supply the Arabs with weapons without pressure and without requiring political commitments. The West should not insist on retaining the power of command in this field; this the Arabs themselves were capable of providing without any alignment.

The Baghdad Pact controversy is significant in at least two respects. According to Nasser, he was talking not only for Egypt but also in the name of a unified Arab strategy. What is characteristic of his speeches at that time is his identification with nationalist Arab aspirations and the transcendence of the interests of individual states and governments.

Second, the controversy between the supporters of pro-Western alignment and those of nonalignment was depicted as synonymous with the battle of "imperialism, zionism and their stooges" against the forces of independence and Arab nationalism. If anyone questioned this equation, Israel's February 28, 1955 attack on the Egyptian-controlled territory of Gaza (killing 38 people and wounding 31) was to "prove" that Egypt was paying the price for its opposition to "imperialist" alliances. This confirmed that Nasser—an Arab champion— was the "target of the Arabs' enemies" and this strengthened his position in the Arab world enormously. Of course, power struggles were not limited to relations between Arabs and non-Arabs, but they permeated inter-Arab relations.

Inter-Arab Balance of Power

The Arab world itself has experienced various forms of balance of power. These variations ranged from hegemonic behavior by one actor (e.g., Egypt 1954–1967) to increasing power diffusion among regional members (e.g., 1967–71, 1988–1990) with some attempts at effective partnership (1971–1977, 1981–1992).

The period 1979–1988 witnessed complete Arab fragmentation. Following President Sadat's decision to adopt "go-it-alone" diplomacy with Israel, Egypt's membership in the Arab League was suspended, and the Arab League itself moved to Tunis. Moreover, the Arab states seemed to be divided about the primary threat facing them: was it Israel or revolutionary Iran (and its possible victory in its war with Iraq)? The agenda and deliberations of the 1987 Arab Summit in Amman revealed these acute divisions. The year 1988 saw the cease-fire between Iran and Iraq, Egypt's reintegration into the Arab world, and the return of the League to its original headquarters in Cairo.

UNILATERAL HEGEMONIC BEHAVIOR 1954-1967

The controversy over the Baghdad Pact was crowned with Egypt's success in establishing its regional preeminence. This preeminence rested on important bases of power—both tangible and intangible. Egypt's population at the time constituted no less than a third of the whole Arab population. (In fact, at the height of their petro-power in 1975, the six countries that coalesced in the Gulf Cooperation Council contained not more than one quarter of the population of Egypt.) Historically, Al-Azhar Islamic University radiated enlightenment all over the Arab and Islamic world; Egypt's many famous authors, poets, and journalists set the literary and intellectual pace; and Egypt's teachers flocked to socialize future Arab elites. Egyptian universities were the goal of promising Arab intellectuals. Many Arab high school students felt they had to work hard and earn high grades to get admitted to Cairo University, otherwise they would be "forced" to go to Oxford or Cambridge!

Egypt's multifaceted predominance in the region was reflected in the Arab League. In Alexandria in 1944, a meeting was convened to establish the League and approve a protocol. The minutes of this meeting are full of speeches affirming Egypt's regional preeminence. And it was in Cairo that the new organization located its headquarters. Until the late 1950s, Egypt's share in the League's budgets was between 40 and 50 percent, and in 1974, of the 253 permanent and non-permanent staff members of the League, 162 were Egyptians. Until the League was forced to move from Cairo to Tunis after Egypt's separate peace with Israel, the three Secretary-Generals had all been Egyptians.

Various quantitative indicators that span a long period in the evolution of the Arab system confirm Egypt's centrality. For instance, the pattern of official visits for the period 1946–1975 confirm Egypt's preeminence among Arab and other Third World countries (Korany 1988, 164–178). Similarly, at the civil society level, in the mid-fifties when Jordanian leaders seemed inclined to join the Pact with their Hashemite cousin, Iraq, huge demonstrations erupted in Jordan and other Arab countries at the instigation of Egypt and its Arab supporters. Consequently, Arab membership in the Pact was limited to Nuri's Iraq, and when this regime was overthrown in 1958, one of the first measures of Iraq's Free Officers was to withdraw from this military alliance (which had then to change its official name to CENTO—Central Treaty Organization).

Egypt's prestige increased and its leadership was confirmed when it managed to nationalize the Suez Canal Company in 1956 and politically defeat the "Tripartite Aggression of Britain, France and Israel." This rising political hegemony was reinforced when Cairo was explicitly solicited to lead the union with Syria in the United Arab Republic (Flory and Korany 1991; Riad 1986,

193–222). Not only were two prominent states combining their capabilities, but two Pan-Arab organizations—the Ba'th and Nasserism—were joining forces to establish an imposing influential pole projecting the future blueprint of Arab society.

Even though the UAR's existence came to an end after only three and a half years, Nasserism survived. It manifested its tangible power by sending troops across the Red Sea to assure the survival of a revolutionary regime in one of the most inhospitable areas for revolutionary change in the Arab world: Yemen. Egyptian troops were thus amassed in the backyard of the leader of Arab conservatism and traditionalism: Saudi Arabia. More than once these troops crossed Saudi frontiers in hot pursuit of Yemen's royalist forces. Increasingly, Arab interactions were polarized. With the main Western powers actively involved on the Saudi side, the Arab world echoed the global bipolar structure. As at the global level, bipolarity did not mean complete parity between the camps. Algeria's 1962 independence, the 1963 coups in Syria and Iraq, followed by tripartite unity talks in the spring and summer of that year, illustrated that Nasserism still represented the regional dominant pole, both at the state and civil society levels. The cracks within the Saudi regime, such as the defection of some Saudi pilots, the activities of "liberal princes," and the departure of King Saud himself for asylum in Egypt, confirmed Egypt's apparent hegemony. In contradiction of the theory of hegemonic stability (Gilpin 1987, 86–92), Egypt's hegemony did not last long.

Egyptian hegemony was overstretched and eventually exhausted. The humiliating defeat in the third war with Israel—the so-called Six-Day War—confirmed this exhaustion (Korany 1988, 164–178).

What Nasser said in November 1967 is still valid. "After this great catastrophe, we were like a man who went out in the street to be hit by a tram or a car and lay both motionless and senseless on the ground." Six months later on April 25, 1968, he described himself as "a man walking in a desert surrounded by moving sands not knowing whether, if he moved, he would be swallowed up by the sands or would find the right path." Indeed, on November 23, 1967, Nasser admitted that his country's direct losses at the hands of a state with one-tenth Egypt's population were 11,500 killed, 5,500 captured, 80 percent of Egypt's armor and 286 of its 340 combat aircraft destroyed. The chaotic collision between two divisions of the Egyptian army in their disorganized race to withdraw to the mountain passes showed that the army as a military corps had ceased to exist. To add insult to injury, Israel's casualties were comparable proportionally to yearly road accidents in any industrialized country or even in Israel itself.

Worse still, there was no diplomatic victory (as in the 1956 Suez war, for instance) to compensate for this military disaster. On the contrary, to this Arab military defeat was added political humiliation. As one observer noted,

> The pre-war picture of Israel as a beleaguered fortress . . . had earned the Israelis wide international sympathy. . . . By the discrepancies between their threats and their performance, the Arabs had invited the world's derision. This had been skillfully encouraged by Israeli psychological warfare and propaganda which stressed the cowardice rather than the lack of skills of the Arabs and took every opportunity of showing the Arab and especially the Egyptian armies in a humiliating light—for example, by photographing Egyptian prisoners stripped to their underwear or in other unheroic situations. (Stephens 1971, 497, 504).

Arab speeches of the time are full of themes of the "ordeal," the "cruelty of our situation," "our great pains," "the greatest test and crisis of our modern history." These expressions are in fact reminiscent of the first wave of writings by Constantine Zureik and others after the first "catastrophe," that of 1948. Similarly, the "setback" in 1967 led to a second wave of lamentation literature (Korany 1988, 164–178; Maddi 1978; Shukri 1970).

In an atmosphere of tightening political control by the existing regimes, it seems that mass protest and lamentation could best be expressed through novels and other literary forms, and thus publications of this genre increased noticeably. Between 1961 and 1966, the number of novels published in the Arab world was 92, between 1968 and 1973, the number was 163. The yearly average thus jumped from 15 novels to 27 annually (Maddi 1978: 26–35).

INCREASING DIFFUSION OF POWER

Nasser's personal popularity notwithstanding, the demise of the Egyptian pole was confirmed and even legitimized during the August 1967 Khartoum Arab Summit. Nasser's Egypt and the radical Arab order was to be subservient to what we can call "political petrolism." Two immediate indications demonstrate the retreat of the radical order: the hurried withdrawal of Egyptian forces from Yemen, and Egypt's financial dependency on subsidies from the oil-rich states. Neither the emergence of a fervorous Muammar al-Qadhafi (1969) in his fragile state, nor the stateless Palestinian revolution could provide an alternative base for the radical order. The power vacuum—to use the language of balance of power adherents—was to be filled by "petro-powers"—at least by default (Korany 1988, 164–178).

Some quantitative indicators confirm the primacy of the oil states in inter-Arab politics (Dessouki 1982, 326–347).

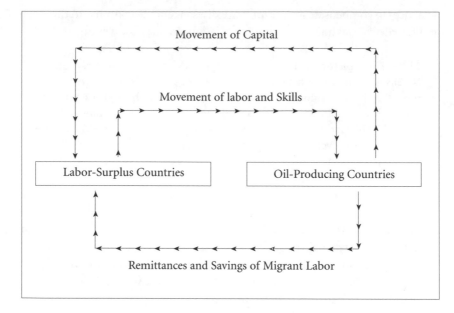

FIGURE 2.1   Mobility of Labor and Capital
Source: Abdel-Fadil 1979, 161.

By 1979, 55 percent of the capital of inter-Arab economic joint ventures was contributed by oil-rich Saudi Arabia, Kuwait, the UAE, Qatar, and Libya; and usually the country that contributes the most capital becomes the host country for any new project headquarters.

Thus, the oil states were becoming the locale of an increasing number of new Arab organizations. In 1970, Cairo was host to 29, or 65 percent, of these organizations; Iraq hosted none and Saudi Arabia only one. Eight years later, Baghdad had become the locale for 12 organizations, thus occupying the second place after Egypt, and Saudi Arabia was in third place with eight organizations.

Fewer Arab League meetings were held in Egypt and more in the oil states. The proportion of meetings held in Cairo decreased from 70.5 percent in 1977 (the year of Sadat's visit to Jerusalem) to 42.2 percent in 1978 (the year of the Camp David Accords).

Egypt's share in the Arab League budget dropped. That share was above 40 percent until the late 1950s but declined until in 1978—the year the Arab League moved to Tunis—it was only 13.7 percent, equivalent to the contribution of Kuwait.

Yet, the rise of oil states created a golden opportunity for a balanced, less monocentric Arab interstate community to develop. For instance, some basic shortages of the newly rich powers were offset by the "excesses" of the old declining powers, enabling the former to create a demand for the surplus labor of the latter (see Figure 2.1).

Moreover, the huge oil revenues were partially redistributed through remittances to the poor labor-exporting countries, with the result of more equally widespread benefits to the region as a whole (see table 2.1). What better basis for an integrated Arab system could there be?

SEEMING ARAB COMPLEMENTARITY IN THE 1970S.

With the exception of Algeria and Iraq, the so-called rich countries were lacking in everything from food to arms. There were huge deficiencies in infrastructure and in established bureaucracy as well as in personnel. Once development projects were envisaged, both skilled and unskilled labor was acutely needed, and importing it was beneficial to the Arab interstate society as a whole since the problem of most Arab countries has been a labor surplus.

Thus, the complementarity among the factors of production, labor, and capital, provided an excellent prod for integration and thus a higher level of resource exploitation. Moreover, the acceleration of the laborers' movement across state frontiers showed the fragility of legal state barriers, and made the different strata of Arab society aware of their interdependence.

Why did this integrative process stop half way despite the factors in its favor? This question touches on one of the most nagging issues of recent social analysis: the transformation of political systems. Although some studies have addressed themselves successfully to the transformation of nation-state systems (Goldstone 1989; Moore 1966), analysis of the transformation of interstate or international systems is still in an embryonic stage (Armstrong 1993). Consequently, the ups and downs in the Arab interstate society can shed light on the conceptual issues of system transformation while also providing information on the important regional dynamics in this part of the world.

Two preliminary explanations answer why the Arab integrative process stopped half way: The inability (even if willingness existed) of oil states to act as an alternative regional base and the absence of a pan-social project to give normative direction and hold the interstate society together. The result of this fragility of a petro-based hub would not be a shift to another hegemon but, rather, power diffusion.

The oil states are not powers in the conventional sense of this concept. If they are powers at all, it is purely in the financial sense. They lack almost all other attributes of power: sizeable population, solid administrative structures, well-trained effective military manpower, and pan-Arab political organizations. Even though Saudi per capita income is 16 times that of Egypt, Saudi Arabia is basi-

TABLE 2.1. Remittances in Select Labor Exporting and Importing Countries
(millions $U.S.)

Country	1973	1974	1975	1976	1977	1978
Export Labor:						
Sudan	6.3	4.9	1.5	36.8	37.0	66.1
Egypt	123.0	310.0	455.0	842.0	988.0	1824.0
N. Yemen	na	135.5	270.2	675.9	987.1	910.1
S. Yemen	32.9	42.8	58.8	119.3	187.3	254.8
Jordan	55.4	82.0	172.0	401.8	420.8	468.0
Import Labor:						
S. Arabia	−391.0	−518.0	−554.0	−989.0	−1506.0	−2844.0
Bahrain	na	na	−227.6	−252.8	−300.3	−387.7
Oman	na	−111.0	−208.0	−220.0	−222.0	−212.0
Libya	−273.0	−350.0	−260.0	−257.0	−856.0	−557.0
Kuwait	na	na	−276.0	−315.0	−370.0	−433.0
Country	1979	1980	1981	1982	1983	1984
Export Labor:						
Sudan	115.7	209.0	322.7	107.1	245.8	275.3
Egypt	2269.0	2791.0	2230.0	2116.0	3315.0	3611.0
N. Yemen	936.7	1069.5	777.4	911.4	1084.4	995.5
S. Yemen	311.5	347.1	406.2	429.7	436.3	479.3
Jordan	509.0	666.5	921.9	932.9	923.9	1053.3
Import Labor:						
S. Arabia	−3365.0	−4064.0	−4100.0	−5211.0	−5236.0	−5284.0
Bahrain	−278.8	−282.8	−317.6	−311.4	−300.0	−345.7
Oman	−249.0	−326.0	−452.0	−684.0	−692.0	−819.0
Libya	−371.0	−622.0	−1314.0	−1597.0	−2098.0	−1544.0
Kuwait	−532.0	−692.0	−689.0	−702.0	−906.0	−855.4

Source: IMF *International Financial Statistics Yearbook*, December 1980, February 1983, December 1985, as adapted from Nazli Choucri, "The Hidden Enemy: A New View of Remittances in the Arab World," in *World Development* 14(6)(1986):697–712.

cally poor in most indices of development. In 1975, Saudi Petroleum Minister Ahmed Zaki Yamani described his country in the following way:

> . . . We are still a poor country . . . we lack industry, agriculture . . . manpower . . . we have to import engineers, technicians, specialized workers that we don't know where to house because we lack hotels. To build hotels we need contractors, but the contractors themselves need hotels to live in. It is a vicious circle that exhausts us. Among other things we lack cement. We lack harbors because we lack cement to build them. Last, but by no means least, we lack water. We haven't a single river, a single lake. We depend on rainfall alone. For one hundred years, it has rained less and less frequently, for the last twenty-five years hardly at all. (Ayubi 1982, 23–24)

Even in purely financial terms, Saudi per capita income is comparable to that of Finland, which is not a particularly rich country, and has lent its name to the political term "Finlandization," indicating almost total marginality and dependence. Until the gigantic projects at Jubail and Yanbu' manage to give an industrial base to the Saudi kingdom, it remains dependent on the outside world. In fact, in all of the oil states, even basic infrastructure is still in the making, and that thanks to foreign labor. For instance, in 1975, foreign workers constituted 81 percent of the labor force in Qatar and 85 percent in the UAE.

Another reason for the fragility of the "petro-based hub" lies with historical patterns of social organization. The process of state-formation rendered those countries family-states rather than nation-states. The economist Hazem El-Beblawi writes: "Though oil wealth has transformed [the Gulf States] into advanced welfare states, they still remain patriarchal in a distinctly familial way. The Sauds, the Sabahs, the Al-Thanis, the Qasimis, the Al-Nahayans, the Al-Maktums, the Al-Khalifas, are not only the ruling families: they embody the legitimacy of the existing regimes" (El Beblawi 1982, 210–11).

Pan-Arabism retreated in front of the *raison d'état*, which was indiscriminately mixed with *raison de famille*. Two results follow from this situation. First, the leadership was characterized by a limited time horizon and an extremely personalized perception of national and international events. Second, inter-Arab relations were contaminated with the long history of interfamily feuds. In short, family frictions imposed extreme limitations on political coordination. Unfortunately, the rising technocratic elite has not been able to change this situation much. Consequently, Arab finance has not been a complement to pan-Arabism. The oil states were unable or unwilling to devise an Arab strategy. If they seemed in control, it was not so much that their achievements have won out, but that the outcome has been determined by the failure and exhaustion of the "radicals." Thus, the oil states' primacy in the Arab interstate society represented victory by default.

This is not a strong base for an international regime. Even if Saudi Arabia, the birthplace of Islam, had become armed with a barrel of oil and was increasingly the site of secular as well as religious pilgrimage, it has not been able to keep a regional system together. As has been said, "the hegemony of mere money unsupported by manpower, cultural attainments, military strength or industrial development may be something of a mirage." (Kerr and Yassin, 1982, 11)

The increasing labor-capital complementarity was not correlated—as the functionalist theory of integration insists—with equivalent political integration. All that could be achieved from 1971 to 1974 was a Cairo-Riyadh axis, based on a tradeoff of Egyptian capabilities and Saudi money. A predominant characteristic of a relationship based on money is constant haggling, which may destroy the relationship at any time. A general mood of "affairism" rivaled nationalist commitment and penetrated the highest echelons of society, even trickling down to the masses in former revolutionary centers like Egypt and Syria. Heikal (1978b, 261–62) summarized the change:

> For a generation the men who directed the course of events in the Arab world had been ideologists or officers from the armed forces—or sometimes officers who turned into ideologists or ideologists who tried to behave as if they were officers . . . (for example, Sadat, Assad, Boumedienne, Qadhafi, Michel Aflaq, Saddam Hussein). . . . Many of these were still there, but they were now being joined by the first installment of a new breed of power brokers, the middlemen, the arms dealers, the wealthy merchants who flitted between East and West, between royal palaces and the offices of royal companies . . . (for example, Kamal Adham, Mahdi Tajir, Adnan Khashoggi) . . . and by royalty itself, for who in the Arab world now exercised more power that Prince Fahd or Prince Sultan of Saudi Arabia? Could not individuals such as these, it was argued, achieve more for the Arab world than mass movements and radical revolutions? It is not surprising if in this changed atmosphere men and women in Egypt and Syria felt that the time had come for them, too, to see some improvement in their material circumstances. They had known hardship; now they looked for their reward—for more to eat and for better houses to live in. Of course, money would have to be found to pay for this, but who would dare to suggest that the Arabs were short of money? It was being said that the Arabs possessed the power to bring the rest of the world to starvation; surely they must have the power to feed themselves? So eyes turned to the oil-producing countries. Oil fields began to loom far bigger in the public mind than battlefields; *tharwa* (riches), it was said, had begun to take over from *thawra* (revolution).

The end result was not then another cycle of hegemony but rather power diffusion. Within this pattern of power diffusion, there were attempts at partnership. Though issue-specific and consequently short-lived, they still went beyond axis-building. A well-known example of such partnership was the Egyptian-Syrian-Saudi coordination for the launching of the 1973 October war with Israel.

The preparation (rather than the performance) of the October war was based on minute planning, systematic information gathering and analysis, and detailed discussion and bargaining among the different participants, notably between Syria and Egypt. These two countries' various negotiations and discussions resulted on January 31, 1973, in the organization of a unified command for their armed forces (Korany 1986, 87–112). Continuous and intense coordination at top political and military leadership levels fixed the specific day and hour of the attack on the ceasefire lines with Israel: Yom Kippur, Saturday, October 6, 1973, 2 p.m., Middle Eastern time.

Along with this politico-military coordination, the war had a wide impact on the global economy because of the accompanying decision to impose an oil embargo. The decision to employ an oil embargo was actually a cluster of several decisions. The announcement on October 17, 1973 by the oil ministers of the Organization of Arab Petroleum Exporting Countries (OPEC) of a monthly 5 percent cut in the flow of oil to the United States and other countries supporting Israel against the Arabs. It also included Saudi Arabia's October 18 announcement to cut oil production by 10 percent at the time the United States especially was pressing oil-producing countries to increase their production to meet the demand of an increasingly oil thirsty world. Also part of the embargo was Saudi Arabia's October 20 announcement to stop all oil exports to the United States following President Richard Nixon's October 19 demand to Congress for $2.2 billion in emergency security assistance to Israel and the continuation of a massive U.S. airlift beginning October 13 to compensate Israel's war losses.

This partnership, however, was already reaching its limit by 1975. In September 1975, Egypt formally initiated its go-it-alone diplomacy with Israel by signing its second disengagement agreement with a political clause amounting to a state of nonbelligerency. The rift between Egypt and Syria was patched up temporarily in a 1976 tripartite summit in Riyadh. Saudi mediation facilitated an Egyptian-Syrian reconciliation where Syria agreed to tone down its critique of the Egyptian move and Egypt accepted the presence of Syrian troops in Lebanon. Egypt's go-it-alone diplomacy with Israel was confirmed and consolidated on the occasion of Sadat's "sacred mission" to Jerusalem. Egypt's membership in the Arab League was suspended and the League moved its headquarters from Cairo to Tunis.

The attempt at partnership was revived again on the occasion of the second Gulf War. The partners were almost the same, except that Saudi Arabian participation was enlarged to include other oil-producing Gulf countries, and Syria brought along Lebanon. In 1992, the number of visits exchanged within this group was 131—compared to 38 visits for the nine-country pro-Iraqi partnership (Arab Strategic Yearbook 1992, 192–96). But this partnership around the March 1991 Damascus Declaration was even more short-lived than the first one. Even though the Damascus Declaration has not been formally abrogated, it was never carried out.

In addition to partnership, this pattern of power diffusion has also witnessed an institutionalized coalition-building. The most notable examples are the various subregional organizations. These were three on the eve of the second Gulf War: the Arab Cooperation Council (Egypt, Iraq, Jordan, and Yemen), the UMA (Union du Maghreb Arabe: Algeria, Libya, Mauritania, Morocco, and Tunisia) and the Gulf Cooperation Council (Bahrain, Kuwait, Oman, Qatar, UAE, and Saudi Arabia). The fifteen Arab countries that were divided among these different suborganizations represented two-thirds of all the Arab population, hosted the highest number of universities and research centers, controlled 90 percent of traditional energy resources and 75 percent of water and agricultural resources.

On the surface, these organizations were active and dynamic. The Arab Cooperation Council, for instance, held no less than seventeen formal meetings at the summit or ministerial level during 1989 (Arab Strategic Yearbook 1989, 259–69). Yet this Council precisely broke down on the occasion of its first policy challenge: Iraq's invasion of Kuwait. The Council members were never consulted or even informed of this decision, and Egypt joined the international coalition against Iraq. Equally divided was the UMA, with Morocco sending troops to Saudi Arabia. Only the GCC kept its ranks unified, but failed to prevent its founding member, Kuwait, from being attacked and occupied.

Regional power diffusion often invites claims for hegemony. The most notable is, of course, Iraq's attempt, of which the 1990 invasion of Kuwait was part and parcel. But this attempt dismally failed, with dire consequences for both Iraq and the Arab interstate society as a whole.

The 1990s Arab Balance of Weakness

A traumatizing result of aborted hegemony—like the one following Iraq's eviction from Kuwait—is not simply a return to the previous pattern of power diffusion. Saddam's Iraq had violated a taboo. It not only initiated inter-Arab war-

fare on a large scale but also sought to cancel out an Arab League member. Moreover, it justified its action by appeals that were attractive to the majority of Arab populations: correcting colonial border demarcation, achieving Arab unity, and redressing flagrant inter-Arab inequalities.

Consequently, the end of the military confrontation did not mean the end of all forms of inter-Arab warfare, either between states or within their societies. Mutual recriminations of "stoogism," "treason," and "adventurism" as well as vendettas still linger on both sides. In a word, Arab society is seriously bruised, with the marks likely to remain for a long time. This is not a political or psychological context conducive to partnerships.

The result at present is a pattern not only of power diffusion but also of weakness diffusion. A minimum of inter-Arab coordination has not only declined but in many cases has been replaced by narrow state interests and interstate competition even in the face of core Arab issues such as the Arab-Israeli Conflict. A prevailing atmosphere of lack of credibility among many Arab leaders—especially between the PLO and Jordan—has been dutifully exploited by Israel's negotiators to emphasize diversity of Arab state interests (Arab Strategic Yearbook 1992, 211–31). Burning Arab issues, like Somalia's disintegration or the civil war in Yemen, have illustrated a glaring absence of any Arab mechanism of conflict resolution or even conflict management.

In this context, it is more appropriate to talk of an Arab balance of weakness, rather than balance of power. This becomes clear when we return to the distinction of Arab versus non-Arab clusters in the region. Already during the 1980s, Iran threatened the Arab status quo not only by virtue of its physical size and strength but also because of its revolutionary Islamic ideology. The support extended by Arab Gulf states and other Arab regimes to Iraq during its eight-year war against Iran stemmed especially from the hope of undermining the credibility of revolutionary Islam. During the 1990–1991 Gulf crisis, Iraq found it necessary to rebuild bridges to its erstwhile enemy. In a desperate bid to minimize the destruction of its military machine, Iraq sent part of its air force—23 planes according to Iran, 135 according to Baghdad—to the safety of Iranian airfields. Teheran's Islamic Republic—after long being considered a pariah state—seemed to be rehabilitated in the wake of the Gulf crisis at Iraq's expense. With Iraq still in disarray, the potential for future regional hegemony by Iran was rendered easier.

The Gulf crisis further consolidated Israel's military predominance in the region. Conventional indicators establishing Israel's military superiority over the Arab world are too well-known and numerous to be repeated here. It suffices to point out that Iraq's defeat obviously tilted the balance even more in Israel's favor. More important, however, is the degree to which the Gulf crisis

furthered Israel's political integration within the region. A few years ago, few would have imagined the signing of formal agreements or even the convening of multilateral Arab-Israeli talks. Visions of Omani delegates speaking publicly with Israeli counterparts in Moscow corridors would have seemed far-fetched as would suggestions that Saudi Arabia's Prince Bandar might coordinate moves with U.S. Jewish leaders or that his country would host visiting Jewish delegates. These events have occurred, and the ongoing Middle East peace talks have moved from discussions of military and political matters to technical and cultural issues. The fact that all of this has transpired with no radical transformation of Israel's approach to some basic conflict issues—the application of the principle of self-determination to the Palestinian people, and the status of Jerusalem—starkly shows how far the balance of power has moved in Israel's favor.

Turkey was one of the greatest winners of the 1991 Gulf War. After the end of the Cold War, Turkey was in danger of losing its strategic importance between the East and West. The Gulf War gave Turkey a new strategic role at the expense of its Arab neighbors. Again, the military gap is too clear to be labored, but Turkey is now capitalizing on a much more important strategic asset: water resources.

In a region of overuse and undersupply, as is the case of the Arab world, water is literally a factor in survival and is at the basis of any program of food security. It is, therefore, notable that 67 percent of the Tigris's sources and 88 percent of the Euphrates's sources originate in Turkey. With the decline of Iraq's military power, Turkey is in an even stronger position to exercise substantial pressures for political concessions on both Iraq and Syria. Turkey's blockage of the Euphrates's water flow for a month in early 1990 not only affected agriculture in Syria and Iraq but also led to frequent electricity cuts in both countries. At present, there are serious concerns over the effects of Turkey's planned $20 billion water control project, a massive undertaking that envisages the construction of 21 dams and 17 power stations. If Turkish hopes of extending water pipelines to Jordan, Palestine, Iraq, and the Gulf are eventually realized, Ankara will be in a good position to barter water for oil and, more important, to dominate daily life in much of the Arab world.

Thus with the elimination of Iraq as a military power for years to come and Arab dispersion, erstwhile Arab power levels have declined in both relative and absolute terms. The result is a higher level of Arab insecurity and multiplicity of threats—military and otherwise: e.g., Syria in relation to Turkey and Israel. Moreover, for some Arab countries threats come now from within the family. Kuwait and other Gulf countries have now to face up to the multiplicity of threats from both Iran and Iraq, including subversive activities. Possibly, such

TABLE 2.2. Political Processes Under Conditions of Realism and
Complex Interdependence

	Realism	Complex Interdependence
Goals of Actors	Military security will be the Dominant goal.	Goals of states will vary by issue area. Transgovernmental politics will make goals difficult to define. Transnational actors will pursue their own goals.
Instruments of state policy	Military force will be most effective, although economic and other instruments will also be used.	Power resources specific to issue areas will be most relevant. Manipulation of interdependence, international organizations, and transnational actors will be major instruments.
Agenda formation	Potential shifts in the balance of power and security threats will set the agenda in high politics and will strongly influence other agendas.	Agenda will be affected by changes in the distribution of power resources within issue areas; the status of international regimes; changes in the importance of transnational actors; linkages from other issues and politicization as a result of rising sensitivity interdependence.
Linkages of issues	Linkages will reduce differences in outcomes among issue areas and reinforce international hierarchy.	Linkages by strong states will be more difficult to make since force will be ineffective. Linkages by weak states through international organizations will erode rather than reinforce hierarchy.
Roles of international organizations	Roles are minor, limited by state power and the importance of military force.	Organizations will set agendas, induce coalition-formation, and act as arenas for political action by weak states. Ability to choose the organizational forum for an issue and to mobilize votes will be an important political resource.

Source: Keohane and Nye 1977, 37

multiplicity of threats could balance each other out, giving rise to what we can call a new balance of threats. Indeed, American policy toward the Gulf in the 1990s has been articulated as a strategy of "dual containment"; of Iraq and Iran. (Indyk 1994; Gause 1994)

If this line of thinking is adopted among Gulf countries, it means that the Arab/non-Arab distinction in regional politics is an increasingly fading line in the sand. The alternative might then well be a reorientation of regional politics toward the adoption of a new conceptual lens: a balance of benefits.

From Balance of Power to Balance of Benefits?

The two proposed conceptual lenses of balance of power versus balance of benefits refer to seemingly two different visions of international relations. They have been dubbed power politics versus interdependence. The first emphasizes the continuity of (violent) history ever since Ancient Greece and the Peloponnesian War. The aim is to attract attention to the ever-present predictability of war among sovereign states (and hence the necessity of power balance). The second, interdependence, aims to understand change at the international level (including regional) and the increasing human interconnectedness (both interstate and intersociety) in the global village. Keohane and Nye's preceding table (1977, 37) synthesizes well the differences between realism based on balance of power and interdependence based on cooperation and the possibility of a balance of benefits.(Table 2–2)

I have shown elsewhere (Korany 1996) that some political practices make the two conceptualizations less mutually exclusive than their developers want them to be. Indeed, interdependence terminology could be used to promote balance of power calculations even by some visionaries of a "New Middle East" (Peres 1993, 21, 33–34). Does this mean that the balance of power conceptual lens is the be-all and end-all and that the analysis of Middle East dynamics cannot be conceived in any other light? This would be a reductionist view of a region as complex as the Middle East.

The "New Middle East's" power calculations notwithstanding, the interdependence conceptual lens is different from the traditional balance of power lens in two main respects: (1) interstate relationships are not pure zero-sum games, where some win all and others lose all. Power is not primarily military but multifaceted; it is not absolute but relative. It can be shared, albeit not equally. (2) interstate relationships are not reduced to violent warfare, where history is defined as the normalization of the use of force—Raymond Aron's *marche à la folie*.

For example, from an interdependence perspective, conflicts between the Arab states and Israel could be managed before escalating to military confrontation, owing to the multiplication of channels of communication between them. Moreover, the emergence of "low politics" (e.g., economic boycott, normalization) make the use of military force less efficacious in settling most of them. "The scale," Peres rightly observes, "has tipped in the direction of economic rather than military might" (Peres 1993, 34–35). Consequently, national security, which conventionally is seen as depending on military and weapons systems, is increasingly "*of necessity* based on political accords and embraces international security and economic considerations" (Peres, 33–34, emphasis added).

Therefore, given (a) the complexity of the Middle East and its multiplicity of issues, and (b) its continuous evolution (indeed, its seeming eternal state of transition!), it seems clear that the two conceptual lenses must be used side by side in order to address the complex dynamics of this region. Some examples will clarify this point. One concerns the prevalence of protracted conflict and the relevance of balance of power reasoning. In the summer of 1997 when reading the regional press (both Arab and Israeli) one was reminded of the late 1960s when the Arab-Israeli conflict dominated the scene. Regional interactions oscillated between peace initiatives (such as Swedish diplomat Gunnar Jarring's fruitless mission) and warfare (such as the "war of attrition" between Egypt and Israel along the Suez Canal). Warlike behavior tended to overshadow fledgling "peace processes."

The situation in the late 1990s is similar. As in the post-1967 Six-Day War context, Arab governments manifest no unified Arab strategy, and major sectors of Arab civil sosciety resent what they perceive as Israeli *dictats*. These inter-Arab divisions (among states and within them) were exemplified by disagreements over attending the fourth Middle East and North Africa Economic Summit, scheduled to be held in Doha, Qatar in November 1997. The disagreement pitted Qatar—committed to Washington's efforts to promote a "new Middle East" regional order, including Israel—against a growing number of Arab governments disenchanted with the policies of the hardline Israeli government of Benyamin Netanyahu. The dissidents even included Saudi Arabia—traditionally very supportive of the "peace process." With such a reintensification of the conflict between the longtime Arab and Israeli protagonists, one is tempted to stick to the balance-of-power conceptual lens in decoding regional politics.

But there is danger in looking at the region as if its main conflict patterns and protagonists have remained unchanged over the years. For important aspects of the seemingly eternal Arab-Israeli conflict have changed considerably

since the Six-Day War. Peace treaties have established a different code of conduct. Diplomatic relations, exchange of top-level visits, mutual investments, and economic relations do create patterns of partnership. Even for the Likud establishment the PLO is no longer entirely reduced to a "terrorist organization." Similarly, Netanyahu's Israel is no longer reduced simply to "the Zionist entity" in the perception of most Palestinian and Arab elites. No less a figure than President Hafiz al-Assad of Syria personally received (in August 1997) a delegation of Israeli Arabs, including Knesset members representing official Israeli political parties. Such an evolution—involving as it does the end of non-recognition and the growth of multiple open and direct contacts at both the state and societal levels—invites and indeed requires us to complement the balance of power analysis by also looking at the region through the interdependence conceptual lens. The relevance of the latter approach is reinforced by the increasing permeability of the state in the Arab world and the increasing political importance of the societal dimension.

If with increasing globalization the state is no longer an island but a crossroads, the Arab/non-Arab dividing line cannot be assumed to include in one bloc monolithic Arab entities behaving like billiard balls on the pool table of international power politics, as Heikal's twenty-year old quotation cited above indicates. The "non-Arab periphery" is increasingly part of intra-Arab and inter-Arab interactions. Israel has been and will increasingly continue to be an explicit factor in inter-Arab politics—in conflict as well as cooperation. Whatever the lapses of the peace process, Israeli penetration of inter-Arab politics will intensify horizontally (covering more sectors of relations) and vertically (becoming deeper in specific sectors). Iran's (Shi'ite) Islamic revolution continues to represent a major attraction for many Arab-Islamic movements, including the Sunni ones. Turkey, either because of its water resources or arms industry, represents a pole of attraction of a different kind.

Similarly, at the level of state-society relations (Hudson 1994), Arab monolithism—for so long an assumed given—is also eroding. Though the *coup d'état* that characterized Arab domestic politics in the 1950s and 1960s have until new blocked major political change at the top, the Arab domestic scene is increasingly dominated by clashes between the incumbent government and armed groups. The case of the Islamic Salvation Front (FIS) in Algeria first comes to mind, but Islamist protest movements are prevalent all across the region. In addition we see growing conflicts pitting incumbent regimes against minority groups ethnic movements, as in the Sudan (against its southernmost population) in 1955–62 and 1983 to the present, and in Iraq (against its Kurdish minority) for extended periods since 1958. Some of these intrastate conflicts

have reached the level of civil war: e.g. Lebanon, 1975–1990; Somalia, 1991–1994; and Djibouti, 1992–1994 (Abdel-Salam 1994). In such situations we are indeed far from the geopolitical thinking of the "national security" "billiard ball" state as depicted through the balance-of-power conceptual lens.

Do these factors of declining state monolithism, growing transstate relations and societal interconnectedness completely invalidate the Arab/non-Arab distinction? The traumatizing Gulf war of 1990–91 has certainly given credence to such a view. Such assertions, however, go against the grain of prevalent cultural norms and the collective psychology in the region. What Paul Noble (1991, 47–48) observed a few years ago is still valid: "In some ways, the Arab system has resembled a vast sound chamber in which information, ideas, and opinions have resonated with little regard for state frontiers. Political developments and changes in one segment of the system have set off reverberations in other segments. . . ."

This multi-level and intense interconnectedness distinguish the Arab core from the Middle East region as a whole. The result is that the prevalent inter-Arab conflicts—which will probably continue—do not seem to diminish this collective Arab identity. These conflicts have been less militarized than in other regions. According to Abdel-Salam (1994), for the period 1945–1990 the greatest number of conflicts (49 percent) were conducted through propaganda campaigns. In only 9 percent of these conflicts were military means employed, and even then they were limited in 86 percent of the cases. Iraq's 1990 invasion of Kuwait is an exceptional rather than representative case of inter-Arab dispute. The Arab/non-Arab distinction, though changing, is still alive and relevant to the balance of power configuration at the wider Middle East regional level.

Conclusion

To reiterate, then, the picture at the end of the century is of a complex region in a continuing state of transition, oscillating between coming together and moving apart, between welfare and warfare, at both the state and society levels. This is what makes the analysis of the region both challenging and stimulating. On the eve of the third millennium Middle East dynamics—in addition to their manifest global importance—constitute an intellectual laboratory offering benefits for both the area specialists concerned with micro-level description and understanding and for the political science/international relations generalists interested in empirically based model building.

References

Abdel-Fadil, Mahmoud. *Oil and Arab Unity*. Beirut: Center for Arab Unity Studies, 1979.
Abdel-Salam, Mohamed. *Inter-Arab Military Conflicts*. Cairo: Al-Ahram Center for Political and Strategic Studies, No. 23, 1994 (in Arabic).
Ahmed, Ahmed Youssef. *Inter-Arab Conflicts: A Heuristic Study*. Beirut: Centre for Arab Unity Studies, 1988 (in Arabic).
Armstrong, David. *Revolution and World Order*. Oxford: Clarendon Press, 1993.
Ayubi, Nazih. "OPEC and the Third World: The Case of Arab Aid." In Robert Stookey, ed. *The Arab Peninsula*. Stanford, CA: The Hoover Institution, 1982.
Barraclough, Geoffrey and Rachel Wall, eds. *Survey of International Affairs 1955–1956*. Oxford: Oxford University Press (for the Royal Institute of International Affairs), 1960.
Choukri, Nazli. "The Hidden Enemy: A New View of Remittances in the Arab World." *World Development*, 14:6 (1986), 697–712.
Cobden, Richard. *Political Writings*, vol. 1. London: Ridgway, 1867.
Dessouki, Ali E. Hillal. "The New Arab Political Order: Implications for the 1980s." In Malcolm H. Kerr and El-Sayed Yassin , eds. *Rich and Poor States in the Middle East*. Boulder, CO: Westview Press, 1982.
El-Beblawi, Hazem. "The Predicament of the Arab Gulf Oil States." In Malcolm H. Kerr and El-Sayed Yassin, eds. *Rich and Poor States in the Middle East*. Boulder, CO: Westview Press, 1982.
Fero, Marc. *Comment on raconte l'histoire a traverse le mode arabe entier*. Paris: Payot, 1986.
Flory, Maurice and Bahgat Korany, et al. *Régimes politiques arabes*. Paris: Presses universitaires de France, 1991.
Gause, F. Gregory, III. "The Illogic of Dual Containment." *Foreign Affairs* 73:2 (March-April 1994), 22–44.
Gilpin, Robert. *The Political Economy of International Relations*. Princeton, NJ: Princeton University Press, 1987.
Goldstone, Jack. *Revolution and Rebellion in the Early Modern World*. Berkeley: University of California Press, 1989.
Haas, Ernest. "The Balance of Power: Prescription, Concept and Propaganda." *World Politics* 5:4 (1953), 442–77.
Heikal, Mohamed. "Egypt's Foreign Policy." *Foreign Affairs* 56 (1978), 714–27.
Heikal, Mohamed. *The Sphinx and the Commissar*. New York: Harper and Row, 1978.
Hudson, Michael C. "Democracy and Foreign Policy in the Arab World." In David Garnham and Mark Tessler, eds. *Democracy, War and Peace in the Middle East*. Bloomington: Indiana University Press 1994.
Indyk, Martin, et al. "Dual Containment." *Middle East Policy*, 3 (1994): 1–26.
Kennedy, Paul. *The Rise and Decline of Great Powers*. New York: Random House, 1988.
Keohane, Robert O. and Joseph S. Nye, Jr. *Power and Interdependence*. Boston: Little, Brown, 1977.

Kerr, Malcolm H. and El-Sayed Yassin, eds. *Rich and Poor States in the Middle East.* Boulder, CO: Westview Press, 1982.

Korany, Bahgat. *Social Change, Charisma and International Behaviour.* Leiden: Sijthoff, 1976.

Korany, Bahgat, et al. *How Foreign Policy Decisions are Made in the Third World.* Boulder, CO: Westview Press, 1986.

Korany, Bahgat. "Hierarchy Within the South: In Search of Theory." *Third World Affairs Yearbook, 1986.* London: Third World Foundation for Social and Economic Studies, 1986.

Korany, Bahgat. "The Dialectics of Inter-Arab Relations 1967–1987." In Y. Lukacs and A. Batta, eds. *The Arab-Israeli Conflict.* Boulder, CO: Westview Press, 1988, 164–78.

Korany, Bahgat. "The Old/New Middle East." In Laura Guazzone, ed. *The Middle East in Global Change.* New York: St. Martin's, 1997.

Maddi, Shukri. *The 1967 June Defeat in the Arab Novel.* Beirut: Al-mu'assasa al 'arabiyya lil-dirasat wal-nashr, 1978 (in Arabic).

Moore, Barrington, Jr. *The Social Origins of Dictatorship and Democracy: Lord and Peasant in the Making of the Modern World.* Boston: Beacon Press, 1966.

Moul, W. "Measuring the Balance of Power: A Look at Some Numbers." *Review of International Studies,* 15 (1989): 101–21.

Nasser, Gamal Abdel. *Speeches 1959.* Cairo: State Department of Information, 1960.

Noble, Paul. "The Arab System: Pressures, Constraints, and Opportunities." In Bahgat Korany et al. *The Foreign Policies of Arab States,* 2nd. ed. Boulder, CO: Westview Press, 1991.

Nye, Joseph S., Jr. *Bound to Lead: The Changing Nature of American Power.* New York: Basic Books, 1989.

Peres, Shimon (with Arye Noar). *The New Middle East.* New York: Henry Holt, 1993.

Riad, Mahmoud. *Memoirs of Mahmoud Riad.* Cairo: Dar el-Moustaqbal el-Arabi, 1982, vol. 2 (in Arabic).

Stephens, Robert. *Nasser.* London: The Penguin Press, 1971.

Shukri, Ghali. *The Resistance Phenomenon in Arab Literature.* Cairo: Dar el-Maarif, 1970 (in Arabic).

Other Sources

Arab Strategic Yearbook. Cairo: Al-Ahram Center for Political and Strategic Studies, various years (in Arabic).

Newspapers: *Al-Ahram* and *Al-Ahram Weekly* (Cairo), *Al-Hayat* (London), and *The Jerusalem Post* (Israel).

chapter 3

The Prospects for Arab Cooperation in a Changing Regional and Global System

Paul Noble

For nearly fifty years students of international relations have concentrated heavily on conflict and conflict-related topics. When attention turned to the subject of cooperation, it often centered on instances of collaborative action undertaken for purposes of conflict, e.g., alliances.[1] In recent years, however, increasing attention has been paid, both theoretically and empirically, to the question of cooperation in world politics (Oye 1986; Keohane 1984, Krasner 1983). This trend has been reinforced by the end of the Cold War and prospects of a new world order, growing interdependence and economic integration, and a new emphasis on shared interests and common security. It is both appropriate and timely, therefore, to turn our attention to the issue of cooperation in the Arab world.

The focus of this inquiry is cooperation rather than integration. Cooperation is a broader, more elastic concept. According to one well-known definition, cooperation occurs when "actors adjust their behavior to the actual or anticipated preferences of others through a process of policy coordination" (Keohane 1984). This definition, however, is a little too broad since it fails to distinguish between accommodation (i.e. the reduction or resolution of incompatibilities of interests/values between actors and/or agreement to limitations in the way actors pursue their incompatible interests/values) and cooperation in the strict sense of the term. It is in this stricter sense that the term cooperation is used here, namely the adoption of common policies and/or the undertaking of concerted/joint action by two or more actors, whether informally or in an institutional framework. This cooperation can occur in a variety of frameworks ranging from informal common fronts/alignments or coalitions/concerts of powers through formalized alliances or international organizations to out-right unions of states (formal integration). Such cooperation can develop at any level, from particular pairs of states to an overall regional system. This chapter seeks to explore the problem not so much through an examination of actual attempts at Arab unity past or present, but rather through an analysis of under-lying conditions both within the Arab world itself and in the larger regional and global environments that impinge on it. Specifically, it seeks to assess the impact of changing conditions in these spheres on the prospects for Arab cooperation.

As one surveys the post-Cold War, post-Gulf War situation in the Middle East, one is immediately confronted by a striking paradox. Conditions in both the Middle Eastern and global systems seem to pose significant challenges to Arab interests and thus presumably should generate clear incentives for coop-eration. Yet the Arab world remains more fragmented than ever. The explana-tion for this, as we shall see, lies partly in the nature of the challenges faced but more importantly in conditions within the Arab world itself, not only at the level of interstate relations but also, at a deeper level, in the relations between Arab societies and, ultimately, conditions within these societies themselves. Consequently, the underlying theme of this chapter is one of considerable skep-ticism regarding the prospects for cooperation.

The Changing Regional System

Within the larger regional arena, Arab states face substantial challenges from non-Arab regional powers, notably Iran and Israel. These pressures, which have been accentuated by a deterioration in the Arab position on both fronts, have tended, however, to generate more divergence than consensus. The result has been continued fragmentation and increased reliance on outside powers.

THE GULF SECTOR

The situation in the Gulf has been of considerable concern given not only the possibility of renewed Iraqi aggressiveness but also the radically altered strate-gic environment (Cordesman 1993; Chubin 1994). Iraq's massive defeat tem-porarily eliminated one major concern of Arab Gulf states but potentially gen-erated another by creating an imbalance in Iran's favor. The situation has been exacerbated by the accentuation of ethnic and religious divisions in Iraq which have rendered it more permeable to Iranian influence. The imbalance will undoubtedly grow if Iran strengthens its military capabilities and puts its eco-nomic house in order. New opportunities have also emerged for Iran elsewhere in the Arab world as well as in neighboring areas (the Caucasus, Central Asia,

Afghanistan) as a result of the growing strength and activism of Islamic move-ments (Sid Ahmed 1992a, 1992b).

The future direction of Iranian policy, however, remains unclear. Many believe that the increasing emphasis on resolving economic problems com-bined with a shifting internal balance of forces will lead to a more pragmatic foreign policy. At the same time, Iran's greatly improved position in the Gulf and increased presence elsewhere may tempt it to pursue a more assertive, if not adventurous, policy. There have been instances of this in the Gulf, notably the pressure on Sharjah over the future of Abu Musa and Iran's opposition to the involvement of non-Gulf Arab states in Gulf security arrangements com-bined with an insistence on its own inclusion in any such arrangements (Jaber 1992; Haeir 1991). Whatever the direction of Iranian policy, its growing weight and expanded involvement in the region clearly pose an important challenge.

Despite the unstable and potentially threatening environment in the Gulf, the level of Arab cooperation in this area has been limited. The weaknesses of the Arab system are evident in the failure to institute proposed joint Arab secu-rity arrangements for the Gulf. Several factors have been responsible for this failure. The security concerns of the Arab Gulf states remain acute after two major wars in the last decade and the accompanying military and power pres-sures. They fear that these pressures could resume when Iraq regains its strength; at the same time they cast an anxious eye toward Iran and its inten-tions. Given these concerns, the Arab Gulf states are eager both to increase their military capabilities and to participate in effective security arrangements (Gause 1994; Tyler 1991; Ibrahim 1991). The Arab system is perceived, however, to have a limited capacity to generate the required support; there are also ques-tions about the reliability of any such commitments. The United States and Western powers, for their part, clearly possess the required military strength and force projection capacity to meet these states' concerns and, in the course of the Gulf crisis, demonstrated their commitment to do so. Consequently, the Gulf states believe that their security in a turbulent area can best be assured through vertical cooperation (with the Western powers) rather than horizontal (inter-Arab) cooperation.

Divergences in approach to dealing with Iran constitute another obstacle (Gause 1994; Jaber 1991a, 1991b, 1992). Some Gulf states are inclined to concil-iate Iran with a view to encouraging moderation in its policy as well as its avail-ability as a counterweight should Iraq regain its strength and embark once again on an adventurous policy. Those who hold this view have been reluctant to proceed with Arab security arrangements if this would antagonize Iran. Others, particularly Egypt, have not necessarily objected to conciliating Iran but believe that this should be accompanied by an Arab security umbrella to reduce imbalances in Iran's favor and limit any temptation on its part to become more assertive in the Gulf. Syria, for its part, supported the proposed arrangements but, as a quasi-ally of Iran, sought to ensure that these were not directed against it. Inter-Arab considerations have undoubtedly also played a role in hampering security cooperation in the Gulf (Sayigh 1991). One is the concern of the Gulf states that such arrangements would obligate them to provide substantial amounts of financial assistance on a continuing basis. Another is possible Saudi reluctance to accept Syrian participation owing to its close ties with Iran, or Egyptian participation because it might dilute Saudi influence among the smaller Gulf states. Internal security concerns may be another factor.

THE ISRAELI SECTOR

Serious pressures have also confronted the Arab states on the Israeli front. In recent years, Israel has enjoyed a decisive advantage in power terms. This has involved a substantial superiority in conventional forces and a monopoly of nuclear weaponry as well as a capacity to project military power far beyond the frontline states into virtually all areas of the Arab world. Israel's demographic capabilities have also been greatly strengthened through Russian Jewish emigration, thereby undercutting one of the principal arguments against an expansionist policy in the occupied territories. Israel's position has been further strengthened by the sharp decline in Russian and East European military and political support for its principal opponents.

The Gulf conflict had a paradoxical effect on the balance of forces on this front. On the one hand, at the regional level, the imbalance was reinforced by a noticeable weakening of the Arab position in the wake of the war. This stemmed from a series of unfavorable developments: the massive defeat of Iraq, which removed one potentially important military counterweight to Israel, and a clear weakening of Jordan, the PLO, and the Palestinian community. On the other hand, at the overall level, Israel's position weakened because it became increasingly dependent on the United States, particularly in the economic sphere. The Gulf conflict and the dynamics of regional politics also led the United States to press seriously for the initiation of negotiations and to use its increased leverage with Israel to ensure progress toward that end. This combination of factors contributed in part to the defeat of the Likud government in the 1992 elections and a reassessment of Israeli policy toward the conflict under the new Labor government. Such a reassessment may have eased one set of threats to Arab frontline parties but in some ways it posed an even more difficult challenge. For a more flexible Israeli policy, even one that still fell short of offering an honorable settlement on some fronts, combined with the advent of a more favorable American administration, produced a marked rapprochement with the United States. Israel thus continued to enjoy clear-cut superiority over the neighboring Arab states and the advantage of ongoing control over the disputed areas, but with little or no pressure from Washington to offset this. Indeed, it benefited from increased U.S. financial assistance as well as diplomatic support for its approach to a resolution of the conflict.

The new Israeli challenge was reflected in its insistence, backed by the United States, that Arab frontline parties agree not only to the normalization of relations but also to the establishment of substantial economic links and cooperation as a condition for an as yet undetermined extent of withdrawal from the occupied territories. Given the substantial disparities in levels of economic and technological development, this could result in relations of economic dependence (particularly on the part of Palestine and Jordan) and consequently a sphere of Israeli economic dominance. This challenge was broadened considerably due in part to the multilateral mechanisms for tackling regional issues that emanated from the Madrid conference. In the context of this broader multilateral framework, Washington has urged, with considerable success, other Arab states (notably in North Africa and the Gulf) to develop contacts or undertake measures of normalization with Israel even before satisfactory final settlements with the frontline states had been negotiated.[2] It also encouraged these rear-line states to develop economic and other links with Israel to create a network of regional economic interdependence that would underpin a potential Arab-Israeli settlement. The substantial dependence of most Arab states on the United States enticed some to undertake such moves in order to strengthen their ties with Washington.

Despite the challenges posed by these developments, the Arab world has experienced difficulty in coordinating policies, let alone developing a common front. Among the frontline parties themselves there have been several obstacles to close cooperation. One is the difference in national situations vis-à-vis Israel, in terms of their recognition as national entities with an acknowledged territorial base and leadership, the relative importance of the territory to be recovered, and the seriousness of the obstacles to the achievement of these aims. Hence the stakes involved in the conflict, the perceived prospects for achieving an honorable settlement and the sense of urgency regarding negotiations have varied considerably among Arab frontline parties, as have views about tactics and the extent to which the United States can be relied on to bring about such a settlement. To these must be added clear differences about relationships among the frontline actors, particularly about their respective position and influence in the Western Fertile Crescent. This has created frictions and rivalry between Syria and all of its smaller neighbors as well as between Jordan and the Palestinians.

These problems have been reflected in differences of approach concerning procedural concessions to be made in order to advance negotiations over substance, the linkages between various bilateral negotiations, and the linkages between multilateral and bilateral negotiations. Initially many of these differences were muted because of Israeli inflexibility on all fronts. They were accentuated, however, under the Labor-led governments of Yitzhak Rabin and Shimon Peres as Israel pursued a more flexible policy, particularly on the Palestinian front. The return of a Likud-led coalition government headed by Benjamin Netanyahu in June 1996 has led to a renewed and much harder-line approach toward Syria and the Palestinians and, consequently, serious blockages and heightened tensions on these fronts (as well as on the Israel-Lebanon border). Whether this new challenge will create a stronger sense of common interest, and hence increased coordination, among Arab frontline parties is debatable given the frictions and suspicions arising from developments in the "peace process" to date. Moreover, the renewed blockages and tensions may alter the domestic balance of forces within one or more neighboring Arab countries, strengthening the position of hardliners as well as generating increased political instability.

The difficulties in developing a common Arab front also increased as a result of frictions between the frontline parties and key rearline states (particularly the Gulf countries). Their respective national situations differ, giving rise to varied interests and perspectives regarding the conflict. Moreover, since the Gulf War some Arab Gulf states have displayed a marked antagonism toward the PLO/Palestinian community and Jordan for their previous sympathy toward Iraq (Jaber 1992). In addition, both the Gulf and North African states have become preoccupied with their own immediate concerns and hence have been less responsive to the problems and interests of Arab frontline countries. The gap between these segments of the Arab world has been reinforced by the widespread interest in strengthening ties with the United States. Rearline Arab states, particularly those in the Gulf, have tended to be more responsive to Washington's views regarding the conflict and consequently more inclined to support procedural concessions or provide assurances to Israel through bilateral discussions and ties before an honorable comprehensive settlement has been reached with the frontline countries. While the advent of a new hardline government in Israel has undoubtedly slowed or even frozen normalization measures by Gulf and North African states, the gap between frontline and rearline countries will continue to provide opportunities which can be exploited by both Israel and the United States.

The Changing Global System

In addition to substantial pressures within the larger regional arena, the Arab states also face challenges arising from major changes in the workings of the dominant system both in the politico-military and economic spheres. These too have had important implications for Arab cooperation.

THE POLITICO-MILITARY SPHERE

During the Cold War years the global politico-military system was characterized by a combination of two-power dominance, intensely conflictual relations between the dominant powers, and the polarization of virtually all major powers into two blocs under their leadership. Within a few short years a dramatic transformation has occurred in major power relations, although the extent, durability, and even the direction of those changes are subject to considerable debate.

The changes in the distribution of power have attracted the greatest attention. Here, the sudden collapse of the Soviet Union as a world power and the absence of any other effective global rival have led to a situation of apparent one-power dominance (Krauthammer 1991). U.S. preeminence is more evident and likely to persist longer in the Middle East than in any other region except the Western Hemisphere. It is the only power that has demonstrated both an ability and a willingness to deploy substantial military strength in the area. While other powers can furnish various types of armaments, only the United States has the capacity to provide a full range of weaponry. Its military technology is also regarded as more advanced than that of other powers, and hence more attractive, because of its superior performance in the Gulf War. Washington's considerable leverage and influence over a wide range of major powers and regional states further strengthen its position in the area. To be sure, questions can be raised about how long this situation will persist. Nevertheless, U.S interests in the Middle East are likely to remain substantial—Israel, oil and the oil-producing states, and the maintenance of a satisfactory distribution of power such that U.S interests or those of key allies are not threatened. This will undoubtedly result in a continuing high level of U.S involvement in the area, far surpassing that of any other power. The military and political needs of key regional states are also likely to be considerable, thereby ensuring heavy reliance on outside support. However, although the United States will remain the preeminent external power in the Middle East for some time, such preeminence does not mean complete dominance over regional actors or control over developments in the area (Hadar 1991).

Equally significant is the change in actual relationships among the leading powers. The most striking development here has been the transformation of relations among former adversaries from intense competition and conflict to accommodation mixed with varying degrees of collaboration (Rosecrance 1992; Miller 1992; Kristof 1992). This new pattern is likely to persist for the foreseeable future. Russia's preoccupation with domestic problems and relations with its former Soviet neighbors combined with heavy reliance on the West to meet its acute economic needs effectively ensure that it will be in no position to antagonize, let alone challenge, the United States for some time. China will undoubtedly have similar, although less serious, preoccupations, but the competition will be less muted and its cooperation more limited. Relations among the leading Western powers will probably not pose any significant problems either.

There is considerable debate about whether the end of the Cold War will result in the erosion or even disappearance of the two core Western alliances (NATO and the U.S-Japanese alliance) (Brown 1988, ch. 11; Tucker 1990; Cumings 1991) Certainly, Western allies may feel less dependence on Washington due to declining military-security concerns. However, if they wish to display greater autonomy and play a larger role in international affairs, they are likely to concentrate their efforts closer to home (Eastern Europe and perhaps Africa in the case of the European powers and Asia in the case of Japan). It is there that they have a more direct interest and a better chance of enhancing their influence. In the Middle East Washington will probably face only muted competition from its Western allies for some time (Hadar 1991). The major exception is North Africa, where France and other European states have significant interests. France, Britain, and others will also compete to supply conventional arms throughout the area.

The United States is likely to retain its preeminent position in the Middle East longer than elsewhere outside the Americas. It has been successful so far in capitalizing on this position to ensure not only muted competition but even a significant degree of cooperation (or at least acquiescence) on the part of other intrusive powers on certain basic issues, notably the handling of the Arab-Israeli conflict, the containment of Libya and, to a large extent, Iraq (but not Iran), and the control of nonconventional arms transfers. Thus, Arab states are confronted not only by U.S preeminence but also varying degrees of concerted action by the major powers on some key issues.[3] However, while the United States will remain the preeminent intrusive power in the region for some time, this does not guarantee either the continued cooperation of other intrusive powers on key issues or the maintenance of a substantial degree of control over regional actors and developments.

THE ECONOMIC SPHERE

The changes in the global economic system, while less dramatic than those in the politico-military sphere, are no less significant. The patterns here differ noticeably, however, from those just outlined (Bergsten 1992). While the United States has become the predominant politico-military power, in the economic sphere its position has slipped as the capabilities of other states and economic units have grown. What has emerged is an unbalanced tripower system with the United States enjoying a clear but diminishing lead. There is a further structural difference. The politico-military sphere has been characterized by the disappearance of the Soviet bloc and attempts to maintain, if not strengthen, a core coalition of Western powers under U.S leadership. In the international economic system, on the other hand, a more complex pattern has arisen with the emergence of two major power-centered economic groupings (the European Union, North American Free Trade Agreement and an embryonic East/Southeast Asian economic network). These regional groupings still operate, however, within an overarching framework of common institutions, giving rise to tensions between trilateral and tripolar tendencies. Finally, the politico-military sphere seems likely to be characterized by accommodation and possibly partial collaboration among the leading powers. In the economic sphere, however, there is a prospect of increasing assertiveness and rivalry among the leading Western powers, given U.S determination to reverse its economic decline, and Europe's and Japan's willingness to pursue their economic interests more forcefully (Garten 1993).

This divergence in global economic and politico-military patterns is reflected in the Middle East although not in full force. In the first place, the pattern of economic involvement in the area is less concentrated than in the politico-military sphere. Regional trade ties are relatively diversified. U.S financial capabilities, while considerable, are not unlimited, as evidenced by its need to turn to Japan, Germany, and the Gulf states to help pay for the cost of the Gulf War. U.S capacity to increase economic assistance to the area is also limited while other Western powers have greater potential and may figure more prominently in this area in the future. Still, the U.S economic position in the Middle East is stronger than it is at the global level. Its decisive action in the Gulf crisis and the continuing reliance of key Gulf producers (and Western consumer states) on the United States for the protection of the area's oil resources have given Washington a strong say on energy issues (Sarkis 1992). Moreover, while its position may be slipping, the United States is still the largest supplier of economic aid to the area and the leading player in international financial institutions dealing with Third World aid and debt. This provides it with important leverage vis-à-vis less well-off Arab states although such leverage is likely to decline if shifts in global economic strength continue.

Because of the better balance in resources, the level of intrusive power competition also tends to be greater in the economic sphere. With their enhanced capabilities, the rising economic powers are in a position to play a more active and independent economic role in the Middle East. Incentives to do so certainly exist in view of the importance of Middle Eastern energy supplies and the presence of substantial markets backed by considerable financial resources. However, there are also constraints. The United States enjoys a decided advantage in much of the area arising from its protective responsibilities in regard to Gulf oil-producers and its central role in the Arab-Israeli conflict. The ensuing special relationships with key Arab states tend to restrict the ability of potential rivals to compete in establishing markets or enhance their trade and influence through economic assistance. Hence, while economic competition among intrusive powers will increase in the Middle East, it is likely to be less intense than elsewhere.

This transformation of major power relations has important consequences for Arab interests and inter-Arab relations although these vary depending on the sector. In the *politico-military* sphere, the ending of superpower rivalry has limited one source of division within the Arab world. However, the new strategic environment has not led to any real increase in Arab politico-military cooperation. In fact, the Gulf War, along with the ensuing postwar problems confronting the Arab world, have tended to generate much greater cooperation (and reliance) between Arab states and the Western powers than among the Arab states themselves. Thus during and after the Gulf War the security and territorial concerns of many Arab states remained acute. This was true not only of Saudi Arabia and the Gulf states but also of the parties on the Israeli front. Both sets of states felt a strong need for tangible support and allies to ensure their security, contain potentially threatening regional powers, or secure Israeli withdrawal from the occupied territories. Based on the experience of the Gulf War and the postwar period, most were convinced that the United States and the Western powers were likely to prove more effective and reliable than fellow Arab states in protecting these basic interests. The resulting intensification of reliance on these intrusive powers limited the potential for meaningful Arab security and political cooperation.

While such widespread shared reliance on the U.S. and Western powers admittedly facilitated accommodation and perhaps some degree of cooperation between Arab states, it tended to remain "dependent cooperation" (i.e., under the aegis of an intrusive power). This situation accorded with the view that cooperation requires a strong leader or hegemon except that in this case it was an external hegemon. This type of cooperation has continued into the postwar period but is problematic because it can develop only as far as the preeminent power is prepared to allow.

Nevertheless, the reshaping of the strategic environment poses significant challenges to many Arab states and thus could potentially create incentives for cooperation. In particular, the combination of one-power dominance and intrusive power cooperation on key issues has clearly limited the options available to regional states (MacFarlane 1991; Selim 1992). The alternatives have been either to turn to the preeminent power or to proceed with little outside assistance. Such a situation has reduced Arab leverage and may limit the responsiveness of the sole remaining superpower, thereby potentially harming Arab interests. This, in turn, might provide a spur to Arab regional cooperation in the long run.

The dynamics of the *global economy* have also generated considerable pressure on the Arab world. The accelerated development of major power centered regional trading blocs, in particular, has posed major challenges. Faced with this trend, the interests of many Arab states would probably be served by developing a common front and negotiating jointly in order to protect or enhance access to these markets (El-Rafei 1992). Cooperation would also be useful in expanding export opportunities within the Arab world to partially offset possible difficulties in access to traditional markets and to develop more competitive enterprises in today's globalized market. Admittedly the better balanced and more competitive three-power structure of the global economy provides Arab states with more options in pursuing their economic interests, thereby reducing some of the impetus for cooperation. Still, these features are by no means fully present yet in the Middle East. Moreover, in spite of *tripolar* tendencies the leading economic powers continue to act substantially in concert *trilaterally* on economic issues of importance to Arab states, notably debt rescheduling and energy questions. Hence the challenge remains.

Compared to the politico-military sphere, the position of Arab states in the economic sphere is more varied and consequently the issue of the framework for cooperation is more complex. The have-not states have experienced serious economic difficulties since the late 1980s due to accelerating development needs and a rapidly accumulating debt burden, a situation exacerbated by the economic strains generated by the Gulf War. The ability of fellow system members to meet the economic needs of these states, at least in the aid sphere, has been substantial. However, the capacity and willingness to do so has been limited in practice due to both economic and political constraints. In fact, the intrusive powers, headed by the United States, took the lead in attempting to alleviate the most pressing concerns of some states, notably in the areas of compensation for losses suffered during the Gulf War and debt restructuring or cancellation (Greenhouse 1991).

These powers are also in a much better position to address problems of market access. Hence, while the regional capacity to meet important national concerns is greater in the economic than in the politico-military sphere, most have-not Arab states have concentrated their economic hopes and efforts at the intrusive power level. The economic concerns of the major oil-producing states are nowhere near as acute as those of the have-not states. They are still important though, especially in an international oil market which has been relatively soft. Since the leading economic powers constitute the major markets for oil exports, considerable emphasis has been placed on relations at this level. However, unlike the situation in the politico-military sphere, these vertical relationships have not prevented the development of varying degrees of cooperation among Arab oil producers.

While collaboration with outside powers may be easier and produce more results in the short term, it is questionable whether quasi-exclusive reliance on this form of cooperation is healthy or stable in the longer run. In a situation of one-power dominance combined with muted competition and partial concert among the intrusive powers, Arab leverage may be limited; consequently the United States may be less responsive to the interests of Arab states. For example, concerted efforts to limit weapons transfers may result in the freezing of serious imbalances (Sayigh 1992). The U.S might lose some of its incentive to press forward and ensure progress toward an honorable settlement of the Arab-Israeli conflict or to act evenhandedly in doing so. The absence of serious major power rivalry could, after a while, reduce the incentive to continue providing substantial support to some Arab states. More worrisome still, Washington may act in an overbearing manner to enforce its views and promote its interests while exerting strong pressures on Arab states deemed to be unfriendly.[4] In all these situations, Arab division would make matters worse—reducing Arab bargaining power even further, increasing the vulnerability of states to pressures, weakening Arab security, and reducing the possibilities for an honorable settlement to the Arab-Israeli conflict or other conflicts with non-Arab regional powers. In short, while the new strategic environment may place obstacles in the way of inter-Arab cooperation in the short to medium term, it may also pose a serious challenge to Arab interests and possibly strengthen the incentives for Arab cooperation in the long run.

Overall then, Arab states face important challenges not only on various regional fronts but also from the dynamics of the global politico-military and economic systems. When a number of states are similarly positioned in relation to conditions in these systems, and more particularly are faced with pressures or threats from the same source, one would normally expect some sense of shared concerns and interests to develop. It is in this sense that we can talk of "Arab" interests, at least on the part of those Arab states most directly affected by particular pressures if not within the Arab world as a whole. The existence of a sense of affinity and common identity, however minimal, among significant segments of Arab societies can also provide a further (subjective) foundation for the notion of "Arab" interests. In any case, the shared concerns and interests might be expected to generate incentives for cooperation.

There have been, however, two major problems in this regard. The first is the fragmentation of concerns within the Arab world, at least between subregions. Owing to the variety of challenges, the Arab states diverge considerably in their hierarchy of concerns. The GCC states have been preoccupied with the situation in the Gulf, involving problems of military and power-security as well as transnational and internal political security. The parties on the Israeli front have been concerned primarily with the achievement of a satisfactory settlement that would result in the recovery of their territory and, in the case of the Palestinians, the achievement of political independence. These states are also burdened by significant internal difficulties. Egypt, for its part, has been concentrating on its internal political and economic problems, while at the same time, for external purposes, trying to demonstrate its value as a force for moderation and stability in the region. Finally, the Maghrib states have been preoccupied with domestic concerns as well as relations with key European states.

The second problem is that even where common concerns exist, as in some subregions, there is both divergence regarding the appropriate response and, ultimately, a pronounced tendency to rely heavily on the lone superpower and other intrusive powers to deal with the concern. In other words, the various regional and domestic challenges which the Arab States face have indeed encouraged them to engage in cooperation, but it has been *vertical* cooperation (with the leading intrusive powers) rather than *horizontal* (inter-Arab) cooperation. This combination of the fragmentation of concerns and the globalization of responses is the most direct and immediate, though probably not the most fundamental, obstacle to Arab cooperation.

The Changing Arab System

Prospects for Arab cooperation depend ultimately on the situation in the Arab world itself. This includes not only prevailing conditions and relationships within the Arab state system but also, at a deeper level, trends in relations between Arab societies and, ultimately, internal developments within these societies.

INTER-STATE RELATIONS

The Legacy of the Past

Relations between states are rarely impressed upon a tabula rasa. The current attitudes of Arab state elites are conditioned to some degree by previous attempts at cooperation and integration. Given the marked linguistic, cultural, and even religious homogeneity among Arab peoples and elites, the idea of unity understandably has had considerable appeal. Unfortunately, at the height of its appeal in the 1950s and 1960s, what might be termed Bismarckian and revolutionary approaches to this goal tended to predominate. Both approaches involved a strong challenge to the legitimacy and autonomy of existing states. The Bismarckian approach involved a core power employing relatively coercive methods to achieve these goals. The revolutionary approach sought to promote unity through internal upheavals in the countries concerned, encouraged and supported by a regime or political movement in a neighboring country. A leading regional state usually sought to assume a predominant role in this process, although other patterns were possible. President Gamal Abdel Nasser's unity efforts involved a mixture of these two approaches, but with greater emphasis on the latter. However attractive the principle, these approaches proved counterproductive. Given both the ends sought and the means by which these were pursued, unity efforts came to be viewed in many countries as highly threatening to a broad range of state, regime, and societal interests. In short, in the context of an ongoing process of consolidation of the postcolonial state system, the idea of Arab unity came to acquire strong negative associations even among elites who originally supported the idea.

Fortunately, approaches to cooperation in the Arab world have moderated significantly. Some key features of what might be termed a European Community approach have emerged in inter-Arab relations. The legitimacy and autonomy of existing state units are now more widely accepted, and the institutional arrangements envisaged reflect this, namely cooperation councils, common fronts, and functional cooperation. Moreover, the methods employed in promoting unity are far less forceful, centering primarily on diplomacy, bargaining, and rewards. Finally, the element of one-power dominance is muted. As a result, the idea of cooperation is now seen as less threatening. Nevertheless, the legacy of earlier approaches has by no means disappeared. These resurfaced in recent years in Saddam Hussein's apparent hegemonic policies in which the Bismarckian approach predominated.

Power and Influence

One factor which has received considerable attention in analyses of international cooperation has been the pattern of power within a system. In the 1950s,

Karl Deutsch underlined the importance of a core state in the development of what he termed "security communities" (Deutsch 1957). A.F.K. Organski and long-cycle theorists have also stressed the pacifying, if not cooperation-generating, effects of the predominance of a single power (Organski 1968, Thompson 1988). This has also been a prominent theme among students of international political economy who have emphasized that cooperation requires the presence of a "hegemon." While the latter argument is expressed in general terms, it is essentially an explanation of economic cooperation, more specifically the development of a liberal (open) international economy. Moreover, some have argued that while the existence of a hegemon may be necessary to initiate international economic cooperation, once established, this cooperation can, under certain circumstances, survive the hegemon's decline (Keohane 1984).

These arguments emphasize two important contributions of the core power. One is the exercise of leadership. The other is the possession of a sufficient concentration of capabilities to provide key services or collective goods to members of a given system. For some it is the provision of politico-military services, such as protection from outsiders or conflict-management within a group. For others, it is the ability to furnish a variety of economic services needed to sustain a liberal economic order. If these arguments have some validity, then conditions in the Arab system at earlier periods were probably more conducive to cooperation than they are today. In the 1950s and 1960s Egypt enjoyed a preeminent position and arguably could have served as a core power.[5] However, the way in which its power was exercised proved detrimental to cooperation. Since the 1970s, though, the Arab system has had no clear leader. More recently, Iraq began to emerge as a potential core state but engaged in a premature and rash drive for predominance. Since its overwhelming defeat, the situation has reverted to a more balanced pattern.

The problem in the Arab system runs deeper, however, than simply the existence of a diffusion rather than a concentration of power. The current relatively balanced multipower pattern is not really a "balance of power" but a "balance of weakness." In other words, all the leading Arab states suffer from substantial inconsistencies with regard to key components of national capabilities. Those possessing significant military capabilities (Egypt, Syria) are burdened by serious economic weaknesses, while the Arab state with the greatest financial capabilities (Saudi Arabia) has major military deficiencies. Iraq has been the only power with significant potential in both areas, but its military and economic capabilities have now been severely damaged. Moreover, all have suffered periodically from uncertain domestic political situations which have further weakened them. In short, none of the key states has had the consistent strength required to be a fully effective and energetic player in the regional system.

Furthermore, even in areas where individual powers are relatively strong, the actual level of capabilities is generally insufficient to provide the relevant collective goods or support required by other members of the system. This is particularly true with respect to military security—where the capacity to project force over distances in a short period of time is limited. The same applies, to a lesser extent, to the capacity to provide economic assistance. The problem is compounded by uncertainty regarding the reliability of system members. Hence, as noted, Arab states have generally turned outside the system to the major powers for the support required to meet their needs.

While the absence of a core power with the requisite capabilities and leadership potential would appear to limit the prospects for cooperation, the emergence of a core coalition of leading Arab states might serve as an effective substitute. In other words, though no individual Arab power might be sufficiently effective due to inconsistent capabilities, a combination of such powers with complementary capabilities arguably could achieve the same effect. While there is much to commend in this argument, there are two major problems. First, regardless of their complementarity, the inadequacy of the capabilities in both military and economic spheres relative to system members' needs would probably preclude primary reliance on Arab support. Secondly, even if a coalition of leading Arab states could be a relatively effective substitute for a core power, such a coalition has yet to emerge. During the Gulf crisis, the joint involvement of Saudi Arabia, Egypt, and Syria in the effort to contain Iraq seemed to create the seeds of such a coalition. Hopes that this alliance might be transformed into an effective long-term coalition were raised by the Damascus Declaration (FBIS 1991; Butt 1991). In this agreement, plans were made for Egyptian and Syrian military contributions to Gulf security paralleled by important Saudi and Gulf state financial contributions to these have-not states. Since the war, however, few, if any, concrete measures have been taken to translate these plans into reality (Jaber 1991; Daoud 1992). As a result, Egypt and Syria withdrew their troops from the Gulf area, and trilateral political cooperation eroded. Postwar developments cast doubt, therefore, on the emergence of an effective coalition of leading powers that could provide direction to the Arab system. Without such a coalition to provide a solid political framework for cooperation, fragmentation is likely to prevail.

Revisionism and Conflict

Another important factor shaping the prospects for cooperation is the degree of compatibility of the interests of Arab states and the level of revisionism and conflict. In this latter area the situation has improved compared to earlier periods when unity figured prominently on the Arab agenda. Previously the level of revisionism was very high, as various states (notably Egypt) and political movements sought to bring about extensive change in virtually all aspects of the status quo. Such policies had considerable appeal among elements of the elite and broad segments of the public in all Arab countries. However, they were viewed as highly threatening by most regimes, whose fundamental interests and values were severely challenged. Proposals for common fronts, mergers, or even increased ties tended to be perceived in this light and were usually resisted. Now, the Arab state system is characterized by relative moderation. While the status quo may not be accepted as fully legitimate even by state elites, no major state is highly revisionist, at least not since the defeat of the Iraqi challenge. This is due in part to the balance of weakness which tends to limit major threats to the status quo.

The substantial decline in revisionism has clearly enhanced the possibilities for accommodation within the Arab system. However, there are still conflicting interests and sources of friction which are an impediment to cooperation. Differences concerning position and influence have been a persistent problem area. As noted, the dramatic weakening of Egypt's position post 1967 and the advent of a more balanced multipower structure contributed to a significant reduction in revisionism. Since then, a combination of inconsistent capabilities and the fluctuating external as well as domestic fortunes of leading Arab states has produced both a leadership vacuum and an unstable power hierarchy in the Arab system. This shifting and uncertain balance of forces has tended to encourage recurrent maneuvering for position as well as periodic assertiveness. This revisionism and competition has been manifested both in the overall system and at the subregional level.

Conflict and rivalries have persisted in varying degrees since the latest Gulf War and continue to serve as an impediment to cooperation. The most profound division has been between Iraq and the other leading Arab powers. The recent experience of extensive Iraqi revisionism accompanied by forceful action has generated acute security concerns, particularly on the part of Saudi Arabia and Kuwait, concerns that are reinforced by fears of a resurgence of such revisionism. Saudi Arabia, Egypt, and Syria will therefore undoubtedly retain a strong interest in the containment of Iraq, at least as long as Saddam Hussein remains in power. This severe split renders an overall concert of Arab powers all but impossible. It might be argued, however, that this persisting conflict, and the accompanying threat perception, should facilitate, if not encourage, cooperation in the form of a core coalition of the remaining powers. In reality, the usual effect of such severe threat perception in the Arab world has been to generate cooperation with outside powers rather than with other Arab states. The present situation is no exception.

The other principal axis of conflict emerging from the Gulf crisis has been the pronounced split between the former Arab coalition partners and countries that sympathized in varying degrees with Iraq (especially Jordan, the Palestinian community, Yemen, and the Sudan). Saudi Arabia and Kuwait in particular, adopted a tough stance toward these parties and have been slow in modifying it. Some of these lines of conflict cut across subregions, but in many cases the Gulf War simply reinforced prior tensions between preeminent sub-regional powers and lesser states in their immediate area. More generally, in the wake of the crisis, some Arab powers adopted a more assertive policy in their subregions in order to improve their security or consolidate their influence. This reassertion of geopolitics has been evident in varying degrees in the case of Saudi Arabia vis-à-vis smaller Gulf and Arabian peninsula states as well as in the case of Syria within the Western Fertile Crescent (historic Syria) and Egypt within the Nile Valley (Salamé 1988). More muted differences also persist to some degree among the former Arab coalition partners, thereby rendering cooperation problematic. Some of this centers on concerns about position and influence. Egypt, not satisfied with its previous isolation or a limited sphere of influence in the Nile Valley, seeks to assume a leading role within the Arab world, albeit in a very different manner than in Nasser's day (Aftandilian 1993). Cairo believes that its capabilities, experience, and diplomatic connections enable it to contribute significantly to the advancement of Arab (and Egyptian) interests, notably in the promotion of stability in the Nile Valley and adjacent areas, the achievement of an honorable settlement on the remaining Arab-Israeli fronts and the development of an Arab security umbrella in the Gulf. It feels that its overall weight, pragmatic policies, and diverse connections enable it to serve as a bridge among Arab states. Other Arab powers, while recognizing Egypt's contribution, are reluctant to see it play too large a role in their respective areas and thus weaken their influence.

Syria seeks to establish itself as the leading power in the Western Fertile Crescent due to its overall weight and historic role and expects other Arab states to accept this preeminence (Drysdale and Hinnebusch 1991). It is also con-vinced that a common front of neighboring states under its leadership is neces-sary to defend Arab interests vis-à-vis Israel. Otherwise Israel would be able to divide these states in any negotiations, seriously weakening the chances for a satisfactory settlement on any front. Syria believes that it must play a leading role here, not only to be taken seriously by Israel and the major powers but also to strengthen its position in the larger Arab system. Other major Arab states appear willing to accept Syria's local preeminence, but only up to a point. Iraq was a major exception but is presently too weak to mount any challenge. Egypt and Saudi Arabia acknowledge Syrian primacy in Lebanon, within limits, but prefer to see Jordan and the Palestinians retain their autonomy, in part to ensure the maintenance of pragmatic policies toward Israel.

Saudi Arabia, for its part, views itself as the leading power among Arab Gulf states as well as within the Arabian peninsula and is determined to preserve, if not enhance, this position. While Riyadh clearly had substantial security concerns in the Gulf, it was hesitant to proceed with the proposed Arab security umbrella. This was due in part to doubts about the effectiveness and reliability of such arrangements, as well as apparent Iranian objections to the abovementioned proposals. Saudi Arabia also had reservations about an Egyptian and Syrian politico-military role in the Gulf, albeit for different reasons. Concerns that such arrangements might create an entitlement to substantial financial aid were also involved. The combination of reservations about Egyptian and Syrian involvement in Gulf security arrangements and a lukewarm view of their economic needs has generated resentments and cast a shadow over both states' relations with Saudi Arabia (Sayigh 1991; Rodenbeck 1991).

Apart from the conflict between Iraq on the one hand and its immediate neighbors as well as the remaining Arab powers on the other, few, if any, of these conflicts are particularly acute or insurmountable. Nevertheless, the frictions they generate clearly contribute to Arab fragmentation.

Regime and Ideological Differences

The Arab world has been characterized not only by pronounced heterogeneity but also by severe challenges on the part of some regimes to the legitimacy and security of others. While welcomed by many Arabs, these challenges were perceived as highly threatening by most Arab regimes. Since unity proposals were frequently viewed as an instrument for the achievement of these ends, they met with strong suspicion and resistance. Now, however, the differences between regimes, at least in regard to the nature of their economic systems, have declined. With the advent of more pragmatic regimes there has also been a pronounced de-ideologization of interstate relations. Certainly no major Arab state presently poses a serious ideological threat to the others, apart possibly from a potentially resurgent Iraq and a somewhat unstable Sudan. The legitimacy of regimes continues to be questioned, even challenged significantly, but the real challenge comes not from other regimes but rather from opposition forces, primarily Islamic fundamentalist movements, linked loosely in a fundamentalist "internationale."

An ideological cold war exists within the Arab world, but for the moment it is being waged primarily *within* Arab states and societies rather than *between* them. Regime differences are not at this point a major source of conflict between Arab states. This could change quickly, however, if an Islamic movement were to come to power or achieve a dominant influence within a key Arab state. Regime differences could also widen and generate increased tensions in the event of more extensive moves toward democratization either in countries currently undergoing limited democratic experiments or in others newly embarking on such a path.

In addition, the 1991 Gulf War and ensuing developments have served to reinforce or intensify differences, both *between* and *within* Arab states, over a number of issues which are likely to become more divisive with the passage of time. These include economic disparities, the role of Islam, and the policy to be pursued toward Israel and Iran as well as the United States. These developments further complicate the task of developing cooperation not only at the overall Arab level, but also within subregions.

INTERSOCIETAL RELATIONS

Intersocietal relations constitute a deeper set of conditions affecting the prospects for Arab cooperation. These consist basically of the degree of complementarity between the peoples, societies, and economies of the area as well as the extent of interconnectedness between the countries involved. Together, these factors determine the strength or weakness of the societal bonds underpinning a state system. At first glance conditions here appear relatively favorable to Arab cooperation—more favorable, seemingly, than in any other regional system of developing states. However, when one probes more deeply, the situation appears more problematic. A steady erosion of these societal bonds occurred over the last two decades and intensified noticeably in the wake of the Gulf War. Indeed, the change in intersocietal relations has been more substantial than that in interstate relations.

The most obvious factor is the *extensive homogeneity* of Arab peoples and elites. This has tended to generate a strong sense of kinship and even common identity within the Arab world. For a considerable period, this broader sense of identity rivaled individual national identities among important sectors in many states. This facilitated the development of a substantial level of transnational social communication in which information and currents of thought circulated widely and resonated strongly across state borders. Membership in the larger Arab family generated a perception of common interests and led to a sense of solidarity when any segment of the community found itself in conflict with a non-Arab actor. Key elements in Arab societies identified closely with, and were responsive to, leaders and movements in other states that gave voice to these common interests. Belief in a common identity also gave rise to the view that political unity was a desirable objective. These bonds created a potentially strong foundation for Arab cooperation.

During the 1970s and 1980s these bonds eroded considerably. Iraq's invasion of Kuwait further weakened the sense of solidarity in important segments of the Arab world. This was particularly noticeable in Kuwait, Saudi Arabia, and other Gulf states, where the crisis had a twofold effect. At one level, the immediacy of the threat and the forcefulness of the assertion of Iraqi interests generated, among elites and publics alike, a stronger sense of identification with their own states and societies. At the same time, it created marked animosity not only toward Iraq but also toward those Arab peoples who sympathized with it, all of whom had been beneficiaries of considerable financial assistance from the Gulf states. The resulting sense of betrayal led to an intensified psychological distancing of these regimes and societies from the rest of the Arab world.[6] This has been reflected not only in punitive measures toward countries siding with Iraq but also in an apparent diminished sensitivity to the concerns and needs of other Arab societies generally. In turn, Saudi Arabian and Kuwaiti pressures on Yemen, Jordan, and the Palestinian community, as well as against nationals of these countries residing in their territory, have generated strong resentment among the target communities. As a result, relationships among these peoples have been badly frayed. Finally, in Egypt, the unfortunate experiences of many of the nearly one million persons who had worked in Iraq during the 1980s tended to undermine feelings of Arab kinship and limit the responsiveness to Iraqi appeals. Egyptians also resented some of the attitudes of their Kuwaiti and Saudi allies after the war (Fandy 1991). In short, the crisis and its aftermath appeared in many cases to accentuate the differences between Arab peoples and elites as well as to intensify attachments to individual states and their interests.

On the other hand, Saddam Hussein's appeal to Arab nationalism and Arab solidarity did strike a responsive chord among substantial sections of the population in many states, including those in the anti-Iraq coalition. The crisis also revealed a heightened sense of Islamic identity which has become an additional and more powerful basis of transnational identification and responsiveness in the Arab world (Piscatori 1991). These broader identities may even be strengthened should the United States and Western powers overplay their current dominant position in the region or, more generally, come to be perceived as hostile to the interests and values of Arab-Islamic countries and indifferent to the fate of Islamic peoples under attack in various parts of the world (e.g., Bosnia, Chechnya). Thus it is premature to proclaim the definitive triumph of local nationalisms and the end of any broader sense of community within the Arab world. Too many common frustrations and concerns remain among Arab peoples. *Raison d'état* may have gained ground at the expense of *raison de la nation* (Khalidi 1992), but the latter has by no means disappeared. Indeed, before long it may emerge reinforced and transformed by *raison de l'"umma"* (the Arab-Islamic community).

The question of *economic complementarity* and *economic links* constitutes another important dimension of intersocietal relations. While this matter is perhaps best left to economists, some points are worth noting. One is that most Third World regions are characterized by considerable similarity in their productive activities, thereby limiting the prospects for economic exchange and cooperation. This holds true to a substantial extent for the Arab world, at least within subregional clusters of states, e.g., the Gulf states with their oil, petrochemical, and banking activities, as well as the Maghrib states and several states in the Nile Valley and Western Fertile Crescent regions, each with their particular concentrations of agricultural activity. Nevertheless, a significant degree of diversity and complementarity exists as well, particularly between these subregional clusters. Some countries have a developed agricultural sector (or the potential to create one) while others have little or none. Some are substantially endowed with energy resources while those of others are modest or nonexistent. The manufacturing and service sectors are developed in varying degrees across the Arab world, sometimes with different concentrations. Finally, certain countries have substantial supplies of capital but only a limited supply of managerial talent and skilled or unskilled workers. Others lack capital but are relatively well-endowed with workers. In short, to a noneconomist at least, there appears to be a potentially meaningful degree of complementarity which could constitute a base for economic cooperation.

This complementarity was translated into a variety of economic links in the 1970s and 1980s. Indeed, the Arab world developed some of the strongest economic links of any regional system of developing states. The intraregional flow of financial resources (from the oil-producing states) and workers and professionals (to the oil-producing states) has arguably been the highest in the developing world (see tables 3.1 and 3.2). However, trade links have been relatively weak (see table 3.3). Since the mid-1980s, these links have declined considerably due largely to a dramatic softening in the international oil market. The economic constraints on cooperation have, if anything, intensified since the recent Gulf crisis. The two wealthiest Arab states (Saudi Arabia and Kuwait) have experienced a substantial drain on their financial resources as a result of costs incurred in supporting the coalition war as well as the expense involved in postwar reconstruction and further development of their military capabilities (Sadowski 1991; Mohamedi 1993; Boustany 1994). Thus their capacity to serve as an engine of Arab economic cooperation is limited at this stage.

In addition to the purely economic constraints on cooperation, political factors have also played an important role. Saudi Arabian and Kuwaiti anger at the stands taken by various Arab states and societies during the Kuwait crisis led to the cessation of financial assistance to these countries. It also resulted in the displacement of large numbers of their nationals from Saudi Arabia and Kuwait

TABLE 3.1   Official Aid Flows (Bilateral and Multilateral) Within the Arab World
(in millions of $US)

	1975	1980	1985	1989
Total Recipients	4708	5534	2567	823
Eastern Arab World	1335	3803	1530	236
Egypt	2525	2	-27	83
Arab Africa	600	1561	973	322
Unspecified	248	168	91	182

Source: Adapted from Pierre van den Boogaerde, Financial Assistance from Arab Countries and
Arab Regional Institutions, Occasional Paper 87 (Washington: International Monetary Fund, 1991),
Table 32. Van den Boogaerde's tables are drawn from IMF and Organization for Economic
Cooperation and Development staff calculations.

(Brynen and Noble 1991). Those displaced are unlikely to be replaced to any significant extent by nationals of other Arab countries. Instead, the wealthy Gulf
states seem inclined either to make do with fewer foreign workers or to rely on
non-Arab replacements who are liable to be less troublesome politically.
Beyond this reaction to recent events, there is a more general political con-
straint on economic cooperation. This involves the apparent unwillingness of
Arab governments to accept any meaningful division of labor or mutual economic dependence for fear that it would be vulnerable to interruption as a
result of political rivalries or tensions. In short, the prospects for economic linkages are probably limited as much by political considerations as by economic
factors. Whatever the cause, the absence of developed economic links clearly
limits the sense of interdependence which is an important foundation stone of
cooperation among states.

DOMESTIC CONDITIONS

Domestic political conditions and state-society relations generally constitute a
further level of factors affecting the prospects for cooperation. In the 1970s, after
many years of internal turbulence, *domestic instability* in the Arab world
declined somewhat. Among the contributing factors were the oil boom, which
reduced socioeconomic tensions in many countries, and the substantial
strengthening of the internal security apparatuses and coercive capabilities of
Arab regimes. By the late 1970s, there were renewed manifestations of instability with the increasing assertiveness of Islamic fundamentalist forces, bolstered
in part by the revolution in Iran. Despite the renewed pressures, Arab states and

TABLE 3.2   Worker Remittances Within the Arab World (millions of $US)

1975	1980	1985	1989
1138	5999	6004	6440

Source: Adapted from Pierre van den Boogaerde, Financial Assistance from Arab Countries and Arab Regional Institutions, Occasional Paper 87 (Washington: International Monetary Fund, 1991), Table 35. This table was derived from the IMF Balance of Payments Statistics, various years.

Notes: The figures represent total remittances received through official channels by Arab countries whose emigrant workers were concentrated heavily within the Arab world, e.g., Egypt, Jordan, Syria, Yemen Arab Republic, Yemen-PDR, Sudan, Tunisia. It does not include Arab African countries where remittances are derived almost entirely from workers in Europe, except for the Sudan and Tunisia, a significant portion of whose workers were located in the Arab world. Actual aid levels were undoubtedly higher because many Arab donor states transfer sizable funds quietly and unofficially; for example, the aid of the Gulf States to Iraq during the 1980s was not included in records of official aid flows. The flow of workers and professionals has also been substantial, with an estimated three million Arabs at work in other Arab countries in the early 1980s. Fred Halliday, "Labor Migration in the Arab World," MERIP Reports (May 1984) which draws from I. Serageldin, J. Socknat, S. Birks, B. Li and C. Sinclair, Manpower and International Migration in the Arab World (Washington, DC: Oxford University Press for the World Bank, 1983). These expatriate workers greatly increased financial flows within the Arab world through their remittances. For an overview of these and other facets of Arab economic integration, see Sami K. Farsoun, "Oil, State and Social Structure in the Middle East," Arab Studies Quarterly (Spring 1988).

regimes proved relatively resilient due to previous improvements in their internal security and economic capabilities. The period was also characterized by an upsurge in cooperation between internal security forces in the Arab world. This was reflected particularly among the GCC states but also among other pairs of states and even at a broader multilateral level within an Arab League framework. This phenomenon deserves further exploration, but it would be ironic indeed if the *mukhabarat* constituted the vanguard of Arab cooperation in the 1980s and 1990s.

Since the late 1980s, domestic tensions have been rising again throughout much of the Arab world. These were accentuated in many cases by the Gulf conflict and its aftermath, which exacerbated not only socioeconomic tensions (due to postwar financial exigencies and sharply reduced intraregional personnel and resource flows) and sociocultural tensions (reflected in the heightened appeal of Islamic fundamentalism stemming both from the search for cultural authenticity and deepening socioeconomic difficulties), but also political frustrations arising from continuing authoritarian rule (Brynen and Noble 1991; Daoud 1991). To these may be added new sources of tension and strain, notably emerging resentment at what is seen in some quarters as domineering behavior and insensitivity to Arab interests on the part of the United States and Western

TABLE 3-3   Intraregional Trade in the Developing World (1989)
(as % of the trading activity of regional states)

	Exports	Imports
Asia	31.1	29.2
Latin America/Caribbean	13.9	17.4
Middle East[a]	6.2	7.2
Africa[b]	5.8	6.1

a Middle East figures include Iran and Israel but exclude Arab Africa.
b Africa figures include North Africa.

Source: Adapted from International Monetary Fund, Direction of Trade Statistics Yearbook 1990 (Washington, DC: International Monetary Fund, 1990), regional tables.

powers as well as potential frustrations in the event of failure to make real progress toward an honorable settlement on the Syrian-Israeli and Palestinian-Israeli fronts. In short, while Arab regimes (including that of Saddam Hussein) have proved resilient to date, we are in a period of increased pressure for change and possibly renewed political turbulence.

What impact is such political instability likely to have on Arab cooperation? On the one hand, these developments may encourage some regimes to work together to prevent movements that constitute a common threat (e.g., political Islamists) from coming to power or to contain them if they are successful in one or two states. Elements of such an approach appear to be present in the reactions of Saudi Arabia, Egypt, Tunisia, and perhaps others to developments in Algeria and the Sudan, in one case quietly supporting a regime that cracked down on fundamentalists, in the other exerting pressure on the regime to moderate its policies. Such cooperation might simply involve parallel activities behind the scenes or might be more closely coordinated in the form of an "anti-holy" alliance or common front.

On the other hand, intensified domestic instability is more likely to impede cooperation. In the first place, it could lead governments to concentrate their attention and energies on the internal front to the detriment of inter-Arab cooperation. If they felt vulnerable domestically, they might avoid joining an overtly antifundamentalist front in order to deflect pressures from themselves. Secondly, states would probably place little faith in regional security cooperation if potential partners suffered from pronounced instability. In such circumstances, questions would undoubtedly arise about the reliability of any commitments made. Thirdly, the presence in one country of strong opposition movements that were regarded as a threat by neighboring regimes could hamper any form of cooperation involving the flow of persons and ideas between these societies. Other regimes would be reluctant to engage in such cooperation for fear of the possible spillover effect of these movements on their societies. Finally, internal instability might also bring about a significant modification or transformation of regimes. The result would be an increased heterogeneity of regimes, either in terms of political structure (e.g., pluralist/liberalized vs. authoritarian regimes) or in terms of the types of elites and directions they were pursuing (e.g., Islamic fundamentalist vs. secularist or moderate Islamic regimes). In the former case, cooperation would be more difficult because political liberalization would probably lead to media criticism directed at the authoritarian partner, which in turn would resort to pressures to have it stopped. In either case, each regime would regard the other as a potential threat. On the whole, therefore, intensified political instability and pressures for change are likely to prove detrimental to cooperation, at least in the short to medium term.

Another factor shaping the potential for cooperation is the evolving character of *Arab domestic economic and political systems*. Previously, the prevalence of state-run command economies may have made the development of economic links and cooperation easier in one sense. Since governments controlled key sectors of the economy, they did not have to contend with autonomous enterprises motivated by their own economic interests. Rather, they could conclude economic agreements relatively easily, based on calculations of "national" political and, to a lesser extent, economic interests, without too many complications or too much bargaining with autonomous societal interests. This may have facilitated economic cooperation in the short run. However, since it represented politically driven intergovernmental cooperation, it was vulnerable to interruption due to changes in relations between the states concerned. The present trend in Arab states toward economic liberalization may make economic cooperation more complicated in the short run since it will require the initiative, or at least the acquiescence, of autonomous interests. Nevertheless, it arguably will lead to more durable economic links since these will be economically, rather than politically, driven and will create interests within the societies themselves that favor cooperation. These should be less vulnerable to interruption in the medium to long run.

Similar paradoxical trends are evident when one turns to developments in Arab political systems. As in the economic sphere, it could be argued that authoritarian political systems make Arab cooperation easier because such cooperation could be undertaken by the principal decisionmakers without having to contend with the views and interests of many autonomous political and social forces. Extending this argument, if pressures for change were to lead to a widening of political participation and the mobilization of new forces in one or more Arab countries, efforts at cooperation by those regimes would become more complicated due to the need for responsiveness to a broader range of political and social forces. From an alternative perspective, however, authoritarian systems are viewed as hindering the growth of civil society. This in turn limits the development of transnational civil society (in the form of transnational associations and movements) which is regarded as a potentially important foundation for Arab cooperation. Political liberalization and democratization, on the other hand, would tend to encourage the development of Arab transnational civil society which could provide a much firmer and more reliable basis for Arab cooperation, especially in the longer run. In the short to medium term though, the burgeoning of transnational civil society could render Arab cooperation more difficult. The primary beneficiaries would undoubtedly be Islamist movements and associations whose linkage in larger transnational groupings would prove destabilizing not only for individual regimes but also for inter-Arab relations.

Perhaps the most serious domestic impediment to Arab cooperation, however, is the absence of any regimes that could serve as *poles of attraction* for other Arab societies. Regimes in key Arab countries, and indeed in the whole of the Arab world, appear to be tired and unable to engage in any significant internal renewal with respect to competence, integrity, political participation, and social justice. As a result they possess little appeal either within their own societies or within other Arab societies. No Arab regime, therefore, enjoys the prestige or moral authority that would enable it to serve as a pole of attraction for the populations of other Arab countries and thus generate some measure of enthusiasm for inter-Arab cooperation.

OVERCOMING OBSTACLES

The end of the Cold War and the subsequent shockwaves of the Gulf War have brought about important changes in both the Middle Eastern regional system and the major power intrusive system. These, in turn, pose serious challenges to the interests of many Arab states, which arguably should provide a substantial incentive for Arab cooperation. Paradoxically, however, the Arab system remains as fragmented as ever. Part of the explanation, as we have seen, lies in the fact that the very multiplicity of the challenges facing Arab states has led to a divergence rather than a convergence of concerns.

Moreover, even where a group of Arab states faces a major common challenge, the very seriousness of the problems confronting them has inevitably led to reliance on, and cooperation with, the leading intrusive power(s) in preference to inter-Arab cooperation. This tendency to rely on the intrusive powers is understandable given their substantial capacities to deal with the concerns in question. However, even if it is evident why vertical ties constitute the primary axis of cooperation, it still remains puzzling why there is so little horizontal cooperation, if only as an insurance policy in the event of uncertain major power support or as a device to limit dependence on or to achieve increased leverage vis-à-vis these powers. The explanation for this lies ultimately, as we have seen, in conditions within the Arab world, not only in the area of interstate relationships but increasingly also in terms of intersocietal relations and domestic conditions. The obstacles to Arab cooperation are clearly formidable.

Overcoming these obstacles will require not just a modification of objective circumstances but, more importantly, some fundamental shifts in approach to international relations within the Arab world. One such shift concerns the bases of cooperation. Underlying notions of common identity and kinship should certainly not be taken lightly since these constitute an important motivation and basis of legitimization for attempts at Arab cooperation. For such attempts to be successful, however, Arab leaders must move beyond purely identitive considerations and give greater prominence to interest-based considerations and appeals. This should be accompanied by a shift in the way interests are defined away from a short-term atomistic approach (focusing only on the interests of the individual states) toward a longer term, interactive or holistic approach (focusing on the linkage of the fortunes of Arab states and larger Arab interests) (Buzan 1991). Such a shift, in turn, should lead to a broadening of security horizons not just in terms of the range of interests to be protected or promoted but also the strategies to be employed; in other words, it should be a shift from simple self-reliance or reliance on outside powers to collaborative approaches in association with other Arab states. This need not entail cessation of cooperation, let alone confrontation, with these powers. Rather what is required is the progressive strengthening of Arab ties and a better balance between horizontal and vertical cooperation.

Acknowledgment

This study is part of a larger research project on The Changing Face of National Security in the Arab World which has been supported by the Fonds pour la Formation de Chercheurs et l'Aide à la Recherche (FCAR), the Social Science and Humanities Research Council of Canada, and the Inter-University

Consortium for Arab Studies. The author is grateful for this support as well as for the comments and constructive criticism of Rex Brynen.

Endnotes

1. Some attention was paid to the topic of cooperation in the work of the functionalist school (1940s–50s) and the integration theorists (1950s–60s). However, these efforts were vastly overshadowed by analyses of conflict, crisis, and war.

2. These steps include high-level Israeli visits to Morocco and Tunisia and the subsequent establishment of diplomatic relations, *New York Times*, September 2 and October 3, 1994; a similar high-level visit to Oman, *Le Monde*, December 28, 1994; the convening of meetings of the multilateral working groups on water issues and arms control in Oman and Qatar respectively (April–May 1994) with large Israeli delegations in attendance; the decision of the GCC states to end the secondary and tertiary economic boycotts of Israel and to ease other restrictions on third parties who deal with Israel (*Le Monde*, October 2 and 3, 1994); the convening of the Casablanca and Amman regional economic conferences (November 1994 and October 1995).

3. In general, controlling the transfer of arms and military-related technology will undoubtedly prove to be the most problematic area for cooperation; see the reports in *The New York Times* of January 21, June 10 and 13, and July 9 and 10, 1991; January 31, May 28 and 31, 1992; and Feldman and Levite 1994.

4. Strong concerns about this were expressed when the U.S, Britain, and France were considering what measures to take against Libya for its alleged role in the explosion of a Western airliner over Lockerbie, Scotland, and related terrorist incidents. These concerns were manifested even in countries like Egypt which are closely associated with the U.S; see Loutfi El-Kholi, "The Libyan-Western Crisis: a Preliminary Reading," *Al-Ahram Weekly*, March 12, 1992 and Mohamed Sid-Ahmed, "Is the New World Order Aimed at the Arabs?," *Al-Ahram Weekly*, April 30–May 6, 1992.

5. Egyptian preeminence rested less on its hard *material* (i.e., military and economic) capabilities than on what might be termed its *political* capabilities, namely the tremendous appeal of its leader and his policies within other Arab countries, and the strong position of the regime at home. Nasser's Egypt sought, but never really achieved, a hegemonic position within the Arab system in part because its material capabilities were insufficient for the purpose. For a more extensive discussion, see Noble in Korany et al., 1991.

6. One indication of this can be found in the *Al-Hayat* survey of Kuwaiti public opinion reprinted in the *Journal of Palestine Studies* (Autumn 1991).

References

Aftandilian, Gregory. *Egypt's Bid for Arab Leadership*. New York: Council on Foreign Relations Press, 1993.

Bergsten, Fred. "The Primacy of Economics." *Foreign Policy* (Summer 1992).

Boustany, Nora. "At Saudis' Rich Table, the Alien Taste of Austerity." *Washington Post* (August 13, 1994).

Brown, Seyom. *New Forces, Old Forces and the Future of World Politics.* Glenview, IL: Scott Foresman, 1988, ch. 11.

Brynen, Rex and Paul Noble "The Gulf Conflict and the Arab State System: A New Regional Order." *Arab Studies Quarterly* (Winter–Spring 1991).

Butt, Gerald. "The Damascus Declaration." *Middle East International* (March 21, 1991).

Buzan, Barry. *People, States, and Fear.* Boulder, CO: Lynne Rienner Press, 1991.

Chubin, Shahram. *Iran's National Security Policy.* Washington, DC: Carnegie Endowment for International Peace, 1994.

Cordesman, Anthony. *Iran and Iraq: The Threat from the Northern Gulf.* Boulder, CO: Westview Press, 1993.

Cumings, Bruce. "Trilateralism and the New World Order." *World Policy Journal* (Spring 1991).

Daoud, Khaled. "Has the Damascus Declaration Anything to Declare?." *Al-Ahram Weekly* (July 23–29, 1992).

Daoud, Zakya. Articles in *Le Monde Diplomatique* (April, June, and November 1991).

Deutsch, Karl, et al. *Political Community and the North Atlantic Area.* Princeton: Princeton University Press, 1957.

Drysdale, Alasdair and Raymond Hinnebusch. *Syria and The Middle East Peace Process.* New York: Council on Foreign Relations Press, 1991.

El-Rafei, Shahira. "Single EC Looms Over Arabs." *Al-Ahram Weekly,* (February 6, 1992).

Fandy, Mamoun. "Egyptians vs. The 'Pure' Arabs." *New York Times* (May 16, 1991).

FBIS, *Daily Report. Near East and South Asia* (March 7, 1991).

Feldman, Shai and Ariel Levite, eds. *Arms Control and the New Middle East Security Environment.* Boulder, CO: Westview Press, 1994.

Feuilherade, Peter. "Row Between Kingdoms." *Middle East International* (April 3, 1992).

Garten, Jeffrey. *A Cold Peace.* New York: Times Books, 1993.

Gause III, F. Gregory. *Oil Monarchies.* New York: Council on Foreign Relations Press, 1994, 134–37, 166–70 and chs. 5 and 6.

Greenhouse, Steven. "Half of Egypt's $20 Billion Debt Being Forgiven by United States and Allies." *New York Times* (May 27, 1991).

Haeir, S. "Kuwait and Iran." *Middle East International* (September 13, 1991).

Hadar, Leon T., "The United States, Europe and the Middle East." *World Policy Journal* (Summer 1991).

Hubbell, Stephen. "Egypt: Keeping Iran at Bay." *Middle East International* (June 12, 1992).

Ibrahim, Youssef. "Gulf Nations Said to be Committed to U.S Alliance." *New York Times* October 25, 1991.

Jaber, Nadim.. "Kuwait: Looking for Protectors." *Middle East International* (August 30, 1991).

_____. "The Gulf: Elusive Security." *Middle East International* (September 27, 1991).

_____. "The Gulf: Conflicting Visions." *Middle East International* (November 22, 1991).

_____. "Iran Flexes Its Muscles." *Middle East International* (May 1, 1992).

Keohane, Robert. *After Hegemony*. Princeton, NJ: Princeton University Press, 1984.

Khalidi, Walid. Keynote address, symposium on Arab integration, Center for Contemporary Arab Studies, Georgetown University, Washington, DC, April 9–10, 1992.

Krasner, Stephen, ed. *International Regimes*. Ithaca, NY: Cornell University Press, 1983.

Krauthammer, Charles. "The Unipolar Moment." *Foreign Affairs* 70,1 (1991).

Kristof, Nicholas. "As China Looks at World Order, It Detects New Struggles Emerging." *New York Times* (April 21, 1992).

MacFarlane, S. Neil. "The Impact of Superpower Collaboration on the Third World" in Thomas G. Weiss and Meryl A. Kessler, eds., *Third World Security in the Post Cold War Era*. Boulder, CO: Lynne Rienner, 1991.

Miller, Benjamin. "A New World Order: From Balancing to Hegemony, Concert or Collective Security?." *International Interactions* 18,1 (1992).

Mohamedi, Fareed. "The Saudi Economy." *Middle East Report* 185 (December 1993).

Organski, A. F. K. *World Politics*. 2nd. ed. New York, NY: Knopf, 1968.

Oye, Kenneth, ed. *Cooperation Under Anarchy*. Princeton: Princeton University Press, 1986.

Noble, Paul. "The Arab System: Pressures, Constraints, and Opportunities" in Bahgat Korany et al. *The Foreign Policies of Arab States*, 2nd. ed. Boulder, CO: Westview Press, 1991.

Piscatori, James, ed. *Islamic Fundamentalisms and the Gulf Crisis*. Chicago, IL: American Academy of Arts and Sciences, 1991.

Rodenbeck, Max. "Why Mubarak did a U-turn on the Gulf." *Middle East International* (May 17, 1991).

Rosecrance, Richard. "A New Concert of Powers." *Foreign Affairs* (Spring 1992).

Sadowski, Yahya. "Arab Economies After the Gulf War." *Middle East Report* (May–June 1991).

Salamé, Ghassan. "Inter-Arab Politics: The Return of Geography" in William Quandt, ed., *Ten Years After Camp David*. Washington, DC: Brookings Institution, 1988.

Sarkis, Nicolas. "Washington renforce son emprise sur la politique pétrolière." *Le Monde Diplomatique* (July 1992).

Sayigh, Yazid. "Regional Security in the Gulf: The Geopolitical Realities." *Middle East International* (May 31, 1991)

_____. "Regional Security in the Gulf." *Middle East International* (August 30, 1991).

_____. "Reversing the Middle East Nuclear Race." *Middle East Report* (July–August 1992).

Selim, Mohammed El-Sayed. "Arabs in a Dangerous World." *Al-Ahram Weekly* July 23–29, 1992.

Sid Ahmed, Abdal Salam. "Tehran–Khartoum: A New Axis or a Warning Shot." *Middle East International* (February 7, 1992).

_____. "Iran, Sudan, Algeria: A Setback in the Grand Plan" *Middle East International* (March 20, 1992).

Thompson, W. R. *On Global War*. Columbia, SC: University of South Carolina Press, 1988.

Tucker, Robert. "1989 and All That." *Foreign Affairs* (Fall 1990).

Tyler, Patrick. "Gulf Security Talks Stall Over Plans for Saudi Army." *New York Times* (October 13, 1991).

chapter 4

From Pan-Arabism to the Community of Sovereign Arab States: Redefining the Arab and Arabism in the Aftermath of the Second Gulf War

Bassam Tibi

Since the creation of the Arab state system in the wake of the decolonization of Arab lands (Fromkin 1989), the rhetoric of pan-Arab unity has been the prevailing pretension in inter-Arab politics (Tibi 1997). Yet, conflict, not cooperation, has been the hallmark of highly competitive Arab state policies, and interstate relations have been characterized more by divisive coalitions than by cooperative integration (Kerr 1971).

Until the Gulf crisis, the basic belief underlying pan-Arab rhetoric was that all Arabs, as an imagined community, share commonalities on every level and thus need only to be unified into one, centrally governed nation-state. The fact that Arab unity is not yet a reality, but remains a dream that falls short of the requirements of a policy, is explained as an outcome of external conspiracies (*mu'amarat*) directed against the Arabs by their Western enemies (Tibi 1993). The prominent Iraqi Ba'th politician Sa'dun Hammadi clearly puts forward this contention: "In the Arab homeland there exists no movement that suffers from the hostility of Western imperialism more than pan-Arabism does. The reason for this is that the West is aware of the consequences that may result for its presence in the area, if a mighty pan-Arab state could be built up" (Hammadi 1970, 166–67). Hammadi also blames the Arabs themselves for the absence of this "mighty Arab state," without, however, giving up on the notion of an external *mu'amarah* (conspiracy) as a major explanation for the lack of Arab unity. This understanding of pan-Arabism perhaps influenced Iraq's decision to invade Kuwait in 1990. In the text of his declaration of the annexation of Kuwait, Iraqi President Saddam Hussein highlighted the pan-Arab perception that the West committed a "major crime" against the Arabs when it divided their lands. Saddam reminded his fellow Arabs that the region was "one entity when it was ruled by Baghdad" (*Al-Muntada* September 1990). The confusion of the Ottoman Empire with the Abbasid Caliphate is striking in this statement based on the perception of a sinister conspiracy. The notion of *mu'amarah* and the threat perception related to it are salient features of pan-Arab rhetoric (Tibi 1993 and Spanish edition 1996). Some of the beliefs underlying the idea of a United Arab State had taken on a quasi-religious character, and to question them was viewed as tantamount to sacrilege.

The Gulf crisis changed this situation decisively, since it was ignited by the invasion of a sovereign Arab state by another Arab state, not by an extraregional power. At the outset, no external forces were involved. Efforts to deal with the conflict on a regional level, i.e., to deescalate the conflict within the framework of a *hall al-'Arabi* ("Arab solution," see Tibi 1993, ch. 16), were hampered by the lack of an Arab institutional framework for conflict management (Kriesberg and Thorson 1991, 267–73). The fact that the Arab state system participates in a regional organization, the Arab League, changes little in reality (Macdonald 1965; Gomaa 1977). The Arab League simply does not have the institutions and the related mechanisms of collective policymaking required for regional conflict resolution. In comparison with the European Union (EU), the Arab state system also lacks the necessary institutional efficacy. Despite its well-known flaws, European integration provides a model from which the Arabs could learn much in their efforts to redefine Arabism in the aftermath of the Gulf crisis. I would argue that, had the Arab League been of the same caliber as the EU (and earlier the EC), both institutionally and in terms of policymaking, the interstate conflict between Iraq and Kuwait over oil and boundaries would not have erupted and escalated, let alone have led to war. But unfortunately the Arab League lacked the capacity to resolve, or even to deescalate, the conflict (Tschirgi and Tibi 1991; Tibi 1993, Part III).

The vision of a pan-Arab state, as it had prevailed until the Gulf crisis, was related to the ideology and rhetoric of pan-Arab nationalism, but not to an existing citizenship pattern nor to a model of integration of regional states. Pan-Arab ideology was directed against the existing institution of the nation-state, along whose lines all discrete states of the region are organized. In the political language of pan-Arab ideology, existing Arab states were not accepted as nation-states. They were downgraded and labeled *al-dawla al-qitriyya* (the domestic state) (Tarabishi 1982). The term meaning "the Arab nation-state" (*al-dawla al-qawmiyya*), was used only to refer to the visionary pan-Arab state aimed at, and allegedly hitherto impeded by, Western conspiracies. Thus, pan-Arab ideology, even though it negates the existing Arab nation-states, remains imprisoned in the nation-state idea. It simply aspires to a larger pan-Arab state that unites all Arabs. In fact, harmony and brotherhood were the central rhetorical themes of pan-Arab ideology, while real interstate Arab politics, as with any other politics, has been characterized by severe conflict.

The difference between Arabs and Europeans has not been the difference between a harmonious and a conflict-ridden group of states. Rather, it has been the difference between European states as a group equipped with mechanisms of conflict resolution and a realistic concept of Europeanness, and Arab states blinded by ideological and extended tribal formulas such as brotherhood and pan-Arab harmony (Tibi 1990), which preoccupy their thoughts and policies. To put it bluntly, one of the lessons of the Gulf crisis ought to be the recognition of the strength of a policy-oriented, rather than an ideology-oriented, redefinition of Arabness.

As noted, pan-Arab ideology denounced the existing nation-states as *dawla qitriyya* (the domestic state). In fact, with the exception of Egypt and Morocco, all existing Arab states can be described as nominal nation-states in that they lack the substance of the nation-state institution first developed in Europe and then—in the course of globalization—adopted by the entire world (for more details, see Giddens 1987, 255ff and Tibi 1990). Third World states often have been described by international relations scholars as "quasi-states" (Jackson 1990). Nevertheless, the existing Arab nation-states are here to stay. Surely, the first lesson of the Gulf crisis must be that any effort to induce boundary changes in the existing Arab state system will erupt in violent conflict. In the case of the Gulf, the conflict cost the Arabs dearly.

To question the ideological concept of pan-Arabism and to plead for a redefinition of Arabness is not to rebuff the Arab aspiration for integration. If this aspiration were to be redefined in policy terms, it could develop into a pragmatic policy of integration that would contribute to Arab development and regional peace. With the aim of redefining Arabness along these realistic lines, I want to explore the usefulness of the European integration experience as a possible model for Arab politics.

Underlying my argument are two propositions. First, redefining Arabness must be aimed at developing a new design for inter-Arab relations: an interstate structure of sovereign states based on mutual respect. In early 1996 the Secretary General of the Arab League, Dr. Esmat Abdel-Meguid, made a proposal urging that the existing sovereignty of the Arab states be unambiguously accepted as a matter of "*sharaf 'arabi*" (Arab honor). The integration pattern ought not question or violate the national sovereignty of the existing Arab states. For this reason, European integration is an experience from which the Arabs could learn.

Second, we must redefine the Arab as a citizen of a democratic state and divorce the notion of the Arab from its hitherto prevailing ethnic connotations. The Kurds of Syria and Iraq, the Dinka of Sudan, and the Berber of Algeria and Morocco could then feel like true Arab citizens, no longer outlawed by a quasi-racist ethnic-exclusive definition of the Arab. Furthermore, the new definition of the Arab should also be secular since not all Arabs are Muslims. A secular redefinition of the Arab smoothes the way for Arab Christians to honor Arabness as a citizenship that puts them on equal footing with their Muslim co-citizens (see the secular position of Christian Lebanese Mughaizel 1980; and the contrary position of the Egyptian fundamentalist 'Imara 1981).

European Integration as a Model

It is common sense to state that the overall problems of the community of Arab states cannot be solved on the level of the existing discrete nation-states. However, regional integration seems to promise new avenues for progress. In this regard, the EU provides a model from which Arab policymakers could learn a great deal. Unfortunately, since these policymakers do not face the threat of being turned out of office by voters, they may not adopt these lessons. Integration is nevertheless not a new theme in Arab politics (see Luciani and Salamé 1988). The problem is that the term "integration" has been consistently used by Arab politicians as equivalent to the blurred concept of pan-Arab state unity. In this understanding, the EU cannot serve as a model for the Arabs since Europeans—as will be shown later in more detail—are not attempting to create a "United States of Europe." In Arabic, there are important nuances between integration (indimaj), cooperation (ta'awun), and unity (wahda). However, in the language of Arab politics, all of these meanings are subsumed under the pan-Arab concept of central unity as designated by the ideology of Arab nationalism. If Arab politicians are to learn from the Gulf War in the context of redefining "Arabness," it becomes imperative for them to take a serious look at the structure and achievements of the European Community and its development to a European Union. This is why I believe it is important to reconsider and redefine "Arabness."

There are two major conflicting paradigms in the Middle East: the pan-Arab and the Islamist (Tibi 1987, 59–74 and Tibi 1997, Part V), along with various ethnic and local-national subdivisions (Khoury and Kostiner 1990), which undermine the structure of the Arab nation-state and thus stand as obstacles to Arab integration.

In an interview with this writer on September 28, 1989, the late Shaykh of Al-

Azhar, Jadulhaq Ali Jadulhaq, responded to a question concerning Muslim unity with his own question: "You come from Europe. What are the Europeans doing there?" In the Shaykh's mind, the EC was then a model for Arab or Muslim unity. The rationale of his question was that if the Europeans are uniting, why cannot the Muslims and Arabs unite as well. This logic can be found elsewhere in pan-Arab political thought. It draws on the model of German unity once described by Sati' al-Husri as an example for the Arabs to emulate and has been expanded to include commentary on the recent European progress toward unity. Yet, a closer look at the EU helps overcome this misconception that the European model is somehow comparable to the pan-Arab goal of a single Arab state. The realities of the ongoing European integration simply "do not fit with the notion of either a 'superstate' or a 'United States of Europe' " (Sbargia 1992, 2). What then is European integration? And to what extent can it serve as a model for the goal of Arab integration under a new definition of Arabness?

A recent Brookings Institution study states that "national governments are prominent actors in the [European] community, integral to its very identity" (Sbargia 1992, 12). This observation may shock or disillusion those Middle Easterners who look to the early EC and the current EU as a model for Arab state unity. Then too, this observation may relieve the fears of those Arab statesmen who pay lip service to pan-Arab unity while deep in their hearts and in their realpolitik, they resent it as a threat to national sovereignty. To reemphasize the true meaning of European integration: the European states are—without great fanfare—pursuing their politics of integration while maintaining and acknowledging the existing state units as the basis of representation within the community. The EU is not like the Arab League; it represents institution-building and substantive integration. The EU has created an internal market encompassing all member states which includes goods, services, capital, and labor. This eliminates all earlier existing nontariff barriers among the participating member states.

The second area of European integration is in policymaking. In substance, the political process of integration in Western Europe means nothing more than the building of institutions as a framework for policymaking. A prominent example is the European Court of Justice. Another is the European Parliament. The other major institutions include the EU Commission, the Council of Ministers, and the European Council. These institutions represent an extraordinarily complex political system of policymaking on all levels which, nevertheless, does not infringe on the sovereignty of decisionmaking and bargaining, and which is capable of translating "institutional capacity . . . into the effective representation of diverse national interests and needs at the community level" (Sbargia 1992, 3).

Most importantly, this system is underpinned by an intrinsically democratic political culture in which qualified majority decisions are recognized and unanimity is not basically required. Democratic leadership, democratic coalitions, diversity, bargaining, convergence, policy differentiation, and national government discretion are the terms around which the system of European integration can be described. Thus, decisionmaking in the European community is an interplay between member states and the institutions of the community (Sbargia 1992, 2–3). In short, European political integration is based on the institutional framework for interplay among sovereign states.

Having unraveled what European integration is all about, it might no longer seem to be attractive to those Arabs for whom *al-wahda* ("unity"—meaning the fusion of existing states into a larger union) is a kind of civil religion. In the aftermath of the Gulf War, the community that believes in this political religion has been diminishing. The different pan-Arab regimes in Syria and Iraq have sought to monopolize the secular religion of Arabism while denying it to the other and viewing the other as an agent of imperialism and Zionism. While waging a war of words and avowing pan-Arabism rhetorically, each regime has jealously protected its own national state sovereignty and concomitant security concerns. The rivalry between the pan-Arab Iraqi Ba'th and the Syrian pan-Arab Ba'th is just a case in point (Kienle 1991). A recent comparison between royal Hashemite and radical pan-Arab unionism leads to the same disillusioning conclusion (Mufti 1996). In light of the Gulf War, this pattern can hardly be considered a model for redefining Arabness. Nor can the invasion of Kuwait by Iraq's Saddam Hussein—the self-proclaimed Arab Bismarck—be an acceptable model for integration.[1]

The Arabs have been talking for decades about integration in terms of pan-Arab unity without progressing toward this rhetorically proclaimed end. In contrast, integration in Europe was a policy issue, not pan-ideological rhetoric. Inherent in this policy has been the consistent honoring of the existing nation-states in Europe. Institutionally supported respect for national differences on all levels, and thus for plurality, has been the hallmark of the EU. Rather than purporting to abolish diversities, which pan-Arab nationalists disregard as *iqlimiyya* (see al-Husri 1963), the Europeans established the institutional framework to deal with the conflicts arising from these diversities in a democratic and pluralistic manner. One of the lessons of the Gulf War is that existing Arab nation-states—regardless of their historical background—are here to stay. This insight makes the European model of integration, which honors diversity as plurality and which views national governments as the major players in the policymaking process, more appealing to pragmatic Arabs who turn away from the conflict-igniting ideologies that have blinded past generations and wasted their energies and their resources. In discussing Arab integration, Ghassan Salamé reminds us that the ideology of pan-Arab nationalism was clearly based on the "utopian idea of a single Arab state" (Luciani and Salamé 1988, 264). Yet all Arab governments that avowed this utopia have instead practiced "isolationist policies with pan-Arab vocabulary." This discrepancy between dishonest rhetoric and realpolitik has been the hallmark of Arab politics since the creation of the Arab state system.

I share Salamé's view that the Arab League has failed to achieve anything worth mentioning with regard to Arab integration because it pays lip service to the utopian idea of the pan-Arab state while simultaneously doing everything possible to prevent it. Even in terms of modest integration goals, such as cooperation frameworks, the Arab League has achieved little. In an environment in which the political culture necessary for practicing democracy is lacking, the rhetorical call for unanimity replaces actual political bargaining on the grounds of mutual acceptance of sovereignty. Salamé refers to the 4,000 resolutions adopted by the Arab League since its creation: "80 percent of them, though adopted by unanimous votes, were never applied. . . . [T]here is no need to establish majority rules since even when unanimity is possible it remains ineffective" (Luciani and Salamé 1988, 75). He also refers to the impressively large number of treaties signed under the auspices of the Arab League:

> Applied, they would have created a very high level of pan-Arab integration. This is obviously not the case. . . . The major obstacle [is] the lack of implementation even of unanimously voted resolutions. . . . It is the discrepancy . . . between the dream of unity and the reality of inter-Arab politics. Arab regimes . . . would be threatened by a higher level of integration in the Arab world. And they clearly, systematically oppose this integration even when the state religion is Arab nationalism. (Luciani and Salamé 1988, 278)

Integration is perceived by Arab regimes as a threat not because the incumbents are traitors, "agents of imperialism and Zionism" and the like. Nation-states have national interests. The utopian and illusionary ideology of pan-Arab nationalism (Tibi 1997) is aimed at abolishing boundaries and establishing an ill-defined central pan-Arab government at the expense of competing national interests. No Arab state honestly wanted to be subjugated to such an unstable polity. However, if integration is understood as a politico-institutional framework for policymaking among equal nation-states—as is the case in the EU— then the threat-perception of Arab policymakers would abate.

The Arabs can learn a great deal from the European process of political and economic integration because no single Arab state can hope to cope with its problems in the absence of such integration. This process of Arab integration could take place while simultaneously maintaining and acknowledging the importance of the national governments participating in this process as sovereign actors. Policymaking within the framework of regional integration along the lines of the EU then would be a democratic process that does not violate the national interests of the member states. Thus conceptualized, "the role of national governments can be incorporated into a fuller understanding of policy making within the community" (Sbargia 1992, 12) as the EC model teaches us. This model could serve as a successful case to emulate while providing the basis for second thoughts on the overall failure of pan-Arabism and its rhetorical concept of Arabness.

Regional Integration in the Light of the Peace Process

In the same year of the Gulf War the Madrid Peace Conference took place and indirectly led to the Oslo Declaration of Principles and the ensuing Israeli-Palestinian peace accords in Washington and Cairo. Within this framework three economic summits—Casablanca in 1994, Amman in 1995, and Cairo in 1996—followed, in which many (but not all) of the Arab states participated, along with the United States, European Union member countries and—significantly—two key non-Arab Middle Eastern states—Israel and Turkey. A regional formula dubbed the "New Middle East" was promoted in these meetings, especially by the United States and Israel. (Indeed Israel's former prime minister Shimon Peres wrote a book with this title [Peres, 1993]). Unlike the Arab state system, the "New Middle East" comprises all the states of the region. A competing formula, which also emerged in the course of the peace process, is Euro-Mediterranean cooperation and integration. As awareness has grown of the significance of the southern and eastern Mediterranean countries for Europe (especially those member states on the northern Mediterranean coast), the European Union started to develop its own approach to the region. One important milestone in this trend was the Mediterranean Summit held in Barcelona in November 1995. The "New Middle East" is considered to be an American policy for the region while "Mediterranean integration" is seen as a European approach. It is clear that both new visions bring to the fore the fact that in the post–Arab-Israeli conflict and post–Cold War eras integration in the Middle East area is no longer an exclusive inter-Arab matter. In all of the aforementioned summits multi-billion-dollar funds were promised for financing the economic development of the Middle East as a whole, not just the Arab states. The establishment of the Regional Bank for Development in the Middle

East in Cairo in March 1996 was the first concrete step for promoting the "New Middle East." This U.S.-supported measure faced tough European opposition.

Irrespective of further developments either in the direction of a "New Middle East" or a "Mediterranean network" (or a combination of the two competing formulas) the real issue is the need for regional cooperation that goes beyond the confines of the Arab state system. Middle Eastern peace can only be enduring if combined with the needed economic underpinning to be achieved through regional integration. The funds promised by the international community can only be made available on these grounds within this context.

In order not to create any tensions between the unfolding of a community of sovereign Arab states and these two new approaches to regional integration Arabs need to be assured that economic cooperation arrangements involving Israel would not serve as an umbrella for promoting Israeli regional hegemony. Similar Arab reservations are also valid concerning the inclusion of Turkey and Iran in a "New Middle East." A substantial water arrangement with Turkey and the abandonment of Iranian expansionist policy in the Gulf are, from the Arab point of view, as important as an honest and wholehearted Israeli commitment to a just peace. Following the 1996 elections in Israel (which brought Benjamin Netanyahu to power) and the ensuing Arab summit meeting in Cairo, the actors in the Arab-Israeli conflict have traded their roles: the Arab states are now asking for peace, and the new Likud government is rejecting the spirit (if not the letter) of the Oslo "peace process." A basic repercussion has been the blocking of both projects—"New Middle East" and "Euro-Mediterranean Integration"— and the freezing of their economic planning.

In short, the development of a community of sovereign Arab states and a structure for comprehensive Middle Eastern regional integration could become complementary rather than antagonistic to one another, but only under conditions of true Arab-Israeli peace based on mutual recognition in all substantive areas. At present the obstacles are tremendous and unlikely to disappear. So for the time being Arab integration must remain the top priority.

Toward a Secular, Non-Ethnic Arab Citizenship

A democratic framework for a new concept of Arab integration could provide a basis for redefining Arabness. A new approach to integration must be directed by and oriented toward the needs of the Arab people rather than by an ideology obsessed with rhetorical political utopias.

In pan-Arab ideology, Sati' al-Husri defined Arabness along the lines of

Herder's German romantic idea of the nation as a *Kulturgemeinschaft*, i.e., a community determined by a common language and a shared history (on the German impact on Husri's thought, see Tibi 1997, 127–38). Basically, al-Husri's concept was a secular one. Nonetheless, this concept became mingled with Islam and Arab ethnicity in Arab politics (Hudson 1977, chs. 2–3). Non-Arab minorities such as the Kurds, the Dinka, and the Berber; non-Sunni Muslims such as the Shi'a; and non-Muslims, either were practically outlawed or were not considered to be full members of the community. Muammar al-Qadhafi put it most blatantly when he said that Arab Christians ought to convert to Islam if they wanted to become true Arabs. While it is possible to switch from one religion to another through conversion, no one can escape their ethnicity. Kurds, Dinkas, and Berbers could never become ethnic Arabs even if they wanted to do so. The uprising of the Kurds and the Shi'a in Iraq (Nakash 1994, 273–81) in the aftermath of the Gulf War reveals the consequences of attaching Arabness to a Sunni-Arab ethnic-sectarian concept. In the light of the Gulf crisis, a redefinition of the Arab is urgently needed. A secular, nonethnic and nonsectarian concept of citizenship in a civil, i.e., democratic, society provides a way out of this dilemma.

Even ethnic Arabs do not share a common identity, given their involvement in subethnic, sectarian, and tribal communities (for more details, see Esman and Rabinovich 1988 and S. E. Ibrahim 1995). Arab societies are still traditional societies characterized by ethnic strife and tribal identities (see Tibi in Khoury and Kostiner 1990, 127 ff). As Giddens tells us: "The population of traditional states did not know themselves to be 'citizens' of those states, nor did it matter particularly to the community of power within them. . . . The expansion of state sovereignty means that those subject to it are in some sense . . . aware of their membership in a political community" (1987, 210). Citizenship is not based on commonly shared ethnic origins but rather "is anchored psychologically in distinctive features of modern societies. . . . The extension of communication cannot occur without the 'conceptual involvement' of the whole community in a way in which traditional states were not" (Giddens 1987, 219).

Redefining the Arab, therefore, in the aftermath of the Gulf crisis needs to take place within the nonethnic and secular features of citizenship. Regrettably, instead, the outcome of the Gulf crisis so far has been a strengthening of Islamic fundamentalism (Piscatori 1991; Tibi 1998, ch. 3) rather than the development of an awareness of the importance of citizenship based on neither religion nor ethnicity.

Once again, the European experience provides a salutary model. In the EU, the collective decisionmaking process rests upon the free and democratic interplay of citizens and interests within each state, and upon the democratic behav-

ior of member-states themselves in regional institutions. When we acknowledge that the EC is neither a state nor an international organization but rather
a state system of policymaking, it becomes clear that in the European model of
integration, "the nation-state truly becomes the member state" (Giddens 1987,
258). If this model seems acceptable to those responsible Arab policymakers
searching for an alternative to failed paths, the following issue areas become relevant to Arab integration as a viable alternative:

- The political culture of decisionmaking in the EC seems an appropriate
  model for promoting integration among Arab states, not in the ideological sense of Arabism, but in the practical sense of creating institutional
  patterns for regional cooperation.
- In such a culture, decisions are made within a framework based on related
  interests, not on primordial notions such as "*ukhuwwa*" ("brotherhood"—no mentioning of the sisters) and the like. If this framework is
  accepted, then the issue would become how to rationally converge the
  interests of sovereign Arab states and how to establish cooperation among
  them within a state community of members linked to one another by a
  system of policymaking.
- In the EC there exists a balanced relationship between the state and the
  overall community structure based on the interplay between national
  governments and community institutions (Peters in Sbargia 1992, 75 ff).
  This pattern seems relevant for establishing inter-Arab relations within a
  framework promoting integration in the sense of an interplay between
  actors seeking stable and tenable common ground.
- One of the lessons of the Gulf War ought to be that the Arab League lacks
  the institutional capacity for regional conflict resolution. It makes no
  sense to argue that the League failed to foster an Arab solution to the Gulf
  crisis without referring to the lack of institutions that would have contributed to this end. The Arab solution, under these conditions, was
  downgraded to an Iraqi propaganda formula. The result was an overwhelming fragmentation of the Arab state system (Tibi in Tschirgi and
  Tibi 1991, 71 ff).
- The European system of integration has been able to solve a variety of
  interstate European conflicts within the existing institutional framework.
  The Arab state system urgently needs an institution similar to the
  European Court of Justice (Shapiro in Sbargia 1992, 123 ff) with all its
  legal-institutional capabilities of peaceful conflict resolution. Integration
  is a system of policymaking that has the institutional capabilities to conduct conflict resolution and deal with discord.
- Credibility is another issue that must be addressed. In Arab politics, credibility is either related to ideologies, such as pan-Arabism as a rhetorical
  superlegitimacy (Hudson 1977, 1–30), or to primordial norms and values,

such as the personal honor of the policymaker. In the EU, credibility is, on the contrary, a pragmatic issue associated with costs (Whooley in Sbargia 1992, 157 ff). If an actor in international relations cannot bear the costs associated with its policies, then the credibility of the actor is jeopardized. No single Arab state nor the Arab League has ever pursued such a linkage between credibility and the capacity and willingness to bear the costs of the policies pronounced. This is the major reason for the lack of credibility in the system of Arab integration. Unlike the Arab state system, the EU treats credibility as a secular issue: it derives from the thoughts and actions of calculating policymakers.

- Before the Gulf War, and in a more intensified manner since, there has been endless talk in Arab politics about the transfer of funds from rich to poor Arab states (see the early debates in Kerr and Yassin 1982). The Europeans have similar discussions: poor EC members in southern Europe, in particular Spain, have asked for a transfer of funds from rich states to poor ones. In the December 1991 Summit of Maastricht, Spain raised this issue again. Instead of unattached transfers of funds by rich to poor European countries, the EU has given prominence to structural policy. The European system places the transfer of funds within a development policy framework (Marks in Sbargia 1992, 191 ff). Formally, there are similar development-oriented funds in the Arab system (Marks in Sbargia 1992, 191 ff), but laden with the rhetoric about "brotherhood." Because those institutions lack capability and credibility they have been ineffective.

The Middle Way

To conclude, under the present process of globalization, the discrete weak Arab nation-states cannot survive on their own. Yet the old Arab dream of a United Arab State has proven to be a fallacy. Between the isolation of some Arab states and the expansionism disguised as pan-Arabism of others there exists a middle way of integration for which the EU can serve as the most successful example. Arabs can learn a great deal from this model while working to redefine Arabness and the Arab. The first thing to be learned from the EU experience is the need for a highly institutionalized structure that is neither a superstate nor a commonly shared citizenship, but is rather, a political culture of policymaking within a civil society. These factors are crucial for the integration of Arab states. Integration, in turn, is badly needed to foster development and the capacity to resolve conflict.

It must be noted that the institutionalization of the policymaking system in Europe would have been unthinkable without one crucial requirement: the

process for which Charles Tilly coined the term "the civilianization of governments" (Tilly 1990, 122). By civilianization is meant the building up of institutionalized statehood and the concommitant depersonalization of power. In this
regard most Arab states have (to varying degrees) weak statehood and a very
low degree of civilianization. This civilianization created the substance of the
nation-state. Elsewhere I have argued that the present nation-states in the
Middle East lack this substance; they remain nominal nation-states (Khoury
and Kostiner 1990). The groundwork for redefining Arabness, then, must be
laid first on this very basic unit of action, the state. The civilianization of governments and the related institutionalization of the nominal Arab nation-states
themselves would be the prerequisite for creating a functioning inter-Arab state
system and democratic citizenship. These, in turn, are the indispensable bases
for Arab integration.

In pursuit of this needed pattern of Arab integration a new definition of the
Arab League is also required. The League, once established by "politicians more
experienced in intrigue than in the debate, mediation and compromise of international relations" (Macdonald 1965, 281) proved to be most unsuccessful during
the Gulf crisis. In addition to its lack of an institutional structure for policymaking, one of the consistent failures of the Arab League has been "its reluctance to
accept its role as a regional organization. The inclination has been to regard the
League as a step along the path to Arab unity" (Macdonald 1965, 300). However,
as we have seen, this inclination never went beyond rhetoric. Arabs need to free
themselves from this rhetoric while making efforts at democratization of their
societies and the civilianization of their governments in order to strengthen the
statehood of existing polities. Anything else would be wishful thinking.

In light of the Gulf crisis, ideological and rhetorical pan-Arabism ought to
be buried once and for all, not for the sake of a further fragmentation of Arab
politics, but rather, with the aim of establishing a stable Arab integration system
based on a democratic, nonethnic, and secular understanding of what it means
to be Arab. Without this buildup there can be neither a stable Middle East nor
real peace in the region.

Acknowledgment

This article is based on papers presented at the Georgetown University Center
for Contemporary Arab Studies and the American University in Cairo. It was
completed at the Center for International Affairs at Harvard University during
my term there as an "Akademie" Fellow of the Volkswagen Foundation.

Endnote

1. In the declaration of the annexation of Kuwait, the terms *wahda* (unity) and *indimaj* (integration) were collapsed into one term to form the title of the text: *Wahda indimajiyya*. The Arabic text can be found in the special issue of *Al-muntada* (September 1990), published by Arab Thought Forum, Amman. The idea of an Arab Bismarck needed to unite the Arabs stems from Sati' al Husri (See Tibi 1991,152, and also the chapter on the Arab Bismarck as a secular Imam in my most recent book, *Der wahre Imam*, Munich: Piper Press, 1997).

References Cited

al-Husri, Sati.' *Al-iqlimiyya: judhuriha wa buzuriha.* Beirut: Dar al-'ilm lil-malayin, 1963.

Esman, Milton J. and Itamar Rabinovich, eds. *Ethnicity, Pluralism and the State in the Middle East.* Ithaca, NY: Cornell University Press, 1988.

Fromkin, David. *A Peace to End all Peace: The Fall of the Ottoman Empire and the Creation of the Modern Middle East.* New York: Avon Books, 1989.

Giddens, Anthony. *The Nation-State and Violence.* Berkeley, CA: University of California Press, 1987.

Gomaa, Ahmed M. *The Foundation of the League of Arab States.* London: Longman, 1977.

Hammadi, Sa'dun. *Qadaya al thawra al-arabiyya: al-thawra al-'arabiyya wa al-wihda.* Beirut: Dar al-tali'a, 1970.

"Hawl 'an al-wahda al-indimajiyya ma'a al-kuwait.' *Al-Muntada.* Amman. (September 1990), 19–20.

Hudson, Michael. *Arab Politics: The Search for Legitimacy.* New Haven, CT: Yale University Press, 1977.

'Imara, Muhammad. *Al-islam wa al-'uruba wa al-'ilmaniyya.* Beirut: Dar al-Wihda, 1981.

Jackson, Robert H. *Quasi-States: Sovereignty, International Relations and the Third World.* Cambridge: Cambridge University Press, 1990.

Ibrahim, S. E., "Ethnic Conflict and State-Building in the Arab World." In Geoffrey Kemp and Janice Gross Stein (eds.), *Powder Keg in the Middle East* . London: Rowman & Littlefield, 1995.

Kerr, Malcolm H. *The Arab Cold War.* New York: Oxford University Press, 1971.

Kerr, Malcolm and Sayid Yassin, eds. *Rich and Poor States in the Middle East.* Boulder, CO: Westview Press, 1982.

Khoury, Philip and Josef Kostiner, eds. *Tribes and State Formation in the Middle East.* Berkeley, CA: University of California Press, 1990.

Kienle, Eberhard. *Ba'th Versus Ba'th.* New York: St. Martin's Press, 1991.

Kriesberg, Louis and Stuart J. Thorson, eds. *Timing the De-escalation of International Conflicts.* Syracuse, New York: Syracuse University Press, 1991.

Luciani, Giacomo and Ghassan Salamé, eds. *The Politics of Arab Integration*. London: Croom Helm, 1988.

Macdonald, Robert W. *The League of the Arab States: A Study in the Dynamic of Regional Organization*. Princeton, NJ: Princeton University Press, 1965.

Mattione, Richard P. *OPEC's Investments and the International Financial System*. Washington, DC: The Brookings Institution, 1985.

Mufti, Malik, *Sovereign Creations: Pan-Arabism and Political Order in Syria and Iraq*. Ithaca, NY: Cornell University Press, 1996.

Mughaizel, Joseph. *Al-'uruba wa al-'ilmaniyya*. Beirut: Dar al-Nahar, 1980.

Nakash, Yitzhak. *The Shi'is of Iraq*. Princeton: Princeton University Press, 1994.

Peres, Shimon (with Aori Naori). *The New Middle East*. New York: Henry Holt, 1993.

Piscatori, James, ed. *Islamic Fundamentalism and the Gulf Crisis*. Chicago: The American Academy of Arts and Sciences, 1991.

Sbargia, Alberta, ed. *Euro-Politics: Institutions and Policymaking in the "New" European Community*. Washington, DC: The Brookings Institution, 1992.

Tarabishi, George. *Al-dawla al-qitriyya wa al-nazariyya al-qawmiyya*. Beirut: Dar al-Talia, 1982.

Tibi, Bassam. "Islam and Arab Nationalism" in Barbara Stowasser, ed., *The Islamic Impulse*. Washington, DC: Center for Contemporary Arab Studies, 1987.

Tibi, Bassam. "The Simultaneity of the Unsimultaneous: Old Tribes and Impaired Nation-States," in Khoury and Kostiner, 1990.

Tibi, Bassam. *Die Verschworung/al-Mu'amarah: Der Trauma arabischer Politik*. Hamburg: Hoffman & Campe, 1993; Spanish edition, *La conspiration*. Barcelona: Edition Herder, 1996.

Tibi, Bassam. *Arab Nationalism: A Critical Inquiry*. New York: St. Martin's Press, second edition,1991. Enlarged 3rd edition with new subtitle: "Between Islam and the Nation State," 1997.

Tibi, Bassam. *The Challenge of Fundamentalism: Political Islam and New World Disorder*. Berkeley: University of California Press, forthcoming 1998.

Tibi, Bassam. *Conflict and War in the Middle East, 1967–1991: Regional Dynamics and the Superpowers*. London: Macmillan, 1993 (second edition forthcoming 1998).

Tilly, Charles. *Coercion, Capital and the European States*. Cambridge, MA: Basil Blackwell, 1990.

Tschirgi, Dan and Bassam Tibi. *Perspectives on the Gulf Crisis*. Cairo: Cairo University Press, 1991.

Mustapha Kamil Al-Sayyid

That one ambitious experiment of political integration in the Arab world has failed occasions no surprise
for observers of Arab politics or integration experiments. Other attempts at integration among Arab
countries have met a similar fate; none managed to
match even the three and one-half year lifespan of the
United Arab Republic. One has only to remember that
the confederation of Arab Republics (Egypt, Syria, and
Libya), which apparently caused a rift between late
president Anwar al-Sadat and his Nasserite ministers
in May 1971, survived a mere two years. That was also
the fate of similar attempts between Syria and Iraq
(1980), and Libya and Tunisia (1981) to mention only a
few examples.

The failure of integration schemes cannot be attributed to some unique feature of Arab culture or the
Arab mind since similar endeavors in the Third World-
-Senegal, Mali, and Guinea; Malaysia and Singapore
(1963–1965)—-also failed. In addition, there are cases in
which countries have split apart or have maintained
their territorial integrity only by suppressing important segments of the population. A weakened "sense of
community" has recently infected some hitherto well-
established multinational states in developed countries
as well, causing the complete disintegration of the
Soviet Union and provoking much tension between
French-speaking Canadians and their federal government. The conclusion of a well-known 1957 study on
cases of integration in Western countries remains:
"The closer we get to modern condition and to our
own time, the more difficult it is to find any instances
of successful amalgamation of two or more previously
sovereign states. Thus far we found not a single full-

fledged modern social service state that has successfully federated or otherwise merged with another" (Deutsch et al. 1957, 23).

Such a lesson is no consolation to many Arabs, and not only those identified with Arab nationalism such as the Ba'thists and the Nasserites. Members of the elite and the masses alike continue to view Arab unity as the best way to promote sound economic development and to gain true Arab independence vis-à-vis great powers. The merger of Syria and Egypt into a constitutionally unitary state demonstrated briefly that Arab unity was no longer a dream; for three-and-half years, it was a concrete reality. The failure of that experiment has continued therefore to inspire many studies, by both Arab and foreign scholars, reflecting on the cause of its failure. On the thirtieth anniversary of the establishment of the United Arab Republic, 90 Arab scholars met in Sanaʿa (the capital of the Yemen Arab Republic), to speculate on the lessons to be learned from that experiment. Their papers and deliberations were published in a volume of more than one thousand pages (CAUS 1989).

The plethora of such studies renders the job of this writer rather challenging. Several accounts have been written of how the United Arab Republic (UAR) came into being and how it floundered, and it is not difficult to piece the story together. This makes it hard to come up with a new perspective not previously suggested or to shed new light on any obscure aspect of this experiment. I will begin, therefore, from the point at which previous studies left off, namely the continued controversies surrounding the major issues raised by the experiment, particularly the formula for Arab unity, the meager performance of the integrative structures, and the causes of disintegration. In discussing such issues, interviews conducted in 1982 and 1983 with key figures in the UAR by the research team of which the author was a member help shed additional light on the events that led to the rise and fall of the UAR. The theoretical framework informing my analysis is inspired by the work of Karl Deutsch, since his approach grants a prominent place to security and political considerations in the genesis and evolution of political communities. Such considerations were—and still are—very important in all attempts to build larger political communities in the Arab world. Functionalist approaches to political integration, which became fashionable in the Arab world after the 1970s, were almost unknown to Arab leaders and the public in the 1950s, when the UAR was established.

The Rise of the UAR

Most accounts of the rise of the UAR would concur on the factors that led to the fusion of Egypt and Syria into one country in February 1958. Whatever date one considers as the point of departure for the march toward political unity, national security considerations, broadly defined, loomed large in the calculations of both Syrian army officers and the Egyptian leadership when they decided in mid-January 1958 to unite their countries in one state. Massive support in Syria for the cause of Arab unity, and expectations of a more powerful position for the Ba'th party in the unified state, constituted important background conditions which weakened any possible resistance to the proposed unity. Given this situation, other sections of the Syrian political elite who would have favored either a federative formula or even unity with Iraq, rather than with Egypt, could not prevail.

The common stand taken by Egypt and Syria against attempts by the United Kingdom and the United States to pressure them into joining Western-dominated military alliances, or to punish them for their opposition to such membership, had brought the two countries closer together since early 1955. Egypt's symbolic gesture of support to Syria—the dispatch of few hundred Egyptian soldiers to that country in a show of solidarity during its confrontation with Turkey—made a very strong impression on both the Syrian public and Syrian army officers. Some sources attribute to members of the Supreme Council of the Armed Forces a feeling of apprehension that disputes among Syrian political parties and their allies in the army could push the country into civil war at a time of fierce rivalry between the superpowers in the Middle East (Seale 1965, chs. 19–22). Other sources suggest that Syrian army officers feared that the Syrian Communist Party would be the only winner in this atmosphere of civil war. According to these sources, the officers concluded that unity with Egypt was the best way to preempt a Communist-inspired takeover (Nasr 1976, 69). Both Syrian and Egyptian sources discount allegations of the fear of the Communist conspiracy, as the communists had—in their view—very few supporters in the armed forces at the time. In interviews, Mahmoud Riad, the Egyptian ambassador to Syria, Abdel Muhsin Abul Nur, the well-connected Egyptian military attaché, and Abdel Hamid al-Sarraj, head of the Second Bureau (military intelligence at the time), all expressed such a view. Most Syrian sources, including those interviewed by the research team, suggest that massive support from the Syrian public as well as the charismatic leadership of Nasser were the most important factors which led the Syrian army and government to ask for unity with Egypt (Asasa 1989, 84–85; Heikal 1988, 1: 280).

Security considerations were also important for the Egyptian leaders. In its confrontation with Western powers after 1955, which led to a military conflict and the abortive invasion of the country by British, French, and Israeli forces in the autumn of 1956, Egypt needed allies. Allies in the Arab world would strengthen its hand in dealing with continued American efforts to enlist all countries in the area, under different guises, in its struggle against communism. Some of those Arab regimes were getting Soviet military, economic, and diplomatic support to face the threat posed by Israel to their security, a threat completely ignored by the United States. Egyptian leaders were reluctant to accept merger with Syria, which would focus Western pressures on the new entity if it continued to reject military alliance with the West. Yet they were also concerned that if they declined the Syrian offer, Syria would move to the opposite camp in the Arab cold war led by Iraq, and supported by both the United States and the United Kingdom. Mahmoud Riad, Hafiz Isma'il, and Muhsin Abul Nur supported this view. Patrick Seale came to the same conclusion, suggesting that President Nasser was interested in controlling Syrian foreign policy without facing the dilemmas of its turbulent domestic politics. As it became clear to Nasser in his talks with Syrian army officers that he could not guarantee continued Syrian support for his foreign policy if Egypt rejected Syrian demand for unity, Nasser opted for the formula that would enable him to exercise complete control over Syrian domestic politics (Seale 1965, ch. 22).

The prominence of security considerations in the minds of Syrian army officers and Egyptian leaders alike would not have provided sufficient impetus for the February 1958 unification were it not for the pressures exerted by actors who favored complete merger over any formula short of political unity. Those actors included foremost the Syrian public, specific groups of army officers in Egypt and Syria, and the Ba'th Party.

Syrian Public Opinion

No nation lightly abandons its historical name, its independence, and all the symbols of its national sovereignty. Yet the Syrian people enthusiastically supported this option in the second half of the 1950s. Charmed by the charismatic leadership of Gamal Abdel Nasser; his opposition to Western influence in the Arab world; Egypt's support under his leadership of liberation movements in the Arab World; his nationalization of the Suez Canal Company; his courageous resistance to armed aggression by Great Britain, France, and Israel in the autumn of 1956; and Egypt's backing of Syria in the face of pressures exerted by regional and foreign powers, the majority of Syrian people ardently wished to see both Syria and Egypt united as a first step toward a larger entity that would include all Arab countries. Unity for them was the only way to consolidate independence for the Arabs and to restore past glories. Syrian politicians and army officers had to reckon with this massive popularity of the cause of unity. Syrians expressed their feelings in huge demonstrations and letter-writing campaigns between 1956 and 1958.

Army Officers. Although public support for unity with Egypt was an overriding consideration in the movement toward unity, the formula for unity initially emerged from meetings between groups of army officers in Egypt and Syria. Not only was the Syrian delegation which carried the demand for immediate fusion of the two countries to President Nasser on January 11, 1958, made up completely of Syrian army officers, but also their official counterparts in Syria and Egypt were all either former or current army officers. All Egyptians involved in talks leading to unity came originally from the armed forces. Syrian army officers used to meet in Damascus with both the late Mahmoud Riad and Mohsen Abul Nur, ambassador and military attaché, respectively, in Egypt's embassy to Syria. They met also in January with General Hafiz Isma'il, chef de cabinet of Abdel Hakim Amer, Egypt's Minister of War. Amer happened then to be the chief of staff of the joint military command of the two countries. More importantly, the top leadership of Egypt at that time was made up exclusively of the remaining members of the Revolutionary Command Council who led the July 1952 Revolution against the monarchy. Abdel Latif al-Baghdadi mentioned in his memoirs that whereas the majority of those former officers favored a more gradual approach to unity with Syria, President Nasser changed his mind and approved complete merger of the two countries, a position taken as well by Amer, his Minister of War (Baghdadi 1977, 2:37–38). Syrian army officers, on the other hand, were represented in these developments by members of the Supreme Council of the Armed Forces, which was established by Lieutenant General Afif al-Bizri, who succeeded General Tawfiq Nizam al-Din as the commander of armed forces in 1955. Membership on this council comprised (according to different sources) twenty-two to twenty-seven officers representing all political groupings in the Syrian army. No important decision, whether of a political or military nature, could be taken in Syria without the support of this council (interview with Abdel Hamid al-Sarraj in Asasa 1989, 83).

Patrick Seale has identified six major groupings within the council. M. H. Heikal has identified the same groupings without citing his source (Seale 1965, 320, 322, ch. 18; Heikal 1988, 258). Thus the major blocs within the Syrian army were the following:

1. Abdel Hamid al-Sarraj, who did not belong to any party, but was a nationalist officer and a strong admirer of Nasser
2. Ba'thist officers, led by Mustapha Hamdoun and Abdel Ghani Qannout
3. Former supporters of the Arab Liberation Party of Adib al-Shishikli, led by Amin al-Nafouri

4. A neutral group wavering between the Ba'thists and the Liberationists, led by To'mat al-Odallah and Ahmed Heneidi
5. The Damascan grouping led by Akram Deiri
6. A small group led by Lt. General Afif al-Bizri who sympathized with the Communists.

Many sources concur on their accounts of tensions among these groups of army officers. All young army officers trained in the Syrian military college of Hama who had replaced the previous generation of less educated officers of the Ottoman army, but their rivalries made them fear each other more than they feared foreign powers. Patrick Seale writes that their rivalries occasionally became too intense to be resolved by any power in Syria and were taken instead to Egyptian War Minister General Amer, the only acceptable judge (Seale 1965, 416–417).

A Syrian author suggests that the Supreme Council of Armed Forces (SCAF) adopted a written statute calling in its second and third articles for "support of the anticolonialist policies of the Government of Sabri al-Asali, consolidation of relations with revolutionary Egypt, and work for union between Egypt and Syria" (Asasa 1989, 83).

How much support did the SCAF enjoy within the Syrian armed forces? It is difficult to answer this question at present. Patrick Seale suggests that the enthusiasm for unity manifested by members of the council was not shared to the same degree by other officers. He adds that whereas the majority of army officers did sympathize with Egypt, members of the SCAF had an additional reason to favor immediate unity with Egypt; namely, their belief that such a move would enable them to rule Syria in the same way that the Revolutionary Command Council ruled Egypt (Seale 1965, 416). Al-Sarraj, for his part, suggests that most of the members of SCAF who went to Egypt in January 1958 for the unity talks were moved, together with the majority of Syrian army officers at that time, by their ardent wish to give concrete shape to the ideal of Arab unity.

The Ba'th Party

Of all the civilian political forces in Syria, the Ba'th Arab Socialist Party worked most energetically for unity with Egypt. Arab unity ranked high among the ideals for which Ba'thists were struggling. In their writings, Ba'thist leaders Michel Aflaq and Salah al-Bitar expressed their belief that the unity cause would gain considerable momentum if Egypt could be persuaded to join a larger Arab entity. This belief in Arab unity was demonstrated when the party insisted that its participation in the national unity cabinet, formed under the premiership of Sabri al-Asali on June 14, 1956, would depend on the cabinet's commitment to initiate unity talks with Egypt. On July 5, 1956, the prime minister announced the constitution of a committee to undertake negotiations with Egypt for that purpose (Hudson 1977, 260–267).

The Ba'th, although a prominent political force in Syria, was by no means the most influential party. It held only 20 seats out of 142 in the national assembly elected in 1955. Within the SCAF, it had perhaps no more than 5 out of 27 members. It could not, therefore, count on its electoral majority or its supporters in the armed forces to seize power in Syria from the conservative parties. These parties sympathized more with Iraq or Saudi Arabia than with Egypt, although they could not declare this position publicly because of the popularity of the Egyptian leadership.

With the prospect of an impending election, which would reveal the incapacity of the Ba'th to attract a majority of votes, Ba'thist ministers submitted a proposal to the cabinet in December 1957 calling for the establishment of a federation between Syria and Egypt. Many observers believed that this move was aimed at accelerating the march toward a type of unity with Egypt that would weaken the Ba'th's adversaries in Syria and leave it a dominant force on the country's political scene. After all, the Ba'th perceived itself to be Nasser's closest ally (Seale 1965, 405–407, 413–418). The party reluctantly had to accept the complete merger of the two countries, since the efforts of its foreign minister to persuade the January 1958 SCAC delegation to Cairo to opt for a federal link with Egypt rather than complete fusion had failed. The Ba'th threw its weight behind complete merger, hoping to turn this option to its own favor. This expectation was to be frustrated (al-Sarraj, interview).

The events that led to the fusion of Egypt and Syria in the UAR have been described in many works (Seale 1965; Wilber 1969; Farsakh 1980; Yusuf 1989). There are two ways of telling the story, depending upon the point of departure one designates as the beginning of the march toward unity. According to one version, the decision to fuse the two countries was taken during the visit of members of the SCAF to Cairo from January 11 to 14, 1958, and was implemented on February 22, 1958, following a referendum on that question carried out in the two countries. In that referendum, between 99.98 percent and 99.99 percent of the people endorsed unity. The other version of the story would claim that the real starting point was the Revolution of July 1952 in Egypt, which stirred a strong wave of sympathy in Syria.

The progressive march toward unity acquired concrete shape on March 2, 1955, when the two countries signed a joint statement calling for cooperation in foreign, economic, and military policy, giving rise to the constitution of a joint military command. A few months later, on October 22, 1955, a mutual defense agreement was signed. The national unity government of Sabri al-Asali carried the process further by approving a draft for federation between the two countries on the basis of which Salah al-Bitar, the Ba'thist foreign minister, was entrusted to negotiate with the Egyptian government. Demonstrations of solidarity between the two peoples multiplied in 1956 and 1957 after the petroleum pipeline—Tapline—passing through Syrian territory was sabotaged during the Suez crisis in November 1956, an action probably ordered by Abdel Hamid al-Sarraj, then head of Syrian military intelligence, but attributed at the time to Syrian workers. Later, Egypt dispatched a few hundred soldiers to Syria on October 13, 1957, during the confrontation between that country and Turkey. The national assemblies of the two countries expressed in November 1957 the wish of the two peoples to be joined in a federation.

The decisive steps leading to the materialization of unity were taken in early 1958. First came the January 11–14 visit of the SCAF to Cairo, and then a visit by senior members of the Syrian government including the premier and the president who signed the treaty establishing the UAR on February 1, 1958. The departure of the SCAF to Cairo was prompted by the impression SCAF members got in meetings with General Hafiz Isma'il who had been sent by Nasser to discuss ways of consolidating cooperation between the two countries. What Isma'il proposed did not satisfy the Syrian military, as it was limited to enlarging cooperation between two countries (Isma'il, interview). They decided to leave for Cairo immediately to try to convince Nasser of the need for complete fusion, and left it to al-Sarraj to inform the government of their departure and to maintain national security in Syria during their absence.

It is interesting to note that the integrative formula proposed by Syrian civilian politicians was that of federation. This was in essence what the Syrian national assembly as well as the cabinet called for. Nasser and most of his colleagues also initially favored a federative formula, to materialize gradually over a period of five years. Both Nasser and Amer changed their minds during the meeting with the Syrian military delegation in Cairo in January 1958. Knowing that Abdel Nasser was not interested in immediate fusion of the two countries, certain Syrian parties and personalities opted precisely for that formula. However, when Nasser changed his mind, some of those personalities— including al-Bizri and even the Ba'thist Bitar—tried to persuade their colleagues to revert to a federation formula. Nasser, however, formulated three conditions for accepting the complete and immediate fusion of the two countries as demanded by the majority of the SCAF and the Syrian cabinet: dissolution of all political parties in Syria; acceptance of a single mass organization—the National Union—as the framework of political activity in the county (as was the case in Egypt); and banning all political activity by the Syrian armed forces, with those army officers willing to engage in politics to assume civilian posts.

After some discussion, the Syrian military and politicians—with few exceptions—had accepted acquiesced to Nasser's conditions, paving the way for the declaration of the UAR following the popular referendum on February 22, 1958 (Baghdadi 1977, 31–47; Nasr 1976, 44).

No matter which version of this story one accepts, whether it took three years, six years, or six weeks, the march toward unity was indeed very short compared to any successful experiment of political integration past or present. It has taken Europe thirty-five years to move from a common market to consideration of full economic unity. Transition to a political union is unlikely to take place before the end of the century. The march toward unity between Egypt and Syria was indeed very brief, as was political unity itself.

The two countries came in February 1958 to establish what Karl Deutsch termed an "amalgamated security community"; in other words, "two previously independent units formally merged to constitute a single larger unit, with some type of common government after amalgamation" (Deutsch et al., 1957, 6).

Some of the helpful background conditions that facilitated this integration were: elements of shared culture and history; the charismatic leadership of Gamal Abdel Nasser; and a perception of foreign threat which induced Syrian leaders to make the necessary concessions for the amalgamated community to take shape. However, both the theory and the practices of political integration suggest that such background conditions are only helpful; but not by any means sufficient for a process of integration to proceed. Out of the ten essential conditions in that process suggested by Deutsch et al., only five could be said to have been met in the particular case of the UAR, namely reluctance to wage "fratricidal" war on each other, linguistic unity if not necessarily ethnic assimilation, expectations of stronger economic ties or gain on the part of both the industrial and commercial bourgeoisie of the two countries (Abdel Malek 1962, 143), a marked increase in the political and administrative capabilities of at least one of the two partners (Egypt, as a result of its successes in foreign policy and political stability since 1954) (Sayigh 1982, 1: 381–384), and an increase in communications and transactions stimulated by expanding and diversified relations between the two countries since 1955 (Al-Mashat 1987, 25–28). Other conditions for integration were not only absent, as will be demonstrated later, but more importantly those conditions which facilitated integration in the first place were to disappear only a few months after the brief takeoff of the integration process in the winter and spring of 1958.

Areas of Integration

The "amalgamated political community" lasted only from February 22, 1958 to September 1961—hardly enough time for integration to proceed in all areas of life in the two regions of the United Arab Republic. However, what was accomplished was quite meager, even for such a short period of time. More could have been done, and done better. This was the conclusion of some the people, close to the president, who saw difficulties accumulating in many areas with no decisive action to remove them (Baghdadi 1977, 120–121). The approach used in dealing with problems was often inconsistent.

The most visible signs of integration were a new organization of some of the central powers of the government, a single president, a central government, a single national assembly, a uniform political system based on the single mass organization, and uniform economic policies with the extension of economic planning, agrarian reform, and nationalization of big private firms to the Syrian region. The authoritarian character of Abdel Nasser's regime experienced by the intelligentsia in Egypt now cast its shadow also on Syria. Some newspapers lost their license; civil and political rights were violated, though the perpetrators in this case were Syrians (Asasa 1989, 134, 149, 260).

An attempt was made also to integrate further the two armies by having officers from one region serve in the other, but this did not go very far. The attempt caused much tension among Syrian army officers, who found this process to be biased in favor of the Egyptian officers (Abul Nur, interview). Similar attempts were made to harmonize the work of administrative and social services, particularly education, and to bring the laws in force in one region more in line with those operative in the other. Such endeavors meet with little success due not only to the short duration of unity, but also to some resistance by Syrian officials.

The areas in which no integration took place were primarily those of monetary and fiscal policies, as each region continued to have its own currency, central bank, and fiscal system, as well as civil as administration and security services. Each region continued to have its own administration, including a separate regional government, until just weeks before secession when the two regional councils were abolished and one central government established on August 16, 1961.

Thus the most visible signs of integration were to be found mostly at the level of the central government. Those signs included the promulgation of a provisional constitution embodying many of the provisions of the constitution of the Republic of Egypt, which endowed the UAR with a presidential regime. The reorganization of government structure which followed fusion did conform to a single pattern, moving from one central government for the two regions on March 6, 1958, to a central government plus a regional executive council for each region on October 7, 1958, and reverting to a single government on August 16, 1961. The task of coordinating government activities in the Syrian region with those of the central government in Cairo was entrusted in Damascus first in April 1958 to Mahmoud Riad, who was appointed as president's adviser, then in December 1958 to a committee including three vice presidents of the republic with very limited powers, and finally in October 1959 to Field Marshal Amer who was delegated presidential powers over Syria. A national assembly for the two regions was appointed in June 1960 with 600 members, one-third of them from Syria, but exercised its functions for less than a year. Judicial authorities in the two countries remained separate.

Finally, political parties were formally abolished in Syria, and a single mass organization, the National Union, was established there to parallel the political structure in Egypt. Members of the abolished political parties continued, however, to meet and to act collectively in politics (Riad, interview).

Although integration did not proceed in many areas, the areas in which it was effected demonstrate its unbalanced nature, for one region predominated to the detriment of the other. Vice presidents chosen from Egypt outnumbered their Syrian counterparts. They were assigned specific tasks while the functions of their Syrian counterparts were ill-defined. Egyptians outnumbered Syrians in the central government and monopolized all key ministries. The same was true in the national assembly. More seriously, that was also the case in the armed forces, with Egyptian officers serving in Syria exercising effective power while their Syrian counterparts in Egypt had no substantive powers at all (Asasa 1989, 141–142, 154–156, 159–168). Besides, the reorganization of the governmental and political structures of the new state followed exclusively Egyptian lines. If one would add to all this that the president of the UAR came from and its capital was located in the bigger unit (Egypt), the inescapable conclusion is that the integration process implied imbalances, with one region losing more than the other in symbols of respect and prestige.

Syria's loss in this process was not, however, limited to respect and prestige. The economic performance of the UAR was quite disappointing in two sectors of vital importance to the Syrian people, agriculture and commerce, both of which stagnated during the unity years. Production of grains and agricultural production in general fell from index numbers of 132 and 114 respectively in 1957 to 71 and 81 respectively in 1961, due to a three-year drought. In addition, benefits from agrarian reform were delayed, because confiscated land was not distributed immediately to its beneficiaries and remained uncultivated for years, a policy that aggravated the food crisis in the Syrian region (Sayigh 1982, 381–384; Asasa 1989, 177–192). Strained relations with Saudi Arabia, Jordan, and Iraq disrupted Syrian trade with them, causing the Syrian commercial bourgeoisie to lose its most important markets.

Thus if a successful process of integration is usually expressed in a new way of life and the building of new loyalties, it would not be an exaggeration to conclude that life under the UAR seemed to many Syrians to be worse than life before unity, and of a quality that would weaken their loyalty to institutions of the larger political community and even their sense of community. It is intriguing that despite such disappointment, many Syrians continued to believe in the cause of unity and the capacity of the UAR to overcome its difficulties. This was demonstrated by the lack of popularity of the military regime which followed secession, and the pretense by successive regimes that they were working to re-create unity with Egypt (Heikal 1988). It should be noted in this respect that the military officers who put an end to the UAR also claimed to be working for Arab unity.

The Fall of the UAR

While a few favorable background conditions did exist in the case of the UAR, such conditions did not give rise to a dynamic process of integration. In fact, the exact opposite happened. The proclamation of the UAR was followed by a dynamic process of disintegration. Other necessary conditions were not to materialize, while the few helpful background conditions that existed at the start were gradually eroded. Instead of achieving a threshold for integration at a certain moment later on in that experience, several alarming signs developed which pointed toward a reversal of the 1955–1958 trend toward closer ties between the two peoples. The collapse of the entire edifice of unity seemed by the summer of 1961 to be only a question of time.

Expectations of stronger economic ties or gains on the part of the Syrian commercial and industrial bourgeoisie were soon to be frustrated as a result of custom regulations that flooded Syrian markets with foreign products imported via Egypt (Asasa 1989, 189–190). The nationalization measures of July 1961 affected few Syrian private companies, the owner of one of which was related to the first prime minister appointed after secession from Egypt (Buzu, interview). The marked increase in the political and administrative capacities of the Egyptian government before integration had little spillover effect in Syria after the establishment of the UAR. The dispatch of Egyptian soldiers, experts, and teachers to the "northern region" (i.e. Syria), which usually had been welcome before unity, was viewed with suspicion after the merger (Sayyid Mar'ei, interview). It is true that a five-year plan was adopted for that region, and a few industrial, infrastructure and agricultural projects were implemented (Mar'ei, interview; Sedki, interview; Sayigh 1982). Relations between Egyptian leaders and their erstwhile allies in Syria dominated debates within the central government, diverting attention and energy from the principal task of shaping a new and a better way of life for citizens of the two regions, particularly the Syrian one. Under such conditions of near-paralysis, aggravated by the central organs of government, aggravated by the whimsical implementation of agrarian reform as well by the effects of the three-year drought (Mar'ei, interview; Buzu, interview), the majority of Syrian citizens felt few concrete benefits from the integration project.

Soon, the factors of disintegration began their work as well. The incompatibility of values between Egyptian and Syrian leaders quickly became manifest. Conservative politicians in Syria, who had dominated both the Syrian national assembly and the cabinet before unity, were initially disregarded in favor of the Ba'thist politicians and army officers who constituted a small minority within the Syrian political elite. The Ba'thists later became disenchanted when the National Union, the mass organization that was to replace the formerly dissolved political parties, was constituted through elections which they lost massively, and were further alienated when they were not given a free hand in the running of the Syrian region. Ba'thist ministers thus resigned collectively from the government in December 1959, less than two years after the establishment of the UAR (Asasa 1989, 219–26).

Links of communication between the two peoples, hampered geographically by the lack of contiguity between their territories, were socially strained as well because of the perceived inequality of treatment between the two regions, manifested at various levels. Syrian personalities appointed to the central government found themselves in unimportant ministries, with no power, and for some time even without places of work. They also had the feeling that former members of the Revolutionary Command Council in Egypt agreed on everything in advance and that meetings of the central government simply ratified decisions reached earlier (Abdel Karim 1962, 281). With ministers from each region shunning consultation with their colleagues from the other region in both the central government and the regional executive councils, such organs ceased to be integrative mechanisms. At lower levels, the disparity of power between Egyptians assigned to the Syrian region and Syrians transferred to Egypt poisoned relations between the Syrian officials and their counterparts.

Disaffection among Syrian military officers was particularly serious, for the whole enterprise had taken shape through their initiative in January 1958. It was also to end through their action in September 1961. It is true that the Syrian military was not a homogeneous body in terms of political affiliations. However,

Egyptian aides to Field Marshal Amer who were assigned to the command of the Syrian army ended up, unwittingly, alienating most Syrian officers in their attempts to get rid of both those officers whom they *perceived* to be politically ambitious and their friends. The first to be alienated was General Afif al-Bizri, commander of the Syrian army, whose proposal to transfer and promote some officers shortly after the proclamation of UAR was rejected by both Amer and Nasser on the advice of Abul Nur, who had been assigned to the Syrian high command. The Egyptians viewed al-Bizri's proposal as excessively favorable to communist officers. Al-Bizri resigned his army post in March 1958, and later left the cabinet-level minister of planning post to which he had been appointed after he quit the army. Abul Nur, together with other Egyptians in the Syrian high command, did their best to remove from the army every Syrian officer reported to be close to any political party (Abul Nur, interview). The only basis for groupings within the Syrian army after this purge of Ba'thist, Liberationist, Neutralist, and "communist" officers was that of birthplace. Abul Nur and his colleagues did not suspect that such "primordial loyalties" would bring officers together. Yet most of the officers who led the coup d'etat of September 28, 1961, were Damascene in origin (Asasa 1989, 296–97).

The last Syrian personality to be alienated from the Egyptian leadership was the very man chiefly responsible for internal security in Syria, both before and during its fusion with Egypt, namely Abdel Hamid al-Sarraj. Trusted by Nasser, he was given a free hand in Syria and allowed to concentrate much power in his own hands. At the zenith of his power, he personally held the ministries of interior, social affairs, and labor in addition to his post as Secretary General of the National Union and his control over the special security apparatus he established after he quit military intelligence. Many of al-Sarraj's practices irritated the Syrian people. His approach was not much different from that of Nasser's minister of interior in Egypt. However, Sarraj's activities in Syria clashed with those of Field Marshal Amer, who was appointed by Nasser on October 21, 1959, to be his deputy in the Syrian region, essentially exercising presidential powers there. A Syrian source mentioned that Amer had another security service working for him and competing with that of al-Sarraj. In order to trim Sarraj's powers, he was appointed on August 16, 1961, a vice president of the republic in charge of internal security, but was to perform his job from Cairo. However, a few days in his new post in Cairo convinced Sarraj that he had no power there, prompting him to decide to return to Damascus. Nasser asked Amer to come with Sarraj to Cairo in order to persuade him to accept the new post. Al-Sarraj adamantly rejected the offer, resigned his post on September 24, 1961, and went back to Syria. The coup d'etat which led to the secession of Syria took place four days later (Baghdadi 1977, 1: 107–12; Asasa 1989, 240–41).

By this time, it could be safely said that most of the Syrian politicians and military officers who had worked for unity had been alienated from President Nasser's leadership. Members of other social groups in Syria who had hoped that fusion of the two countries would mean a better standard of living had seen their position worsen or little improved. No wonder these actors watched indifferently, or even heaved a sigh of relief, as the final act of this play of Arab unity came to an end.

Lessons of the Experience

Maintaining an "amalgamated political community" is indeed a challenging enterprise. The dramatic breakup of the USSR and of Yugoslavia as well as tensions in relations between French-speaking Quebecois and Canadian federal authorities attest to the validity of this observation. However it should be also recognized that the minimal conditions for the survival of this type of political community were not met in the case of the UAR.

The formula for the merger itself was quite ambitious. Syrian politicians talked mostly of a federal framework for the unity of the two countries but had to acquiesce to the determination of the leading group of Syrian army officers to effect an immediate and total fusion of the two countries. President Nasser himself was quite apprehensive about any kind of unity, preferring to proceed gradually. He was supported in this view by most of his colleagues. Not only did Nasser dramatically and somewhat unconvincingly change his mind as a result of conversations with members of the Syrian Supreme Council of the Armed Forces, but he also soon treated anyone who expressed preference for the federal framework as a traitor. This was the case with Egyptian and Syrian communists, many of whom were jailed partly for expressing a federalist view (Mursi, interview; Hussein, interview; Yusuf, interview). A federal framework would have enabled the Syrians to be masters of their own country; benefiting from whatever help or advice they could get from the Egyptians, while taking specific Syrian conditions into consideration. The presence of Egyptians in the army, as well as in government departments in Syria with direct links to Egyptian policymakers in Cairo and in Damascus, did not make the Syrians feel they were masters of their own affairs in the UAR.

A more open political system, permitting opposition views to be expressed, all complaints to be aired, and the appointment of elites to government posts on the basis of some degree of popular consent would have offered a second safety valve to this amalgamated community. It is true that Nasser knew of the difficulties agrarian reform was facing in the Syrian region and of the resentment caused by al-Sarraj's methods of imposing law and order there. However, it is only in an open political system that the gravity of such problems could be felt and remedial action taken in time, rather than too late as was the case with the removal of al-Sarraj from his security job in Syria. An open political system would have enabled various political forces to remain active, seeking to mobilize popular support while contesting the policies of incumbent parties. A stronger sense of community and commitment to the UAR's continued existence could have thus been stimulated. From this point of view, the outlawing of political parties in the UAR was not a wise decision, for it left no other option but underground opposition to those Syrian political leaders who were alienated from Nasser's policies but wanted to mobilize public opinion to change them. The single mass organization could not have served as a framework for oppositional political activity, as it was strictly controlled by al-Sarraj's security services. The weak appointed national assembly functioned for just one year.

Deutsch (1957, 55) speaks of "a balance of respect—or of symbols standing for respect" as a likely important condition for successful amalgamation of sovereign states. Such a balance was definitely missing in the UAR. The Syrians wanted definitely to have part of the prestige the creation of this larger territorial entity created in the Arab world. The Syrian politicians and senior army officers wanted to exchange their allegiance to Nasser's leadership for a free hand in their own country and Nasser's endorsement of a prominent position for the Ba'th Party in particular in Syria. They wanted also to be seen as taking part in directing affairs of the new integrated community. Obviously, this was not the case. Both prestige as well as effective power went mostly to the Egyptians. Egyptians outnumbered Syrians in all organs of the central government, and among vice presidents, ministers, and members of the legislature. The Egyptians also monopolized positions of prestige and respect. All key posts were in the hands of Egyptians: supreme command of the armed forces, and the ministries of foreign affairs, interior, economy, and treasury. Even the vice president for the affairs of the Syrian region was Egyptian. Baghdadi recounted that Nasser contemplated appointing him as head of the Executive Council, i.e., the Council of Ministers, for the Syrian region, an offer Baghdadi wisely declined. Moreover, Egyptian aides and advisers sometimes vetoed the decisions of their Syrian superiors in the army as well as in the Executive Council, as was the case of Abul Nur and Mahmoud Riad respectively (Abul Nur, interview; Asasa 1989, 134–44). Syrians who were dispatched to Egypt either as ministers or senior officials had no parallel powers. One need only add that the capital of the UAR and its president were identical to those of the Republic of Egypt before unity to complete the picture of unbalanced distribution of power and prestige between the two regions.

However, even these three conditions—a federal framework, a more open political system, and a more balanced division of power and prestige—might not have been sufficient to maintain this "amalgamated Political Community." They do not guarantee consolidation of links and cultivation of ties between the two formerly separate entities. Such links are usually weak and limited among countries of the "periphery," compared to their multiple and intensive ties with the economically dominant countries of the "center." It is instructive in this regard that data published by those Arab scholars who suggest that the unity enterprise between Egypt and Syria evolved gradually also indicate that interaction between the two entities was more intense before fusion and declined after unity failed (Al-Mashat 1987, 27–28). However, a more complete picture of such transactions would reveal still stronger links with countries of the "center" (Galtung 1976). If Arab unity is ever to be rebuilt, it cannot be founded exclusively on shared culture and common aspirations, but must rather be grounded in concrete interests interwoven into thick and multiple webs of interactions among Arab peoples in all areas of human activity.

References

Abdel Dayim, Abdallah. "Experience of Egyptian-Syrian Unity, 1958–1961" (in Arabic). *Shu'un 'arabiyya* (September 1985) 43, 109–129.

Abdel Karim, Ahmad. *Shedding Light on the Unity Experience* (in Arabic). Damascus: Dar Atlas, 1962.

Abdel Malek, Anouar. *L'Egypte, Société Militaire*. Paris: Editions du Seuil, 1962.

Asasa, Sami. *Secrets of Secession, Egypt and Syria* (in Arabic). Cairo: Dar al-Sha'b, 1989.

Awad, Ibrahim. "Théorie de L'intégration Politique et Application au monde Arabe." *Etudes, Politiques du Monde Arabe, Approches Globales et Approches Spécifiques*. Dossiers du CEDEJ. Cairo: CEDEJ, 1991, 315–357.

al-Baghdadi, Abdel Latif. *Memoirs of Abdel Latif al-Baghdadi* (in Arabic) 2 vols. Cairo: Al-Maktab al-Hadith, 1977.

Center of Arab Unity Studies [CAUS]. *Arab Unity, Its Experiments and Expectations* (symposium, in Arabic). Beirut: CAUS, November 1989.

Deutsch, Karl, Sidney A. Burrell, et al, *Political Community and the North Atlantic Area. International Organization in the Light of Historical Experience*. Princeton, NJ: Princeton University Press, 1957.

Draz, Nada. *The United Arab Republic 1958–1961. The Problem of Defining National Interest* (M.A. dissertation). London: School of African and Oriental Studies, University of London, 1991.

Farsakh, Awni. *Unity in Practice: An Analytical Study of the Unity of 1958* (in Arabic). Beirut: Dar al-Masirah, 1980.

Galtung, Johan. "The Lome Convention and Neo-Capitalism." *University of Oslo Papers* 20 (1976).

Heikal, Mohamed Hassanein. *Years of Upheaval* (in Arabic). Cairo: Dar al-Ahram, 1988.

Hudson, Michael C. *Arab Politics: The Search for Legitimacy*. New Haven, CT: Yale University Press, 1977.

Al-Mashat, Abdel Mon'eim, "Thirty Years after the Egyptian-Syrian Unity: Retest of its Premises" (in Arabic). *Al-mustaqbal al-'arabi* 2. Beirut: CAUS (February 1987) 4–33.

Naf'a, Hasan, "The Experiment of Egyptian Syrian Unity" (in Arabic). *Shu'un 'arabiyya* 46 Tunis: General Secretariat of the Arab League (June 1986) 155–74.

Nasr, Salah. *Abdel Nasser and the Unity Experience* (in Arabic). Beirut: Dar al-watan al-arabi, 1976.

Roberts, D. *The Ba'th and the Creation of Modern Syria*. London: Croom Helm, 1987.

Sayigh, Yusif A. *Economics of the Arab World: Development Since 1945* . 2 vols. (in Arabic). Beirut: Al-mu'assasa al-'arabiyya lil-dirasat wal-nashr, 1982.

Seale, Patrick. *The Struggle for Syria*. London: Oxford University Press, 1965.

Yusuf, Ahmed. "The Experiment of the UAR: A Contribution Toward a New Assessment," in Center of Arab Unity Studies, *Its Experiments and Expectations* (symposium, in Arabic). Beirut: CAUS, November 1989, 205–236.

Wilber, Donald N. *United Arab Republic*. New Haven: Human Relations Area Files Press, 1969.

Syrian and Egyptian Politicians Interviewed by the Research Team on Arab Unity 1982–1983

INTERVIEWED BY THE AUTHOR:

Abdel Muhsin Abul Nur
Abdel Hamid al-Sarraj
Adel Hussein
Hafiz Isma'il
Sayyid Mar'ei
Fu'ad Mursi
Aziz Sedki
Abu Seif Yusuf

INTERVIEWED BY OTHER MEMBERS OF THE TEAM:

Ali Buzu
Khaled Mohieddin
Mahmoud Riad
Ali Sabri
Omar Talmesani

MEMBERS OF THE RESEARCH TEAM ON ARAB UNITY:

Dr. Ahmad Yusuf Ahmad
Dr. Mustapha Kamil al-Sayyid
Dr. Ali Mukhtas
Dr. Hasan Naf'a

chapter 6   The United Arab Emirates: A Quarter Century
              of Federation

Frauke Heard-Bey

There are many criteria by which to measure the performance of a country. These might range from its economic development to its record on human rights.
Internal cohesion is not usually the first yardstick that
comes to mind, except perhaps when dealing with a
federal state. A federation requires consensus and a
continuous effort on the part of its constituent members: Each of them must want to remain part of it, and
those institutions which are the function of the central
body alone must be given adequate power because it is
only through them that the concept of federation can
become a meaningful reality.

From the beginning the unity of the United Arab
Emirates was based on a great many compromises, but
after two decades and a half the federation has not
fallen apart despite the predictions of doubters and
detractors. Measured on the experience of Arab integration in recent times it must be considered a success.
The three underlying factors that have contributed to
the success of the seven shaykhdoms now forming the
UAE (Abu Dhabi, Dubai, Sharjah, Ra's al-Khaimah,
Fujairah, Ajman and Umm al-Qawain) are its population structure (with only around 15 percent of the
inhabitants being nationals), the uneven distribution
of wealth, and the traditional structure of the local
society. In addition to these basic factors, however, the
success of the UAE must be explained in terms of pragmatic institution-building in response to structural
changes, respect for tradition, and a leadership with
the ability to adapt to challenging situations.

The UAE came into being in 1971 in response to an
externally created political situation described in the
first part of this paper. In the second part, the institutionalization of unification, the nature of federation,

mechanisms of political participation, and the constitution are analyzed. The third part examines the federation in action, discussing how it coped with a constitutional crisis, regional instability, economic issues and foreign policy challenges.

Establishing the Federation

The following historical points are of importance in terms of the situation prior to the federation process which began in the late 1960s:

- All political power and executive authority had become concentrated in the rulers of the coastal-based shaykhdoms and their families, as a consequence of historical developments in eastern Arabia, and in particular the interaction with the British Indian empire.
- Due to the chance distribution of natural wealth, the seven formerly comparable shaykhdoms became increasingly unequal in terms of wealth, population structure, and development prospects.
- The local population was about to become outnumbered by immigrants.
- In terms of institutions, infrastructure, and any other development, the seven states were still almost at the very beginning, when they suddenly had to face the decisions of how and with whom to shape their political future.

THE BRITISH WITHDRAWAL

On January 16, 1968, the British government announced its decision to withdraw from all obligations east of Suez. This meant repatriating some 6,000 British troops from Sharjah and Bahrain, and relinquishing British responsibility for the security and the foreign affairs of the seven Trucial States, Qatar, and Bahrain.

There had been extensive discussions in Westminster about withdrawal, but by the end of 1967, it had seemed certain that the Gulf region would not be affected. Therefore, the British decision to leave the Gulf as well came as a complete surprise to the rulers and the people of these nine states. They were ill-prepared to face a number of unresolved territorial claims, to defend the growing oil-wealth of the region against possible predators, to deal with the different ideological trends sweeping the Arab world, and to guard against the possibility of subversion.

Two major unresolved questions faced the Trucial States: first, the Iranian claim to Bahrain, which the Iranians referred to as "our crown jewel," and to three islands belonging to the emirates of Sharjah and Ra's al-Khaimah; second, the persistent claim by Saudi Arabia to large tracts of Abu Dhabi territory, although in 1955 Britain had unilaterally brought the Buraimi issue to a close.

The decision to withdraw the troops and to cancel all commitments was bound to have an effect on the entire region. Qatar and Bahrain had almost identical treaty arrangements with the British government as with the seven Trucial States; Kuwait had since 1961 a treaty of friendship with a clause promising British military assistance in case of an attack. For a long time, the rulers of Oman had relied on a British umbrella. Both Saudi Arabia and Iran were likely to redefine their security objectives and assume a higher profile in the Gulf region.

REGIONAL RESPONSE

The future of "the Gulf after 1971" was widely discussed in British government circles, in particular among the Conservatives. The Gulf rulers were made aware of British thinking on these matters. But there also emerged an awareness among many of the decisionmakers in the Gulf that the time had come to actively shape the future political landscape of the region. The idea of some kind of Gulf-wide federation favored by Britain began to be discussed. The Ruler of Bahrain and the Foreign Minister of Kuwait took the initiative by visiting several neighboring Gulf states to sound out their views. The first decisive step was, however, taken by the rulers of Abu Dhabi and Dubai when they met on February 18, 1968 on the border between their two states, resolved their frontier difficulties, and declared their two states united. Foreign affairs, defense, social services, and the very important matter of immigration were to be the responsibility of this new "Union." It is interesting to note that the two rulers did not want their newly declared Union to be the final structure in shape and size. Instead, they invited other rulers to join. Both were well aware that there was not yet much reason for euphoria—rather that they had started a process that would lead them into uncharted waters.

The response to this invitation was very favorable, and a week later, on February 25, 1968, the rulers of Bahrain and Qatar joined the rulers of the seven Trucial States in Dubai. The result was the agreement to establish a federation of the nine emirates effective March 30, 1968, while the drafting of a constitution continued (Rumaihi 1986, 55–65; Taryam 1987, 64–189; al-Alkim 1989, 8–15).

At the time most observers were surprised that the meeting resulted in considerably more than the universally expected declaration of an intention to sound out the possibilities of a federation. In fact, the 12 points of the February agreement were the skeleton of a constitution. From then on, the nine member-states were under an obligation to come eventually to an agreement on the constitution of this, their new union. There followed more than three years of searching for constitutional formulae that would be acceptable to all members.

This process of constitution-making took place under fairly unconventional conditions for such a momentous but also highly specialized task. Not only had the seven emirates of the Trucial States rapidly become so very unequal in size of population, economic capability, and ability to sustain development, but the addition of Bahrain and Qatar also introduced unexpected complications. These ranged from the striking differences in the levels of education—Bahrain and Qatar were far ahead at that time—to the readiness to hold elections for representatives to sit in a council or parliament. Bahrain, and to a lesser extent Qatar, had well-tried institutions for all essential manifestations of governmental authority.

During the next three years there were not only the rather too infrequent meetings of the nine rulers as the "Supreme Union Council," but also meetings of the deputy rulers, and a staff of negotiators delegated from each emirate, who in turn named various committees which met frequently. Some of the negotiators took upon themselves the heavy burden of traveling all over the Gulf region on "federation business" in additional to their government positions back home, because there was no one else to stand in for them. For many of them this was not only a taxing but also an exhilarating experience: They were involved in building something worthwhile for their own people—and for the first time with little outside help. Grave responsibilities were carried, often on young shoulders, but invariably with dignity and a keen desire to "get it right." The spirit of these years is a treasured memory for those who experienced them.

THE DECISIONMAKERS

The ultimate decisions in each of the constitutional issues at stake were taken by the nine rulers. Who were they at that crucial time, and what was the environment in which they lived?

In August 1966, Shaykh Zayid bin Sultan al-Nahayan had taken over the rulership of Abu Dhabi from his brother Shaykh Shakhbout, who had ruled for thirty-eight years—witnessing the peak of the pearling industry and the subsequent devastating economic recession, followed by the gathering pace of the oil boom. Shaykh Zayid was expected to give the inhabitants some immediate signs of the long-awaited benefits from the new oil wealth in the country—while his brother had held back from fear the fickle world market for this commodity, oil, like the pearls before it, would not always produce enough revenue for the country. Shaykh Zayid engaged straightaway in comprehensive developments on all fronts—infrastructure, education, health, services, and institution-building. His vision, however, from the outset extended beyond the emirate of Abu Dhabi. With the assurance of steadily growing oil exports, he planned to share much of the emirate's wealth in the spirit of Arab brotherhood; already in 1966 he donated relatively large sums to the Trucial States Development Fund, established by Britain for the seven states in the 1950s. From the inception of the federation, he made it known that a large share of Abu Dhabi's growing funds would be available to build a viable union. Other Arab, Islamic, and Third World countries were to experience his generosity too. But already it was obvious that he saw the new federation as the most important political goal and was willing to pledge almost total dedication from Abu Dhabi's side to its success.

Shaykh Rashid bin Sa'id al-Maktum of Dubai had a longstanding reputation for being farsighted and economically astute. Dubai's trade had gone from strength to strength even before he succeeded his father as ruler in 1958. Before oil was found in Dubai (and was first exported in 1969). Shaykh Rashid had devoted his considerable energy to improving Dubai's infrastructure in order to consolidate Dubai's position as the leading trading port for the region. At times his efforts were helped by grants and loans from his son-in-law, the Ruler of Qatar. In consequence, the two emirates that had a common currency, the Qatar and Dubai riyal, often formed one interest group in the discussions about the constitution of the new union. If the ruler of Abu Dhabi was motivated by idealism, the ruler of Dubai provided the realism.

Qatar, the second of these nine Gulf states to find oil, started exporting in 1949. In the 1950s, it became a welcoming haven for many families from the poverty-stricken Trucial States who were seeking better living conditions, a job, and education. Government institutions had already been set up, the process of legislation was underway, and at the end of the 1960s, Qatar was more "developed" than any of the other emirates except Bahrain. Qatar's ruler, Shaykh Ahmad bin Ali al-Thani, shared much of the responsibility for the state with his deputy, Khalifah bin Hamad al-Thani, by whom he was eventually deposed in 1972. Qatar brought the most professional approach to the conference tables—which did not always impress the other participants, who were inclined to seek what was politically possible, rather than what was constitutionally correct.

The ruler of Bahrain, Shaykh Isa bin Salman al-Khalifah, was in charge of the most sophisticated of the nine emirates and also the largest, with about 200,000 inhabitants. Formal education had been introduced in Bahrain by 1919. In consequence, there were already well-established government institutions. Oil was first discovered in 1932, and Bahrainis worked at all levels in the oil extraction and refinery industry. But above all, the population as a whole was considerably more politicized than anywhere else in the Gulf. The people were following the negotiations on the ultimate shape of the new union, and they expected to have their say. Shaykh Isa did not intend to deny them certain political rights and led his country's plea for a fair representation of Bahrainis, the largest population. Yet, Bahrain was situated a considerable distance from most of the states of the Union—it is, for instance, 330 miles to Ra's al-Khaimah. As an island, it is not only difficult of access, but also is traditionally very much involved with other littoral states of the Gulf such as Kuwait. Bahrain and Qatar had an unresolved dispute over some sandbanks and small islands. The ruler and the people of Bahrain were interested in the progress toward a union of their liking, but they followed even more eagerly the developments with regard to the Iranian claims to their island.

The ruler of Sharjah, Shaykh Khalid bin Muhammad al-Qasimi, had replaced his pro-Nasserite predecessor in 1965, at the behest of the British. While the federation negotiations were going on, exploration for oil in the vicinity of the disputed island of Abu Musa was starting, and Iran's claims to this island introduced further complications. Sharjah had the best educated population of all the shaykhdoms of the Trucial States. A school was established there in 1952, and by 1968, many secondary school graduates had already obtained higher education abroad. Their experience was particularly valuable during the federation negotiations.

Ra's al Khaimah, which in the past had been united with Sharjah under some of the influential and powerful Qasimi rulers, approached the negotiations with the attitude that it was therefore still one of the most important of the Trucial States. Moreover, there were reports that the exploration for oil in Ra's al-Khaimah would lead to a big discovery, enabling the emirate to be once again on a par with Abu Dhabi and Dubai. The ruler, Shaykh Saqr bin Muhammad al-Qasimi, was keen to maintain his own contacts with some of the neighboring states, such as Iraq and Saudi Arabia.

The only emirate of the Trucial States which is situated on the Indian Ocean coast is Fujairah. The ruler at the time, Shaykh Hamad bin Muhammad al-Sharqi, was the first to be recognized by Britain as another "Trucial Ruler"—after agreeing to give the multinational but London-based Iraq Petroleum Company's (IPC) a concession to prospect for oil in 1952. Communications with Fujairah were still difficult because the rough track over the mountains was sometimes washed away by flash floods. The emirate asked Abu Dhabi's delegation to speak on its behalf at some meetings. Finally, the two smallest emirates, Umm al-Qawain and 'Ajman, had rulers, Shaykh Ahmad bin Rashid al Mualla and Shaykh Rashid bin Humaid al Nuaimi, who were both very elderly but contributed continually to the ongoing discussions.

FAILURE OF THE UNION OF THE NINE

The Conservative election victory in Britain of June 1970 again raised questions about the program for withdrawal. Finally in March 1971, the British foreign secretary announced that Britain would adhere to the timetable, previously set by the Labour government, to complete withdrawal by the end of 1971. During this period of uncertainty, some of the emirates lacked the incentive to work wholeheartedly for the establishment of the Union; some even considered the possibility of opting out.

With the help of the United Nations, whose representative, V. W. Guiccicardi, conducted an informal survey, it was ascertained that the population of Bahrain did not want to be under Iranian rule. In May of 1970, the uncertainty over Bahrain's future was removed when Iran formally renounced its claim. By June of the following year, it became clear that Bahrain would no longer participate in the union of the nine states because on August 14, 1971, Bahrain declared its independence. Qatar in turn followed suit on September 1, 1971.

Abu Dhabi had already announced the formation of the emirate's first Council of Ministers on July 1, 1971 (it was abolished in 1973 in a move to give greater prominence to the federal government). A few days later, the seven rulers of the Trucial States met for a series of marathon sessions in Dubai, and the formation of the state of the United Arab Emirates was announced on July 18, 1971. One of the Trucial States, Ra's al-Khaimah, delayed joining until February 1972.

After the completion of the transfer of authority from the British government to the new state, a provisional constitution came into effect on December 2, 1971, the day which is now celebrated as the National Day of the United Arab Emirates. The experience gained over the years of negotiation as a group of nine and the results of their efforts were the very building blocks for the union of seven. The loose nature of the new federal state reflected to a certain extent the geographical, social, and political diversities of the group of nine. There was considerable temptation to gloss over the differences and to continue with an increasingly meaningless union in order to please the rest of the Arab World, which was looking for a symbol of Arab unity. The leaders and the people of the Gulf emirates were more concerned with political realism and with best preparing themselves to conduct their own affairs than with impracticable political gestures.

PROVISIONAL CONSTITUTION

The constitution eventually adopted by the seven emirates of the UAE differs little from the document that had been discussed over the years by the nine emirates. The constitutional drafts were molded in later stages by a number of expatriate Arab legal advisers and by the delegates of the nine emirates. Looking in detail at the genesis of this material over the three years, one finds that indeed a large part of the work of shaping this constitution was done by the two absent participants, Qatar and Bahrain.

The constitution of the UAE reflects the political reality of the time. First and foremost it was meant to be in force only for the first five years, to be replaced by a permanent constitution tailored more precisely to what was hoped to be, by then, a political entity well on its way to becoming a centralized state. The political reality of the time was that the individual emirates were not yet ready to give up their identity, and their rulers could certainly not imagine relinquishing their authority in the face of such crucial changes. This is nowhere more manifest than in article 23 of the Provisional Constitution, which states that "the natural resources and wealth in each emirate shall be considered to be the public property of that emirate." In consequence, those emirates which were lucky enough to derive wealth from exporting oil or from trading are constitutionally in sole possession of that wealth. It is indicated elsewhere in the constitution that regulations would be made to ensure that a certain proportion of that wealth is put at the disposal of the federation as a whole. Not stating what that proportion was to cause considerable problems in later years. Moreover, when the wealth also enhances disproportionately the more fortunate emirates' political power, this encourages erosion rather than growth of national unity.

A further reflection of the political reality of the time was the weak role given by this constitution to the population's representatives. In 1971, it seemed unrealistic to provide for elections (although the constitution allowed for an emirate to choose its representatives in that way). At the time, the majority of the potential electorate was totally unprepared for such an innovation. It was assumed that the small local population of each emirate would be adequately represented by a few people chosen from among the leading merchant families and tribal elders, who had always had the confidence of their people and were seen as the community leaders. Thus only forty delegates constitute the Federal National Council (FNC). Of these, eight represent Abu Dhabi, eight Dubai, and six or four the smaller emirates respectively. The powers of the Council are consultative: it is not expected to initiate bills but can comment on them and may amend them before they become law.

According to the provisional constitution, the ultimate authority in the land is the Supreme Council of Rulers, who approve all legislation and by their meeting provide a manifestation of centralized unity. But the constitution lacks any provision for enforcing regular meetings of this highest authority. Over the years, the rulers preferred the ease of informal meetings to the constraints of an imposed routine. In the absence of a mechanism that enforces debate and decision at the highest level, controversial issues can be simply left in abeyance.

The provisional constitution does not stand the test of constitutional experts—it is a weak and incomplete document. But it was for that reason that it could be adopted without further long discussion by the seven emirates' delegations in the summer of 1971. Its very vagueness constituted the room for compromise that made the handshake, the deal, and the signature possible. A more sophisticated written constitution, at a time when the venture into a modern unified political structure was still perceived as a tentative experiment, would have meant a less honest inception of this federal state. It can be argued that the fact that this rather imperfect provisional constitution has yet to be replaced may indicate that the political environment has still not matured enough to make such a replacement meaningful. An answer may lie in an assessment of the political developments of the UAE over the past quarter century.

Institutionalizing Unification

THE FEDERATION

The establishment of the United Arab Emirates in the final months of 1971 was the response to a political necessity. For the population of these emirates it was also an economic and social convenience. But whether the young states would survive as a federation, whether it would grow from being merely the sum-total of seven tribal societies to become a genuine "motherland," and whether the inhabitants of the coastal population centers as well as of the many remote villages would become a nation would all depend on the interplay of a great number of factors.

The UAE was based on a constitution over which the notion "compromise" was written in large letters. The rulers and their advisers made commitments to the new state on behalf of their emirates, but the people themselves participated little. Most observers expected only a minimum of federal governmental structure at that time. That absolute minimum had to include the matters over which the British government had held authority, such as defense, foreign affairs, and immigration.

Since 1971 the UAE government has extended its authority to the extent that it affects every citizen's day-to-day life. One may point to a great number of imperfections and to many still unfulfilled hopes and expectations such as greater economic equality, less autocratic rule, or better decisionmaking processes, but there is now no doubt that the government of the UAE is able to respond to demands in the same way as any other government. The most recent demonstration of this ability was the role played by the UAE during the 1990–91 Gulf crisis, both during the war and afterward. There were internal consultations during the crisis at different appropriate levels. The federal decisionmaking process—though it might be expected to be slow—came up with results in a way undistinguishable from those of the governments of any of its centrally ruled neighbors. The UAE took an unequivocal stand with regard to the Iraqi invasion, welcomed Arab and other initiatives to find a peaceful solution, and was decisive in its support for the allies when it came to the military confrontation.

GROWING POLITICAL PARTICIPATION

The federation was set up by the traditional decisionmakers, assisted by a group of educated nationals with the support of the established merchant community and encouraged by the British Foreign Office. At the time the people were neither in conflict with, nor critical of these traditional authorities, but saw them as acting on their behalf within the framework of the familiar tribal system. Many warmly welcomed the federal state and there was no active opposition to it. Such positive but largely passive attitudes soon gave way to expectations which a growing number of UAE nationals actively voiced as they became more aware of the political scene in their country.

The 1973 October War involving Israel and its Arab neighbors was the first occasion when the UAE experienced the full impact of being swept up in the tidal wave of Arab politics. These events also heightened people's awareness of, for instance, the expectations of the other Arab countries that they would share in the oil wealth, the need to distribute the wealth more evenly inside the UAE, the possibilities for more formal—as opposed to traditional tribal—participation in the decisionmaking process, and the desire to have one strong UAE force rather than a number of defense forces.

THE PERMANENT CONSTITUTION

When the time came in 1976 to replace the provisional constitution with a permanent constitution, a lively public debate ensued for the first time about the future political scene in the UAE. (Heard-Bey 1996, 378ff; Taryam 1987, 234ff; Peck 1986, 131ff). A committee of twenty-eight was charged with drafting the permanent constitution with the help of a legal expert. The committee was divided between those who saw themselves as delegates of their home emirate and sought to promote the particular preferences of their ruler and others who saw an opportunity to change a great many things in the political life of the UAE, which they perceived as outdated, divisive, and inappropriate for the future. This second group—what one might call the "independents"—sought as the first objective for the new constitution greater centralization at the expense of the powers exercised by each ruler and his court. They also hoped to introduce more direct and democratic participation by the people in deciding the affairs of the federation. The independents wanted more efficient distribution of the wealth of the country. Some among them suggested abolishing Article 23 of the provisional constitution, thereby making the income from oil or any other natural resource the property of the whole nation. The committee's draft of the permanent constitution envisaged a compromise, requiring each emirate to transfer 75 percent of its income to the federal treasury.

The committee also agreed on a compromise for the composition of the Federal National Council, which would have done away with the allocation of a fixed number of representatives for each particular emirate. Instead the assembly was to have a large number of seats divided among the emirates according to the number of nationals in each of them. The role of the Council was also hotly debated since several committee members had hoped to give it full legislative functions. The question of national security, another burning issue, was not resolved in favor of the maximalists, who wanted to forbid the individual emirates from retaining a local force. The draft permanent constitution did go a long way in this direction, though, saying that only the federal authorities may establish and maintain a military force. Private Emiri guards, whose number would have to be limited by law, would still be allowed.

One of the main issues throughout this exercise was the extent to which the centralized powers (always referred to as "federal") should be strengthened at the expense of the emirates' individual powers. Some members of the drafting committee vigorously opposed such proposals, especially those who represented Dubai and Ra's al-Khaimah. The debate then widened to the question of whether or not there should even be a new constitution—whether it was not better to continue with the provisional one, gradually changing it over time. It eventually transpired that Dubai would reject the new constitution.

This constitutional controversy, together with a dispute over immigration policy and the general reluctance of some of the other rulers to follow Abu Dhabi's example and give up regional powers in favor of a stronger and more unified central state, motivated President Shaykh Zayid to announce that under those circumstances he would not accept a further term of office when his five-year term expired in December 1976. In any event, the Supreme Council of Rulers decided at its meeting in July 1976 not to approve the draft permanent constitution but to extend the validity of the Provisional Constitution for another five years. Fearful of the possibility of the disintegration of the fledgling federation and of the dire consequences for the entire region, Shaykh Zayid did accept a further term of office as president.

Managing Domestic and Regional Pressures

CONSTITUTIONAL CRISIS

Thus the changes that a group of nationals, chiefly from Sharjah, had worked for and that many people in the region had hoped for, were not adopted. But the spirit of reform remained alive after December 1976, most obviously in the newly constituted Federal National Council. The Council of Ministers, too, benefited from the presence of fifteen university graduates in its midst. Between these two institutions, the ideas that had been discussed in preparing the draft of the permanent constitution were taken up again at a time when it was obvious that the country needed decisive leadership and cohesion in view of the growing instability of the Shah's regime in Iran in 1978. The Council of Ministers and the Federal National Council formed a joint committee, with the hope of convincing the rulers individually that it was time to give up their particularism and support a strong national government. The group visited each court on more than one occasion and also arranged for a joint debate of the Federal National Council and the Ministers on June 27, 1978. Eventually, a memorandum was prepared by this joint committee and submitted to all the rulers, suggesting—even demanding—the speedy resolution of these issues which had been pending since 1976. (Taryam 1987, 240–42; Heard-Bey 1996, 407–14).

These suggestions gained the enthusiastic support of the president of Abu Dhabi and the rulers of Sharjah, Fujairah, and 'Ajman, which led to a confrontation between Abu Dhabi and Dubai in March of 1979. The matter had to be put to the Supreme Council of Rulers, which convened in Abu Dhabi on March 19, 1979, to study the memorandum of the joint committee as a first step toward resolving the brewing constitutional crisis. While the Supreme Council was in session in the guest palace in Abu Dhabi, a large number of students, citizens, and tribesmen demonstrated outside in support of the points raised in the memorandum, but also in support of the president, who was seen as the guarantor for a more unified, hence more effective government of the UAE.

The urge to rush to the street to demonstrate was a novelty in the UAE, and was most certainly provoked by the daily television footage of demonstrations in Iran. But otherwise, there was nothing in common with the events on the other side of the Gulf. When the president interrupted the session of the Supreme Council to speak to the people outside, there was a wave of sympathy between them. All the demonstrators wanted was for Shaykh Zayid to take the government of the entire union more firmly into his own hands and thereby—it was hoped—to deliver the benefits of Abu Dhabi's wealth more directly to the entire country, to render its defense arrangements more effective, to prevent duplication of infrastructure and industrial projects, and to regulate the influx of immigrants. The president was ready to comply, but not all the members of the Supreme Council were as ready to give up so many of their traditional powers, which were still considered to be the hallmark of each emirate's statehood.

Compromise could not be achieved for some days, during which the demonstrations continued, and Shaykh Rashid, the ruler of Dubai, published a counter-memorandum. In essence, his statement was an equally convincing plea for unity within the federation. In his view, this had to be achieved by first concentrating on better services for all parts of the country; only when there were no longer such huge differences in the living standards of the national population throughout the federation did it make sense to unify more completely.

The intervention of mediators, in particular the foreign minister of Kuwait, Shaykh Sabah al-Ahmad al-Sabah, finally resolved the impasse. The cabinet was dissolved on April 26, 1979, and Shaykh Rashid, ruler of Dubai, formed the new government as prime minister. This solution, although a very helpful compromise, was yet typical of the way in which confrontations so often have been overcome: instead of clinging to a principle with the tenacity of one's conviction, one embraces and thereby silences the opposition. In this case, the astute manager of Dubai's economic successes, the realist with a team of practical people behind him, undertook to improve matters where he had seen them lacking. Shaykh Rashid's cabinet turned out to be effective, in particular in improving conditions in remote areas. Far from harboring any resentments over the earlier differences of opinion, the president and the prime minister worked very effectively together. Dubai also started to contribute to the federal budget.

Although the "activists" of the 1976–1979 period had not achieved many of their objectives, they were ready to give the new government time to implement changes in its own way. After all, the constitutional crisis had never developed into an all-out confrontation. The supporters of the memorandum never opposed their rulers but urged them to take more positive, even bold, political decisions rather than clinging to their routines. Thus, the issue was settled quietly. Not only was the president ready to stand for another term in office (his third), but the prime minister was also reelected in 1981, and the validity of the Provisional Constitution was extended for yet another five years at that same time. It was therefore a sad blow for the entire country when the prime minister became very ill and increasingly unable to discharge his duties; yet it was not deemed right to confer the premiership on anyone else during his lifetime. Shaykh Rashid died in October 1990.

THE WAR YEARS OF THE 1980s AND AFTER

The 1980s witnessed no serious attempt to reform the political system of the UAE. There was even a noticeable decline in the role of the Federal National Council, which met less frequently, and spent much of its time on routine business. Thus the assembly did not develop many initiatives. This does not mean, however, that there was less constructive political will at work. While the Iran-Iraq War was raging dangerously close, the UAE had to try to keep out of the firing line—literally so far as shipping and petroleum exports were concerned, and figuratively in the sense that it was caught in a difficult political balancing act between the two nations at war. In such circumstances, building political unity in the UAE could not fruitfully be achieved through public memoranda, debates, and demonstrations. It was obvious to everyone that internal dissension of any kind would have been detrimental to each member state and every institution in the federation. Throughout the Iran-Iraq War, then, the status quo in domestic politics remained unchallenged. However, this pragmatic way of dealing with an exceptional war situation had become the universally accepted norm by the beginning of the 1990s. Thus it came as no surprise that the text of the provisional constitution of 1971 was declared the permanent constitution in the course of celebrations for the twenty-fifth anniversary of the federation in December 1996.

Whereas the young UAE nationals of the 1970s were largely educated in Arab universities, and had been exposed to the political ideas prevalent in those universities in the 1960s, the new generation of young technocrats taking over in the 1980s and early 1990s have been educated for the most part in Western universities and have learned the value of pragmatism. Members of this generation have moved into positions in the ministries, the military, the newly formed Central Bank, and the oil industry, where they worked effectively for the benefit of the UAE. While abroad, they identify themselves with the UAE rather than with their home emirate. Returning home, they work in the central administration in Abu Dhabi or Dubai. This is the generation that identifies practical ways of advancing the interests of the state of the UAE. It is no coincidence, therefore, that the constitution is now rarely mentioned in public. Reality has overtaken its shortcomings.

One day a new generation of young visionaries will take up the task of bringing the constitutional document, on which the federation should rest, in line with reality-and thereby chart a clearly marked route for the political future.

ECONOMIC ISSUES

The years since 1971 have seen steady progress in consolidating unity, which began as a fragile statement of intent. It should not be forgotten, however, that the fledgling federal state started off with a very rosy economic future. (Khalifa 1979, 62–74). Abu Dhabi's and to a lesser extent Dubai's growing income from oil helped to encourage the other emirates to join with them in 1971, and ever since oil money has remained an essential factor in maintaining the momentum of building the federal state. Soon after the UAE was formed, an unexpected fourfold rise in price and the considerable oil production increases generated a windfall of oil revenues, which peaked in 1980 at $14.3 billion before declining as the oil price fell. During the Gulf crisis, increased production again resulted in an estimated $15.6 billion of oil revenues for the UAE in 1990.

This is not to say that economic issues have never been a problem for the federation over the last two decades and a half. On the contrary, the fact that the lion's share of income accrued to only two of the seven emirates has caused tension. But the extent to which the non-oil emirates have benefitted has to be judged by comparison with conditions in these emirates before 1971 (Heard-Bey 1996, 164–237). Success in the federation was nevertheless not an automatic consequence of the country's income from oil, in particular because the people have anyway learned to expect from the central authorities tangible improvements in their lifestyle.

THE FOREIGN POLICY COMPONENT

As soon as the UAE was declared in December 1971, steps were taken to impress on foreign nations that this was not another of the loose and short-lived British constructed federal states. The UAE immediately became a member of the Arab League, the United Nations, and various UN bodies. Diplomatic relations were established with many countries. Patient diplomacy brought results where they were most urgently needed. In 1974, Saudi Arabia recognized the UAE after their common border had finally been agreed upon, and the friendship of this most important and powerful neighbor was confirmed.

The UAE as an independent state was primarily interested in confirming its credentials as a good Arab and Islamic country. The 1973 war and its aftermath gave the UAE the opportunity to demonstrate its commitment to the Arab world-even though its conservative system of government differed from those of many Arab nations. Declarations of all kinds, acts of solidarity such as the oil boycott of the U.S. and the Netherlands, and above all, the generous aid to many Arab countries and communities from the early 1970s onward—were usually made in the name of the UAE, thereby strengthening the image of unity at home and abroad. The UAE has also provided considerable financial aid to a number of Islamic and Third World countries. There was a flurry of involvement in international conferences, and the establishment of diplomatic relations with many more countries. Some foreign relations decisions had to be handled carefully because different emirates attached different importance to relations with particular countries for historical reasons. Relations with Iran fall into this category because of Dubai's traditional trade across the Gulf (al-Alkim 1989).

In recounting the efforts of the late 1970s to forge a much more effectively structured union for the UAE, in which he was personally involved, Abdullah Taryam writes: "the citizens themselves remained faithful to the union and worked for its preservation. Far from accepting existence within the narrow limits of a provisional constitution, they behaved in a spirit of unity." (1987, 247). This underlines the fact that the federation is a success at least where it matters most—in the hearts and minds of the local population. Its success since its very inception in presenting itself abroad as a fully integrated political entity is equally impressive. Such positive experiences are relevant for the Arab world in general and will be highlighted below.

Relevance of the UAE's Experience

LEADERSHIP STYLE

The UAE's success in building a federation that has already survived longer than any other Arab union in modern times is due primarily to strong leadership. On the twenty-fifth anniversary of the UAE in December 1996, the by-now usual media outpouring of sycophantic praise for the president, who had returned from abroad on account of ill health to a tumultuous welcome in November, reached unprecedented proportions. This should not distract us from trying to understand a leadership style that has proved so successful—both at home and abroad. The strength of leadership in this region has rarely been a function of its might, but rather of its ability to strike a good compromise at the right time. To cite a historical example, Abu Dhabi's main tribal confederation, the Bani Yas, wedged between the Wahabis and the Qawasim, managed to maintain its independence from both—staying aloof from their escapades and quarrels throughout much of the eighteenth and nineteenth centuries or patiently negotiating with one or the other party until compromise was reached.

Tracing the ups and downs of more than a quarter century of federation, one could rarely find an instance when Abu Dhabi used its wealth to foist a decision on others. Instead, the prevalent political management style in the UAE largely depends on a plethora of meetings—the formal ones with all their much-loved protocol, and the informal ones at the camel racetrack or in the desert—as well as on telephone calls, messages, intermediaries, and go-betweens. From the outset, all parties recognize that a compromise must be achieved and that it does not really matter how long it takes. What is important is to help the other side to save face, compromising in a positive spirit so that all parties feel that they have achieved a "happy ending." In March 1979 the constitutional crisis could easily have led to a clash between Dubai and Ra's al-Khaimah on one side and Abu Dhabi and other emirates on the other side, but this was avoided because the two leaders holding contrary views stayed away from the crucial meeting. Subsequent attempts at solving the impasse followed the usual pattern of bilateral contacts, delegations, and mediators all testing out various configurations of compromise. All parties made use of the fact that contemporaneous developments in Iran, the Arab world, and Pakistan put their domestic differences into perspective. The solutions reached—in this instance in a painstaking behind-the-scenes search for compromise—provided a good basis for further and better cooperation between the two emirates within the federation from 1979 onward.

The strength of this political style is an attitude of tolerance, the absence of doctrinal or ideological fixation, and infinite patience. Its weakness is that success or failure ultimately depends on the leaders alone. There is little room for a corporate approach or for teamwork, although advisers may be consulted. Also in this system, the time factor is obviously of relatively little importance, yet not all developments wait for compromises to be worked out in their own time. This political style is common elsewhere in public life throughout the federation—where it may be manifested not as a purposeful search for a compromise but rather as the unnecessary delay of a much-needed decision.

TRADITIONAL DEMOCRACY

While a tribesman now has little influence on the choice of the next ruler in his emirate, and has little say in who represents his emirate in the Federal National Council, he nevertheless remains confident that if he has a substantive grievance, he can put it to his shaykh. UAE society is small enough and structured enough that this line of communication for all intents and purposes should be open in both directions. The shaykh's *majlis* was and is an institution designed to facilitate this vital privilege: direct communication. Thus, even now, people voluntarily acknowledge a ruler's authority. Criticism is aimed not at the traditional structures and their proponents, but increasingly at the inadequacy of the people around them and at the way in which the rest of the public machinery functions.

It is important to note that such voluntary continuation of this grassroots type of democracy still works and is operational for most of the nationals in the country, though not for the expatriates. For example, the chairman or the manager of a business may hold an open *majlis*, to which staff, employees, and others are expected to come occasionally. Throughout the Arab world there is a ready understanding of this voluntary interaction between the people and those whom they acknowledge to be their leaders.

STABILIZING INFLUENCE

Would the Gulf's stability have suffered if the UAE had split apart? The unified stance that the federation has presented to its neighbors and to the world in itself has had a stabilizing influence on the area. By the 1970s, the UAE was already involved in efforts to mediate within or between other Arab states. The question of the form the union of the nine emirates should take was of paramount importance to their immediate neighbors in the Gulf. In the three years before 1971, the politicians and rulers of the nine emirates thus became engaged in intensive diplomatic activity with each other and the neighboring states of Kuwait, Saudi Arabia, and Iran. They visited each others' countries frequently and thus became knowledgeable about each other in a way that might otherwise not have happened. When, in subsequent years, matters of Gulf-wide importance, for instance oil prices, had to be discussed, leaders followed this pattern of easy, ad-hoc, mutual consultation that had been established while preparing for the federation before 1971. The decision to form the Gulf Cooperation Council (GCC) in May 1981 is likely to have been inspired by the example of unity in diversity in the UAE (see chapter 7).

In setting up the UAE, the principle of solidarity among the seven shaykhdoms was very important. It is most likely that even if the federation had not come about in this form, the poorer emirates would have benefitted from the wealth of the richer ones. It is well-known that the UAE has generously aided other Arab countries, but it has also always been a keen participant in Arab issues, forthcoming with demonstrations of political solidarity. Both were offered even while the memory was still alive of the critical if not deprecatory Nasserite and Ba'thist comments about the conservative governments of the Gulf which had been made in the past by some of the current recipients of aid. The selfsame principle of focusing on the future rather than the past was again evident when the UAE joined with Saudi Arabia and Kuwait in an International Monetary Fund–sponsored plan to help the ailing economies of those Arab states which suffered most as a consequence of the Gulf War.

The UAE and Oman were the two GCC countries most active in keeping the lines of communication open to both sides during the first Gulf War of 1980–88, when it was recognized that ideological differences with Iran should not detract from the fact that the Iranian people would always remain neighbors with whom the UAE would want to have a peaceful relationship.

MANAGING A MULTINATIONAL STATE

The UAE probably has the most varied population mix of any of the Arab countries; dozens of foreign nationalities account for well over 80 percent of its population. While watching the rapid changes in the population structure of the country during the 1970s, a great many local politicians were very concerned about the consequences for the national identity of the local population, their security, and the additional burden on the government-provided services. Today such issues are still discussed, but there is now more confidence that the problem of the population structure is manageable. A great deal of effort has been made to regulate immigration and labor matters with the aim of making it extremely difficult for immigrant workers to put down roots. Most of these economic migrants from all over the Third World are badly off back home and are willing to accept a low status in the host country so long as they can earn enough to support their families at home. Should they leave, they are easily replaced by other migrants ready to work for even less. This "over the horizon" labor force potential encourages the authorities and the people of the UAE to view labor as a mere commodity governed by market forces, and effective measures to deal with the population structure are deferred to an ever later date.

In the UAE, as in some other Arab countries of the Gulf, the original tribal population will probably never again be numerically dominant. The Kuwait crisis highlighted the question of whether the small local populations of these countries might some day allow immigrant inhabitants to qualify for nationality, equal citizenship, and a share of the nationals' rights and obligations. Being the most acutely affected, the UAE may need to consider earnestly the status in particular of the many long-term Arab residents in their midst, whose loyalty to the country is a valuable asset for its future development.

FREEDOM OF INFORMATION AND A NEW REALISM

Educational facilities in the UAE are at present still too limiting for exceptionally clever students, but the obstacles that so often stand in the way of students seeking further education abroad—in particular, lack of funds or ideological constraints—are absent in the case of young UAE nationals. The availability of funds, both governmental and private, for citizens to travel, study abroad, or benefit from the latest in educational technology is primarily a direct consequence of the country's oil wealth.

The fact is that no shackles are put on the individual's quest for knowledge and information, which is a credit to the country's tolerance compared to some of its neighbors. In many countries, government policy or pressures from within the society prevent citizens from trying to understand the rest of the world sufficiently well to form a balanced view; the new generation is thus subjected to ideological limitations and as a consequence is not well-equipped to think independently. In contrast, the UAE authorities initiated a dramatic reappraisal of information services at the outbreak of the Gulf War and (initially to preempt rumors) began transmitting CNN uncensored for 24 hours a day. With television sets in almost every building being now connected to satellites and the Internet, information from around the world enters the UAE unhindered.

The openness and tolerance practiced in the UAE are appreciated by expatriates, who find it possible to practice their own religion and lifestyle and to choose from a great number of international newspapers or television programs. Those limitations which are being imposed where possible are predicated on moral rather than ideological grounds. However, this tolerance is of particular importance for the new generation of citizens who are expected to lead the country in its economic and political interaction with the rest of the world. Many young people are fascinated by wealth and lack the motivation to achieve through hard work. But many others—often the deeply religious—have already made the most of their opportunities to combine the heritage of their resourceful ancestors with the skills and knowledge that modern education, information, and travel can offer. This will be a very valuable asset for the future, and may eventually give this young country an advantage over some of the traditionally leading but now sadly self-limiting Arab countries.

Conclusion

Strange as it may seem at first, the three main factors that contribute to this country's success as a federal state are its population structure, with only around 15 percent of the inhabitants being nationals, the unevenly distributed wealth, and the traditional structure of the local society.

Every UAE national—however humble his or her material and educational circumstances and status within this society—by virtue of *not* being part of the non-national majority, has a vested interest in the continued integrity of the traditional society with tribal shaykhs and rulers at its apex. Being part of this structure is the basic reason why a national family is able today to lead a life in which poverty has been left behind—indeed *a priori* none can be lower than "middle class" because all manual laborers are immigrants. In dress, lifestyle, tastes, and a host of traditional customs as well as newly acquired habits, nationals endeavor to set themselves apart from the immigrant majority.

An inseparable feature of this social structure is, however, that it has the tribally legitimized leadership with its increasingly material vested interests and patronage as its focus. The seven ruling families in principle still have equal political power, and this is borne out by the fact that the 1971 constitution, which not only gives the emirates much independent political status, but also confirms and consolidates the individual rulers in their positions, has not been superseded. A society with a more normal population mix would have taken steps to constitutionally redefine the role of the traditional leaders, and a natural consequence of such steps would have been reshaping the federation from within.

The wealth of some of the emirates has been a mainstay for the federation's continued cohesion. The practical benefit of oil revenues to the less wealthy is an invaluable asset for the federation; it is also important that the not so fortunate emirates have little option but to continue to operate within the existing framework because they cannot hope to survive outside the federation. Given the spirit of the early 1970s, the issue was rarely whether giving to the "have-nots" was generous enough; but rather that the "have not" tribal leaders did not want to give up any of their sovereignty in exchange. A more institutionalized routine for distributing the wealth within the country could have been established if there had been a more ready reduction in the attributes of regional particularism and sovereignty. At times such issues may be hotly debated, but are unlikely to lead to confrontation under the current circumstances primarily because the basis of the local society's minority structure cannot be called into question. Then too, this rapidly developing wealthy state has built up practical, nonpolitical ways to administer the benefits of a modern way of life throughout all the emirates, to all nationals, and to a large extent, to immigrants, too. Thus for many practical purposes, the federation is becoming increasingly centralized.

When the UAE was set up, it was essentially a creation of the rulers, and could not have been built without them. Now the national society, by dint of being in a position quite "apart from" the rest of the population, preserves and confirms those very features which make the country continue to adhere to the conditions under which the federation was created and thereby continues to legitimize its rulers' role within the federation. Under those circumstances, there seems to be no urgency even to change an outdated written constitution or to upgrade political institutions which are still to some extent rudimentary. In spite of such imperfections, but due largely to the society's ingrained tolerance and sense of realism, the UAE has indeed thrived, and more than a quarter-century after its establishment can be considered a successful experience in Arab integration.

References

al-Alkim, Hassan Hamdan. *The Foreign Policy of the United Arab Emirates*. London: Al-Saqi, 1989.

Heard-Bey, Frauke. *From Trucial States to United Arab Emirates: A Society in Transition*. London: Longman, 1982; 2nd edition, 1996

Khalifa, Ali Mohammed. *The United Arab Emirates: Unity in Fragmentation*. Boulder, CO: Westview, 1979.

Peck, Malcolm C. *The United Arab Emirates*. London: Croom Helm, 1986.

Rumaihi, Muhammad. *Beyond Oil*. London: Al-Saqi, 1986.

Taryam, Abdullah Omran. *The Establishment of the United Arab Emirates 1950–1985*. London: Croom Helm, 1987.

chapter 7

The Gulf Cooperation Council: Nature Origin, and Process

Abdul Khaleq Abdulla

Few other comparable groups of states have more in common than the six Arab Gulf states that decided in May 1981 to launch their own integration venture and establish the Gulf Cooperation Council (GCC). These states; Bahrain, Kuwait, Oman, Qatar, Saudi Arabia and the United Arab Emirates—have almost every conceivable commonality and a strikingly deep homogeneity. Despite their sociopolitical similarities, however, these states have found it difficult in the years since the GCC's establishment to advance their integration and develop the organization to a point that it serves as more than merely a forum for yearly summit meetings that issues innocuous communiqués on current events in the Gulf and the wider Arab-Islamic world.

Even these largely ceremonial summits experienced a sudden deadlock during its sixteenth annual meeting in Muscat in December 1995, when Qatar withdrew from the closing session. The Qataris declared their intention to boycott any future GCC meetings attended by the newly appointed General Secretary Jamil al-Hujailan of Saudi Arabia (*Al-Ahram Weekly* 1995). In the wake of this discord, Bahrain and Qatar, two of the smallest GCC states, decided to step up their ongoing political feud. Bahrain extended a high-profile official welcome to the deposed ruler of Qatar, Shaykh Khalifah bin Hamad. Qatar instantly retaliated by giving a rare one-hour live television interview to two leading exiled Bahraini opposition leaders.

These and other instances of open conflict inevitably renew doubts about the viability and longevity of the GCC, especially among the legion of self-professed skeptics on prospects for Arab integration. These events indicate that the GCC states have yet to settle many of their outstanding historical and political, as well as petty personal, frictions. Qatar's unprecedented and surely embarrassing walkout at the Muscat summit fundamentally shattered the tightly guarded consensual fabric of the GCC. It was a further sign of a recently growing internal power struggle and of disenchantment with the lack of any genuine integrationist breakthroughs.

Clearly the GCC is entering a critical stage of uncertainty. Its internal cohesiveness will be severely tested. It is desperately searching for a common denominator beyond the external threat that gave birth to the GCC in 1981, when the Arab Gulf states essentially huddled together in a crisis situation that resulted from, among other things, the fall of the Shah of Iran and the subsequent Islamic revolution. But since 1991, and as the Gulf region and the whole Middle East experience persistent tensions beneath a deceptively calm appearance, fresh anxieties over long dormant disputes among the GCC states, and between the GCC and its neighbors, have been creeping into the foreground.

These mounting apprehensions, old and new, are exposing the GCC's inability to fulfill its most ambitious integrationist objectives and to deliver on its often grandiose political and security declarations. Progress toward economic integration of the GCC is almost flat. Its oft-repeated claim that the security and defense of its members is exclusively a GCC affair finds its ultimate denial in the excessive reliance of the Arab Gulf states on United States protection. Political coordination, once the hallmark of the GCC, has declined sharply. Today the institution suffers from a credibility gap.

Furthermore, the GCC states appear to be more protective of their national sovereignty and its attendant symbols than ever before. These states are growing steadily more inward-looking and preoccupied with domestic concerns. These include, among other things, financial constraints, rising social tensions, emerging Islamic radicalism, mounting youth unemployment, desperately needed economic restructuring, and the newly assertive popular demand for greater accountability, political institutionalization, and participation. These critical internal issues, rather than the external ones (which are also serious), should be of greatest concern to the GCC's leaders and citizens alike as the "holiday ends in the Gulf" and the GCC states gradually move away from the exceptionality of the super-rich to normality, with all its problems (Zanoyan 1995). The conventional wisdom in the Gulf today is that from now on, as the basic political and economic logic dictates, everybody tends to his own interests. It is these new realities that are making the mission of the GCC distinctly burdensome. For some observers of Gulf affairs the GCC, particularly after the Muscat stalemate, is at a turning point and may be sinking into irrelevancy.

For those less skeptical, the latest setbacks, momentous as they appear, are not sufficient to declare the GCC politically dead. The Muscat episode was surely irksome but not necessarily terminal. It was probably a timely reminder to Gulf integration enthusiasts that the political and economic coming together of the six Arab Gulf states has been and will be, as are most integration experiments, an agonizing and protracted process with many breakdowns and few breakthroughs. In the opinion of this writer, the GCC is neither dead nor moribund, and the historical process of integrating and ultimately uniting the six Arab Gulf states continues. The GCC has already, for all practical purposes, passed the test of "to be or not to be." It has amply proven its survivability. There is, to begin with, an intense sense of the durability of common interests that acts as a coalescing force. In addition, these states have made enormous tangible commitments of resources toward integration. Despite the difficulties, there is now an irreversibility in the common concerns and activities of the GCC which are essential to its welfare. Indeed, one can argue that the organization is approaching the threshold stage of implementing a common agenda of social and economic policies.

Although it is relatively new, even integration skeptics must admit that the GCC is here to stay. Indeed it has been remarkable in its durability. It is definitely proving to be one of those few cases—perhaps the only case—in the Arab world where genuine cooperation is not only working but actually substantially deepening, albeit in fits and starts (Christie 1987, 13). The fundamental operative logic of the GCC has been simple: if total political unity—theoretically at least the ultimate goal—is a practical impossibility and complete economic integration is not immediately attainable, then cooperation is the second best goal (al-Qasimi 1988, 1). This kind of ideological pragmatism in the midst of entrenched political conservatism was responsible for the birth and evolution of the GCC in a most unlikely region. This acute blend of pragmatism and conservatism has also been germane for the inner cohesiveness of the GCC and its success in surviving the daunting challenges it has faced.

During these delicate formative years, the GCC has gotten a toehold and can now begin to climb. Its members collectively faced up to the imminent threats of the Iranian revolution. They outlasted the surmountable daily dangers of the eight-year Iran-Iraq war. They even bravely dug in together during the subsequent short-lived Iraqi invasion of Kuwait. In addition, the GCC managed to reduce violent tensions among its member states by developing a nascent security community, albeit an imperfect one, that has enjoyed a decade-and-a-half of relatively peaceful coexistence. Economically, it created its own customs union, imposed a common external tariff, and is incrementally delivering on its unified economic agreement. In foreign affairs, the GCC has become a recognized regional organization in international politics, projecting an image, which has been noted by both friends and foes, of a somewhat collective foreign policy . Domestically, there is an evolving sense of "oneness" (Bishara 1983–84, 41), a psychological affinity to the community, and a common regional identity that spontaneously distinguishes between what happens within and what happens outside of the GCC's geographic and political confinement.[1] The GCC states are easily identifiable as the six traditional monarchies with a unique political culture and distinct way of life that possess a commodity of vital strategic value to the rest of the world.

At its inception, the GCC was viewed by political observers, scholars and the press as a regional organization that was born to die. Ten years later, many believed that the GCC had already outlived its usefulness and had few successes to its credit. Now, many are still predicting gloom and doom for the GCC, yet it has not only survived, but has also found a receptive audience within the Gulf region and beyond.[2] The GCC continues to contradict the implication of the realist perspective in international relations theory that attempts at voluntary cooperation and integration among sovereign states in the anarchical environment of world politics generally are doomed to failure. The GCC's persistence instead confirms the more liberal assertion that cooperation and integration are not only attainable but are part and parcel of contemporary international relations, maybe more so now than ever.

Achievements and failures notwithstanding, the GCC, like other attempts at institutionalized cooperation, remains bedeviled by profound strategic uncertainties. This situation raises some legitimate questions with uncertain answers. First, what is the nature of the GCC? Does it represent political unification or economic integration? Is it a military alliance or a security community? Or is it more a uniquely Gulf phenomenon? Second, what is the origin of the GCC? Is it a force or voluntary association? Which accounts more for its origin—internal or external factors, ideological affinity or objective necessity? Third, what are the basic objectives of the GCC and to what extent has it fulfilled them? What accounts for its achievements and failures, for its breakthroughs and breakdowns? Finally, what is ahead for the GCC? Is it going to persevere or dissolve? Will Arab Gulf integration survive or stagnate? Will it reach its ultimate goal or will it break down?

The Nature of the GCC: Contending Perceptions

The GCC, even to many of its constituent ruling elites, is something of a riddle. It occasionally eludes them as much as it puzzles close observers of Gulf affairs. Its nature and what it stands for was hardly clear at the outset, and it is certainly no clearer today. If anything, the riddle is increasingly becoming wrapped in mystery. What precisely did the six Arab Gulf states have in mind when they decided to join together to form the GCC? The thinking behind the formation of the GCC remains a closely guarded secret. Most likely, however, there was not so much sober thinking as there was an immediate, ad hoc reaction to the turbulent regional events of 1979–80—the Iranian revolution and the beginning of the Iraq-Iran war.

It is critical to note that the typically recalcitrant and normally conservative Arab Gulf states took less than three months (February to May 1981) to unanimously agree on the broad ideas and goals of the GCC, approve of its final charter, sign many intricate documents on rules and structures, and hastily announce its formal birth in May 25, 1981 (Christie 1987, 10). Such extraordinary speed is practically unheard of in the history of regional integration and is particularly uncharacteristic of the rulers of the six Arab Gulf states whose normal tendency is to procrastinate on a decision with potential ramifications for their sovereignty.

If anything, this speedy implementation of the yet-to-be refined and comprehended ideas of cooperation only confirms the widely held belief that the GCC was more of a hasty reaction than a calculated initiative (al-Alkim 1994). It also indicates that abnormal circumstances were decisive in defining the GCC's initial scope and vision. In essence, the GCC was a panic response to a situation of profound uncertainty which enormously shaped its nature and its subsequent unfolding.

When the GCC was originally conceived, there were at least three contending perceptions of its nature and what it should stand for (Ramazani 1988, 1–3). The three were hurriedly juxtaposed and incorporated in the GCC Charter. This lumping together of plainly contradictory ideas further complicated the question as to what was being created, what it should be doing, and what it was for and what it was against. Initially, Kuwait advanced its vision of the GCC. It had in mind virtually nothing specific beyond a nonbinding Gulf common market, perhaps loosely analogous to the European community but not necessarily a replica of the European Economic Common Market. The principal emphasis in this version of the GCC was economic and social integration.

On the other hand, Oman's view of the nature of the GCC was pointedly specific. It had in mind a purely military alliance. Oman was keen on creating nothing short of a Gulf version of NATO or the Warsaw Pact. The regional and international enemies against whom this military alliance was directed were perfectly clear to Oman: Iran, South Yemen, and the Soviet Union. That is why Oman unequivocally stressed that this military alliance should openly and intimately coordinate its activities and strategies with the United States, the only superpower supposedly friendly to the six Arab Gulf states.

Saudi Arabia also had plans for the GCC. The Saudis were eager neither for economic integration nor formal military cooperation between the six Arab Gulf states. Their priority was political and it was twofold. First and foremost was internal security and the preservation of the political status quo in the region. The GCC, according to the Saudi plan, would primarily provide the six states with a sense of collective security while each individually pursued its own policies and interests. Secondly, Saudi Arabia viewed the GCC as a fairly pliable and probably useful vehicle to promote its own foreign policy and diplomatic interests. The GCC would boost Saudi Arabia's political standing vis-à-vis its regional power competitors—Iran and Iraq—in a region that was beginning to be thought of as a Saudi sphere of influence.

The relatively smaller states of the GCC—Bahrain, Qatar and the United Arab Emirates—did not have specific plans of their own. To them, the regional threat loomed large, and it mingled in their minds with those positive ideals and goals that are rightly associated with cooperation and integration. In retrospect, it is obvious that they knew little of what was taking place. Some even suspected that the GCC might be a maneuver to bring them either into the Saudi saddlebag or into what was then considered an "unholy alliance" with the United States (Graz 1990, 228). However, they happily followed the lead of the others, especially Saudi Arabia. Quite predictably, they could not openly oppose the wishes of their purportedly trustworthy bigger neighbors. To them the GCC was potentially an added insurance policy. It provided a convenient shelter for their monarchical regimes and helped to prevent radical groups or movements from gaining momentum in their newly independent states. As small states they stood to gain handsomely from economic and military cooperation, as well as security coordination, both immediately and in the long run.

All Things To All People

Even today the nature of the GCC has yet to be clearly defined. It has clearly evolved into all things to all people. Each of the member states has its own perceptions and expectations. Some now, more than before, emphasize its economic integration function. Others vigorously advocate greater military cooperation. Still others remain exclusively fixated on internal security as the principal objective of the GCC. Periodically, the GCC has vacillated among all these tenuous functions and expectations. It has yet to drop anchor at any one of them for a sustained period of time. However, as it exists today, the GCC is none of the above: it is not an economic integration body, nor a military alliance, nor a full-fledged security community.

The GCC hardly qualifies as an integration venture. Integration refers to that process by which supernational institutions come to replace national ones. It is the gradual shifting upward of sovereignty from the state to a regional structure. The ultimate expression of integration would be the merger of several states into a single state. Functionally, integration proceeds from economic and technological developments which lead to more supernational interactions and structures. This necessitates greater political involvement, which in turn drives integration further (Haas 1958, 16). Integration is clearly too generous a term to apply to the GCC, except to point it out as a classic failure of economic and political integration. After a careful review of the GCC's economic achievements Erik Peterson concludes, "Because of these considerations it can not be said that the GCC economic program has transcended national sovereignty" (Peterson 1988, 229).

The GCC is manifestly neither a political nor a military alliance. An alliance is a formal pact between sovereign states. It stems from formal treaties between or among two or more states, binding them to collaborate on purely military or political issues. It is formed quickly during a period of intense ideological and political conflict in anticipation of a war for which collective resources and domestic energies and emotions are mobilized. A peculiar feature of an alliance is that it is formed deliberately against rather than for something. It is a determined collective effort to overcome an ideological, political, and military rival and to score a decisive victory. Short of that, one of the most pressing goals of alliance formation is to prevent an adversary from achieving a dominant international or regional position (Holsti et al. 1985). Clearly, while the GCC was partly conceived as a means of thwarting a bid for political and military hegemony by the larger regional states, it does not qualify as an alliance per se. It was probably never intended to be an alliance of any sort, let alone a military one. Since its inception the GCC has studiously done everything conceivable, in both word and deed, to avoid being perceived as an alliance against any nation.

If it is not an integration nor an alliance, is the GCC a security community? A security community refers to the attainment of a sense of community and institutions and practices that are strong and deep enough to assure durable and dependable expectations of peaceful exchange among the states in a given regional system. The bottom-line requirement for the formation of a security community is a reliable expectation of nonviolent relations between the involved states (Deutsch 1957). Beyond this, a security community can take many forms. Some involve formal mergers between members and the development of supreme central institutions with power to take binding decisions. The GCC, while ensuring relatively peaceful coexistence between its member states, does not add up to this form of security community. It patently lacks a central institution capable of making legally binding decisions (Angel in Sandwick 1987, 106–49). Even the decisions of the Supreme Council, the highest authority in the GCC's hierarchy, are not legally binding. The Secretariat General, furthermore, has no enforcement power apart from moral suasion, and even this moral authority is becoming increasingly marginal.

The GCC does, however, qualify as a fairly loose and heterogeneous security community. This type of security community falls short of legal merger and opts instead for close cooperation among its essentially autonomous member states. Even so, while the GCC enjoys a strong sense of community and peaceful coexistence, there have been a number of unexpected hostile incidents between GCC member states. Most of these violent conflicts were short-lived clashes limited to border disputes. Yet they nearly shattered the tranquility of peaceful coexistence within the community. These lingering border disputes—between Bahrain and Qatar, for example—have yet to be satisfactorily addressed. They likely will resurface, and hence remain a potential trigger for further violent incidents and community disintegration.

The Charter of the GCC is of no help in clarifying its nature and specifying its political philosophy. The Charter generously employs lofty terms such as unity, integration, cooperation, and coordination. These are used casually and interchangeably to describe the immediate objectives and the ultimate goals of the GCC. In the two-paragraph preamble of the Charter, the term "unity" appears twice, "integration" and "coordination" each appear three times, and "cooperation" is mentioned five times. The term "unity," referring to the political unity of the six Arab Gulf states, is described as the ultimate goal of the GCC. "Integration" is reserved for the more mundane social and economic fields. "Cooperation" and "coordination" turn up in connection with political and policy-related interests. The Charter speaks openly of the ultimate aim of unity and of an eventual confederal union of the GCC states. As to the more immediate objectives, article four of the Charter mentions such far-reaching goals as achieving cooperation in all fields, strengthening links in different fields, establishing similar systems in all fields including the economy, commerce, communications, legislation, administration, and, not least, technology. Conspicuously missing in the Charter is any specific reference to cooperation in the field of security and defense. Yet security has been consistently the most visible preoccupation of the GCC. It is an open secret that while volumes of press releases and official statements have kept up the charade of a focus on economic cooperation, the urgent concerns and discussions within the GCC have actually focused on defense and internal security (Nakhleh 1986, 8).

This seemingly unwitting constitutional ambiguity inevitably heightens the confusion about the actual nature of the GCC. It is tempting to simply brand the GCC as a one-of-a-kind institution (Christie 1987, 14). But this characterization only evades the need to seriously scrutinize the GCC, especially when it claims to have pioneered an era of regional integration in the Arab world. In short, whether it is a unique or a standard cooperation and integration initiative, today it is manifestly easier to identify what the GCC is not than affirm what it is.

This lingering doubt about the GCC's true nature is of course linked to the still more ambiguous issue of its origin. Even today, the origin of the GCC is open to dispute. The central unresolved question is: what factor(s) precisely gave rise to the GCC? Was affinity or necessity fundamentally responsible? Was the GCC a natural product of a long history of association between the six Arab Gulf states or was it basically an immediate response to the sudden turbulent regional events of 1979–80? In other words, was internal or external cause more important in the final decision to establish the GCC? The more general and perhaps more relevant question is: under what conditions are cooperation and integration among states likely to occur?

The Origin of the GCC

According to the realist theory of international politics, states rarely engage in cooperation and integration (Waltz 1979, 106). The gains to states are not sufficient to initiate cooperation, which is ordinarily permeated with strategic uncertainties (Lida 1993). Interestingly, states often become even more reluctant when one state realizes in the process of cooperation that possible gains may favor others more than itself. Even in the most unlikely case, where there are absolute gains to all members, states do not promote cooperation so long as each fears how the other will use its increased capabilities. The "self-centered" nature of international politics is such that it rarely encourages nations, especially newly independent states, such as the GCC states, to initiate regional cooperation and integration.

The GCC rather is a deviation from this allegedly ironclad rule of international politics. Despite the theoretical improbability, the GCC was born. Its member states are earnestly engaged in conscious policy coordination in all fields. These states, despite uncertainties, have found it desirable to cooperate to pursue mutual interests and to realize potential tangible gains. They willingly, though incrementally, adjust their expectations and actions and adopt to the logic of policy harmonization, so that all eventually end up better off than they would have otherwise. They seem to appreciate the largely beneficial consequences of interstate cooperation and coordination.

The GCC seems to be not only a theoretical but also an empirical oddity. It is possibly the only contemporary cooperation venture for which objective domestic realities had absolutely no relevance for its initiation. Strangely enough, the GCC is not a product of local social pressure since there are virtually no political parties or interest groups, apart from the ruling families, credible enough to push the GCC states toward regional cooperation. The GCC is detached from internal social realities. It has no broad popular base. Its social base is nearly as narrow as the ruling families and as limited as the six heads of state. Equally, the GCC is not a product of any particular economic development or technological advancement. It is not demand driven, and it does not follow the usual logic of spillover, as the liberal and functionalist theory of integration would maintain (See Keohane 1984). Technological and industrial advances, which liberal theorists posit as the principal cause of regional integration (witness the European common market), have little if any relevance to the creation of the GCC. Functional and structural spillover did not directly launch the GCC.

The GCC is equally an anomaly in its regional setting. Contrary to a widely held belief, the Gulf region is not conducive to ideas of peaceful coexistence and regional cooperation. The Gulf, which is composed of eight states (the GCC countries, Iran, and Iraq) that vary in size and importance, is a chronically conflict-oriented region (Abdulla 1994). There have been more serious occasions of conflict and dispute than occasions of cooperation and peaceful coexistence among these eight states. Throughout their modern history, these geographically clustered states have engaged in conflicts in many forms: tribal wars, border wars, oil wars, and not least, political and ideological wars (Litwak 1993). Notwithstanding the settlement of some border issues in recent years, most of these ongoing conflicts remain dormant and regularly reemerge to catalyze fresh conflict.

Hence, when it comes to the Gulf region, dispute is the rule, whereas institutionalized peaceful coexistence and cooperation is the exception (Abdulla 1994, 2). One might say that the GCC as an integration project was certainly a rational idea, but that it was established in an inhospitable environment. Its purposes seem antithetical to the fractious and parochial characteristic of Gulf politics. Certainly, such an endemically conflict-oriented region desperately needs confidence-building initiatives such as the GCC. The only problem is the essentially exclusivist predilection of the GCC ruling elites. In addition, of course, the current GCC formula notably excludes the Gulf's two largest states: Iran and Iraq.

In the absence of a region-wide expansion of the GCC, the Gulf will remain a tense region. The GCC's creation has only deepened political rifts among the major regional powers because Iran and Iraq are understandably suspicious of GCC intentions and motivations (al-Alkim 1994). They justifiably view the GCC as a tool of Saudi diplomacy which aims to assume a greater regional role at their expense. It is precisely since the birth of the GCC that Gulf conflicts have become distinctly more violent and bloody. The last two tragic Gulf wars amply testify to this higher level of brutality. Since the creation of the GCC, Gulf disputes have also tended to attract unusual international interest. Purely Gulf conflicts instantly transcend regional confinement and are transformed into acute crises with massive global consequences (Heikal 1993).

The GCC was born despite overwhelming odds and can only be attributed to complex sets of internal and external causes. These include, among other things: unique family and tribal ties, deep socioeconomic similarities, identical political and cultural values and beliefs, shared historical experience, intense dependency on oil and oil revenues, geographic proximity, a distinct pattern of interstate interactions, a common perception of friends and enemies, a sudden change in the regional balance of power, the emergence of an anti–status-quo regime in Iran, the outbreak of the Iran-Iraq war, the Soviet invasion of Afghanistan, intensified superpower rivalries in and around the Gulf region, emerging Saudi diplomatic assertiveness, and growing American apprehension about the Gulf security and its vital interests in this highly strategic region.

Each one of these important factors played a role in the making of the GCC. Undoubtedly, considering the many odds against its creation, all of these factors had to combine to create a decisive push in the direction of its official launching. The question as to which one of these factors or combination of factors is more decisive is still as valid as it was in 1981. One way to resolve this question would be to classify all the possible causal factors into two broad variables: ideological affinity and objective necessity. The GCC is a product of both these variables. They have contributed equally to its birth, first as mere idea and then as actual reality. Cultural and ideological affinity is structurally the constant cause. It has been around for centuries and most likely will persist as an ongoing source of harmony among the six Arab Gulf states. Ideological affinity unequivocally set the idea of the cooperation in motion well before the official establishment of the GCC. Objective necessity, however, was and is the catalyst behind the GCC's creation and continuance. It invariably asserts its primacy and urgency under specific circumstances and at given historical junctures. It usually plays a decisive role in transforming latent ideas into action. Hence, factors of affinity as the background cause, and factors of necessity as the efficient cause, jointly gave rise to the GCC in 1981.

Building Blocks for Cooperation

A sense of community, or what Deutsch (1957, 123) calls "compatibility of major values," is an essential condition for the formation of amalgamated or pluralistic security communities; clearly it is also necessary for regional cooperation in general. Any serious attempt at cooperation and integration presupposes the existence of national and ideological affinity that goes well beyond expediency and rationally calculated self-interest. It is universally acknowledged that states with similar characteristics are more likely to cooperate than dissimilar ones (Axelrod 1984). In the case of the GCC states, their political and ideological affinity is, quite simply, exceptional.

What binds them together is a common religion, Islam, a common language, Arabic, and a common heritage and tribal background which is earnestly preserved despite rapid modernization. They also enjoy a common system of governments which are basically single-family, single-tribe centered (Gause 1994). Except perhaps for Saudi Arabia, they all fit neatly into the category of physically, militarily, and even psychologically small states (al-Ebrahim 1983). In addition, there is a shared history, geographic proximity, and a roughly equal standard of living, which has been inflated by oil revenues. Similarly, their economies are totally oil based and their societies are predominantly subsidized, which has created a "rentier mentality" and a relaxed way of life peculiar to the GCC states (al-Naqeeb 1990). These and many other sociopolitical commonalities and exceptional qualities bind the GCC states together. They have effectively and skillfully used their unique political and ideological attributes to their advantage and formed an apparently exclusive club.

Beyond the visible harmony of its states, the GCC benefited greatly from the personal and psychological affinity of its founding fathers. Elite affinity in this case is unprecedented, and certainly more true and relevant to the formation of the GCC than the normal and perhaps exaggerated affinity between its states. The GCC leaders live next to each other not only in space and time, but also quite palpably in cognitive framework. Epistemologically and psychologically, they belong to the same paradigm. They are a group of rulers who speak, think, and act in tandem and usually have no fear of being misunderstood by each other. This is especially so when it comes to the question of preserving their way of life and the one-family form of government. Understandably, the ruling families take an active interest in each other's welfare and longevity.

These rulers made the right decision at precisely the right moment with hardly a ripple of dissent. Their decision to establish the GCC instantly proved a winner. There was an element of enormous simplicity in the formation of the

GCC: it was conceived purely as a process of elite integration. Its conception was entirely consistent with the unusually personalized politics of the GCC states (Gause 1994, 143), and despite rigorous bureaucratic attempts to deepen its scope and mandate, it has been and will remain deliberately elitist.

While ideological and personal affinity are essential ingredients here, hardcore interests rather than sentimental ties are what eventually led to the development of cooperation. States formally join together to achieve tangible domestic and foreign policy goals and cooperate to enhance each other's security. That is why cooperation becomes not merely desirable but actually indispensable under acute circumstances. A specific situation must exist to justify the development of cooperation. Indeed, cooperation is entirely unnecessary under normal circumstances: when relative harmony prevails, a state might be unwilling to cooperate in such a way as to benefit its partner state. However, failure to cooperate under acute circumstances may lead to devastating consequences, especially for vulnerable states such as those constituting the GCC (Ahrari and Noyes 1993).

The extraordinary regional and international circumstances of 1979–80 left the six small Arab Gulf states with no choice but to coordinate policies. The GCC was at the time an objective necessity. The unstable situation in the region triggered the process of the formalization of cooperation. Rapidly unfolding events presented the GCC states with formidable challenges, dangers, and ultimately choices that necessitated a major transformation of the usual thought process. The logic of the situation demanded a higher degree of security and military consultation and closer political coordination.

The most threatening aspect of the 1979–80 events was surely the Islamic revolution in Iran, which quickly led to the downfall of the Shah (Ramazani 1988, 6). The Arab Gulf rulers viewed with utmost alarm this abrupt termination of the most powerful monarchic regime in the Gulf. These rulers, for better or worse, had grown accustomed to the Shah and his somewhat grandiose regional design. In many ways the Shah was just like them: a monarch, a strategic ally of the West, a relentless enemy of communism, a cogent defender of the regional status quo. His sudden downfall was shocking and believed to be a bad omen.

Worse yet was his replacement. A menacing Islamic revolutionary republic was a complete contrast to the largely moderate regime of the Shah. The new revolutionary regime in Iran did everything possible to heighten fears among the already timid and vulnerable Arab Gulf states. It immediately raised questions about their Islamic credentials—long an indispensable pillar of their legitimacy. It exposed their "unholy" ties with the West, particularly the United States, which formed the bedrock of their security underpinnings. Furthermore, the new revolutionary regime made it amply clear that it intended to actively export its Islamic revolution to its neighboring countries and, with God's help, to the rest of the world (Manashri 1990). For the Arab Gulf states to face up to this radical and revolutionary regime, cooperation was inevitable. It was no longer a luxury, nor even a free choice. It was simply an urgent objective necessity.

On top of this political and ideological challenge came the Iran-Iraq War in September 1980, a direct consequence of the downfall of the Shah. The war proved to be not only the longest interstate war of the twentieth century but, more important, the bloodiest conflict in the recorded history of the Gulf (Hiro 1990). The human, social, and economic destruction it caused far exceeded any imaginable expectations (al-Nasrawi 1986). It shattered the relaxed and easygoing mode of the Gulf of the 1970s. All these benign feelings—the general sense of optimism associated with the 1973 oil boom and the dreams of building the new and modern welfare state—vanished as the war raged and grew ever more threatening. The whole region was in state of untenable war; defense and security instantly became the top priority. The commitment of the regimes to sociopolitical change waned. Foreign involvement in Gulf affairs reached an all-time high. Oil prices plummeted, and oil, once the supreme element of bargaining power, was no longer a credible resource.

At such an incredible moment, the mood inescapably supported a collective response and concrete cooperation, especially since there were no psychological impediments to policy coordination at the decisionmaking level. A summit of cooperation-makers was promptly convened in Abu Dhabi on May 25, 1981. In a tableau of unity the six rulers initialed the official establishment of the GCC and proclaimed a new era of cooperation which no one had thought was possible in such a tension-prone region. It is now time to ask: has the GCC fulfilled its economic, political, and military objectives?

GCC Process: Euphoria and Stalemate

Given the right blend of affinity and necessity, states can engage in regional cooperation and integration. But once cooperation is officially put in motion, it invariably experiences moments of both noticeable breakthrough and dismal breakdown. Failures and successes alternate, and both are an integral part of the process of building and consolidating integration and cooperation (See Nye 1968, 859). At the center of all cooperation and integration processes runs an underlying tension between national and supranational loyalties. This tension accounts for the frequent go and occasional stop of cooperation between states, those of the GCC included. Since its inception, the GCC has routinely oscillated between short-lived euphoria and agonizing protracted stalemate. Yet one thing did not happen: the GCC did not break apart.

At the most fundamental level, then, the GCC's principal achievement has been the fact of its establishment and its endurance thereafter. Its sustainability since its inception, in and of itself, is impressive. The six GCC states, remarkably, have maintained their apparent cohesiveness. No defection has occurred nor was one seriously contemplated by any member state, no matter how dissatisfied.

As fundamental as this achievement sounds, it is markedly timid and marginal compared to the grandiose stated goals of the GCC. In this context, survival is a nonachievement achievement. The GCC, as illustrated, came into being as the result of objective necessity, not free choice. Necessity is the cement that binds them still. Dangers lurk ominously just around the corner: Iran, Iraq, foreign workers, Islamic fundamentalism, and social tensions. The internal and external threats are sufficient to keep these states within the boundaries of the GCC shelter, a calculatedly worthwhile political and security guarantee in times of crisis as well as in more normal times.

More specifically, the GCC has achieved one of its overriding individual and collective objectives, namely to make it through the turbulent period following the events of 1979–80. The central goal of the GCC during this extraordinary period was survival of its member states. The GCC states survived the ideological onslaughts of the Islamic revolution in Iran. They stayed as clear as possible from the eight-year-long Iran-Iraq war without having been sucked into it. They dealt wisely with the regional and international consequences of the 1980 Soviet invasion of Afghanistan, and stayed out of the entangled superpower rivalries steadily submerging the Gulf region. They even survived the end of the oil boom era and the subsequent economic and financial austerity of the 1980s. At the end of a turbulent decade, GCC states found themselves surprisingly unscathed. This was an undeniable success, and a great deal of the credit for it deservedly goes to the GCC (Graz 1990, 262).

Nonetheless, these states frankly admit that they do not place significant faith in the GCC's ability to guarantee their security and survivability. This became particularly clear after the August 2, 1990, Iraqi invasion of Kuwait, which severely tested GCC's security and military credentials. It is damning evidence of the GCC's failure in security matters that its states unilaterally opted for foreign protection and are now more hopelessly dependent on external military protection than ever before (al-Alkim 1994). Foreign, primarily American, military protection is an ever-present and embarrassing reminder to the GCC states that in its absence they would not likely survive for long.

This issue of security and survival aside, the GCC, true to its stated goals, has measurably increased official coordination and interstate interactions in almost every field since its inception. In terms of consistency and frequency of official meetings, the GCC's record is outstanding. The meetings of the Supreme Council—the GCC's highest authority, composed exclusively of heads of states—are extremely regular. Their frequency is probably unmatched by any other meetings of Arab heads of state (Anthony in Sindlar 1988; and Peterson 1988, 43). Since the creation of the GCC until 1996, the Supreme Council has been convened 17 times.

Equally important is the frequency of the meetings of the Ministerial Council, composed of the foreign ministers of each state. The Ministerial Council, which acts as the executive branch of the GCC, had met 59 times as of March 1996—nearly four meetings per year. Resolutions on substantive matters have been discussed and approved, which in turn has deepened cooperation in economic, social, and political fields. Other cabinet-level meetings have been as prolific and as productive as the Ministerial Council meetings. During the GGC's existence, for example, GCC ministers of finance have met 40 times; minister of commerce and economics 22 times; ministers of petroleum 21 times; ministers of transportation and communication 20 times; ministers of information 17 times; ministers of interior 15 times; ministers of defense 14 times; ministers of education 12 times; and ministers of justice 7 times. In addition, there have been hundreds of other regular cabinet and high-level official and unofficial meetings, and thousands of lower-level meetings to deliberate issues of common concern (GCC Documents 1995).

These meetings have had a certain significance. They have achieved at least a modicum of the institutional integration necessary to turn mutual ideas into joint legislation. Sadly, however, they have been typically high on talk and low on action. Putting words into action is proving to be extraordinarily difficult. The GCC is only forward-looking when it comes to high-profile summit meetings that produce ceremonious declarations and lofty pronouncements. Very few of these words have been matched by substance. Hence, the GCC is far from acting in concert on either domestic or foreign policy. On the contrary, and in spite of elegant meetings and declarations, absolutely none of the traditional prerogatives of national sovereignty have been forfeited in favor of the supranational authority. In fact, the GCC rulers seem to have studiously avoided this, as the GCC is already irritating some sensitive nerves of national interests (Peterson 1988, 232).

Implicitly, the ground rule among the founding fathers was that the GCC would not be allowed to develop beyond its point of origin, that is, as a malleable organization designed to promote the harmonization of elite concerns.

The six rulers, while they may settle for increased coordination among their officials and states, watchfully guard against any further institutional and policy integration that threatens their uneasy personal and constitutional authority (*World Press* 1995). This lends the GCC a brittle quality. What the rulers once did, they can also—at any moment—undo. The GCC remains structurally foundationless. It is, like many other grand projects in the Gulf, a house perilously built on sand. But as long as it remains convenient and the six rulers find it politically expedient and personally satisfying to announce, now and then, broad policy outlines that are high on declaratory rhetoric, but pointedly low on specifics, the GCC will stand.

Economically, the GCC's most concrete achievement has been the unified economic agreement that was adopted with great ceremony during its second summit meeting in 1981. This 28-article document was proclaimed the concrete framework for the economic integration of the GCC states. The nonbinding agreement, typically replete with generalities, calls for elimination of custom duties, coordination of import and export policies, free movement of labor and capital, joint oil, industrial, and technological policies, construction of a common economic infrastructure, establishment of a unified investment strategy, and coordination of financial and monetary policies. As it turns out, very few of these ambitious plans have advanced beyond voluminous quantities of paper work and uncounted hours of technical committee meetings. The once-vigorous talk of immediate economic integration of the GCC states remains just talk (al-Kuwaiz 1983–84, 45). More disappointingly, even economic cooperation has fallen sharply on the GCC's list of priorities. The GCC states realize that there is little need for the integration of their essentially self-propelled oil-based economies. Furthermore, each GCC state is currently overwhelmed by its own recurring budget deficits and unusual financial hardship.

Militarily, regional events have given the GCC no choice but to focus almost exclusively on defense and security concerns. Despite a high proclivity for cooperation in the military field, even here no major breakthrough has been forthcoming. The most noticeable achievement is the regular annual meeting between the armed forces chiefs of staff and ministers of defense. Additionally, pan-GCC military exercises were conducted in 1983, 1984, and 1987. In 1984, the GCC established the Peninsular Shield, a purely symbolic and inherently impotent joint force combining units of all six states. The GCC has yet to build a credible system of deterrence and defense (Dietl 1991). Ironically, conventional wisdom now considers it more prudent for each GCC state to strengthen its own security and defense infrastructure and separately negotiate and sign defense agreements with the United States, the ultimate military power in the Gulf (Yetiv 1995), as a first step toward an integrated military system.

Politically, the GCC has scored some major achievements by diligently creating images of unity both in domestic policy and foreign affairs. The GCC deliberately promotes itself as a group of exceptionally similar states that are not only interacting and coordinating regularly through shared institutions, but also significantly developing an unmistakable sense of common regional identity. The gradual centralization of regional identity, which is a natural outcome of an increase in interstate interactions, is the GCC's principal political achievement.

The GCC has also emerged by now as an internationally recognized regional organization with clout. In the Arab world, the GCC is envied for its record-breaking endurance (al-Shraidah 1995). It is considered as an illustrative example, if not a prototype, of a potentially successful Arab regional integration experiment. The GCC is readily perceived, at least by the international community, as a unified political actor. It certainly appears to act as a body in the United Nations and similar international governmental and nongovernmental gatherings (See al-Alkim 1994). The wide range of diplomatic activities carried out by the GCC since 1981 has acquired a distinct and recognizable Gulf character. The GCC, and needless to say oil, are the most visible vehicles for so-called Gulf diplomacy, which is branching out well beyond the confines of the region and the Arab world. The GCC has been effectively utilized as a tool to achieve the goals of Gulf diplomacy through close and productive consultation between its states.

Disintegrative Pressures

Even in the political field, the GCC has by no means replaced the individual foreign policies of its member states. It is, of course, difficult to gauge just how far the GCC states sincerely want commonality in their foreign policy. Oman continues to maintain a rather peculiar foreign policy orientation toward Iran, Iraq, the Palestinian issue, and alliance with the United States. Kuwait, certainly before the Gulf War, had its own interpretation of world politics. The UAE, too, perhaps influenced by Oman, has ventured into an independent foreign policy. More recently, the small state of Qatar has emerged as the unlikely maverick member of the GCC. It is fiercely asserting its unilateral foreign policy strategy vis-à-vis Iran, Iraq, and even Israel without undue regard for other GCC states' interests and sensitivities. Saudi Arabia, however, still exerts, at least behind the scenes, the greatest political influence within the GCC. Most GCC states at least pay lip service to the Saudi view of world politics. But Saudi influence is eroding measurably and the junior partners are acting more autonomously in defiance of Saudi political hegemony.

In short, the process of cooperation between the six Arab Gulf states is unexpectedly producing its exact opposite. The GCC states are visibly asserting their peculiarities and asserting their autonomy not only in foreign affairs but actually in all fields. These states are finding it extremely difficult to maintain even the minimum degree of cooperation. Lately, the chemistry among GCC states has not been great even at the elite level, as so clearly indicated by the Muscat fiasco and the controversy in 1997 over Qatar's decision to host the fourth annual Middle East regional economic meeting, with Israel in attendance, at a moment when the Arab-Israeli peace process was in a state of acute crisis. Appearances notwithstanding, on many policy issues the GCC states are clearly more divergent and less homogeneous than it was once assumed.

Disparities in views and capabilities between these states not only exist but in several crucial respects are also compelling. It is not true that all the GCC states are oil states: some (Saudi Arabia, Kuwait, and the UAE) are major oil producers, but others (Oman and Qatar are much smaller producers, and one (Bahrain) is effectively a non-oil state. It is not true, either, that all six of them are equally rich: some are super-rich, some are not so rich, and some are relatively poor. Nor is it true that all these states are monarchies. There is only one king among the six rulers; three others are emirs, one is a sultan (the only and perhaps the last sultan in the Arab world), and there is one lonely "president" (the UAE's Shaykh Zayid, who is periodically reelected by his own Supreme Council which is composed of six relatively independent shaykhs). Equally, it is not true that all the GCC states are conservative or traditional: some are indeed socially and politically conservative, and even reactionary; some are part modern and part traditional; and some are either socially or politically liberal. Furthermore, they are sharply different in size, stage of development, political experience and maturity, level of education, demographic composition, and economic and military capabilities. As a matter of fact, there is also considerable hidden animosity and flagrant suspicion among them. This is especially true of the smaller states, which invariably seek protection from being politically absorbed by the larger and more dominant states. Most significantly, even elite cohesiveness, the bedrock of the GCC, is cracking as a new and younger generation of rulers begin to replace the aging founding fathers. In this respect, the case of Qatar going off on its own is only an indication of things to come.

These diversities and differences are neither peripheral nor easily glossed over. They have existed all along but are now becoming more potent as disintegrative factors. They explain why integration has not been forthcoming and why cooperation has been and probably will remain bumpy. Nevertheless, it was undoubtedly a historical moment when the six GCC rulers first came together in Abu Dhabi. It is still a considerable achievement that they are able to stand united and meet annually in a spirit of politeness to discuss matters of mutual concern.

Endnotes

1. The topic of Gulf identity has generated lively discussions. For different views on this subject see the special edition of *Journal of Social Affairs* 9, 35 (Spring 1992) (In Arabic).

2. The first opinion survey to measure public attitudes toward the GCC was conducted by Shamlan Y. Al-Isa and Kamal al-Manufi in 1985, " Trends in Kuwaiti Public Opinion Regarding the GCC" (In Arabic). For a brief discussion of its findings see Emile Nakhleh, *The Gulf Cooperation Council, Policies, Problems an Prospects* (New York: Praeger, 1986), pp. 87–94.

References

Abdulla, Abdulkhaleq. "Gulf War: The Sociopolitical Background."*Arab Studies Quarterly*. (Summer 1994), 1–13.

Ahrari, M. E. and James H. Noyes, eds.*The Persian Gulf after the Cold War*. London: Praeger, 1993.

Al-Ahram Weekly. December 7–13, 1995.

Al-Alkim, Hassan.*The GCC States in An Unstable World*. London: Al-Saqi Books, 1994.

Al-Ebrahim, Hassan. *Kuwait and the Gulf*. Washington, DC: Center for Contemporary Arab Studies, Georgetown University, 1983.

"GCC Documents." GCC Secretariat, Riyadh, No. 40 (December 1995).

Al-Kuwaiz, Abdulla. "The GCC and Economic Integration."*American Arab Affairs* (Winter 1983), 84.

Al-Naqeeb, Khaldoun.*Society and State in the Gulf and Arabian Peninsular*. New York: Routledge, 1990.

Al-Nasrawi, Abbas. "Economic Consequences of the Iran-Iraq War."*Third World Quarterly* (July 1986).

Al-Qasimi, Sultan Bin Mohammed in R. K. Ramazani, ed. *The Gulf Cooperation Council: Records and Analysis*. Charlottesville, VA: University of Virginia, 1988.

Al-Shraidah, Abdulhadi.*The Gulf Cooperation Council*. Cairo: Madbouli Books, 1995. (in Arabic).

Al-Sharq al-Awsat. London (February 17, 1996),

Axelrod, Robert.*The Evolution of Cooperation*. New York: Basic Books, 1984.

Bishara, Abdulla. "The Gulf Cooperation Council: Achievements and Challenges."*American Arab Affairs* (Winter 1983–4), 41.

Christie, John. "History and Development of the GCC: a Brief Overview." In John A. Sandwick, ed. *The Gulf Cooperation Council*. Boulder: Westview Press, 1987, 10.

Deutsch, Karl. *Political Community and the North Atlantic Area: International Organization in the Light of Historical Experience.* Princeton, NJ: Princeton University Press, 1957.

Dietl, Gulshan.*Through Two Wars and Beyond: A Study of Gulf Cooperation Council.* New Delhi: Lancers Books, 1991.

Gause III, Gregory.*Oil Monarchies.* New York: Council of Foreign Affairs Books, 1994.

Graz, Liesl.*The Turbulent Gulf.* London: I. B. Tauris & Co., 1990.

———.*"Gulf Build Up."The Washington Post.* November 18, 1995.

———.*"The Gulf's Uneasy Rulers."World Press Review.* August 1995.

Haas, Ernest B.*The Uniting of Europe.* Stanford, CA: Stanford University Press, 1958, 16.

Heikal, Mohammed Hasanayn.*Gulf War: The Illusion of Power and Victory.* (In Arabic) Cairo: Al-Ahram Press, 1993.

Hiro, Dilip.*The Longest War.* London: Paladino, 1990.

Holsti, Ole, and P. Terrence Hopmann, and John D. Sullivan, eds.*Unity and Disintegration in International Alliances.* Lanham, MD: University Press of America, 1985.

Keohane, Robert. *After Hegemony: Cooperation and Discord in World Political Economy.* Princeton, NJ: Princeton University Press, 1984.

Lida, Keisuke. "Analytical Uncertainty and International Cooperation."*International Studies Quarterly* (December 1993), 431–57.

Litwak, Robert. *Security in the Gulf: Sources of Inter-State Conflicts.* London: Institute of International and Strategic Studies, 1993.

Manashri, David. *Iran: A Decade of War and Revolution.* New York: Holmes and Meier, 1990.

Nakhleh, Emile.*The Gulf Cooperation Council. Policies. Problems an Prospects.* New York: Praeger, 1986.

Nye, Joseph. "Comparative Regional Integration."*International Organization.* 22:4 (1968).

Peterson, Erik R. *The Gulf Cooperation Council: Search for Unity in a Dynamic Region.* Boulder, CO: Westview Press, 1988.

Ramazani, R. K., ed. *The Gulf Cooperation Council: Records and Analysis.* Charlottesville, VA: University of Virginia, 1988.

Sandwick, John A., ed. *The Gulf Cooperation Council.* Boulder, CO: Westview Press, 1987.

Sindlar, H. Richard III, and J. E. Peterson. *Crosscurrents in the Gulf.* New York: Routledge, 1988.

Waltz, Kenneth N.*Theory of International Politics.* Reading, MA: Addison-Wesley Co., 1979.

Yetiv, Steve A. *America and the Persian Gulf.* London: Praeger, 1995.

Zanoyan, Vahan. "After the Oil Boom, The Holiday Ends In the Gulf,"*Foreign Affairs* (Nov.–Dec. 1995).

I. William Zartman

Like much of the developing world, North Africa approaches regional integration on a number of levels. These levels differ from the economists' classical progression from free-trade zone to common economic area (Viner 1950; Belassa 1962) and also from the political scientists' notions of spillover and hegemony (Haas 1964, Lindberg and Scheingold 1970, Nye 1968).

The highest level is full political integration, with state commitments to reduce individual sovereignty in favor of a larger state formation. A second level, developmental integration, involves trade creation through larger market economies. Beneath these lies a third and looser level of diplomatic cooperation, characterized by momentary acts of unity that are not necessarily expected to endure. North African integration is firmly rooted in this lower level; it occasionally reaches into the second level but has never broached the commitments of the third. At the same time, each level creates its own counterpressures to downscale the cooperation, creating the cyclical dynamic so evident in the political evolution of the region.

The Region of the Maghrib

Unlike some groups of states pursuing integration—the United Arab Republic for example, or even the European Community (EC) or the Association of Southeast Asian Nations—the Maghrib constitutes a region, an island of similar and self-identifying people, mutually interacting and interdependent (Belaid and Zartman 1993). Although there is no single simple identifying term for North Africans in Arabic—

maghribi means "Moroccan," and national identifications are still the most widely used—there is still a sense of regional belonging and interaction when viewed from within as well as from without. Although North African states do not engage in much trade with each other (not more than 5 percent) and their currencies have long been mutually inconvertible, they meet in regional conferences, in Europe, and in transborder exchanges whenever possible, always with a great sense of *rétrouvailles* (reunion). Although their books and newspapers penetrate customs controls only with great difficulty and they intermarry relatively infrequently (no statistics are available), they live in each other's countries, speak mutually intelligible languages, and follow with apprehension the twists and turns of each other's political systems.

Many of the states in the region are long-established entities, as historic as any European state. Morocco is ruled by the oldest dynasty in the world (from 1666), and Morocco and Tunisia were consolidating their monarchies at the same time as were the nations of Europe. Their position as protectorates under colonial rule both attested to and helped to preserve their historic integrity. Algeria and Libya are newer creations (as states, not as societies), and Algeria's coherence as a state derives from its double revolutionary origins—one revolution at the hands of the French rulers who destroyed the Algerian polity, landownership, social structure, and cultural institutions, and the second at the hand of the Algerian nationalists who destroyed French rule. Mauritania is a very new and at best a very weak state even today, while Libya's strength as a state is hard to judge. Even established states show sudden and surprising weaknesses on occasion: Algeria was long a case where a "hard" state was confused with a "strong" state, in the technical sense of the terms (Rothchild and Chazan 1988; Migdal 1988); in fact, the state had ceased to function as a decisionmaking institution after the October 1988 riots. Nonetheless, even in such cases, state weakness does not promote the region as an alternative institution, but rather makes regional integration more difficult.

The region where these states are located has a clear structure. It begins with a population concentrated along the Mediterranean coast from Tripoli to Tangier, and the Atlantic coast from Tangier to Agadir, with the only populous penetrations into the interior being in the Gharb plain to Fes-Meknes and the Haouz plateau to Marrakesh. This means that the populous core of the region is parceled out among Morocco, Algeria, and Tunisia, and that the northern ends of their boundaries cross relatively heavily populated areas. As a result, Algeria occupies a keystone position in the region; it is the only state to border on more than two others and indeed the only one to be contiguous with all the states in the region, and some others as well. Morocco and Tunisia are entirely contained by their regional neighbors, whereas the other states of the region break out into other areas; Morocco's "breakout" is to the Atlantic, which gives it a different perspective than the others. However, the coastal core is not evenly apportioned among the component states: Morocco and Algeria have equivalent populations (about 24 million), whereas Tunisia is only a third their size. Both the equivalence and the disequilibrium are crucial elements in the region's dynamics, as will be pursued below.

The other determining feature of the region's structure is the population and power vacuum that surrounds the core. This periphery begins at the Atlas and Tell mountains to the north and west and runs south and east until it meets another region—West Africa and the Nile border of the Mashriq, respectively. This buffer zone forms an area of protection and expansion for the core, for population growth, development, and exploitation, all the more so because it contains rich resources (notably oil, gas, and phosphates). Like the core, however, the periphery is not evenly apportioned among the component states, nor is it even fully incorporated into the region. The keystone position of Algeria is reinforced by its possession of a large and central part of the Sahara, making it at 919,595 square miles nearly half again as large as Libya, three times as large as Morocco (including the Western Sahara) and nearly 15 times as large as Tunisia, which also has a small part of the periphery. Libya is mostly periphery and Mauritania is entirely so. The rest of the periphery is the territory of weak states of the Sahel—Mali, Niger, and Chad. The power vacuum in the Saharan periphery and its uneven apportionment among strong core and weak peripheral states also constitute a major element in regional dynamics.

The resulting dynamics arise from the result of a need among entities new as modern states to establish a sense of rank and relation among themselves in the region. This drive is a basic element in any regional relations and it becomes the powerful motor of history, as centuries of politics of the evolving state system in Europe and half a century of rivalry between Cold War superpowers have shown. In the Maghrib, the dynamic begins with the mixed equality (in population) and inequality (in territory and resources) between Morocco and Algeria, consecrated (but not initiated) by ideological differences between their regimes. The rivalry takes on all forms, from direct military confrontation to contestation for control of the periphery, from leadership of contending Third World alliances to competition for a favored position vis-à-vis the former metropole and Europe, and association with opposing superpowers. It also involves different views of regional integration, the Moroccan view being more pluralistic and the Algerian more hegemonistic (Zartman 1987).

Tunisia's position in this unfolding structure is clear and awkward. By its position, it is condemned to be a potential ally of Morocco's, under the Kautilyan dictum that "my neighbor is my enemy and my neighbor's neighbor is my friend" (Kautilya 1960; Modelski 1964). But its lack of weight forces it to defend its security by being a neutral peacemaker, as a protection both against domination by a powerful Algeria and against destruction of the region through bilateral conflict. As a result, Tunisia's view of regional relations is loosely integrationist, more egalitarian than Algeria's but more supranationalist than Morocco's.

Until the 1970s, Libya's position in the regional structure was as peripheral as Mauritania's is today (and Mauritania was not even in the region at the time). Libya functioned only as a kind of hinge between the Maghrib and the Mashriq. With oil and Muammar al-Qadhafi came the means and the ends for a new active role in the region, posing in its turn the question of rank and relations for Libya and hence its entry into the regional dynamics (Deeb 1991; Zartman and Kluge 1991). In Kautilyan terms, reinforced again by ideology, Libya is both a friend and an enemy of Algeria, a potential ally of Morocco, a meddler in the peripheral areas of the Western Sahara, Mali, Niger, and Chad, and a security threat to Tunisia. Before it ever invented its ideology, its role was structurally determined. Ideologically, however, its view of regional relations is tightly integrationist, since Qadhafi dislikes state divisions of the Arab (or Maghribi) nation and since Libya can only gain from acquiring what it lacks (new populations and territory) in exchange for what it has (correct leadership) through union with its neighbors.

As a result of this structural dynamic and of the attractiveness of the myth of unity, Maghribi states continually pursue the mythical goal in their fashion, yet often turn the search for unity into a cause for division. As Gamal Abdel Nasser learned when he vacillated between "Unity of Ranks" and "Unity of Purpose" (Kerr 1967), there is nothing so divisive as the pursuit of "proper" unity. Various North African states have frequently captured the regional flag as a rallying point for rivalry, bringing in some member states in an effort to isolate others. This remains the state of relations, as will be developed below. Thus both the ups and the downs of integration have been achieved in the name of a commitment to unity; they mark high and low points along the all-embracing path toward the achievement of the goal, not a waxing or waning of attachment to the goal itself. By the same token, as an integral part of the dynamic, when the pursuit of favorable unity (Unity of Purpose) becomes too divisive, and threatens to blow the region apart, one of the members—usually Tunisia, because of its calling born of its position— raises the banner of comprehensive unity with a call to pursue Unity of Ranks and overcome conflict.

Cycles of Integration

The interaction of these views of Maghrib unity with the structurally driven dynamics of the region has led to the ups and downs that have marked intra-Maghribi relations since before independence. In these cycles the most notable form of integration has been the diplomatic event, a meeting with no essential concern for institutionalization and continuity, whose main impact is achieved through the meeting itself. Even subsequent meetings of any organization established at the first meeting have been primarily further cases of diplomatic integration, where attendance was the matter of prime importance and durable decisions were suspect.

It must be emphasized that diplomatic integration is not just a meaningless formality. The very fact of attendance serves to reduce conflict, and further specific measures of conflict management may well take place during the meeting. These conflict-related meetings and decisions are not fraudulent or unimportant; to the contrary. But they are not accompanied by any expectation of or commitment to ongoing cooperation, which would constitute the next phase of integration. In the few cases where developmental integration, the next stage, has been reached, it has had to confront the counterpressures of conflict born of the structural dynamics already discussed.

Much has been written about the second and third phases of integration (Cantori and Spiegel 1970; Falk and Mendlovits 1973; Robson 1983; Mazzeo 1984; Onwuka and Sesay 1985; Wriggins 1992), but little of it has any relevance to the Maghrib because its integration has never reached firmly beyond the first stage. Developmental, or functional, integration involves the transfer of some economic and infrastructural activities to the regional level so that normal national activity in the same sector can no longer be accomplished alone. Such activities can remain under some control by individual states, and indeed the activities can be undertaken by nongovernmental organizations and nonstate actors pulling the state into greater integration. It can also be expected to arouse equivalent opposition from either private or public sectors who see benefit in the national status quo; the rise of this "equivalent and opposite force" is an aspect of integration that has generally not been given enough attention in the literature on integration. Only when that inertia and opposition is overcome and the balance of felt benefits tips in favor of cooperation can the second phase be said to be fully underway. Even then, developmental integration is an unstable intermediate stage, always under pressure either to fall back into national activities punctuated by diplomatic integration or to fall forward into political integration. Since the state is still the unit of the second stage, however, the tendency to back away from developmental integration is the greater of the two.

The decade of the 1950s was characterized by cooperation among the nationalist movements of the French colonial territories (Algeria, Morocco, Tunisia) and then by support for each other as Libya (in 1951) and then Morocco and Tunisia (in 1956) gained their independence. The highlight of the period was the Tangier conference of 1958, where the three countries' nationalist movements—two of them the major government parties—pledged common efforts in support of Algerian independence and other coordinated policy goals (Zartman 1987, 1–8). The meeting was a major instance of diplomatic integration, with no further effect.

The first half of the 1960s was a time of conflict, with major territorial disputes erupting between Tunisia and not-yet-independent Algeria in 1961, and between Morocco and newly independent Algeria in 1963. In between, the region was split between the two competing African Unity groups: the "radical" Casablanca Group (including Morocco, the Algerian Provisional Government, and, initially, Libya) and the "moderate" Monrovia Group (including Tunisia) (Zartman 1987, ch. 1). The pan-African split was resolved in the formation of the Organization for African Unity (OAU) in 1963, and the OAU in turn managed the Moroccan-Algerian border dispute (Wilde 1966; Touval 1972).

The second half of the decade was a period of cooperation reaching the level of developmental integration. The vehicle was the Maghribi Permanent Consultative Committee and its adjunct, the Committee for Industrial Cooperation, founded in 1964 (Slim 1980). The two organs continued to meet at the ministerial and experts' level throughout the decade until Qadhafi gained power in Libya and the autarkist developmental policies of Boumedienne in Algeria ended the participation of those nations in 1969.

In the early 1970s cyclical logic promised a period of renewed conflict followed by reconciliation, but the reverse occurred. The beginning of the decade saw attempts to restore cooperation by dampening conflict, with Tunisia taking the lead role in mediation. Morocco recognized Mauritania in 1969 and started a process of border settlement with Algeria which came to fruition in 1972 when they established, for the first time, a border across the Sahara between the two countries. These were important preconditions to any construction of closer unity. However, the process was interrupted by an extended period of fluctuating conflict between Tunisia and Libya, beginning in 1974 with the aborted Jerba union between the two countries, and, even more seriously, by the deep-seated conflict between Morocco and Algeria over the Western Sahara, after an initial agreement in 1974 to support Morocco's claims. The Saharan dispute was so important because it reflected the basic conflict between the two rivals over size (territory and resources) and over spatial relations, each seeing the other as "encircling" it (Damis 1983a; Zartman 1989, ch. 2).

Soon after the outbreak of the Western Sahara conflict in 1975, Algeria and Libya signed an agreement at Hassi Messaoud to share the burden of supporting the Polisario Front, the Western Saharan independence movement, and unite in supporting other causes. As the conflict raged, raising the danger of an open war between Algeria and Morocco despite their tacit agreement to avoid direct hostilities, Algeria again took Maghrib unity under its wing. In 1983 Algeria established a friendship treaty with Tunisia and Mauritania, explicitly refusing membership to Morocco and Libya (Meliani 1985; Ibrahimi 1988). To Algeria's surprise—and no one else's—Morocco and Libya united in turn in 1984, in a very similar treaty, which, again to no one's surprise, fell apart two years later (Deeb 1989). The call for integration which one would have expected Tunisia to sound, in order to dampen the conflict, was slow to come for inherent reasons: Tunisia felt threatened by its neighbors and feared that each might take integration as a pretext for dominance; while on the other side, the hostility between Morocco and Algeria was too deep and personalized under Hourani Boumedienne's reign (to 1978) and then too politicized under Chadli Benjedid (thereafter) to be susceptible to early reconciliation. It was not until the mid-1980s that a new wave of diplomatic integration was launched (Zartman 1989, ch. 20)[1].

In all of these ups and downs, there had been no effort to move beyond the level of diplomatic integration, where every meeting is its own reward, except for a few years under the auspices of the Maghribi Permanent Consultative Committee (CPCM, in its French abbreviation) in the late 1960s. The dominant motor in cycles of relations has been the search for security within a structural dynamic, in which cooperation is as threatening as conflict, and unity as divisive as dispute. By leaving the CPCM in the hands of economic ministers, whose credits were to be won primarily by tending the domestic economy, even this level of developmental integration became an exercise in defense rather than in construction. At its best, Maghrib unity became a superpatriotic call for a momentary truce, rather like playing the national anthem to control a postgame melee. If integration was ever to move to the next level, something more would be required beyond merely the need to suspend escalating conflict that threatened to break up the family.

The UMA: A New Phase?

Maghribi states draw together in an exercise of diplomatic integration when they need to emerge from a conflict that threatens the integrity of the region. Such integration is only momentary: although the event can be repeated several times if necessary and mutually useful, it carries no presumption of durability. For integration to climb to the next level, one of two conditions is necessary— either an external challenge or an internal hegemon (Deutsch 1957). Although the latter possibility is theoretically conceivable, no state can or will play the hegemonic role for North African integration in the current situation. Algeria is the obvious candidate, but it is so deeply caught up in the structural dynamics of rank and rivalry that it cannot act as a unifier, and any attempt by it to do so would merely provoke even greater opposition and structural dynamics. The Algeria-Tunisia-Mauritania friendship treaty of 1983, renewed in spirit in 1996, is a case in point. However, because of its dynamism, its weight, and its central position, any Maghribi cooperation scheme would require Algerian commitment and participation. Algerian defection undid the CPCM in 1969, and Algerian support is crucial for the success of any pan-Maghribi integration, whether developmental or political.

A mild external challenge—or rather a competition—played a role in each of the peaks in the cycle. The 1958 Tangier meeting with Algeria, Tunisia, and Morocco was stimulated in part by competing challenges from the Mashriq, where both the United Arab Republic joining Egypt and Syria and the Union of Arab States (UAS) between Jordan and Iraq were formed in February 1958 (al-Sayyid, chapter 5 in this volume; Deeb 1991). Similarly, the CPCM corresponded—and responded—to efforts to build an Egyptian-Syrian-Iraqi union in 1963 (Kerr 1967, 69–95; Deeb 1991). Similar conditions were present in 1989, when the Gulf Cooperation Council stimulated the creation of an Arab Cooperation Council of Egypt, Jordan and Iraq (Dessouki 1994).

For the first time at the end of the 1980s, however, a stronger and truly external threat was present. It took the form of an enlarging and closing Europe that contained its major suppliers of Mediterranean products within harmonized tariff walls and excluded their competitors (Aghrout and Sutton 1990). The admission of the Iberian countries to the then EC and the passage of the Single Europe Act (SEA), both in 1986, posed the challenge to North Africa that it must combat Europe with a united front and build trade and industry through an integrated region. The target date for meeting the challenge was 1992, when the SEA was to take effect. The closing of Europe to North African emigrants, rising racial animosity against those already established in Europe, and the shift of European attention to the more developed product and labor markets of the East all compounded the external challenge.

The stalemate in the Western Saharan war by 1981 led the parties to seek a political solution and to find ways to get on with Maghribi business. The Morocco-Algerian summits at Akid Lotfi and Zouj Bghal in May 1987, their joint declaration of May 1988, and the five-state Maghribi summit during the larger Arab summit in Zeralda in June 1988 bore fruit. The Algerian friendship treaties with Tunisia and Mauritania and with Libya were superseded by a new, all-Maghribi summit and commitment among the five states on February 17, 1989, at Marrakesh. The Maghrib Arab Union (UMA) was formed to develop institutionalized cooperation among its members (treaty text in Daoud 1989).

The treaty of Marrakesh overcame many of the problems of past attempts at integration. It provided for a regular twice-yearly meeting of the heads of state, the only figures capable of taking binding decisions. It also provided for a secretariat and planned for periodic agreements on further, specific areas of cooperation and integration. Yet, despite these wise elements, the UMA has still not moved beyond the dominating characteristics of diplomatic integration to developmental integration.

Seven regular summits have been held to date, including Marrakesh.[2] Only the first and third had full attendance: Maaouya Ould Taya was absent from Tunis, King Hassan II from Ras Lanuf, and Qadhafi from Casablanca, each for those minor political reasons typical of diplomatic integration disputes. The twice-yearly rotating presidency occasioned much complicated maneuvering among the heads of state; Hassan II claimed the first 10 and a half months, Qadhafi lost his place in the order, Ould Taya lost his turn completely.

It took two summits to confront and three summits to make the important institutional decisions, again linked to the allocation of positions within the Union. The third summit issued agreements on an agricultural common market, investment guarantees, phytosanitary coordination, elimination of double taxation, and land transit and transport measures (Soudan 1990). The fourth summit decided to create a free trade area by 1992 and a common market by 1995, as proposed by Algeria during its presidency (Soudan 1991a). But no implementing decisions for either have been undertaken. The last three summits were taken up with political problems, including the Gulf War in 1991, the alleged Libyan terrorist destruction of the airliner over Lockerbie after 1992, and the Saharan conflict after 1994. At the end of 1995, Morocco called for a suspension of the Union over the Saharan issue, and there was another round of diplomatic maneuvering. The following two years were spent reaffirming the existence of the Union by the other members and gradually trying to win from Morocco an acknowledgement that the UMA's inactivity did not warrant suspension but rather that its potential merited continued support.

As the summit of the Union, the twice-yearly presidential council meetings (prepared and assisted by more frequent council of foreign ministers' meetings) originally made decisions only by consensus. Since the fifth summit they have agreed to decide by majority (except in case of hostilities). The secretariat, with members from all five states, was located in Morocco by decision of the fifth summit, with a Tunisian secretary general, Mohammed Amamou, for the first three-year term (after Tunis lost the competition for the venue). The consultative committee, composed of ten members from each state's parliamentary body, is situated in Algiers. The tribunal of ten judges appointed in May 1991 is to hold sessions in Nouakchott, the Academy of Sciences and Universities is to meet in Tripoli, and the Maghribi Bank for Investment and Foreign Trade is to operate in Tunis. This allocation of venues was proposed by Morocco at the fifth summit, except for the seat of the secretariat, originally to be in Algiers and then offered by Benjedid to Tunis (Soudan 1991a). Among these institutions, the only one to show any real activity to date has been the presidential council.

Another level of institutions, however, has invigorated the Union with creditable signs of life. These are its commissions and functional meetings. Between the Zeralda and Marrakesh summits, an interministerial commission of the five states met in Tripoli in September 1988, in Rabat in October 1988, and in Tunis in January 1989 to prepare a plan, adopted at Marrakesh, for five commissions, on financial and customs matters, on economics, on social and human affairs, on culture (information, education, and instruction), and on organic and structural affairs. Other specialized commissions on mining, transportation, tourism and handicrafts, and maritime affairs meet frequently. Commissions on interior affairs (internal security) and defense (external security) have never met, although cooperation on internal security among some of the members has been intense. Beyond the commissions, various interministerial meetings among the five countries give serious study to measures of coordination and harmonization.

Other Maghribi institutions have been created under the auspices of the UMA. The Union of Arab Maghrib Labor Organizations was formed in 1989 of all five countries' labor unions, and has met regularly, in June 1991 issuing a charter of basic social rights of Maghribi workers. The third summit approved plans to create a common airline, not yet implemented. The improvement of trans-Maghribi road, rail, and pipeline networks has been studied.

Possibly the most sustained line of activity among the commissions and councils of the UMA has been in regard to Europe, the external challenge. While the initial programs and declarations made no mention of the European Community, the second summit discussed the matter of UMA-EC relations and Zine Labidine Ben Ali used his turn at the presidency in the first half of 1990 to press united Maghribi policy toward Europe. On the first anniversary of the founding of the Union, he called for a joint Maghribi mission in Brussels, and at the end of his term he proposed to EC Commission President Jacques Delors a UMA-EC charter of social rights for North African emigrants in Europe, and a Mediterranean Development Fund to recycle Maghribi public debt for the creation of employment in North Africa to reduce emigration. In May 1990, the human resources commission meeting in Tunis had proposed a consultative council for the North African colony in Europe, as well as the UMA-EC charter.

Both ideas were pursued in a series of Euro-Maghribi meetings in Majorca in October and in Brussels and Tunis in November, and then a year later in further ministerial meetings on Mediterranean cooperation in Rabat and Algiers in September and October, respectively. These meetings have turned into the "5 + 5" Conferences of the European and Maghribi states of the Western Mediterranean, culminating in the Barcelona Conference of November 1995 where significant sums of aid were promised for allocations from the northern to the southern shore, in an effort to keep Maghribi workers at home. UMA insistence, accompanied by growing European resentment of North African immigrants, has kept the matter alive among EC members.

On the other hand, three Maghribi political issues have crowded more productive concerns off the agenda during the short life of the UMA to date, rendering cooperation more difficult. One was the Gulf War, which dominated Maghribi preoccupations for a year from mid-1990 into 1991. During the Algerian presidency of the UMA in the second half of 1990, the war was the subject of Maghribi attempts at mediation; when they failed, optimism over the diplomatic potential of the Union dropped. The shift in attention explains in part the gap in discussions of EC-UMA cooperation during the period. Even before the war was over, the new political issue of Islamist opposition had arisen to trouble the states' relations (Soudan 1990), and in Algeria's case to weaken its capacity for making decisions. The Libyan Lockerbie crisis of early 1992 elicited a cool response from the UMA (Soudan 1992a); the extraordinary summit of support that Qadhafi demanded that year was never held, and the Maghrib states have been troubled by the effect of the affair on their own cooperation and on their relations with the West.

Finally, the shadow of the Saharan conflict still hangs over Maghribi cooperation. Once the treaty of Marrakesh had been signed, King Hassan II began to feel that the issue was under control, a feeling encouraged by the return of a number of Polisario leaders to the Moroccan fold over the following years. The persistence of UN Secretaries General Javier Perez de Cuellar, then Boutros Boutros Ghali, and then Kofi Annan kept the referendum on track, even if slowly, as the UN Mission took up its position and the electoral lists, including Saharans who had fled to Morocco, began to be drawn up. The military-backed takeover of power in Algeria installed a government that Morocco regarded with extreme wariness and considered to be generally less favorable to a solution than an Islamist government might have been.

Then, in the summer of 1994, relations between Morocco and Algeria deteriorated sharply. A terrorist attack on tourists in Marrakesh in August convinced Morocco of Algerian intentions to destabilize the monarchy using Islamists as hired guns; Morocco reimposed the visa requirement for Algerians, and Algeria closed the border in retaliation. Algeria, which had been reviving a hard line on the Western Sahara from time to time as a means of placating its own military, turned toward an even harder position in support of the Polisario Front and in November 1995 rose in the UN to block a plan for an early referendum. On December 22, Morocco formally requested suspension of the UMA. Libya and Tunisia attempted to mediate and Egypt tried to arrange an informal meeting of the five during an Arab League meeting scheduled for March 1996; instead, Algeria (president for the year) called a ministerial council meeting of the UMA in early February 1996, which only Tunisia and Mauritania attended (Ouazzani 1996). Throughout 1996 and 1997, the UMA was in catalepsy as a political organization, although its commissions continued to meet. Integration in the Maghrib had fallen back to the diplomatic level, following the dynamics of the basic structural rivalries.

Maghrib Integration—Up or Down?

It would be unrealistic to expect the path from new statehood to economic and political integration to be free from mines and potholes. The challenge is rather to evaluate whether the political obstacles are more compelling than the road itself. In the process, it should be remembered that whatever form the integration takes—diplomatic, economic, and/or political—it will still contain, not erase, the structural dynamics that characterize current Maghribi relations. Moroccan-Algerian rivalry, Libyan interference, Tunisian mediation, and Mauritanian vulnerability will all characterize the workings of an integrating Maghribi entity as much as they have marked the pre-UMA interactions. Similarly, the cyclical rise and fall of cooperation will also continue, whether or not the trend line itself is rising. Finally, the issues will remain the same, only to be handled in new forms. It should not be thought that a referendum will "solve" or "end" the Saharan question: No matter how it goes, the vote will merely transform the age-old question of nomadic vs. sedentary relations across the desert into new problems for Moroccan, Mauritanian, and Maghribi politics.

It is also important to separate instances and themes of Maghribi cooperation from still or moving pictures of the whole. As it nears the end of its first decade, the UMA shows no greater overall integration than it did at any of its birthdays. Indeed, compared to the plans and timetables, it is behind schedule and stagnating, much like the attempts at regional cooperation which the

Economic Commission for Africa has encouraged elsewhere (such as the Economic Community of West African States, and the Economic Community of Central African States) (Lancaster 1995). When the Maghrib states negotiated new free trade agreements with the European Union in 1995, they did it individually, with little coordination, just as they always had done. All three countries vie with each other for special ties and preferential rights in the European market. Both Morocco and Tunisia have defected from Maghribi economic cooperation and opted for closer integration with Europe, a position Algeria also seeks to claim once its governmental coherence is restored (White 1996).

Sectorially the picture is somewhat different. There is a growing solidarity vis-à-vis Europe which meets European concerns and leads to bilateral cooperation between the two shores of the western Mediterranean on some areas of common concern, even if it does not extend to the joint negotiation of trade agreements. There are a number of small areas of intra-Maghribi coordination and cooperation, not mentioned here in detail, which create familiarities and interdependencies, scarcely irreversible but still influential. There is the increasing reflex of thinking and acting Maghribi in diplomacy. And there are public commitments, as yet unrealized, to eliminate customs, passports, currency controls, and support for opposition movements among the members. (There is even a pan-Maghribist party in Morocco, the Arab Maghrib Unionist Party, though it won no seats in the 1993 election. More important, thirteen nongovernmental parties in the four Maghrib countries met regularly in a "reflection committee" beginning in April 1996 to pressure their governments to revive the UMA, and created a permanent interparty structure (*Jeune Afrique* 1996). The more these developments continue, the more they lift the general trend of integration out of the merely diplomatic and into the economic and, perhaps someday, the political.

But the political is still trumps. North Africa is not a security community (Deutsch 1957), and suggestions from abroad that it work toward that end have been met with understandable incredulity from the Maghribis themselves (Lewis 1994). The structural dynamics of rank and rivalry have and will continue to dominate the region, tearing unity apart and then again making it necessary from time to time, but for the moment keeping it firmly on the level of diplomatic integration, never reaching the developmental or political level.

Endnotes

1. For a conflict that blew a region apart, the collapse of the East African Community and the withdrawal of Tanzania to southern Africa, see C. P. Potholm, "Who Killed Cock

Robin? Perceptions Concerning the Collapse of the East African Community," *World Affairs* 142 (Summer 1979), 45–56.

2. The second summit was on January 22, 1990 in Tunis, the third on July 22–23, 1990 in Algiers, the fourth on March 10–11, 1991 in Ras Lanuf, Libya (originally planned for January 22, in Tripoli), the fifth on September 15–16, 1991 in Casablanca (originally planned for June–July in Nouakchott), the sixth finally in Nouakchott on November 10-ll, 1992 (originally scheduled for January, March, April, and then June); and the last to date in Tunis on April 2–3, 1994. Françoise Soudan, *Jeune Afrique* 1633 (April 23, 1992a), 6–7 and 1640 (June 11, 1992b), 18–23; Tunisia Today May 1994, 4–5.

References

Aghrout, Ahmed and Keith Sutton. "Regional Economic Union in the Maghreb." *Journal of Modern African Studies* 28:1 (March 1990), 115–140.

Belaid, Sadok and I. William Zartman, eds. *Les expériences d'intégration regionale dans les pays du Tiers-monde*. Tunis: Université de Tunis, Centre d'études, de recherches et de publications, 1993.

Belassa, Bela. *The Theory of Economic Integration*. London: Allen and Unwin, 1962.

Cantori, Louis and Steven Spiegel. *The International Politics of Regions*. Englewood Cliffs, NJ: Prentice Hall, 1970.

Damis, John. *Conflict in Northwest Africa*. Stanford, CA: Hoover Institute, Stanford University, 1983a.

Damis, John. "Prospects for Unity/Disunity in North Africa." *American Arab Affairs* 6:1 (1983b).

Daoud, Zakya. "La création de l'Union du Maghreb Arabe-texte du projet d'unité." *Maghreb-Machrek* 124 (1989), 120–38.

Deeb, Mary Jane. "Inter-Maghribi Relations since 1969: A Study of the Modalities of Unions and Mergers." *Middle East Journal* 43:1 (1989), 20–33.

Deeb, Mary Jane. *Libya's Foreign Policy in North Africa*. Boulder, CO: Westview Press, 1991.

Dessouki, Ali E. Hillal. "Regional Organizations and Gulf Security." *Political Science Research Papers* 1:3 (July 1994). Cairo: Cairo University Centre for Political Research and Studies.

Deutsch, Karl. *Political Community in the North Atlantic Area*. Princeton, NJ: Princeton University Press, 1957.

Falk, Richard and Saul Mendlovitz, eds., *Regional Politics and World Order*. San Francisco: Freeman, 1973.

Haas, Ernst. *Beyond the Nation State*. Stanford: Stanford University Press, 1964.

Ibrahimi, A.T. "Le Traité de fraternité et de concorde ou le Maghreb en mouvement." *Revue algérienne de droit international* 9:1 (1988), 7–8.

Jeune Afrique 1845 (May 15, 1996), 10.

Kautilya, translated by R. Shamasastry. *Arthasastra*. Mysore: Mysore Publishing House, 1960.

Kerr, Malcolm. *The Arab Cold War*. Oxford, UK: Oxford University Press, 1967.

Lancaster, Carol. "The Lagos Three: Economic Regionalism in Sub-Saharan Africa." In *Africa in World Politics*. Edited by John Harbeson and Donald Rothchild. Boulder, CO: Westview Press, 1995.

Lewis, William. "Security Community in North Africa." Paper presented to a conference organized by the US Defense Intelligence College and the Tunisian Defense Ministry, Tunis, June 1994.

Lindberg, Leon and Stuart Seheingold, eds. *Regional Integration: Theory and Research*. Cambridge: Harvard University Press, 1970.

Mazzeo, Dominico, ed. *African Regional Organization*. New York: Cambridge University Press, 1984.

Meliani, Habib. "Le Traité de fraternité et de concorde de 1983 ou un nouveau droit de la coopération maghrébine." *Annuaire de l'Afrique du Nord*, Paris: CNRS, 1985.

Migdal, Joel. *Strong Societies, Weak States*. Princeton, NJ: Princeton University Press, 1990.

Modelski, George. "Kautilya: Foreign Policy and International System in the Ancient Hindu World." *American Political Science Review* 58:3 (September 1964), 549–60.

Nye, Joseph, ed. *International Regionalism*. Boston: Little Brown, 1968.

Onwuka, R. I. and Amadu Sesay, eds. *The Future of Regionalism in Africa* (New York: St. Martin's Press, 1985).

Ouazzani, Cherif. "Les dissensions au sein de l'UMA se crystalisent." *Jeune Afrique* 1832 (February 14, 1996), 25–27.

Potholm, C. P. "Who Killed Cock Robin? Perceptions Concerning the Collapse of the East African Community." *World Affairs* 142 (Summer 1979), 45–56.

Robson, Peter. *Integration, Development and Equity*. London: Allen and Unwin, 1983.

Rothchild, Donald and Naomi Chazan, eds. *The Precarious Balance: State Society in Africa*. Boulder, CO: Westview Press, 1988.

Slim, Habib. "Comité permanent consultatif du Maghreb entre le présent et l'avenir." *Revue tunisienne du droit* 3 (1980), 247–72.

Soudan, Françoise. *Jeune Afrique* 1544 (August 1, 1990), 29.

———. *Jeune Afrique* 1577 (March 20, 1991a), 34–37.

———. *Jeune Afrique* 1604 (September 28, 1991b), 4–5.

———. *Jeune Afrique* 1633 (April 23, 1992a), 6–7.

———. *Jeune Afrique* 1640 (June 11, 1992b), 18–23.

Sutton, Keith. "Political Association and the Maghreb Economic Development." *Journal of Modern African Studies* 10:2 (June 1972), 191–202.

Touval, Saadia. *The Boundary Politics of Independent Africa*. Cambridge: Harvard University Press, 1972.

Viner, Jacob, *The Customs Union Issue*. Washington, DC: Carnegie Endowment for International Peace, 1950.

White, Gregory. "The Mexico of Europe Morocco's partnership with the European Union." In *North Africa: Development and Reform in a Changing Global Economy*, edited by Dirk Vandewalle. New York: St. Martin's Press, 1996.

Wilde, Patricia Becko. "The OAU and the Algerian-Morocco Border Conflict." *International Organization* 1 (1966), 18–36.

Wriggins, W. Howard, ed. *Dynamics of Regional Politics*. New York: Columbia University Press, 1992.

Wright, Stephen. "Maghrib 1984—a Region Divided." In *Africa Contemporary Record 1984–85*. New York: Holmes and Meier, 89–94.

Zartman, I. William. "Foreign Relations of North Africa." *Annals AAPSS* 485 (January 1987), 13–27.

Zartman, I. William. *Ripe for Resolution: Conflict and Intervention in Africa*. New York: Oxford University Press, 1989.

Zartman, I. William and A. G. Kluge. "Heroic Politics: The Foreign Policy of Libya." In *The Foreign Policies of Arab States*, edited by Bahgat Korany and Ali E. Hillal Dessouki. Boulder, CO: Westview Press, 1991.

The Republic of Yemen: The Politics of Unification and Civil War, 1989–1995

chapter 9

Robert D. Burrowes

In 1987, the Yemen Arab Republic (YAR) and the People's Democratic Republic of Yemen (PDRY) celebrated their twenty-fifth and twentieth anniversaries, respectively. On May 22, 1990, they united to form the Republic of Yemen (ROY) and the two ceased to exist formally as independent states. Most observers were taken by surprise at this sudden shift from simply improving inter-Yemeni relations to full Yemeni unification. As surprising as the decision to unify was the decision to do it through the democratization of political life and multiparty politics. Relatively free and fair legislative elections were held in April 1993. Unhappily, these elections were followed quickly by a deepening political crisis and by a civil war that by mid-1994 threatened the future of Yemeni unification. The ROY survived and—after nearly three years of demanding financial reforms, economic hardship, and political strife—held a second round of relatively free and fair elections in April 1997. This chapter attempts to chronicle this historic period of Yemen's political life, and to analyze and explain the various stages between 1989 and 1995.

Background to Unification

Yemeni unification—and it was more a matter of unification than of reunification—was confounded by a contradictory political legacy: the ancient idea of Yemen as a place and the Yemeni people, on the one hand, and two distinct national political struggles and resultant territorial states in the twentieth century, on the other (Stookey 1978; Bidwell 1983). Yemen has constituted a single political entity for only short periods over the past two millennia, the last occasion coming after the first period of Ottoman Turkish rule in the seventeenth century. Nevertheless, the ideas of "the Yemen" and of being "Yemeni" were old ones, similar to the situations in Italy and Germany prior to their unifications in the nineteenth century. The port of Aden was certainly seen as part of "the Yemen," and long known in Arabic literature as "the eye of the Yemen." In the twentieth century, moreover, the goal of Yemeni unification was espoused by North Yemen's two strong *imams* and, since the 1940s, by most modern nationalists in both Yemens. In addition, in the first two-thirds of this century increased trade and labor migration between the burgeoning port of Britain's Aden Colony and the southern part of North Yemen—Taiz and Ibb provinces, in particular—provided substructure to the old idea of one Yemen.[1] They provided the buckle that increasingly joined together North Yemen and South Yemen, or at least major parts thereof.

Diametrically opposed to this trend was the bisecting of Yemen by a boundary drawn in the early twentieth century by the British in Aden and the Ottomans in their second occupation in the north. This served to foster the division of Yemen and the Yemeni people into two very different polities and two different political cultures, each with its own values, beliefs, interests, and preoccupations. Although the struggles against the *imams* in the north and the British in the south seemed to many in the 1940s and later to be the two sides of the same Yemeni political coin, the YAR and the PDRY, created in 1962 and 1967 respectively, emerged out of mostly separate and qualitatively different struggles; after their creation, each turned inward and followed a different political path after its creation. The result, quite rapidly achieved, was considerable political and socioeconomic differentiation. There evolved in the north an ill-defined, bumbling, moderate "republican" state (See Burrowes 1987 and 1991; Wenner 1991). In the south there tumbled onto the scene the only avowedly Marxist-Leninist regime in the Arab world (See Burrowes 1989; Ismael and Ismael 1986; Cigar 1985).

This tangle of cross-pressures fostered a confusing, shifting pattern of inter-Yemeni relations from the 1960s onward. Confounded from the start by the bad fit between state and nation, relations between the two Yemens swung wildly between conflict, even war, at the one extreme, and agreements for Yemeni unification, at the other. Indeed, the fifteen years that followed the creation of the PDRY in 1967 contained major border wars in 1972 and 1979, and the PDRY-backed National Democratic Front (NDF) rebellion against the YAR. Both border wars ended oddly in formal political agreements to unify and detailed steps toward that goal. In each instance, the bid for unification proved to be a disguise quickly shed when it ceased to be useful to either or both sides (See Halliday 1984, 1989; Gause 1987, 1988; Burrowes 1987, 1989, 1991).

Although similarly camouflaged by an agreement on new steps toward unification, the suppression of the NDF rebellion and the ending of related conflict
between the two Yemens in 1982 did usher in a new era of improving inter-
Yemeni relations. This era was marked by practical, discrete steps toward
greater cooperation and by close ties between the YAR's President Ali Abdullah
Salih and the PDRY's President Ali Nasir Muhammad.

Given these personal ties, it was inevitable that inter-Yemeni relations would
be strained by the bloodbath inside the ruling Yemeni Socialist Party (YSP) in
Aden in January 1986, a convulsion that caused President Muhammad and
thousands of his followers to flee north to the safety of the YAR (See Burrowes
1989). For the next two years, the new leaders of the YSP in the PDRY tried to
wrap themselves in the legitimizing rhetoric of Yemeni unification and the YAR
just as adamantly refused to reciprocate in both statement and action. The main
barrier to good relations was the unwillingness or inability of the weak and
divided leadership in Aden to ease the burden of the new refugees on the YAR
through reconciliation with the ex-president and his followers.

A serious crisis erupted in late 1987 when the continued failure of the PDRY
to ease the refugee problem through reconciliation combined with renewed
tensions along the undemarcated border separating the YAR's oil fields in the
Marib/al-Jawf basin, discovered only in 1984, from oil fields found even more
recently by the Russians in the PDRY's Shabwa region. Amid reports that rival
oil exploration teams were surveying the disputed borderland for the PDRY
and the YAR, the dispute took a turn for the worse when both Yemens massed
armed forces in the area in March 1988. In mid-April, a summit meeting was
held between President Salih and the new secretary-general of the YSP, Ali Salim
al-Baydh. On May 4, after a second summit, the two leaders signed major inter-
Yemeni agreements.

One of the May 4 Agreements resolved the pressing conflict over the borderland. It called for demilitarization of a "neutral zone" between Marib and
Shabwa and for creation of a joint oil exploration and development company
specifically for the zone. Another agreement provided for the free movement of
Yemenis between the two Yemens, joint border posts, and the requirement of
only domestic identity cards to cross the border in either direction. Finally,
there was an agreement that called for reviving the joint institutions previously
identified with the unification process, setting a new timetable for the draft
unity constitution, and forming a joint committee for a unified political organization (FBIS 1988).

As in the past, the two Yemens in May 1988 used the sweeping rhetoric of, and
small steps toward, unification to camouflage an exercise in crisis management
and problem solving in inter-Yemen relations. The real achievement was the

defusing of a border dispute that had threatened to escalate into serious fighting. Implementation of the military and economic agreements on the neutral
zone began almost immediately. The new regimen for border crossing began in
July and proved immensely popular with the citizens of both Yemens.

Subsequent events emphasized further the revival of the pattern of increased
inter-Yemeni cooperation that had begun in 1982. The two Yemens agreed in
late 1988 on a major project to link their electrical power grids. The new joint
oil company for the neutral zone began operations in early 1989, and negotiations with oil companies to explore in the zone began almost immediately. In
spring 1989, the secretariat of the highest joint body for unity affairs met for the
first time since the 1986 bloodbath in Aden; the PDRY also announced plans to
release many of those convicted for involvement in that episode, a move hailed
by the YAR. There was even talk about the possibility of soon using the Aden
refinery to process crude oil from the YAR.

The Unification Process, 1989–1995

The recently reestablished pattern of improving inter-Yemeni relations was
transformed dramatically—and, to most observers, myself included, unexpectedly—into the politics of unification in late 1989. After a lull of several months,
unification activity began at the end of October with the first-ever meeting of a
body first called for in the original unification agreement in 1972, the Joint
Committee for a Unified Political Organization. During a much-publicized
summit in Aden only four weeks later, President Salih and Secretary-General al-
Baydh committed "the two parts of Yemen" to a series of steps designed to result
in unification in roughly one year. The November 30 Agreement prescribed that
the draft unity constitution, shelved since its completion in late 1981, would be
submitted for ratification by the legislatures of the two Yemens and then to a
popular referendum within two successive six-month periods-i.e., by the end of
November 1990. If the new constitution were approved in this two-step
sequence, then the "Republic of Yemen" was to be proclaimed, the new constitution declared in force, and a transitional government established in the new
capital, San'a. This government was to remain in place only until early elections
for an all-Yemen legislature, which would then select a president and vote
approval of a regular government.[2]

Political parties sprang up like weeds during the months before and after
formal unification, by different counts the total coming to between 30 and 40.
Partisan newspapers and magazines also flourished, and the government came
in for unprecedented scrutiny and criticism in these organs as well as in the

Council of Deputies. The Yemenis took to the rights to speak, write, and organize with a vengeance, and the two-party coalition regime probably got more
democratic politics than bargained for.

The intense, highly focused Yemeni unification process was blindsided on
August 2, 1990, by Iraq's unexpected invasion of Kuwait, only a little more than
two months after the ROY was proclaimed. Foreign Minister Abd al-Karim al-
Iryani was quoted as having said that Yemeni unification had been "ambushed"
by the invasion. The ensuing Gulf crisis and war both diverted the attentions of
Yemenis from the unification process and placed great, unanticipated burdens
upon that process. The impact of the crisis on the new regime was magnified
greatly by its membership at this time on the UN Security Council, assuring it
unavoidable visibility. Arguing and voting throughout for an "Arab solution"—
a negotiated end to Iraq's occupation of Kuwait, and refusing to endorse the
decision by the U.S.- and Saudi-led coalition to expel Iraq by armed force (See
al-Ashtal 1991), Yemen soon found itself bereft of most development aid as well
as budgetary and balance-of-payments support from, most notably, Saudi
Arabia and the other oil-rich Arab Gulf states. More important was the loss of
the far more considerable remittances of the several hundred thousand Yemeni
workers and many businessmen—more than 5 percent of Yemen's total population—who were forced by the Saudis to return to Yemen and likely unemployment.

Relations between the ROY and both Saudi Arabia and Kuwait became
extremely hostile over these months. The exchange of public accusations and
criticism between the Saudis and the Yemenis rose to a level not seen since the
years of the Yemen Civil War in the 1960s, and the underlying hostility persisted
through the mid-1990s. The ROY's relations with the U.S. also suffered.
Moments after Yemen failed to support the U.S.'s use-of-force resolution in the
Security Council in November 1990, its delegate was informed by a high U.S.
official that the vote "was the most expensive 'no' vote you ever cast"-and U.S.
aid was then cut practically to nothing.

The all-Yemeni referendum on the new constitution, the step dropped from
those leading up to formal unification in May 1990, was held with fanfare in
mid-May 1991, a few days before the ROY's first anniversary. From the stand-
point of the coalition regime, the good news was that the constitution had been
approved by an overwhelming majority of those voting; the bad news was that
less than half of the eligible voters voted, in part because of the boycott called
by Islamists and other conservatives who were demanding certain changes in
the constitution. This opposition to the constitution, if not to unification itself,
had surfaced in the months before formal unification in May 1990; it peaked
just before and after the referendum, and continued thereafter at a lower level.

Opposition to the regime's stand on the Gulf crisis, and support for the anti-Iraq coalition, tended to go hand-in-hand with what was alleged to be the insufficiently Islamic character of the constitution. The main opposition vehicle was the Islamic Grouping for Reform (Islah), a party formed in late 1990 that brought together major tribal and religious elements in the north. Islah was headed by Yemen's leading tribal leader, Shaykh Abdullah ibn Husayn al-Ahmar, and by longtime political Islamist Abd al-Majid al-Zindani; both were longtime friends and clients of the Saudi royal family.

After the referendum, the attention of the unification regime turned to the crucial legislative elections set for the end of the transition period in November 1992, some eighteen months hence. President Salih and his colleagues acknowledged repeatedly the dire effects of both the Gulf crisis and "errors" in the unification process at the same time that they claimed that the ROY could and would cope with them successfully.

Despite their surprising collaboration, the two equal partners in the unification regime—the GPC and the YSP—competed against each other at the same time that they joined forces against the several other major political forces and parties, new and old, during the transition period. Worsening economic conditions as well as problems in the effort to merge the two states and to reorganize politics heightened competition and strained cooperation between them in the second half of this period, after the summer of 1991. In particular, the return of the expelled workers and the sharp drops in remittance income and external aid in 1990 gradually but predictably brought economic crisis and hard times to both parts of Yemen in the following year. This worsening of the socioeconomic setting confounded the unification process and distracted the government; it also poisoned the political atmosphere and made cooperation between the two partners more difficult.

Specifically, beginning in late 1991, day-to-day politics was increasingly punctuated by acrimony, popular protests, strikes, riots, bombings, and assassinations that placed the unification regime under great strain. Most of the assassins' targets were YSP leaders, and growing concern about the "security problem" was accompanied by questions of why GPC leaders seemed unwilling or unable to respond vigorously to these crimes. The kidnapping of foreigners—often oil company workers—and the theft of their vehicles became epidemic, providing added evidence of a growing "lawlessness." Rumors of rifts between the GPC and the YSP leadership became frequent. Finally, in August 1992, citing the absence of public safety and the failure of the regime to address major problems, al-Baydh withdrew to Aden, beginning what was to be a long, awkward boycott of the government in San'a.

So great was the political turmoil during the second half of 1992 that the partners in the unification regime seemed to lose sight of the fast approaching date for the legislative elections that were supposed to mark the end of the transition to a unified Yemen. The elections were postponed twice, further adding to the acrimony, particularly between the regime and the increasingly restive opposition. The political crisis came to a head in late 1992 with fatal price riots in cities in the North and a series of terrorist acts, hotel bombings among them, in the South, apparently by militant Islamists with ties beyond the Arabian Peninsula.

These events served well as wake-up calls. They sobered both the partners in the unification regime and its moderate opponents, and led to a general closing of ranks and a respite in the political crisis. As a result, the regime successfully organized and held the elections on April 27, 1993, an event that served to legitimate anew Yemeni unification and the regime, both at home and abroad. No major Yemeni players boycotted the balloting. The big losers at the polls accepted the results after only brief grumbling and cries of fraud; they seemed prepared, if not eager, to assume the role of opposition.

As expected, President Salih and his centrist GPC were the big winners, taking about 40 percent of the seats. The other half of the unification regime, the YSP, while much diminished, survived in good order with 20 percent. Finally, and as important, the tribal and moderate Islamic critics of the regime, represented by Islah, made a strong showing, but not overly so (also about 20 percent).[3]

Although its formation took more than a month of intense politicking, the three-party coalition government made possible by the election results seemed potentially able both to stay together and to address at least some of Yemen's pressing problems. The government announced on May 30, again with the YSP's al-Attas as prime Minister, was a broad coalition ranging from center-left to center-right, the "big tent" apparently favored by President Salih. (Interestingly, the 2:1:1 ratio of GPC to YSP to Islah in the Majlis translated roughly into a 3:2:1 ratio in the new cabinet, suggesting that Islah's strength relative to that of the YPS was perhaps more apparent than real—or that representation in either or both the Majlis and the cabinet were not good measures of power.)

During its first months, the new government emphasized new initiatives and, in particular, launched a concerted effort to restore good relations with Saudi Arabia, Kuwait, and the other Arab Gulf states, an effort that produced only modest results. Popular demonstrations and strikes during the summer and fall, protesting inflation and the late payment of salaries and wages, indicated that the government was under the gun to meet quickly campaign pledges to ease the "pains" of unification and hard times. Vehicle thefts and kidnappings by the tribes resumed, causing chagrin to the regime that had made the end of "lawlessness" a campaign promise. Most worrisome, assassination attempts and other political violence resumed sporadically.

It was soon apparent that the elections had not provided passage to a more complete, more permanent stage of unification, or to more effective government. Strains in the tripartite coalition were evident in the resignation of the armed forces chief-of-staff (a northerner) over the alleged failure of the defense minister (a southerner) to get on with the long-delayed merger of the armed forces, another priority electoral promise. Some YSP leaders were urging the party to join the opposition rather than continue to serve as a junior partner in a coalition dominated by an alleged alliance between the GPC and Islah, the two "northern" parties. This urging came only a few months after an extensive pre-election debate over whether the YSP and the GPC should "merge" or simply continue to "coordinate" and, shortly after the elections, the formal announcement that they had decided to merge into a single party.

In mid-August 1993, about ten weeks after the government was formed, Vice President al-Baydh again retired to Aden and began a new boycott, one that led to a second full-blown political crisis. He left behind a list of eighteen conditions for his return, a rather full plate of political, military, economic, and administrative reforms. Efforts to mediate by Arab friends and expressions of concern by the United States, the Russian Federation, and others were to no avail. Al-Baydh's refusal to come north and be inaugurated as vice president in October 1993, nearly six months after the elections, underlined the stalemate. As a result, the political climate in late 1993 was as bad or worse than a year earlier.

Unlike the crisis of late 1992, moreover, this crisis did not cause the combatants inside the ruling coalition to close ranks, put aside their differences, and take joint action to save both the regime and Yemeni unity when the alarms sounded in early 1994. Despite the efforts and desires of many of the leaders of the unification regime and the opposition—most notably the Political Forces Dialogue Committee formed in late 1993—the second political crisis defied solution.

The attempt by the senior *ulama* to bring al-Baydh and Salih—"the two Alis"—together near Taiz in early January 1994 failed when al-Baydh balked at the last minute. By early January, most of the other YSP leaders in the regime had quietly left San'a and joined al-Baydh in Aden, adding further to the de facto creation of a separate "state" government in the old capital of the PDRY. The southern leaders by this time were openly expressing their demand for decentralization in terms of federation; the northerners translated this as a call for a big step back from unification. The political crisis was paralleled by a simmering military crisis between the unmerged armed forces, with each side accusing the other of resupplying its units and of redeploying them along the former border.

The failed effort by the *ulama* was followed by mediation by Jordan's King Hussein that led on February 20 to a meeting in Amman of al-Baydh and Salih and their signing of the Document of Pledge and Accord, an agreement hammered out over two months by the Political Forces Dialogue Committee. The next day, fighting occurred between army units of the north and south stationed in the Abyan province of the former South Yemen, putting off implementation of the agreement and leading to the formation of a military committee consisting of Jordanian, Omani, and North and South Yemeni officers as well as the military attachés of the U.S. and France, a mission that achieved very little over the next month. Moreover, on the very day that the agreement was signed, the leaders of the two parts of Yemen launched what amounted to separate, conflicting diplomatic initiatives in the Arab world.

In early April, hastily arranged talks between "the two Ali's" in Oman, under the sponsorship of Sultan Qabus, failed to get the reconciliation process back on course, causing the Omanis and then the Jordanians to end their mediation efforts. Shortly after this disappointment, a serious armed incident occurred in Dhamar, in the north, involving a southern unit stationed in that town. By this time, as the fiction of a troubled unity gave way to the apparent physical separation, the wagers of the war of words dropped the euphemisms of the recent past: al-Baydh accused Salih and his "clan" of abandoning unification for "annexation," of conspiring to "marginalize" the YSP; Salih accused al-Baydh and his greedy "secessionist" friends of forsaking the unity of Yemen and the Yemeni people for "a mini oil-state."

Egypt and the UAE started another mediation effort in May, and talk turned to the possibility of a summit in Cairo. Then, on April 27, the first anniversary of the elections, a bloody four-day battle between northern and southern units erupted in an army camp near the town of Amran, north of San'a. Tanks and artillery were involved at close range, and the casualties—civilian and military—were very high. Despite efforts to contain the conflict, fighting again broke out a week later in Dhamar on May 4. The fighting quickly escalated to civil war, spreading to other locations and becoming more or less continuous.

After more than two weeks of fighting, during which the forces of the north got the upper hand and drove deep into the south, al-Baydh was welcoming outside mediation and urging an immediate ceasefire and separation of forces. On his side, Salih opposed efforts to "internationalize" an internal conflict and demanded surrender of the "secessionists" and the trial or exile of about fifteen top "rebels," including al-Baydh. On May 21, with Aden and its environs increasingly cut off from the rest of the south, al-Baydh formally announced secession and the creation of a separate Democratic Republic of Yemen. Salih replied with a pledge to crush the new state and to restore unity. It was the day before the fourth anniversary of the unified Republic of Yemen.

The civil war sputtered on through June, and the fate of Yemeni unification remained undecided. Suddenly, at the end of the first week in July, Mukalla and then Aden fell to the unionists and the southern leaders and many of their armed forces fled the country, marking the complete collapse of the secession (See Warburton 1995; al-Suwaidi 1995).

During the rest of the year there were protracted efforts to get economics and politics—external as will as domestic—back to "normal" in unified Yemen. By early October, the constitution was amended at several points, President Salih was elected to a new term by the legislature, and a new government was appointed and approved. The new coalition government included members of the GPC and Islah—and not the YSP.

Although the coalition held, and talked-of guerrilla warfare from within and without Yemen did not materialize, neither politics nor economics were back to normal by early summer 1995. Serious border conflicts with Saudi Arabia in early 1995 and the further deterioration of the economic situation over the entire period combined to place great demands—and serious strains—on the Salih regime. Despite successful efforts to introduce structural reforms and austerity measures in 1995 and 1996, the regime's ability to get Yemen to turn the corner, and to begin the return to the more promising conditions of 1990, remained in doubt.

The Unification Process Analyzed

Despite the prominent place of unification in public discourse, the more important theme in private in Yemen in the late 1980s was prospects for further cooperation and coordination between the two Yemens. Good inter-Yemeni relations were even being touted by many as the preferred alternative to formal political unification, the latter being regarded as too unlikely, difficult, and even dangerous; to try seriously to unify, they reasoned, would be to overreach—and to put improving inter-Yemeni relations in jeopardy. To these persons, the rhetoric and theatrics of the unification process provided useful cover for the "real" news—the series of concrete steps toward close, mutually beneficial ties between the two Yemens. Most of even those Yemeni leaders who favored and expected Yemeni unification were surprised by the events of late 1989, having come to assume a long time frame and an incremental process. As one high YAR official, almost certainly Foreign Minister Abd al-Karim al-Iryani, put it in

October 1987: "Except by some historical accident, unification will come about over a long period of time. . . . [It] will not be realized through grandiose discussions, but is more attainable through slowly creating concrete links, beginning modestly with areas such as trade and tourism" (*Le Monde* 1987) Assuming the soundness of this judgment when made in October 1987, apparently something out of the ordinary—some "historical accident"—did occur in the two Yemens at some point over the next two years.

HOW AND WHY IT CAME WHEN IT DID

Initiated in this setting, the process that sped to formal unification in May 1990 was neither inevitable nor the next step in a logical, incremental series. Instead, the revived unification process that began in the fall of 1989 involved a big, abrupt change—a step-level change according to systems theorists. The change between the fall of 1989 and just months earlier, at least as much qualitative as quantitative, involved a shift in goals or end values from improved inter-Yemeni relations to the destruction of the two Yemens through their merger. Unlike past unification flurries, this one was not meant to mask a pragmatic effort at conflict resolution or another mundane, practical advance in inter-Yemeni relations. Nor was it designed by either or both Yemens primarily as a device to build domestic political support or as a weapon for use against—or a means to gain advantage over—the other Yemen. In the fall of 1989, the bid for unification was, for the most part, for real.

The YAR was the initiator of this sudden change, and this in itself was part of the difference. In the past it had usually been the PDRY that seized the initiative and acted on the charged issue of unification, forcing the YAR to react. In 1989, however, the roles of pursuer and pursued, wooer and wooed, were reversed, and stayed that way during the fast-paced negotiations leading to formal unification.

Why did the YAR suddenly opt for unification at this time and not before or later? In part it was an act of human will, most certainly a matter of willfulness on the part of President Salih. Possessed of impressive political instincts, he had a string of recent successes behind him, from the celebration of the YAR's twenty-fifth anniversary and the export of its first oil in 1987, through the long awaited elections of a new Consultative Council and his selection for a third 5-year term in mid-1988, to the hosting in San'a of the summit meeting of the newly formed Arab Cooperation Council. It appears that at about the time of this latest triumph, in September 1989, Salih was faced with the question: What's next? Apparently, the answer was a serious bid for Yemeni unification.

Changed conditions caused Salih and his advisers to perceive such a bid as both worth going for and possible of attainment. Combined, these conditions created a window of opportunity for unification. For one thing, the balance of power in inter-Yemeni affairs had gradually, but nonetheless decisively, shifted in favor of the YAR over the course of the 1980s. Significant political construction, which notably increased the strength and legitimacy of the Salih regime in the mid-1980s and thereafter, allowed certain latent YAR advantages to assert themselves: a much larger population; a greater economic development potential, especially in agriculture; and a much larger, albeit declining, inflow of workers' remittances and development aid. The clincher was the discovery and rapid, almost textbook-perfect exploitation of the YAR's modest but ample oil reserves in 1984 and thereafter. Although the YAR experienced serious economic problems in the late 1980s, problems that probably worsened rather than improved in 1989, its prospects for the future looked bright and there was reason for optimism and confidence.

By contrast, the already poor state of the PDRY's economy had worsened decidedly since the mid-1980s and the likely benefits from its newly discovered oil were less certain and farther in the future. Of greater importance, the PDRY had suffered a number of staggering political setbacks just as the YAR was getting on its feet, causing a widening power gap between the two Yemens. Arguably, the regimes headed by presidents Muhammad and Salih were of roughly equal weight in the mid-1980s, and a serious attempt at unity at this time would have had to contend with the presence of two strong-willed candidates for the top post in a unified Yemen. Parity ended abruptly when the YSP decapitated itself in the 1986 bloodbath. In the course of only a few days, Muhammad fled the country, and nearly all of the other top leaders were killed, jailed, or in exile. As a consequence, President Salih stood alone atop the Yemeni leadership pyramid, his stature unequaled by that of YSP Secretary-General al-Baydh or any group of YSP leaders in the south. Despite efforts to repair the damage, culminating in major political and economic reforms and a clear victory for al-Baydh and the moderates in mid-1989, the YSP remained greatly weakened and discredited in South Yemen, and, as important, was perceived as such by political observers in North Yemen.

Probably more important to the undermining of the PDRY regime than the intraparty leadership fight was the sudden withdrawal of Soviet support and the rapid crumbling of the socialist camp in the late 1980s (See Halliday 1989; Cigar 1989; Pollack 1986). Moscow informed the Aden regime in early 1989 that it could no longer grant the PDRY preferential economic and political treatment. The Soviet Union's sharp cutback in its global commitments and the preoccupation of East European countries with their internal problems caused the PDRY regime to feel isolated and without either moral or material support. This loss of aid made it seem all but impossible for the PDRY to survive the wait for oil export revenues, especially since it was the Soviet Union that was developing the country's oil resources—and because the PDRY had lost confidence in Soviet capabilities in this area. The only remaining option was dependence on Saudi Arabia.

This window of opportunity for unification opened in the late 1980s just as political leaders in San'a became increasingly concerned about the need to arrange domestic and external affairs so as to lessen the likelihood of events that might threaten plans to quickly translate the new oil wealth into long-term development and prosperity. To this end, unification was perceived as serving to "domesticate" the question of access to, and the sharing of, the oil resources of the two Yemens in general and the newly created neutral zone between them in particular, thereby preventing the inter-Yemeni conflict that could deny both Yemens the fruits of oil wealth. Recent history suggested that the neutral zone could again become a disputed borderland as long as the two Yemens existed side by side; containing this potentially explosive issue within a unified Yemen, while not eliminating the issue per se, would eliminate the chance that it would again become a matter of state against state, army against army.[4]

The same logic for this domestication through unification applied to other issues that could, with unpredictable results, pit the two parts of Yemen against one another or otherwise involve one of the Yemens in the affairs of the other. For example, mindful of the turmoil of the 1986 bloodbath, some leaders in the north in 1989 feared that the regime in Aden was on the verge of total collapse; for them, the risks involved in unification would be less than those involved in the likely need, were collapse to occur, for the YAR to intervene militarily to prevent the turmoil and outside meddling that could easily spill over the border into the YAR.

Finally, a measure of opportunism on both sides helps to explain the decision to go for unity. The relative strength of the YAR and its leadership in 1989 made its unification initiative a win-win situation: if the effort was successful, the leaders of the YAR could take most of the credit and set most of the terms; if it failed, they could take credit for trying and place blame on their old enemies in the PDRY. For their part, the YSP and its leaders were so weakened and discredited that they could not afford to say no to a call for unification; they had little choice but to buy time by committing themselves now to the goal, hoping that with time their political fortunes would improve, permitting them either to prosper in the union or to slip out before it became final. Accordingly, the YAR forced the issue of merger during the summit in November 1989; and its position in the negotiations leading up to formal unification was for complete merger and the sooner the better. For its part, the PDRY favored commitment to unification now and the later the implementation the better. Sure that the weakened PDRY leadership had tried to use the unification cause primarily to strengthen itself after the 1986 bloodbath, President Salih and his advisers were determined not to give al-Baydh and his colleagues a free political ride; their insistence on moving up the unification date to May in exchange for the long transition period reflected this, at least in part. In the end, however, the leaders of both Yemens got so swept up in the euphoria engendered by their joint effort to unify that their initial opportunism counted for little—at least at the time.

THE HONEYMOON PHASE OF TRANSITION

Negotiations and other events over the several months between the November 30 Agreement and formal unity provided the Yemeni leadership with a heavy dose of practical in-service training in the unfamiliar arts of unifying and pluralizing. In the course of their self-interested jockeying for position, the leaders of the GPC and the YSP converged in their acceptance of the "unify now/go to the people later" formula. By advancing the date, they presented internal and external enemies of unification with a fait accompli, and by putting off national parliamentary elections for thirty months they gave themselves time to "work out the bugs" and demonstrate the benefits of Yemeni unification. Most of them realized that the two economies were in bad shape, would probably get worse before they got better, and that some of the worsening would be caused by the hard choices, confusion, and mistakes that would inevitably accompany the attempt to implement unification. They were also aware that unification placed demands on the state, and raised popular expectations regarding it, at precisely the same time that the many inevitable defects in the merger process were sure initially to weaken if not immobilize the state.

The leadership had reason for feeling cursed as well as blessed by the initial popularity of unification. The likelihood that it would be judged later a success was made problematical by the unrealistically high expectations it raised in many Yemenis. Some thought that unification itself would solve economic ills and bring good times. They maintained that a stable, peaceful, enlarged Yemen would act as a magnet for the funds of foreign investors as well as wealthy Yemenis with funds abroad; in particular, they made much of the untapped potential of Aden, the "economic capital" of unified Yemen, as a free port and industrial zone. Similarly, many idealistic North Yemenis embraced unification as the vehicle for ending the corruption, favoritism, disorder, and lack of organization that they deemed of crisis proportions in the YAR in the late 1980s; the infusion of southerners, reputedly untainted on these counts, would help the northerners effect the needed reforms that they could not effect alone. These expectations were wildly inflated, and the near certainty that they would go largely unmet made it likely that many would judge unification a failure and the regime identified with it as illegitimate and unworthy of support.

Despite these concerns, most of the political leaders, north and south, were confident in mid-1990 that the unification process would come to a successful conclusion and that they individually stood good chances of being among its political beneficiaries. Most of them had been truly surprised by the great popularity of the border opening in 1988—whereby the citizens of both parts were voting for one Yemen with their feet—and were keenly aware of the apparent upsurge in their own popularity in the months after the November 30 Agreement. Noted especially were both the new near-hero status accorded President Salih in the south as well as in the north and the rapid revival of the all-but-spent political fortunes of Vice President al-Baydh and his southern colleagues.

These optimistic conclusions, only wishful thinking on the part of some, were the result of cold calculation by other Yemeni leaders. Although mindful that hard times and economic grievances would place heavy burdens on the unification process, the latter were convinced that most of the populace would give them until the end of the transition period in late 1992 to show the positive effects of unification. They thought that this 30-month grace period would be sufficient to effect the merger of state institutions and the reorganization of political life. Further, they thought that remittances at current levels and the revenue from as much as a doubling of oil output in the ROY to about 400,000 barrels per day would begin to revive the economy by the eve of their first electoral test as the leaders of unified Yemen. Aware that this would be cutting it close, most of them thought nonetheless that they had a better-than-even chance that their moment of truth at the polls would take place in a setting marked by convincing signs of renewed prosperity and development.

The most worrisome and least answerable questions for the leaders of the two Yemens after November 1989 involved the possible impact of unification on politics and the organization of political life. The future of the GPC and the YSP in particular and of past political construction in the two Yemens in general was thrown into question by Yemeni unification. Would the fragile umbrella organization that the Salih regime used with some success to order and contain politics in the YAR remain a dominant force in the enlarged and more challenging environment created by the ROY? Of only limited political relevance even in the 1980s in the north, could the GPC be made to have as much or more (or any) relevance in the 1990s in a setting that included the southern part of Yemen and politically advanced Aden? Would the YSP, largely discredited in Aden and the rest of the old PDRY, revive and survive in united Yemen? Would it establish a major base of support in the north? What would be the relationship between these two ruling parties: would they remain separate, continue to coordinate on politics and policy, merge, or otherwise join forces formally or informally in a new, broad umbrella political organization? What would their relationship be, singly or together, to the many old and new political parties that had already surfaced by early 1990? Would the two compete with each other for power and, somehow at the same time, conspire together to exclude the others from sharing significantly in power?

That the leaders of both Yemens were aware that they were heading into the politically unknown led them to defer for many months of recourse to the people through elections or referenda and to shelve the idea of a "unified political organization" in favor of a multiparty system. The leaders had been uncomfortable with the prospect of letting the people decide their fate in the very near future. If elections were held as early as originally planned, dark humor in San'a had it, Vice President al-Baydh would win in the north and get voted out in the south while President Salih and the GPC would take the south and lose the north. Similarly, realization that the political configuration of united Yemen was uncharted, and likely to change rapidly for some time to come, led the leadership to conclude that the vagaries of an untried multiparty system were in all likelihood safer than the consequences of a probably futile attempt to contain politics in a "unified political organization," however open and broad in theory.

Neither versed nor experienced in multiparty politics, politicians from the two Yemens were unsure and uncomfortable with this abstraction. While most of them were convinced nearly from the outset that political change toward a more open, "pluralist" system was unavoidable and even desirable, they had a more difficult time sketching the broad outlines much less the details of this emerging political order and the path to it. They wondered among themselves where the balance between unity and diversity (or multiplicity) should be struck, and, as important, how it could be maintained and institutionalized.

The leaders of the GPC and the YSP went from wishful thinking in late 1989—e.g., thinking they could, in effect, "federalize" politics so that each of the two parties could continue to enjoy a virtual political monopoly in its respective part of Yemen, at least during the transition—to a rather frantic effort to keep up with a fast changing (fast "pluralizing") political reality in which new and old parties were popping up all over the political map. The alternatives proposed by those in the ruling coalition all tried, implicitly or explicitly, to reserve some special position or advantage for both the GPC and the YSP; they ranged from a broad national front or umbrella organization into which the various parties would largely merge—a super-GPC for all Yemen or something like the Unified Political Organization/National Front in the PDRY in the mid-1970s—to a system of many separate, independent parties over which some sort of official gatekeeper would still have considerable say as to which parties qualified for inclusion. The ruling parties were soon under great pressure from the other parties to give up the former for the latter alternative; some of these parties were even objecting to a gatekeeper or anything else that might favor the *status quo ante*—i.e., the GPC and the YSP. Indeed, the ruling parties were accused publicly in early 1990 by opposition parties of coordinating their affairs so as to monopolize political life, and at mid-year they were still trying to fashion a political party law with registration criteria that would both seem neutral and actually serve to exclude or cripple certain parties—e.g., any party claiming to be *the* Islamic party or having certain kinds of foreign connections.

During the months before and just after formal unity in May 1990, the critics of unification were on the defensive, forced to mute or qualify their criticisms, because of the great popularity of the ideas of unity and democracy. Initially, opposition to unification in general or in its particulars was speculative and theoretical. The Islamic fundamentalists and other conservatives, mostly in the north, focused on the draft constitution and judged it wanting for its failure to make the *shari'a* the sole source of legislation, rather than merely "the main source" (Article 3), and for its sanctioning of parties in an Islamic society (Article 39). Understandably, much of the initial opposition in both parts of Yemen turned on calculations of winners and losers, present and future. Some in the north objected to the parity formula for the allocation of top positions during the transition period, only to be told by its defenders that, in exchange for a few ministries and some offices given to the south, the north was really winning the whole south. At the same time, many of those who realized that the stronger and more populous north was absorbing the south also realized that the minorities that had defined and dominated the north for centuries—the Zaydis and the tribes—were going to be overwhelmed numerically by Shafi'is and nontribesmen in this process. The political left, mostly in the south, protested that unification was going to be achieved at the expense of past gains and future goals, secular and socialist; liberated women in the south feared that they would have to pay a particularly high price for unity.

The coalition of the GPC and YSP needed all the internal cohesion it could muster because, as predicted, the attempt to merge the two previously separate socioeconomic systems produced new strains and problems; also as predicted, the attempt to merge the institutions, personnel, and practices of the two states undermined the already limited capacity of the state to deal with social and economic matters. Since the economy of the north was bigger and more robust and flexible, much of the burden of adjustment fell on the southerners; families in Aden had to cope with price decontrols and civil servants coming north had to cope with the cost of living in San'a. In the north as well, the new problems and tasks brought on by the merger were added to the hard times and austerity many were already experiencing.

The swift and easy appointment of ministers, their deputies, and other top officials in the first weeks after unification masked problems and concerns that were out in the open in a few months. The assurances that during the transition period jobs would be distributed equally between northerners and southerners caused some to fear that a pernicious Lebanese-style quota system would persist beyond the transition. Similar assurances that during this period no one would be dismissed as redundant caused some to conclude that the choice deferred until after the transition was between a bloated public bureaucracy and a period of bitter job competition and wholesale dismissals. By late fall 1990, the talk was of unfilled posts at the level of department head and below, confusion over chains of command, disputes about duties and procedures, and preoccupation with job security and jockeying for position. The capacity of the state to make and implement public policy in the the socioeconomic sphere, after having improved in both Yemens in recent years, suffered a setback. Routine government operations were reduced to a snail's pace if not a standstill. Were it not for the fact that Yemen is still at a level of development where the lives of most citizens are not closely dependent on the quality and quantity of government, the situation would have been a disaster.

Not surprisingly, Yemen's stand on the 1990–91 Gulf crisis proved costly in socioeconomic terms, compounding the problems caused by the unification process itself. The impact, cushioned for a time by the hard currency and possessions brought back by Yemenis forced to repatriate, included serious social as well as economic strains, dislocations, and deprivations. Because few of the workers went to their villages or found work in the cities, the most notable new problems were the staggering increase in unemployment and the growth of vast shantytowns on the outskirts of San'a and al-Hudayda. The virtual end of remittances, the cutoff of most development and financial aid, and a drop in oil prices (and oil export revenues) soon produced a severe shortage of hard currency, and this then caused the Yemeni rial to plummet in value and inflation to soar. Much of the declining hard currency had to go for increased food imports to feed the returnees, leaving little for production and development activities that depended on hard currency for imports. Many projects, public and private, had to be put on hold for want of financing, thereby costing additional jobs. Essential services also had to be cut, and a minimal system of relief and humanitarian aid was stretched to its limits by the growing demand.

These acute problems and the unification regime's feeble efforts to cope with them fostered popular discontent and public protests. Bread-and-butter issues took their place beside the speculative and ideological debate over unification, and were pressed vigorously. Taxi owners protested steep rises in gasoline prices, and work stoppages occurred in the oil fields and at the oil refinery. In early 1992, unified Yemen's main trade union grouping successfully held a 24-hour general strike to protest the government's failure to deal with widespread corruption, soaring prices, and other problems.

The ROY's refusal to join the U.S.- and Saudi-led coalition against Iraq seemed to play into the hands of enemies of unification in Yemen. After August 2, 1990, many of the naysayers who had protested that unified Yemen and its new constitution were not sufficiently "Islamic" added to their litany the failure of the unification regime to take sides with Saudi Arabia, Kuwait, and the other Gulf states against Iraq; they blamed this failure for the hard economic times. In particular, Islah leveled harsh criticism at the regime for its Gulf stand and the domestic effects of that stand. It joined with the League of the Sons of Yemen, led by Abd al-Rahman Ali al-Jifri, and several other smaller opposition parties to fight against the constitutional referendum as well as the regime's Gulf stance in mid-1991. Earlier, these and other pro-Saudi elements had formed a Committee for the Defense of the Rights of Kuwait.

Initially, however, the Gulf crisis may have generated as much support for unification and the unification regime as it eroded that support. The quick and undisguised punishing of Yemen by the Saudis and Americans enabled President Salih and his colleagues to sound a convincing call to all Yemenis to rally and close ranks against a real challenge to unified Yemen and the Yemeni people. The latent anti-Saudi sentiment of many Yemenis became manifest, and the regime turned it to its political advantage. Although disavowed by the regime, the scores of demonstrations and other forms of protest against the anti-Iraq coalition throughout the country during the crisis channeled much anger and frustration harmlessly away from the regime. Moreover, the economic hardships and austerity that had preceded and continued after unification, as well as those that inevitably accompanied the process of merger, could now be partly blamed on or masked by the Gulf crisis and its effects on Yemen.

The negative economic effects of the Gulf crisis were mitigated somewhat by the degree to which the quickly unified petroleum sector was self-standing, insulated from the rest of the economy, and the object of the intense interest of many international oil companies, an interest which, if anything, grew over the course of the crisis. Lowered export earnings, largely caused by the diversion of part of the Marib/al-Jawf production to the Aden refinery in order to cover domestic energy needs previously met with concessionary crude from Iraq and Kuwait, were gradually offset by rising production and slightly higher crude prices. In addition, several hundred million dollars flowed into the Yemeni treasury in 1990–91 as the result of both the lucrative sale of exploration rights to several new blocks in the south and the large cost reimbursement paid by the company that won the right to replace the Russians in Shabwa. Finally, new exploration continued at a fast pace, and produced important new commercial oil finds, strengthening Yemen's longer-term economic prospects at the same time that it further whetted the appetites of the oil companies. Most important was the strike in 1990 in the Masilah Block in the Hadhramawt, a field that was scheduled to begin production in late 1993 and promised to be as big as Marib/al-Jawf in the north. Finally, the expansion of oil production was projected from the roughly 200,000 b/d in 1991 to about 1,000,000 b/d by the year 2000, with the figure of 400,000 b/d estimated for the end of 1993.

Most important, the united front of the two-party ruling coalition was maintained in the face of problems and discontents as a matter of political will. In response to an inchoate and fast-changing political environment, the coalition that negotiated and achieved formal unity between late 1989 and mid-1990 rapidly evolved ad hoc into a unification regime. The competition and antagonism between the GPC and the YSP, the two halves of this regime, while not expunged, were largely overridden by their mutual interest in surviving the growing challenge of a host of other old and new political players. Leaders who had not liked or respected—and often had not really known—one another learned to work together for this purpose. Moreover, the "us against each other and us together against all the others" *modus vivendi*, though contradictory and potentially unstable, worked because the early stages of unification appeared to be a non-zero-sum situation for the two parties. By working together, both ruling parties stood to gain vis-à-vis the array of upstarts that wanted to share power. The heady sense of success and accomplishment, and then the sense of embattlement during the worst days of the Gulf crisis, made for solidarity within the unification regime. The centripetal forces prevailed over the centrifugal ones—at least initially.

AFTER THE HONEYMOON

The unraveling of the original unification regime, marked by political crisis and followed by civil war, began in mid-1991, less than halfway through the transition period. The process by which the centripetal forces keeping the two parties together was gradually countered by the centrifugal ones pulling them apart follows a secular trend, but one around which there was considerable fluctuation.[5] The referendum on the constitution in mid-May 1991 was an event for which the parties put aside their differences and closed ranks in defense of unification and the unification process—and their unification regime. They more dramatically closed ranks again in late 1992, when they interrupted the growing political crisis in order to hold the postponed legislative elections in April 1993. The Document of Pledge and Accord notwithstanding, they did *not* close ranks in the post-election tripartite regime during the more profound political crisis in late 1993 and early 1994—and a consequence was civil war.

The unraveling was not just a matter of "the two Alis." Although both leaders played big roles in it, the process involved the growing hostility and the loss of trust between two groups of political leaders, each able to command a largely loyal military establishment. In the course of the final political crisis, moreover, the two groups changed character as key figures withdrew from the fray and other players joined it. This was especially true of the "secessionist group" which both lost key YSP figures and took on the appearance of a living museum of nearly a half century of South Yemeni politics.[6]

Although a full grasp of the sequence of events that led to the dissolution of the unification regime needs further study, some of the key elements in the process can be identified. In early 1990, both halves of the unification regime discovered that unequivocal identification with unification was an almost instant source of new support and legitimacy because *wahda* (unity) was popularly regarded as both a most desirable end and as a means to other desirable ends; conversely, and just as quickly learned, opposition to unification initially meant the loss of support and legitimacy. By contrast, by late 1992, indifference and opposition to either or both unification and the unification regime were widespread and growing fast, largely because of worsening socioeconomic conditions and the apparent failure of the regime to address those conditions credibly. As a result, it became politically possible for YSP leaders to opt out of unification or the unification regime.

Similarly, like the drowning man to whom a life preserver is thrown, the YSP had little choice in 1989 but to die or to embrace unification, regardless of its costs and risks; the political and economic bankruptcy of the PDRY regime at the time dictated this. By contrast, there was a very attractive, seemingly feasible alternative available to the southern leaders by late 1992: an oil-rich ministate in which one-fifth of the Yemeni population would control and benefit from a disproportionate share of Yemen's oil resources. Beginning with the oil strike in Masilah in 1990, perceptions of where the oil was in Yemen—fed partly by dreams and estimates spun of estimates—shifted east from Marib/al-Jawf, the "neutral zone," and Shabwa to the Hadhramawt, an area well within the borders of the old South Yemen. This shift east probably correlates well with the revival of, and increasing commitment to, the idea of an independent South Yemen among southern politicians. The material basis for independence seemed to be there. In addition, there was material as well as political support from Saudi Arabia for an independent South Yemen, the offer of which probably came sometime in 1992.

Another aspect of the process by which centrifugal forces came to override the centripetal ones involved the transformation of the unification process from a non-zero-sum to a zero-sum situation—i.e., to one in which a gain for one party must result in an equal loss for the other party. By late 1992, the balance in the unification regime's "us against each other and us together against all the others" *modus vivendi* had tipped decisively toward "us against each other." Al-Baydh and those close to him became convinced that for the GPC to get its way would mean their demise and the complete subordination of South Yemen, its people, and the YSP, whereas Salih and those close to him became equally convinced that for al-Baydh and his friends to get their way meant the end of unity and the national development of Yemen. Increasingly, those who became the "secessionists" came to the conclusion that the politics of the situation is zero-sum: the oil *is* in the south, and the choice is between leadership of an oil-rich mini-state or an uncertain place in unified Yemen. Framing them differently, the "unionists" increasingly came to the same conclusions.

The results of the relatively free and fair elections in 1993 probably reflected the support of the three biggest parties quite accurately—and that was the problem. The elections, instead of reaffirming unification and marking the beginning of the post-transition future of Yemeni politics, revealed political realities that some—maybe all—of the political leaders were unwilling to accept. The options before them were three: A minority government headed by the GPC; a two-party coalition government consisting of the GPC and either the YSP or Islah; or, the choice finally selected, a three-party coalition of the GPC, YSP, and Islah. Unfortunately, each of the options involved a leap of faith—faith in peaceful, democratic politics. In turn, that faith depended upon political trust. By mid-1993 if not sooner, that trust simply was not there. Public denials notwithstanding, evidence abounds that the leaders of the GPC and the YSP were aware of the hole they had dug for themselves. Hence the unguarded outbursts of candor and the inconclusive discussions and actions regarding opposition, merger, coordination, or something else. They simply did not know what to do (democratically), given the level of mutual distrust. In this instance, at least, it was the leaders, not the people, who were "not ready for democracy."

As a consequence, the election results became irrelevant and were ignored. Without facing the chicken and egg question, what mattered ultimately was that al-Baydh and the leaders with him believed that the great equalizer was a loyal military establishment which was perceived to be as good, if not better, than that loyal to Salih and his colleagues, and that Salih and his colleagues ascribed this belief to al-Baydh and were also thinking in military terms. In the absence of trust, Yemeni politics increasingly came to be perceived by Yemeni politicians as similar to the game in which Thomas Hobbes said "clubs are trump."

By early 1994, the situation was one in which the two parties were leveling serious, undisguised charges at each other. The southern leaders were publicly questioning in radical terms the form of unification, if not unification itself. That it felt politically free to do this, in a way that critics of unification did not in 1990–91, probably indicates the degree to which unification had lost its cachet and not met expectations. Two sets of rump bodies, the one in San'a and the other in Aden, were acting in place of the formal institutions of unified Yemen. In addition, each of the two parts of Yemen were separately conducting international relations against, not just independently of, the other; each was seeking external support against the other, thereby regionalizing if not internationalizing the unification crisis. Finally, on the ground, the army of each part of Yemen was trying to protect its portion of the oil patch from the other or to encroach on the other's portion—i.e., doing exactly what they had done in 1985 and 1987–88 with such explosive potential.

Hard decisions and actions deferred in 1990 in the name of getting on with the formal process of unification came back later to haunt all of the leaders, and to spawn fear, distrust, and hostility. In retrospect, it might have been better to take some of these decisions and actions—e.g., merger of the armed services and the internal security forces—in 1990 and 1991 when the popularity of the leaders of the unification regime and of unification itself were at their peak. Perhaps the power-sharing formula based on parity for the transition period was a mistake, creating a fiction that would be harder to undo later than to have faced the apparent reality of political inequality in 1990. But this is speculation on paths not taken, paths that, even if available—and this is by no means certain—had their own pitfalls.

Problems and Prospects

"Something wonderful has happened in Yemen," the *The New York Times* rhapsodized in early May 1993-unification *and* democratization, and both now crowned and advanced further by fair, open national elections. The events of the first half of 1994 rendered this eulogy premature.

Unity and democracy may still prevail in Yemen in the near future. However, to say that the leaders of Yemen chose unity and democracy in late 1989 risks obscuring a possible dilemma. More correctly, they chose unity as their goal, and *then* chose to do it democratically; the former preceded the latter on the scale of values as well as in time. Accordingly, the question for the Yemenis at the end of the 1990s is not so much whether unified Yemen will prevail—it quite probably will. Rather, the question is how much of the new, fragile, and not yet internalized democracy might they have to sacrifice in order to restore and maintain that unity (See Carapico 1994; Lerner 1992).

With or without unity, the strengthening of Yemeni democracy probably depends politically upon the ability of a coalition government not unlike the posttransition coalition to preside over, and take some credit for, the development and growing prosperity of Yemen. The trick will be to match North Yemen's success from the mid-1970s to the mid-1980s, and to do this without the peculiar benefits of remittances is now probably a thing of the past. In this less generous environment, the political leaders will have to make the hard choices required by prevailing conditions at the same time that they will be competing for the support of people whose pain and fears are shaped by those conditions. Will the Yemeni leaders be able to meet these contradictory demands? Will leaders who were not ready for democracy in 1994 be ready for it in the coming years?

With or without Yemeni unification or democracy, questions of further socioeconomic development in Yemen and the application of oil and gas revenues to that goal over the next quarter century turn largely on whether the political leadership is able to minimize waste and corruption, resist the temptation to borrow excessively against future revenues, and hold to the stated gospel of agricultural development and light industry. Thus far at least, Yemen's entrance into the oil age has been for the most part cautious and prudent, but this age is just starting and over time oil has intoxicated and seduced seemingly reasonable leaders in Mexico, Nigeria, Algeria, and other developing nations.

There is also the question of how much oil and gas there is—in Marib/al-Jawf, Shabwa, the former neutral zone, and the Hadhramawt—to be cautious and prudent about. Enough to fuel Yemen's development for a generation? For decades into the next century? Recoverable oil and gas reserves may prove to be considerably more than those verified as of the mid-1990s; production of the equivalent of one million b/d of oil early in the next decade is not an unreasonable projection. Even so, this would not leave a big margin for error in pursuit of self-sustaining development. Accordingly, Yemen can ill afford to make too many big mistakes on the path to this goal.

Finally, mention of future development in Yemen leads to questions of the uses to which oil revenues will be put. Unlike the remittance economy of the 1970s and most of the 1980s, which had a leveling effect by distributing benefits widely to many people in many parts of Yemen, the capital-intensive oil industry and much of the rest of the oil-fueled economy that are emerging probably have built-in biases toward greater inequality as well as greed and corruption. Will the oil revenues passing through government hands be put to the good use of Yemeni society as a whole, or be used and even squandered by and for the few? Will state and polity prove strong enough and so structured as to favor the broad distribution of benefits? And with unity, will the egalitarianism of the ideology that for two decades informed the southern part of Yemen, and the degree of order, organization, and honesty that seems to have marked its public life, tip the balance in that direction? Answers to these questions should begin to emerge by the year 2000.

Endnotes

1. This sort of change is predicted by the theory of nation-building based on communications theory (see Deutsch 1966).

2. There for research, I witnessed this process in the two parts of Yemen between late May and mid-July 1990. Awed and sobered by it all, my thoughts often turned for analogy to the time between the adoption and the implementation of the U.S. Constitution in the late eighteenth century. The number of things, large and small, momentous and mundane, that had to be rethought and redone was simply staggering, in the private and mixed sectors as well as the public sector. For an analysis of Yemeni politics, based on a visit to San'a and Aden in June 1990, see Hudson 1991.

3. Most of the remaining 20 percent of the seats were won by "independents," although the Ba'th Party did take several of them. For an early analysis of the election results, see Carapico 1994.

4. Concern about access suddenly crystallized at the end of the 1980s as it became apparent to some leaders in the north that the YAR's oil reserves were growing more slowly than those of the PDRY and as predictions of the bounty of the neutral zone grew to exceed the combined reserves of both Yemens. These leaders saw as potentially destabilizing a population ratio of more than 3:1 for the YAR to the PDRY set against an oil reserve ratio of 1:3:5 for the YAR, the PDRY, and the neutral zone. They concluded that the Yemens should act now to unite before the YAR attempted to get "our fair share" and the PDRY acted to keep "what's ours."

5. For another analysis of the descent into civil war, one taking a somewhat different approach to arrive at similar conclusions, see Hudson 1995.

6. For example, Abd al-Rahman Ali al-Jifri and his League of the Sons of Yemen were throwbacks to the Federation of South Arabia days and Abdulla al-Asnag had been the leader of the Front For the Liberation of South Yemen (FLOSY), the movement that lost out at independence in 1967 to the NLF, the predecessor of the YSP. Less dramatic, such northern political stalwarts as Shaykh Mujahid Abu Shuwarib and Shaykh Sinan Abu Luhum simply withdrew from the fray in disgust.

References

Al-Ashtal, Abdullah. "Eventually There Can Only Be an Arab Solution." *Middle East Report* 21:2 No. 169 (March–April 1991), 8–10.

Al-Suwaidi, Jamal S., ed. *The Yemeni War of 1994*. London: Saqi Books, 1995.

Bidwell, Robin. *The Two Yemens*. Essex, UK: Longman Group, 1983.

Burrowes, Robert D. *The Yemen Arab Republic: The Politics of Development, 1962–1986*. Boulder, CO: Westview Press, 1987.

Burrowes, Robert D. "Oil Strike and Leadership Struggle in South Yemen: 1986 and Beyond." *Middle East Journal* 43:3 (Summer 1989), 437–54.

Burrowes, Robert D. "Prelude to Unification: The Yemen Arab Republic, 1962–1990." *International Journal of Middle Eastern Studies* 23:4 (November 1991), 483–506.

Carapico, Sheila. "Yemen: Human Rights in Yemen During and After the 1994 War." *Human Rights Watch—Middle East*, 6:1 (October 1994).

Carapico, Sheila. "Elections and Mass Politics in Yemen." *Middle East Report* 23:6 No. 185 (November–December 1994), 2–6.

Cigar, Norman. "State and Society in South Yemen." *Problems of Communism* 34 (May–June 1985), 41–58.

Cigar, Norman. "Soviet-South Yemeni Relations: The Gorbachev Years." *Journal of South Asian and Middle Eastern Studies* 12:4 (Summer 1989), 3–38.

Deutsch. Karl W. *Nationalism and Social Communication*. Cambridge: M.I.T. Press, 1966.

Foreign Broadcast Information Service (FBIS): Daily Reports-Middle East and Africa. Washington, D.C., May 5, 1988.

Gause, F. Gregory III. "The Idea of Yemeni Unity." *Journal of Arab Affairs* 6 (Spring 1987), 55–87.

Gause, F. Gregory III. "Yemeni Unity: Past and Future." *Middle East Journal* 42:1 (Winter 1988), 33–47.

Halliday, Fred. "The Yemens: Conflict and Coexistence." *World Today* 40 (August–September 1984), 355–362.

Halliday, Fred. *Revolution and Foreign Policy: The Case of South Yemen*. London: Cambridge University Press, 1989.

Hudson, Michael. After the Gulf War: Prospects for Democratization in the Arab World." *Middle East Journal* 45:3 (Summer 1991), 407–426.

Hudson, Michael. "Bipolarity, Rational Calculation, and War in Yemen." *Arab Studies Journal* 3:1 (Spring 1995), 9–19.

Ismael, Tareq and Jacqueline Ismael. *The People's Democratic Republic of Yemen: Politics, Economics and Society*. London: Frances Pinter, 1986.

Le Monde, October 14, 1987, 7.

Lerner, George. Yemen: Steps Toward Civil Society." *Human Rights Watch—Middle East* 4:10 (November 1992).

New York Times, May 8, 1993.

Pollack, David. "Moscow and Aden: Coping with a Coup." *Problems of Communism* 35 (May–June 1986), 50–70.

Stookey, Robert W. *Yemen: The Politics of the United Arab Republic.* Boulder, CO: Westview Press, 1978.

Warburton, David. The Conventional War in Yemen." *Arab Studies Journal,* 3:1 (Spring 1995), 20–44.

Wenner, Manfred W. *The Yemen Arab Republic: Development and Change in an Ancient Land.* Boulder, CO: Westview Press, 1991.

Inter-Arab Economic Relations During the Twentieth Century: World Market vs. Regional Market?

chapter 10

Roger Owen

The historical arguments used to explain the Arab world's low level of economic integration are well known. They usually begin by pointing to its division into separate units as a result of its incorporation into the world market in the nineteenth century via a process of expanding trade followed by other financial and commercial linkages. These arguments then point to how these divisions were solidified during the colonial period as a result of the creation of new state frontiers and British and French attempts to monopolize the economic relations between themselves and their mandates, protectorates, or colonies. After this, independence is seen to have encouraged efforts to reintegrate the Arab economies through such mechanisms as a free trade area and a common market. However, such attempts did little to promote interregional trade, for both economic and political reasons. Finally, the oil price explosion of the early 1970s provided another and more powerful set of complementarities which are exploited through the development of mechanisms for the exchange of labor for capital (Sayigh 1983).

All this is largely true and I have no quarrel with most of it. Nevertheless, there is some advantage in returning to these arguments at regular intervals in order to see how they have stood the test of time. Like all generalizations, they are open to criticisms as to detail. They may also hide some interesting insights that closer examination could bring to light. Just as important, they may still have something to say about the situation now facing the Arab world in which the end of the Cold War, the Middle East peace process, and accelerated movement toward a new global economic order have created challenges and opportunities that demand serious attention at both the state and the regional level.

I will begin by reviewing some of the historical data with particular reference to such important topics as the absolute level of intra-Arab trade and the relationship between trade and trade agreements. I will then go on to see if the lessons of the past have anything new to tell us about the economic options now facing Arab policymakers at the very end of the twentieth century.

The History: Trade, Economic Division, and Colonialism

The integration of the Arab East into the world market in the nineteenth century had a number of important effects. First, as is well known, it led to a process of uneven regional development in which certain parts of the region began to specialize in the production of crops for export to Europe and North America while others continued to concentrate on preexisting patterns of production and exchange. The most obvious examples of the first type were Egypt, whose economy increasingly came to depend on the international sale of long staple cotton, Mount Lebanon with its concentration on the spinning of locally produced silk, Palestine with its focus on citrus fruits, and the Ottoman provinces of Basra, Baghdad, and Mosul with their growing exports of dates, wool, and barley. This left just the interior of some Syrian provinces subject to older patterns of trade, and even there the economy participated in regular export booms, for example, those for cereals in the 1850s and again in the latter part of the century.

With the increase in exports came the establishment of complex mechanisms for providing the necessary credit, processing, and transport. These involved the creation of banks, the building of ginning plants and storage facilities, and the construction of new rail and other transport networks, all leading to the coastal ports. The result was the growth of what economists have called "export sectors," enclaves that existed physically in the Middle East but were also integrally related to the European economy. By and large, there was a close connection between the major sources of credit required to finance this process and the markets to which Middle Eastern products were then sent. Thus, British merchants and bankers dominated the export sectors in Egypt and Iran, and their French counterparts dominated those of Mount Lebanon.

Several writers have used the existence of such sectors to make the argument that, over time, they came to constitute spheres of European influence that anticipated the division of the Arab East during World War I and so the creation of the separate British- and French-dominated states shortly thereafter (Khalidi 1980). This is certainly a compelling argument. Similar arguments have been put forward to link Britain's growing economic interest in Egypt with its occupation of that country in 1882, but the subject remains a controversial one among historians and theorists of imperialism (Owen 1976; Hopkins 1986).

The creation of the new Arab state system under foreign control had two major economic consequences. On the one hand, it cemented the relationship between the local economy and a particular metropolis. On the other, it began a process of creating barriers to intraregional economic exchange, many of which remain to this day. As far as the first point is concerned, the British and French made every effort to monopolize economic relations with their mandates and protectorates, linking their currencies, acting as sole providers of credit, and trying to ensure that all major contracts for public works and public utilities were awarded to their own nationals. Incorporation into the Franc and Sterling Areas during the 1930s served much the same purpose. Similar constraints were then built into the treaties governing post-independence relations, for example with Iraq in 1931 and Egypt in 1936, to be further reinforced by the military control exercised over the region by British forces during World War II.

Equally important were the barriers which the creation of separate national economies placed in the way of inter-Arab exchange. These included not just the use of tariffs to protect local markets, particularly during the depressed economic conditions of the 1930s, but also the creation of a whole gamut of associated differences—different educational and legal systems, different forms of taxation, different types of business and professional associations—which drove further powerful wedges between the various Arab states. This was underpinned by the establishment of locally powerful financial, commercial, and industrial sectors with strong links with the colonial economic order and with the structure of resource allocation which it had engendered. A good example of this are the Egyptian business empires identified by Vitalis—those like the Abbud, Misr and Cattaui/Suares groups—which vied with one another for the monopoly profits to be obtained by dominating different sections of the domestic market (Vitalis 1990, 291–315). Much the same logic still obtained after their nationalization in the late 1950s and early 1960s when what were often unchanged management teams strove to maintain their position of dominance within a highly protected national economy.

Nevertheless, just what the impact of all this was on inter-Arab economic relations has not been the subject of any very precise study. We know something of the macro situation but much less about the individual countries and individual flows of goods, labor, and capital. In these circumstances I must content myself with stressing two of the more obvious points. The first begins with the observation that while the Egyptian economy was the most closely connected with those of Western Europe, the United States, and, increasingly, Japan, it was still large enough to play a significant role in inter-Arab trade as well. Thus, if we look simply at the direction of trade expressed in proportional terms, we find that only 5 percent of Egyptian trade was with the rest of the Arab world in the 1920s compared with a third of that of Syria/Lebanon (Musrey 1969, 15–16). Looked at in quantitative terms, however, the picture appears quite different. The huge size of the Egyptian economy and its much larger volume of trade meant that it still remained a very important partner for its eastern Arab neighbors, until they too began to introduce significant levels of tariff protection in the 1930s on both industrial and agricultural goods. Restricted access to the Egyptian market was of particular importance for Syria/Lebanon whose exports to Egypt fell from 700,000 Egyptian pounds (£E) in the 1920s to only £E200,000 in the late 1930s and for Palestine/Trans-Jordan whose exports fell from 400,000 Palestinian pounds (£P) to £P200,000 during the same period (Musrey 1969, 22–23).

The second point concerns Syria/Lebanon, which remained at the center of what was virtually a free trade area including Palestine and Trans-Jordan until 1939. Over time, its trade with neighbors assumed further importance when new roads built during the Mandate period greatly improved communications with Jerusalem, Amman, and Baghdad. Syria/Lebanon was thus able to play an important role as an entrepôt, a fact vividly underlined by the political power wielded by its truckers and merchants (many of whom went on strike in 1933 in a partially successful effort to prevent a rise in import duties that they believed would harm their own business) (Shimizu 1986). Thus, a third of Syria's exports went to its Arab neighbors in the 1920s while such trade became even more important in the 1930s as access to the increasingly protected Egyptian market became ever more difficult (Musrey 1969, 26–28).

The situation of declining inter-Arab trade was then briefly reversed during World War II as a result of the efforts of Britain and the United States to manage the whole Middle Eastern economy (the Arab countries of the Mashriq plus Iran, Ethiopia, and Cyprus) as a single unit. Using the Middle East Supply Center (MESC), created in Cairo in April 1941, as their principal agent they managed to save scarce shipping space by reducing imports into the region from their prewar level of 5.5 million tons to just 1.5 million tons in 1944, while encouraging a sharp rise in local production and trade to make up the gap (MESC 1945). In this sense the war acted as a vast form of protection—a point later emphasized by André Gunder Frank—cutting off the Middle East from competition from the world economy while, at the same time, greatly increasing the domestic market via the presence of large armies of Allied troops (1969).

The result was a huge increase in intraregional trade from which Palestine and Iraq seem to have benefited the most. In the case of Palestine, whose proportion of exports going to Middle Eastern markets rose from 10 percent in 1939 to 75 percent in 1942 and 60 percent in 1944, its most important asset was its (mainly Jewish) industrial base which was much more developed and diversified than anything else to be found in the Middle East (Government of Palestine 1946–47). Meanwhile, Iraq's increased exports were based mainly on the passage of its oil through the new transdesert pipelines to the refineries at Tripoli and Haifa on the Mediterranean coast. Here were complementarities that were easily possible to exploit, given overall British and American control.

Nevertheless, Alfred Musrey is rightly skeptical about the longer-term impact of the war in promoting intra-Arab trade, seeing it as no more than a good opportunity for most Arab countries to develop their own productive facilities behind still formidable tariff barriers (1969, 34–37). The reestablishment of the Arab boycott of Jewish industry in 1946, followed by the expulsion of most of Palestine's Arab population and the creation of the state of Israel, then effectively removed the Palestinian economy from the positive role it could well have played in schemes to rebuild the wartime pattern of economic exchange. Meanwhile, British attempts to use the achievements of the MESC as a basis for postwar regional cooperation soon came to nothing in the face of both U.S. and Arab suspicion.

Independence: State vs. Regional Development Before the Oil Era

One of the essential ingredients of almost all the local nationalist struggles against foreign control was a critique of colonial economic management. Beginning in Egypt before World War I, Arab spokesmen increasingly accused Britain and France of encouraging the export of just a few agricultural exports, hindering industry, and expending far too tiny a proportion of the revenue on education and welfare. Thus Habib Bourguiba, writing to the French Under Secretary of State for Foreign Affairs in 1936, spoke of France's creation of great economic inequalities in Tunisia, of the ruin of the *fellah*, and of a customs policy that had put Tunisian workmen at the mercy of certain French, Italian, and Czech capitalists (Bourguiba 1936). Similar criticisms were voiced in Syria and Egypt. This in turn began to provide the basis of a program of industrialization and economic development supported, after World War II, by the introduction of the powerful new notions of planning, technical assistance, and development.

An equally important feature of the Arab critique of colonialism was, of course, its attack on the divisions between the new states symbolized by their "artificial boundaries." It was thus natural to believe that, in the post-independence period, the Arab League should provide a mechanism for reintegrating the region, economically as well as politically. Another influence came from the efforts of the United Nations to promote regional cooperation and, later, from the 1957 creation of the European Common Market.

Arab attempts to create a multilateral framework for greater regional economic integration are generally seen as proceeding in two stages (Diab 1963, chs. 1 and 2; Musrey 1969, chs. 5 and 6). The first, or free-trade, stage began at the 1950 meeting of the League's Economic Council with the ratification of the Treaty for Joint Defense and Economic Cooperation by the ministers of Egypt, Jordan, Lebanon, Syria, Saudi Arabia, and (North) Yemen. This placed a major emphasis on tariff reductions and on measures to facilitate the free movement of people and capital. It was followed in 1953 by the Convention for Facilitating Trade and Regulating Transit, which represented an agreement to abolish tariffs on agricultural products and minerals between League members. Efforts to remove existing barriers to the trade in manufactured goods were not successful, however. Some states, like Iraq, insisted on being able to protect their own industry, while others, like Saudi Arabia and Yemen, insisted that they had to raise a substantial part of their public revenues from duties on imported goods.

The next stage, the attempt to create an Arab Common Market, began in the late 1950s. New conditions had been created by Arab solidarity with Egypt during its struggle against the Anglo-French and Israeli attack on the Suez Canal as well as by the successful launch of the European Economic Community. The 1958 meeting of the Arab League's Economic Council reached an agreement in principle, and was followed in 1962 by the joint declaration of five states— Egypt, Jordan, Morocco, Syria, and Kuwait—to commit themselves to move towards both unified economic policies and unified economic legislation. Finally, in August 1964, representatives of all five states signed the treaty to establish the Arab Common Market on January 1, 1965, with an agreement to a staged abolition of all duties and quantitative restrictions between them by January 1974. This treaty was then officially ratified by all states except Kuwait.

In any event, movement toward reducing tariffs and restrictions proved extremely difficult. During four rounds of discussions each partner produced lengthy lists of goods it wished to exempt from tariff reduction while only minimal progress was made on quantitative restrictions. There was similar lack of progress toward the creation of a common external tariff until, in 1971, the whole notion was officially abandoned. What was left of the arrangement reverted to a putative free trade area (Sayigh 1983, 151).

It has seemed easy to demonstrate, statistically, that the impact of both schemes on inter-Arab trade was negligible. This is Muhammad Diab's conclusion after his detailed study of the impact of both multilateral and bilateral agreements between the Arab states from 1951 to 1960 (Diab 1963, ch. 4). Yusif Sayigh has made the same point about both the 1950s and 1960s noting that inter-Arab trade never became more than a tenth of the Arab total (1983, 149). The argument then moves quickly on to why this should have been so. As far as the literature is concerned, there are two favored culprits. One is the similar economic structures of the Arab states concerned and thus the lack of economic complementarities to exploit by way of greater trade. The other is the obvious lack of political will.

There is clearly much truth in this. Once Kuwait withdrew from the attempt to create a common market, the project was left with members that produced roughly the same range of agricultural goods and aspired to produce roughly the same range of manufactured ones as well. We may also note that similarly ambitious schemes for institutionalizing regional economic cooperation failed in many other parts of the non-European world at this same time, for example in North Africa and in Latin America, for exactly the same reasons (Robana 1978; Finch 1982). Nevertheless, once again, this is not quite the whole story. I will mention just two important qualifications.

First, most post-independence Arab regimes behaved no differently from the vast bulk of their Third World compatriots: they based their strategies for rapid economic development on a version of Import-Substituting Industrialization (ISI), that is, the production of a relatively simple range of previously imported manufactured goods for sale in a protected local market. Looked at in historical perspective, the attractions of such a model must have had something to do with the apparent success of the Soviet Union's drive for rapid industrialization, and something to do with the lessons drawn from colonial economic policy, which was to have barred development by discouraging industry and emphasizing the export of a few agricultural goods. If we add that the ISI strategy could also be recommended as a way of protecting newly independent countries from the rigors of a fiercely competitive world market, with its disturbing movements in the price of primary commodities and its powerful multinational corporations, we can appreciate its apparent advantages for unconfident, uncertain regimes that were already moving toward political strategies of containment and control.

The implications of such a strategy for trade are important. Exports receive low priority, foreign exchange is scarce, and what little there is must be reserved for essential imports of capital goods and raw materials. In addition, for the Arabs, as in most other cases, periodic balance-of-payments crises lead to reduced convertibility for the local currency and an increasing number of controls that, on occasion, leave them with no option but to try to obtain what they need by barter. Meanwhile, the people chosen to manage the increasingly state-owned industries possess few skills or incentives to market their goods abroad. In these circumstances, freer regional trade would become practical only when the industrial base is strong and diverse, and flexible enough to survive, and even prosper, in the competitive conditions of the outside world.

In the Arab context there were only two exceptions to this argument in the 1950s and 1960s: Lebanon, whose tiny domestic market and general free trade orientation encouraged the growth of manufacturing for export, and the oil-rich shaykhdoms of the Gulf, whose one-asset economies also required them to be able to buy where it was cheapest and sell where their oil would obtain the highest price. Both represent economic success stories, at least in their early decades. Whether this success was bought at acceptable social or political cost is more debatable.

Elsewhere, in both the Maghrib and the Mashriq, attempts to create Arab Common Markets during the high tide of ISI during the 1960s quickly foundered on the unwillingness of any regime to surrender control over its own economic policies or access to its own domestic markets. This was the lesson in the Arab East. It was also the lesson of the attempts to form a Maghrib Union which began with the establishment of a Permanent Consultative Council in Tunis in 1966, charged with promoting greater regional integration. In spite of the considerable effort put into identifying industries that might benefit from the creation of a North African market no substantial progress could be achieved. Individual states were too committed to their own programs of industrialization through import substitution. They were also worried that multinationals might establish plants in another member state of the union and use this as a springboard from which to penetrate their own markets. And in the case of Algeria, with the greatest commitment to centralized planning and control, there was the additional difficulty posed by the existence of state trading organizations with monopolies over the import of many strategic foreign products (Robana 1978).

The second qualification concerns the relationship between commercial treaties and economic reality. It can certainly be argued that the emphasis usually placed on the need to create Arab institutions like a free trade area or a common market tends to direct attention away from the trade flows that already exist and from the real barriers to their increase. In other words, if you have trade you may not need treaties, and if you have treaties they may not necessarily increase trade.

With this in mind we can return to an examination of the actual flows of inter-Arab commerce in the 1950s and 1960s without condemning them in advance as too small. Diab's averages for the 1950s for trade between Egypt, Iraq, Jordan, Lebanon, Saudi Arabia, and Syria allow one to make a number of points

(Diab 1963, app. D). First, there was a continuum in terms of the importance of intraregional trade: Syria was the largest in terms of absolute value and Jordan was the largest in proportion of trade with its Arab neighbors. To give just a few examples, 95 percent of Jordanian exports went to its Arab neighbors at the beginning of the 1950s and 47 percent in 1960, while the average for Syria over the whole decade was 37 percent of exports and that for Iraq between 15 and 20 percent. At the other end of the scale was Egypt with only 1.1 percent of its exports sold to its Arab partners in 1951, rising to 5.8 percent in 1960, but mostly as a result of the creation of the United Arab Republic with Syria. Second, Diab's figures show that primary products took a huge share of this trade, with only small amounts coming from textiles and, in the case of Lebanon, simple manufactured products made from (often imported) asbestos, aluminum, wood, and iron, mostly for building. Third, in global terms, the proportion of intra-Arab to total trade was growing over the whole decade.

Later, in the 1960s, the attempt to create an Arab Common Market coincided with the establishment of tightly controlled, planned economies in Syria and Iraq, as well as a worsening of political relations between these two states which reduced their mutual trade to a trickle (Musrey 1969, 113). Hence the main area of intraregional trade continued to be that of Syria/Lebanon/Jordan, with growing links to the Gulf. In addition, as Musrey notes, there was a sudden spurt of trade between Egypt and Iraq that he attributes to the moves to harmonize their economic structures as a prelude to political union (1969, 114). The situation was then changed completely, first by the destruction and disruptions caused by the 1967 war and then by the progressive rise in the price of oil during the early 1970s.

Integration vs. Disintegration in the Oil Era

The impact of the oil price rise and the huge revenues of the 1970s on the Arab economy has been discussed so often that I will simply mention what seem to me the most salient points. The first is its stimulus to a huge increase in the flows of capital and labor between states, though much less to an increase in trade. The second is that only a small part of these new flows were regulated by any of the new Arab banks, funds, and development agencies that mushroomed at this time. With the possible exception of some of the Egyptian labor making its way to Iraq in the early 1980s, Arab workers moved from one part of the region to the other in an unplanned and purely private fashion. As for capital, only a small part of it was channeled through the 237 joint ventures as Sayigh has noted (1983, 149–50). He has also pointed out that the one attempt at an overall plan—the Strategy for Joint Arab Economic Action discussed at the 11th Arab Summit in Amman in November 1980—was first watered down and then never properly implemented (159–64). Thus most movements and transfers were unplanned, unpredictable, and subject to the political interests of the separate states concerned.

The basic shortcomings of pan-Arab economic institutions were also highlighted by the move toward smaller subregional groupings like the Gulf Cooperation Council (GCC), the Maghrib Union, and the short-lived Arab Cooperation Council created in the late 1980s among Egypt, Iraq, Jordan, and Yemen. Of these, the economic component of the GCC was not only the most ambitious but also the only one to survive for more than a few years. It projected the formation of a genuine common market, with a common external tariff and common internal laws and regulations to be established somewhere around the year 2000. We may also note that these putative arrangements were based solidly on the prior existence of a significant amount of trade among the member states of the council.

The results of this situation can be illustrated using figures provided by members of some of the various Arab organizations—as well as individual Arab economists—who remained committed to the idea of further economic integration. On the one hand, the proportion of intra-Arab to total Arab trade, though growing during the 1980s, remained small, particularly if compared with other regions of the non-European world. As Muhammad Abu al-Khail, the Saudi Minister of Finance and National Economy, noted in his address to the Arab Economic Council in 1987, only 5.2 percent of total Arab exports in 1980 and 6.6 percent in 1984 were sent to another Arab country. And even here, as he noted, the absolute values involved were declining as a result of the falling price of oil. Thus, inter-Arab exports were worth $12 billion in 1980 but only $8.4 billion in 1984 (Quoted in CAABU 1987). On the other hand, a huge proportion of what little intra-Arab trade that did take place at this time was among the Gulf oil producers themselves (Riorden et al. 1995).

Other processes were at work to reinforce this pattern. One was the debt crisis that hit a number of Arab countries during the 1980s as a result of falling oil prices. This was particularly severe in states like Egypt and Jordan, which relied heavily on money from Arab aid and from the remittances sent home by their migrant workers in the Gulf. In the short run these crises had the effect of shrinking domestic markets while directing the attention of each regime toward programs of economic stabilization, and then structural adjustment, to the exclusion of almost all else. A second process was the exacerbation of intra-Arab political divisions as a result of the second Gulf War, notably the widening gap among the Gulf states and their western Arab neighbors, as well as between the GCC states themselves. The result was not only a significant reduction in capital flows from the Gulf to countries like Jordan, Yemen and, of course, Iraq but also a further blow to the prospects for intra-Arab cooperation and the revival of moribund institutions like the Arab League.

Nevertheless, the situation was not entirely without hope. Looking at these same developments from a somewhat longer time perspective, it is also possible to argue that they might have paved the way for the removal of some of the existing barriers to increased Arab integration over time. For one thing, there is the way in which the debt crisis encouraged a general movement toward deregulation, the reduction of tariffs and a greater emphasis on production for export. For another, the difficulties involved in trying to revive the Maghrib Union at the end of the 1980s—notably the international isolation of Libya followed by the political crisis in Algeria—as well as the lack of further progress toward the creation of a GCC Common Market may have made it easier for some states to contemplate exchanging their arrangements for participation in some wider Arab economic framework. It is to considerations of this kind that I now turn.

Present and the Future: the Pull of Rival Economic Architecture

The 1990s have seen the emergence of two new, and possibly rival, schemes for the economic organization of the Middle East and North Africa. The first is the plan for a Euro-Mediterranean free trade area put forward by the European Union (EU). This consists of two related sets of initiatives. One is the upgrading, as well as the mutual harmonization, of the existing agreements between the EU and individual southern Mediterranean states. By the beginning of 1996 the Europeans had signed new treaties with Israel, Morocco, and Tunisia while negotiations were underway with Egypt, Jordan, Lebanon, and the Palestinian National Authority (PNA). The second more general scheme unveiled in Barcelona in November 1995 to establish a Euro-Mediterranean free trade area in manufactured goods no later than the year 2010. Signatories included the members of the EU as well as Turkey, Israel, Cyprus, and Malta, the Arab states of Mauritania, Morocco, Tunisia, Egypt, Jordan, Syria, and Lebanon, and the PNA.

As far as these Arab states are concerned the EU's initiative has several obvious disadvantages. It promises no greater preferential access to the European market than most of them already possessed as a result of earlier agreements, yet it commits them to opening up their own markets to what will obviously be intense international competition. It does nothing to lower present EU barriers to either their migrant workers or their agricultural exports. And it commits them to negotiating the necessary treaties with Europe on a bilateral basis, and so without support from their regional or subregional allies.

Nevertheless, all the southern Mediterranean states that attended the Barcelona conference signed the initial treaty, either because they saw no alternative to the new arrangements or because they anticipated particular advantages such as European financial and technical assistance to upgrade key industries in order to prepare them for the coming international competition. It has also been argued that such states might hope to benefit from the fact that their signature alone will provide extra confidence for potential foreign investors in that it commits them to a fixed timetable of reforms from which it will be very difficult to withdraw without incurring huge penalties from the EU (Economic Research Forum 1995). To this we might add that many of the same commitments—for example to reduce tariffs or to introduce new regulations governing protection of intellectual property—are more or less the same as those which most have already agreed to under the Uruguay Round and as part of their membership in the new World Trade Organization (WTO).

Two other features of the Euro-Mediterranean Agreement are also significant from an Arab point of view. One is the built-in incentives toward freer trade among the southern Mediterranean states themselves, notably the promise of better access to the European market for goods produced jointly with other members. Turkey and Israel have already taken advantage of the provision in early 1996 by signing a treaty agreeing to eliminate all trade barriers between them by the year 2000. Among other things this will allow Israeli firms to produce textiles in Turkey and then receive preferential treatment from the European market. The second feature is that the scheme leaves room for both Algeria and Libya to join once their present political difficulties are over.

The second recent initiative stems directly from the Arab-Israeli peace process and involves a plan for a region-wide free-trade area as a way of underpinning the political agreements once they are finally in place. However, this scheme faces a number of serious problems in the years ahead. It is almost wholly dependent on the establishment of a satisfactory peace. It also lacks an institutional mechanism that could be used to guide it to fruition. All that existed as of 1996 was the machinery provided by the annual Middle East business conferences (i.e., those held in Casablanca in 1994 and Amman in 1995) to be supplemented, so its sponsors hope, by the work of the Middle East Development Bank being set up in Cairo. Furthermore, the scheme continues to excite a great deal of suspicion; many Arabs see it as an essentially political project designed to end the boycotts and to ease Israel's integration into the Arab world. Hence, although it looks as though both Jordan and the new

Palestinian state must inevitably become founding members of whatever free trade area may eventually be created, other regimes like the Egyptian will probably continue to reach agreements with Israel on a project-by-project basis rather than under some larger, institutionalized umbrella. In this way they can take advantage of the various geographical economies of scale involved in the creation of joint transport, electric, and gas facilities without committing themselves to a full-scale economic and political partnership.

The existence of the two schemes provides Arab policymakers with any number of difficult choices for the future. This can be demonstrated by listing the various options that confront them. There are the three Middle East-specific subregional schemes already on the table: the Gulf Cooperation Council, the Maghrib Union, and the peace process formula of Israel plus some or all of the Arab states. There is the Euro-Mediterranean free trade area for those eligible to participate. And there are the options of either not joining any scheme at all or belonging to a global organization like the WTO or of joining two at once, as Israel, Jordan, and the PNA seem presently disposed to do. In addition, there is the possibility of reviving a specifically Arab scheme, a subject to which I will return below.

To make matters still more complicated, Arab policy makers have to plan their strategies on the basis of very incomplete information. Work on various economic models designed to provide data about regional trade flows and how they might best be augmented came to an end in the late 1980s and has only just been restarted (See comments in al-Kawaz and Limam 1996). Furthermore, few regimes feel comfortable permitting the kind of informed public discussion that would provide valuable evidence concerning the potential impact of particular commercial policies on particular domestic interests. In addition, most Arab regimes are only just beginning to grapple with the need to create the new institutional and legal frameworks required not just by their own programs of domestic liberalization but also by the international commitments they have already made to the WTO or the EU. In these circumstances, the definition of national economic goals and the creation of mechanisms by which to pursue them in an effective fashion become not just a difficult set of political problems but one of the great challenges facing the Arab states as they position themselves to enter the twenty-first century.

Whether Arab regimes, faced with all these new problems developing will also have the time and the energy to think creatively about developing new inter-Arab economic structures remains an open question. For some the notion may have been made redundant: they are committed to one of the existing schemes to the extent that there is no going back. For some of the others, like the Syrians and the Egyptians, however, it is still a pressing subject for discussion and debate. What lessons can possibly be learned from past intra-Arab schemes, and past failures?

The first lesson is the importance of attending to changed international circumstances. Whatever freedom of action the newly independent Arab states may have had in the 1950s and 1960s, policymaking is now constrained by the existence of other regional and subregional schemes and by the trend embodied in institutions like the WTO toward the establishment of global trading practices. It follows that no new project for Arab economic integration is likely to succeed unless it embodies those same principles which are central to good international commercial practice. By the same token it seems unlikely that such a project could take the form of a common market or customs union which provided preferential treatment simply for its own members.

Second, it is vital that any new Arab project contain a clear economic rationale. Politically inspired schemes have failed in the past and will no doubt fail again. What is required is a proper examination of the present complementarities that await exploitation as well those that may be reasonably expected to emerge as Arab economies, particularly their manufacturing sectors, grow and develop over time.

Third, it is important that the planning of such a project involve public discussion and the identification of those interests that might either profit from it or be harmed by it. Not only have past schemes suffered from a general lack of public support—even of public awareness—they have also failed to identify those groups which would profit directly from them and so have a good reason to help see them through. Too often intra-Arab projects have been perceived by the public as designed to give advantage to just one political regime or just one set of economic actors when what is really required is a plan from which all-or nearly all-would clearly gain.

Given present constraints it would seem that the countries most interested in a new Arab project—and those that would expect to derive most immediate benefit—would be Egypt, Syria, and Lebanon. But, if its planners were wise, they would also design it in such a way that other neighboring states, notably Iraq and Libya, could attach themselves in the future. Could this be achieved, the grouping would contain economies with the mix of resources to provide the basis for greatly increased exchange. Nevertheless, such a partnership would act only as a pole of attraction for new Arab members once it proved its worth. This is the fundamental challenge that states seeking to revive regional economic integration must inevitably face.

Gone are the days when regional groupings could be seen as mechanisms for protecting developing economies from the hostile movements of the world economy outside. Globalism is here to stay and Arab countries will have to find their major markets and major sources of capital investment outside the Middle East itself. What they can aspire to, however, is a replication of the situation that existed in the nineteenth century, when regional economic exchange expanded in tandem with the growing commerce of the outside world.

References

Al-Kawaz, Ahmad and Imed Limam. "The Arab Economies in Multi-country Models: Survey of Some Regional and Global Experiences." *ERF Working Paper Series*, 9602. Cairo: Economic Research Institute, [1996].

Bourguiba, Habib to Pierre Vienot, August 28, 1936, translated in J.C. Hurewitz, ed., *The Middle East and North Africa in World Politics: A Documentary Record*. New Haven, CT: Yale University Press, 1979, 2nd ed., 2 vols. Vol. 2, 496–99.

Diab, Muhammad A. *Inter-Arab Cooperation 1951–1960*. Beirut: Economic Research Institute, American University of Beirut, 1963.

The Economic Research Forum. "Trade with Europe" section at Second Annual Conference, Istanbul, September 16–18, 1995. In *ERF Forum*, 2:4 (December 1995), 7–8.

Finch, M.H.J. "The Latin American Free Trade Association." In Ali M. El-Agraa, ed. *International Economic Integration*. London: Macmillan, 1982.

Government of Palestine, *A Survey of Palestine* (Prepared in December 1945 and January 1946 for the information of the Anglo-American Committee of Inquiry), 1. Jerusalem(?), 1946–1947, 480.

Gunder Frank, André. *Capitalism and Underdevelopment in Latin America: Historical Studies of Chile and Brazil.* New York and London: Modern Reader Paperbacks 1969.

Hopkins, A.G. "The Victorians and Africa: A Reconsideration of the Occupation of Egypt, 1882." *Journal of African History*, 27 (1986).

Khalidi, Rashid Ismail. *British Policy Towards Syria and Palestine 1906–1914: A Study of the Antecedents of the Hussein-MacMahon Correspondence, the Sykes-Picot Agreement and the Balfour Declaration*. London: Ithaca Press for the Middle East Center, St. Antony's College Oxford, 1980, Conclusion.

Middle East Supply Centre. *Some Facts About the MESC*. Cairo 1945.

Musrey, Alfred G. *An Arab Common Market: A Study in Inter-Arab Trade Flows*. New York, Washington, London: Frederick J. Praeger, 1969.

Owen, Roger. "Robinson and Gallagher and Egyptian Nationalism: The Egyptian Argument." In William Roger Louis, ed., *The Robinson and Gallagher Controversy*. London: New Viewpoints, 1976.

Riorden, E. Mick, et al. *The World Economy and Implications for the Middle East and North Africa Region*. Washington, DC: World Bank, International Economics Department, Analysis and Prospects Division (June 1995), 14–15 and Table 23, on 53.

Robana, Abderrahman. "The Maghreb economic cooperation in retrospect." *The Maghreb Review* 3, 7:8 (May-Aug. 1978).

Sayigh, Yusif A. "A new framework for complementarily among the Arab economies." In Ibrahim Ibrahim, ed., *Arab Resources: The Transformation of a Society*. Washington, DC and London: Center for Contemporary Arab Studies, Washington DC and London: Croom Helm, 1983, 147–55.

Shimizu, Hiroshi. *Anglo-Japanese Rivalry in the Middle East in the Inter-War Period* London: Ithaca Press for the Middle East Centre, St. Antony's College Oxford, 1986.

Vitalis, Robert, "On the Theory and Practice of Compradors: The Role of Abbud Pasha in the Egyptian Political Economy." *International Journal of Middle East Studies* 22:3 (August 1990).

Arab Economic Integration: The Poor Harvest of the 1980s

chapter 11

Yusif A. Sayigh

In 1981, I gave a paper at Georgetown University entitled "New Framework for Complementarity Among the Arab Economies (Ibrahim 1983)," which included an assessment of the extent of Arab economic integration and complementarity achieved during the years 1945–1980. My emphasis was on the years 1973–1980, which witnessed the correction of oil prices from October 1973 onward and the parallel rise in oil revenues accruing to the Arab oil exporters. Although the achievement had been quite modest, even during the 1970s, it was sufficient to create rosy expectations, especially when in late November 1980, the Arab heads of state in a summit meeting in Jordan approved a "Strategy for Joint Arab Economic Action" along with twenty-six other documents supportive of the Strategy.

Here I take stock of what has happened in the intervening decade with respect to economic complementarity and integration in the Arab region. Unfortunately, very little has been achieved. The shortfall between the high level at which hopes and expectations stood in 1980, and the much lower level of concrete performance by the summer of 1990 is vast. Yet before I proceed to trace the main steps taken during the 1980s to promote integration and complementarity and to assess their reach and significance, I must make two observations, meant to sharpen understanding of the cautious evaluation I made of the "new framework" in my earlier paper, even though I myself was directly and intensely involved in the formulation of the "Strategy" and the documents prepared for and around it.

The first observation is that I had expressed grave misgivings about the chances that the "New Framework" would be fleshed out by substantive and concrete achievement. My concern was that the framework would remain a largely-unfilled container—however elaborate, rationally reasoned and carefully designed. This fear was generated by the persistence of a number of deep-rooted cultural, political, and structural factors in Arab society, most particularly within the circles of political leadership and parts of the business community in which integration was not deemed desirable.

The second observation is that, in the short to medium term, it is imperative to greatly restrain expectations of marked achievement toward integration and complementarity among the Arab economies. The reason for this gloomy projection is that, in addition to cultural, political, and structural factors, Iraq's occupation of Kuwait in August 1990, along with the crisis and war that occupation generated, resulted in further political fragmentation of the Arab region and far-reaching economic isolationism within virtually every country in the region. In fact, official statements supportive of complementarity and integration, however perfunctory and devoid of purposefulness they often were, are no longer even being uttered. A cloud of gloom, frustration, fear, and cynicism has descended on much of the Arab region since August 1990, blocking any significant rays of hope for either close political or economic cooperation. And, it should be remembered, cooperation and joint Arab economic action are distinctly less ambitious notions than complementarity or integration. There is, however, one notable exception to this very grim generalization which I will discuss in the review and evaluation of the records of the 1980s, to which I now turn. Later, I will attempt to explore the causes for what I have termed the "poor harvest" of the 1980s.

The Record of the 1980s

A review of the development of the 1980s with respect to the process of Arab economic complementarity and integration could easily become bogged down in detail. To spare the reader excessive quantification, I will generally restrict myself to a presentation of the broad findings of research undertaken on the components of the process in question. My main source of information has been *The Consolidated Arab Economic Report*. This official publication appears annually, and contains information relating to the previous year.[1] In addition, I have perused other reports and analytical articles in journals, particularly *Al-Mustaqbal al-'arabi* (*The Arab Future*), a monthly published in Beirut by the Center for Arab Unity Studies), *Shu'un 'arabiyya* (*Arab Affairs*), a monthly published by the Secretariat-General of the League of Arab States), and *Al-Muntada* (*The Forum*), a monthly published by the Arab Thought Forum in Amman). And finally, I have benefited from discussions with a number of Arab scholars, intellectuals, and business leaders who follow Arab economic developments closely and evaluate them analytically. As I do not have the space necessary for specific reporting on the research and the discussions undertaken, the reader may have to depend on the generalizations and conclusions I derive from the findings of my work.

The record of the 1980s will be examined under nine broad headings which feature prominently in the sources perused, particularly the *Consolidated Report*, for the years 1980 through 1990. The headings in question refer to sectors or activities; in other words, a functional classification is adopted. However, the *Consolidated Report, 1989* contained a review of the history of joint Arab economic action and a listing of its main landmarks, from 1945 when the League of Arab States was founded up to the preparation of the *Report* in question. This was the first time such a full review had been attempted. Though useful as a list of agreements drawn up, institutions formed, broad politico-economic structures established, and resolutions taken by Arab officialdom, the review is mainly descriptive, with exceedingly little critical evaluation (*The Consolidated Report 1989*, Part 8).

The *Consolidated Report, 1990* also includes a chapter that, among other things, surveys the activities, but only during 1989, of the bodies involved in joint Arab economic action. The survey follows a mixed institutional and functional (or sectoral) classification and comprises six broad headings, with a large number of subheadings (*The Consolidated Report 1990*, Part 8).

Although the survey claims to record the activities under the headings identified in the *Report* of 1989, the institutions, bodies, agreements, or resolutions listed and discussed all relate to the entire decade. However, there is special concentration on their activities (or the activities undertaken within their stipulations in the case of agreements and resolutions) which relates to the year 1989, but almost invariably with some reference to their background as well. The review of joint Arab economic action during the 1980s, which follows, combines the information available in the two surveys presented in the *Consolidated Report* of 1989 and that of 1990 though their classificatory systems are different. The combination is necessary in order to provide a complete picture for the decade of the 1980s.

THE JAEA: AN INSTITUTIONAL FRAMEWORK

The terminology that is "in style" at any one moment is a clear indication of the position which the body politic takes with regard to Arab economic relations. Thus, it was "cooperation" that was highlighted in the early 1950s, and this choice reflected something less than complementarity or integration. The term cooperation was elastic enough to allow more than one interpretation and therefore to suit the preferences of different Arab governments and intellectual leaderships closely associated with political leaderships. Later in the 1950s, the emphasis shifted radically, and outright unity became the new objective. The shift was reflected in the resolution taken in June 1957 by the Council of the Arab League, the highest ministerial body, approving a project for Arab economic unity and subsequently the formation of the Council for Arab Economic Unity.

We need not survey the smaller shifts in outlook and ambition that occurred between the mid-1950s and the end of the 1960s or the early 1970s. However, the main concern that began to emerge in the intervening years was for something more purposeful than mere cooperation, but less ambitious (and therefore more realistic) than outright unity. Hence the emphasis on complementarity. But with the change in mood after the correction of oil prices in October 1973, and the inflow of vastly increased oil revenues, and with the accelerated formation of specialized regional organizations and federations and hundreds of joint Arab (and Arab-international) projects and companies, joint Arab economic action began to take precedence in the institutional vocabulary of Arab economic structures and relationships. Hence the emergence and subsequent prominence of the designation "Joint Arab Economic Action" (JAEA) which was embodied concretely in the "Joint Arab Economic Sector" (JAES). These two designations were the substance of the Strategy for Joint Arab Economic Action (the Strategy) which was finally drawn up in 1980 and approved at the summit of the Arab heads of state held in Jordan in November 1980.

However, the predominance of JAEA, which continues to be recognized today, has not been free of rivalry. Thus, complementarity and integration continue to be desirable objectives of intellectuals and some business leaders outside the dominant, political mainstream in the Arab region. JAEA, in the eyes of these intellectuals and business leaders, is a diluted formula deliberately designed to draw attention away from the quest for complementarity and integration, which they view as higher than JAEA. Nevertheless, JAEA seems to be a satisfactory objective for mainstream, less highly politicized Arab thinkers and action groups. To conclude, the 1980s opened with the crowning of JAEA and the main modality in its service, the JAES, and has continued to reserve for JAEA the same place of honor it came to occupy at the decisive 1980 summit meeting.

So far we have concentrated only on the conceptual and semantic part of the institutional framework, whether of JAEA or of integration and complementarity. (The Strategy does not clearly differentiate between JAEA, which is a rather generic term, and complementarity or integration, each of which has a specific, clearly identifiable connotation. We will continue to refer to integration, complementarity, and JAEA as though they were interchangeable concepts, processes, or states.)

Two substantive matters remain with respect to the institutional framework. The first is the identity of the tools or instruments through which JAEA unfolds and the JAES operates. The second is the record of JAEA during the 1980s as a whole: the directions, the reach, and the effectiveness of its activities. This record will be traced in the discussion that follows.

By far, most JAEA is governmental, involving two or more Arab governments (and in the case of joint companies and projects, often involving international, non-Arab parties as well). Most of the structures that currently function as instruments of JAEA were formed before the 1980s. They range in their powers of authority and control from the Arab heads of state at the top of the pyramid—acting and taking resolutions at their summit meetings—down to small joint projects and companies at the bottom. In between, there are ministerial councils, specialized regional organizations, joint companies and projects, subregional councils and federations, and ministerial councils without specialized regional organizations of their own.

The most important part of the institutional machinery is the Economic and Social Council of the League of Arab States, which is the kingpin of the machinery of JAEA, positioned as it is between the heads of state on the one hand and the Secretariat-General of the Arab League on the other, with control and coordinative functions and powers over the specialized regional organizations. Its concerns and authority embrace all the sectors directly involved in economic activity and development.

While there has been very little if any change in the institutional framework and structures of JAEA since the economic summit meeting of November 1980, the thrust of JAEA and of the JAES has slackened considerably though in varying degrees between one sector and another, or from one part of the machinery to another. The areas of notable activity during the 1980s will be singled out below. For the moment, let us focus on one important part of the institutional framework and machinery of JAEA. This is the three subregional bodies formed in the 1980s, namely, the Cooperation Council of the Arab States of the Gulf (GCC), formed in 1981; the Arab Cooperation Council, also in the Mashriq, formed in 1989; and the Union of the Arab Maghrib, also formed in 1989.

There has been heated debate by intellectuals, and within some political circles, around the rationale or "philosophy" of the formation of subregional councils. Specifically, the debate has centered around whether such councils, each consisting of small groups of Arab states, are meant to replace the Arab League or to marginalize it, and by the same token to marginalize the goals and objectives it (supposedly) stands for. Or are they merely meant to be more efficient, homogenous, and practical-minded than the League's often overambitious purposes and targets, in the economic as well as the political areas of Arab life? The new bodies themselves claim that they supplement the Arab League and serve its long-term goals.

The debate was hottest with respect to the GCC, as its critics attributed to its members somewhat isolationist tendencies, inasmuch as most of them are important oil exporters eager to shelter their relatively recent financial opulence. The GCC countries' quite substantial aid to capital-short Arab countries during most of the 1970s, and their continued aid (though on a smaller scale) in the 1980s, has created among the capital-short countries a mixed feeling of gratefulness, envy, and displeasure in the face of the conspicuous consumption that has characterized GCC societies since the "oil era" began in 1973–74. In addition, many Arabs are very critical of the outflow of vast financial resources to western money markets instead of the allocation of a larger volume of aid to Arab development. In response, particularly after the second Gulf crisis and war of 1990–91, the GCC members have expressed resentment at the lukewarm popular support that they got from other Mashriq and Maghrib countries, and are set today to restrict their aid considerably, if not stop it altogether, as punishment for what they consider ungratefulness by aid receivers. JAEA will necessarily shrink and suffer for several years to come, given the present feeling on both sides of the political, emotional, and economic divide.

Yet, even if the Gulf War had not occurred, aid outflows from the GCC would have continued to be distinctly reduced in the 1990s, as they have been in most of the 1980s. The basic reason for the drop in the volume of aid during the 1980s was the drop in the price of oil as well as in the volume of exports, and therefore in oil revenues. The drop was so steep that it forced countries like Saudi Arabia and Kuwait to dig into their current and capital budgets in the second half of the 1980s.[2] Aggregate Arab oil revenues reached an all-high level of $209.5 billion for 1980, but dropped to $74.5 billion for 1987 (see OAPEC 1981 and *Consolidated Report 1988*, Table 4/3). (The situation was much more critical in the spring of 1992, after the campaign against Iraq had cost GCC members, particularly Saudi Arabia and Kuwait, tens of billions of dollars which they contributed to the overall financing of the allied military campaign.)

The special financial circumstances of the GCC apart, the Council has taken certain steps since 1983, when its members approved the Unified Economic Agreement in a drive toward complementarity and subregional economic action. These have aimed at:

1. Achieving "economic citizenship," that is, equality among the citizens of each GCC member country with the citizens of other member countries,

with respect to freedom of economic enterprise, and freedom of movement across GCC frontiers by goods and means of transport.

2. Targeting the narrowing of differences among economic policies in the
   various GCC countries and ultimately standardizing them. The policies
   involved included those relating to development objectives and planning,
   agricultural policies, and industrial development policies.

3. Linkage of infrastructural networks and facilities, particularly those that
   promote the intermeshing of economies.

4. The establishment of joint projects. A large number of proposed projects
   have been studied, and reportedly many have been formed (with an aggregate capital of about $21 billion) (*Consolidated Report 1990*, 206).[3]

5. Creation of institutions that serve the GCC as a whole. Three of these have
   already been formed, in the fields of investment, specifications and standards, and a technical bureau for telecommunications.

6. Movement toward the standardization of certain laws, measures, and procedures. This has been achieved with respect to records and forms relating
   to customs, quarantine rules and regulations (agricultural and veterinary), water development and conservation, the use of pesticides, fertiliz-
   ers, medicines, and veterinary immunization, and rules and procedures
   relating to seaports.

7. Taking a common stand vis-à-vis international issues, such as negotiating
   trade agreements, coordinating foreign aid policies, and bulk purchases of
   basic commodities for the GCC as a whole. In addition, the GCC approved
   a contingency plan in December 1988 for the production and marketing of
   petroleum products (*Consolidated Report 1989*, 213–16).

In conclusion, all of these seven avenues of action are on the whole being
translated into agreements and operational modalities. But they are still far
from full implementation, particularly with regard to the "economic citizenship" envisaged under point one.

The two other subregional bodies, the Arab Cooperation Council (ACC) in
the Mashriq and the Union of the Arab Maghrib, have stirred less concern than
the GCC with regard to their real purposes and the implications of their emergence for regional Arab economic complementarity and integration. By the end
of the 1980s, they were still shaping their internal structures and designing their
initial priorities (in terms of activities to be targeted and agreements to be
entered into). The ACC, in fact, can hardly be said to still exist since its two
senior members, Egypt and Iraq, faced each other as enemies on the battlefield
during the Gulf War.

One positive comment in defense of subregional councils must be added.
According to a careful and authoritative observer, such councils provide an
essential intermediate stage between narrowly defined single-country concerns

(a *qutriyya* tendency), and a too-broad regional concern that encompasses the whole Arab region and thus becomes unmanageable (Al-Hamad 1988).

The machinery of JAEA encompasses a number of other parts as well. These include the ministerial councils which have no specialized regional organizations of their own such as those responsible for housing and construction, transport, and the environment. The Secretariat-General of the Arab League acts as an executive secretariat for those councils *in lieu* of specialized regional organizations. Not much can be said of the activities of the councils in question although they have generated sizable stacks of paper relating to the three sectors that fall under their authority. The annual issues of the *Consolidated Report* point to no concrete achievement, however, apart from holding conferences, seminars, and meetings, and some preparation of plans and programs.

The group of specialized regional organizations can lay claim to greater achievements during the 1980s. However, those consist mainly of formulating long-term strategies and programs, providing technical assistance and training, and holding seminars and meetings (as in the case of the organizations for agricultural development, industrial development, and labor, and ALECSO-the Arab League Educational, Cultural, and Scientific Organization). All of them, except the Arab Labor Organization, have carried out extensive and diversified programs within their competence.

All Arab specialized organizations without exception suffer from insufficient budgets and inadequate high-level staffing, and from counterproductive interference or outright neglect by the ministers within whose field of authority they operate. Without fully diagnosing the root causes of the weaknesses and limitations of these organizations, we can say here that what delays and severely limits the development of the various productive sectors served by the specialized organizations is not a shortage of studies, strategies, programs, and plans, nor insufficient understanding of the problems associated with sectoral development, but rather insufficient determination within the government system, misdirected action, and discontinuity of efforts.

Finally, relationships between the organizations as a group, and with the Secretariat-General of the Arab League and the Economic and Social (ministerial) Council which is the titular coordinator and supervisor of the organizations, have never been flawless. Overlapping functions among the organizations, directors-general chosen by political bargaining among ministers rather than on the basis of professionalism and capability, disputes over fair and appropriate budgeting, bureaucratic heavy-handedness—all of these combine to slow down the activities and marginalize the performance of the specialized organizations. For several years now, the Arab League has been studying these problems. A report on the subject by a team of distinguished experts was completed in the late 1980s and has been accepted in principle by the Economic and Social Council, but its recommendations have yet to be implemented.

Joint projects and companies, those capitalized jointly by two or more Arab governments, and in many cases by the Arab private sector as well, are estimated to number 252, with an estimated paid-up capital of $17.9 billion. Another 269 joint projects and companies in which (non-Arab) international parties are shareholders along with Arab parties, are estimated to have an aggregate paid-up capital of $12.3 billion. The authorized and declared capital of both groups combined is larger than paid-up capital by about $4.6 billion. This brings total authorized capital of all joint projects and companies to $34.8 billion (all information on joint projects from *Consolidated Report 1989*, tables and Part 8). The capital of joint holding companies, as well as that of the two regional funds (the Arab Fund for Economic and Social Development and the Arab Monetary Fund), and of national development funds (although these provide development financing to needy Arab countries) have been excluded. (The combined capital of the two regional and five national funds is estimated by the *Consolidated Report 1983* to be $24.2 billion for the mid-1980s.) If the excluded aggregate capital is added to the total of $34.8 billion referred to above, the grand total would exceed $65 billion (Sayigh 1991, 130, quoting Samih Mas'oud 1987; Mas'oud 1987).

Considering the size of the aggregate Gross Domestic Product for the twenty-one Arab countries (excluding Palestine), which stood at $362.4 billion at current prices for 1988 (but at $385.5 billion for 1987) (*The Consolidated Report 1988*, Table 2.1), and considering aggregate investment by the Arab countries within their own frontiers, which in spite of the decline in GDP from its higher level in 1980 and 1981 totaled $93.1 billion in 1987 (*The Consolidated Report 1988*, Table 2.1), and finally considering that Arab financial holdings abroad reached a total of $374 billion by the end of 1982 (OAPEC 1982), the last year for which such information was available, the aggregate capital of the hundreds of joint projects and companies, some $65 billion, seems quite small.

Another cause of dissatisfaction with joint projects as part of the machinery of JAEA is that, although by far the largest proportion of them were established before the 1980s, there is very little difference between the estimate of their aggregate paid-up capital at the end of the 1970s and its level at the end of the 1980s. Furthermore, well-informed authorities both at the Secretariat-General of the League of Arab States and at the Council for Arab Economic Unity, and Samih Mas'oud, the scholar who has done most of the research in hand on joint projects, all agree that most of the projects in question are not functioning well. They are brisk on work programs and declaratory statements, but very sluggish on execution; at the top, they are on the whole bureaucratic in outlook and administration, though there were in the 1980s outstanding examples among them of efficiency and creditable performance, such as the companies formed by the Organization of Arab Petroleum Exporting Countries (OAPEC) to participate in various aspects of oil sector activity.

The Arab private sector has a significant share in the capital of joint projects, whether these are totally Arab, or combined Arab and international. The most notable part of the private-sector machinery in JAEA is the General Union of Arab Chambers of Commerce, Industry, and Agriculture for the Arab Countries—a sort of federation of the individual-country chambers for each of the three sectors mentioned in the Union name. In November 1983, this Union signed an ambitious agreement that approved the establishment of the "Arab Company for Agricultural Investment" with an authorized capital of $1 billion. However, concrete progress has not been reported since then, except that the *Consolidated Report 1985* mentioned that the Company was in the process of completing the formalities for its establishment.

The last part of the machinery of JAEA to be mentioned are the two regional funds: the Arab Fund for Economic and Social Development (AFESD) and the Arab Monetary Fund (AMF). These funds have been the most active JAEA institutions whose performance remained at a creditable level during the 1980s while that of most other parts of the institutional framework of JAEA declined, compared with the 1970s. Other parts of the framework involved in financing and investment will also be dealt with below, however. The distinct importance of these two regional funds warrants a detailed discussion.

FINANCING AND INVESTMENT

If loans and other financial transfers from some of the GCC countries to Iraq during its war with Iran in the 1980s are excluded from this discussion, then by far the largest part of financial transfers (mostly in loans but also to a much smaller extent in nonreimbursable technical assistance grants) from capital-surplus to capital-short Arab countries was effected by the two regional funds, the AFESD and the AMF, together with national development funds. The national development funds include five institutions established by Kuwait, Saudi Arabia, United Arab Emirates, Iraq, and Libya. The Iraqi Fund was inactive during the 1980s as the country's resources were committed entirely to the war effort. In addition to the institutions listed, the finance and investment sector of JAEA includes the Arab Authority for Agricultural Investment and Development, AAAID (with a declared capital of $500 million), the program for financing external trade established in 1989 by the AMF (with private Arab and international participation and a working capital of $500 million), and the Arab Institution for the Insurance of Investments (established in the 1970s) whose activities in the 1980s totaled insurance coverage of about $500 million ((*The Consolidated Report 1989* and *1990*).

The six development funds listed above, plus the AMF, are reported to have had an aggregate declared capital of $24.2 billion by the early 1980s (*The Consolidated Report 1983*). AFESD has a capital of one billion Kuwaiti dinars (KD) or about $3 billion, while AMF has a capital of about $2 billion. The AMF's capital fund is generally considered too modest when set against the many functions the Fund is designed to shoulder, including correcting structural and temporary balance-of-payments imbalances or distortions, and participation in the capital of the program of trade promotion and of investment insurance. The total capital of the six development funds is considerable if one bears in mind that these funds generally try to lend only a part of the investment requirements of the projects for which financing is sought. (AFESD provided loans totaling KD1,152 million during the period 1974–89, for projects whose total cost was KD5,230 million (*The Consolidated Report 1990*, 190). Thus, its financial participation amounted to 22 percent of total cost.) In other words, though the total capital of the development funds is quite substantial in its own right, it serves as a catalytic agent for a much larger volume of investment— indeed, a fivefold volume—if the record of AFESD is representative of the operations of the whole group of Arab development funds.

Arab development assistance to needy Arab countries (both direct government-to-government and through regional and national development funds) amounted to an average of $5.1 billion a year during 1976–89, or a total of $70.8 billion (World Bank 1991, Table 19). But this did not represent the whole volume of aid. Considerable aid is directed by the Islamic Bank for Development (IBD) to needy Arab countries. Likewise, the OPEC Fund for International Development (OFID) had extensive lending operations during the 1970s, though these shrank in significance during the 1980s owing to the crisis the oil sector experienced in prices, volume of production, and revenues earned by the exporters. Both the IBD and OFID receive by far most of their resources from Arab oil exporters. Consequently, aid received by Arab countries from these two institutions is in fact mostly from Arab countries. Finally, the Arab oil-exporting countries made substantial resources available to the World Bank and the International Monetary Fund during the second part of the 1970s. This enabled these two bodies to expand their operations. To the extent that certain Arab countries benefited from the expansion of aid facilities, it has been Arab resources in effect that generated the benefit.

To sum up: it is clear that financial resources accruing to Arab oil-exporting countries have resulted, since the mid-1970s, in a vast inflow of loans and considerable grants to capital-short Arab countries, as well as to a number of non-

Arab countries, thanks to the aid policies of the Kuwait Fund and the Saudi Fund, both of which extended aid to non-Arab Third World countries. And, as Arab resources constituted the largest part of the lending resources available to the IBD and OFID, and these two institutions extended aid to non-Arab as well as to capital-short Arab countries, Arab resources have reached out to help Third World countries beyond the Arab region.

In short, Arab oil revenues have been an important source of financial assistance to the Third World at large, but—quite naturally—to the Arab world more particularly. This can be seen all the more dramatically in the proportion of Arab GDP or GNP which such assistance constituted, compared with its counterpart from the rich Western industrial countries. Thus, in 1987, Arab development assistance amounted to 3.5 percent of the GDP of the donor countries as a group, while Western aid was less than half of one percent of the GDP of the Western industrial countries. Arab assistance also represented 14.5 percent of the volume of oil exports in 1987 (data on Arab donors from *The Consolidated Report 1989*, table entitled, "General Indicators of the Arab Homeland"; data on western countries from World Bank 1991, Table 19). Of course, Arab financial assistance arises from the sale of a depleting asset, not from renewable resources as in the case of the rich Western countries.

ARAB OIL POLICIES AND OIL-RELATED DEVELOPMENT

Any Arab coordination that can be discerned with regard to oil production and pricing policies is undertaken by the seven Arab members of the thirteen-member Organization of Petroleum Exporting Countries. OAPEC, which is purely Arab in membership, is quite restricted to studies, research, some training, and organizing professional seminars on oil and other energy matters. The Arab members of OPEC probably favor this division of labor between OPEC and OAPEC because they believe that pricing and production matters ought to be dealt with by a body that includes non-Arab producers, and thus can claim to speak for a much larger oil constituency.

As a result of this division of labor, the use of oil revenues for development, particularly within the oil sector itself, fell between the cracks: it was deemed to be the responsibility of neither OPEC nor OAPEC. This is part of the reason why the rush to develop petrochemical industries in the Arab oil-exporting countries resulted in a number of industries that had not been pre-planned on a regional or sectoral basis, and that had failed to coordinate either specialization or production capacity with regional oil producers. As a general result, the Arab petrochemical industry now reaps the adverse consequences. These include excessive capacity, duplication of establishments, and marketing problems abroad.

We should not end our discussion of the field of energy without noting its one substantive achievement. This is the linkage effected during the 1980s between the electricity networks of Lebanon, Syria, and Jordan. The linkage serves to reduce sharp seasonal shortages and surpluses in the supply of power.

LABOR VS. REMITTANCES

From 1973 to 1983, an Arab workforce "estimated at three to four million strong moved to the oil-rich countries to take part in the very extensive construction and development activity which the expanded oil revenues have permitted" (Sayigh 1991, 130)[4]. The remittances sent back home by this workforce, or the savings made by it, are estimated to have been $3 to 4 billion a year. However, the size of the workforce and its remittances and/or savings have dropped significantly as a result of the oil crisis in the Gulf countries since the mid-1980s.

The movement in opposite directions of labor and factor payments abroad has reflected a very clear case of complementarity between the oil-exporting but labor-importing countries on the one hand (Iraq, Kuwait, Saudi Arabia, the United Arab Emirates, Qatar, and Libya), and labor-exporting countries (Egypt, [North] Yemen, Palestine-Jordan, Lebanon, and Syria) on the other. However, the Gulf crisis and war of 1990–91 have brought about a drastic reduction in the size of the expatriate labor force and therefore in remittances and/or savings effected by it. Kuwait and Iraq both saw their expatriate labor forces depart, and Saudi Arabia expelled an estimated one million Yemeni workers. The prospects seem very poor for Arab labor (especially for Palestinians and Jordanians) to return to Kuwait in large numbers; the indications are strong that most of the departing labor will be largely replaced by East and Southeast Asians. Thus an aspect of complementarity which had been remarkable and beneficial to all the parties concerned, politically, economically, and symbolically, is threatened by erosion, at least for several years to come.

INTRAREGIONAL TRADE

Although some institutional improvements were made during the 1980s to promote intraregional trade, there was hardly any change by the end of the decade in the proportion of the region's total external trade moving inside it; this proportion has remained at a low 6 to 7 percent. Among the improvements was a new agreement to facilitate trade (approved in November 1980 at the Arab summit meeting devoted wholly to intra-Arab economic affairs and JAEA). The AMF also launched a program to promote intraregional trade, with a revolving fund of $500 million to provide short-term finance to exporters who were waiting to be paid for their sales, and to importers to help them pay for their purchases. Finally, an amendment to the terms of reference of the Institution for the Insurance of Investments within the region, which had been restricted to noncommercial risks, made the Institution capable of insuring commercial risks as well.

The persistence of the limited value of intraregional trade during the 1980s is explained by the slow change in the range of diversification of Arab production, and the weak competitiveness of Arab products, particularly manufactures, compared with their imported counterparts. Another possible reason is the failure of the Arab countries to improve the lines and facilities of transport among themselves to an extent that would reduce transport costs. Finally, most shoppers retain a built-in preference for imported goods, even when national (or regional) products are as good and cheaper. Obviously, there is a very wide scope for the intensification of intraregional trade, but the most essential and pressing prerequisite is the production of more and better goods and services to begin with, so that Arab countries would potentially have much more to offer to each other.

AGRICULTURE AND FOOD PRODUCTION

Failure to achieve an effective measure of joint Arab economic action and complementarity in the area of agriculture and food production has had a most adverse effect on food security and is also very costly to the Arab region at large. In the mid-1980s, the bill for food imports for the region reached $23 billion (15.3 percent of total imports). However, it fell to $14 billion for 1987. The fall generally characterized the period 1979–87, thanks essentially to two factors: "the rise in food production over ... [1981 to 1987] and the drop in oil revenues. The latter forced the Arab countries to compress their food imports and restrict them to the more essential items" (Sayigh 1991, 141; data for the expansion of food production per capita from FAO 1989, Table 4).

Yet the rise in food production per capita, which was partly behind the drop in food imports, was the result of country-by-country action, not collective Arab action. The agricultural sector is one of the largest beneficiaries among all sectors of studies, programs, suggestions, and injunctions by intellectuals and specialized regional organizations (such as the Arab Agricultural Development Organization, and the Arab Authority for Agricultural Investment and Development, along with their programs and subsidiary units). The case for agricultural development through collective Arab action is very compelling, since it uses the danger to food security as its main support. With about one-half of the food it consumes coming from abroad, the Arab region cannot underestimate the gravity of the danger that food security poses.

Specialized organizations—in agriculture as in other sectors—can contemplate, undertake research, design strategies and programs, prepare projects, and make strong appeals to the government ministries under which they operate. But they can do nothing beyond that: action remains the prerogative of the governments, and it is here that the tightest bottleneck is located.

Seeing official hesitation, if not outright lethargy and inaction, the private sector becomes even more hesitant. It ought to be remembered that the size of the food programs envisaged is enormous in terms of investment and working capital, running into many billions of dollars over several years. It is no wonder that the private sector balks when it sees that official action is not forthcoming.

As things stood by the end of the 1980s, the countries with the most promising potential for agricultural and food production, in terms of cultivable and irrigable land, and water—Sudan, Morocco, Syria, and Iraq—were still engaged in their own country programs, while regional programs involving collective action were collecting dust in their files. At the same time, almost every country in the region is vitally interested in the promotion of food production, and could have some role in such promotion, whether as supplier of investment finance (as in the case of most oil-exporting countries), of land and water (as in the case of the four countries listed above), of manpower (as in the case of Egypt, Jordan, Tunisia, and several other countries), or of markets and purchasing power, as in the case of every single Arab country.

MANUFACTURING INDUSTRY

The Arab Industrial Development Organization, AIDO, has been probably as active as the Arab Agricultural Development Organization (AADO), but much more active than the Arab Authority for Agricultural Investment and Development in terms of formulating strategies, designing programs and projects, providing training, and generally stressing the importance of industrialization. It cannot invoke an appeal that relates directly to the physical viability of Arab society, as AADO can when stressing the urgency of expanded food production in order to feed the Arab millions and to stop the massive erosion in Arab financial resources now paying for the import of foodstuffs. But AIDO can invoke the criticality for development of industrialization and the absorption of the existing excess labor supply. Agriculture is providing employment to a continuously shrinking proportion of the labor force, while manufacturing industry, at the stage where it stands today in the Arab region, can claim to be labor-intensive.

AIDO's strategies and programs are largely based on the premise that the process of industrialization involves the development of basic and engineering industries, the training and retraining of skilled labor to meet the requirements of advanced technology in manufacturing, and the widening of the very narrow and inadequate bases of science and technology, and research and development now in existence. Such overwhelming needs require massive investment in addition to the design and building of institutions and services needed for achieving the target of industrialization. This demands collective action by groups of Arab countries, if not by all of them in one massive operation. Industrial complementarity can be achieved, if seriously thought out and sought, both at the horizontal and the vertical levels. The first would involve the grouping of similar undertakings or industries or of research and training facilities. The second requires the division of labor within the same industry, whereby the various processes and phases within it can be assigned to different countries on the basis of the logic of comparative advantage and the availability of appropriate manpower and technology or physical resources.

The record of the 1980s shows that some progress has been achieved in industrial development, but again on a country-by-country, not a regional, basis. The increased export potential of Arab manufacturing has begun to be blocked by protectionist policies imposed by many Western industrial countries. A notable example is the barriers that the Arab petrochemical industry encountered when attempting to market its products in Europe. The GCC has taken the lead in approaching the European Community *as a body* to try to work out a mutually agreeable formula that would allow Arab exports to enter the European market. However, the general tendency with regard to industrialization is still for individual countries to act alone; in the area of industrial development, JAEA is still very marginal.

One feasible and very promising approach to speedier industrialization would be to establish those capital goods industries for the machines, equipment, and spare parts for which there is already a wide enough market to enable the industries in question to be viable and profitable. These might include products for the sectors of transport and communication, construction, tourism and hotel-keeping, agriculture, public works, and printing.[5]

TRANSPORT, COMMUNICATION, AND TELECOMMUNICATION

This sector has no specialized organization to prepare strategies, programs, and networks for it on a regional or subregional basis. However, a number of ambitious projects are at different points of readiness, involving the unification or at least a pooling of the services of some airlines, the construction of roads and/or railroads connecting countries in the Fertile Crescent, and the beginnings of programs to link Arab telecommunication networks. It is as true today as it was at the beginning of the 1970s to say that it is easier for someone in Beirut, Amman, or Damascus to telephone Bonn, Paris, or London than either of the two to telephone other nearby Arab capitals. Intraregional air transport connections are easier and more frequent now than during the 1970s, but still less so than between the Arab region and Western Europe.

Insufficient and inadequate transport facilities within the region serve to hinder intraregional trade, since they increase costs for the transport of goods across national boundaries. Yet, as indicated above, there are other probably stronger determining factors for the small proportion of intraregional trade out of total foreign trade. The rise in the intensity of Arab divisiveness since the 1991 Gulf War has certainly led to the postponement of any linkages, whether by road, railroad, airplane, or ship, which were at an advanced stage of preparation on the drafting board.

Furthermore, the sluggishness in the expansion of economic activity in the region, and the very small growth in GDP during the second half of the 1980s—indeed, its negative growth at times—will combine to postpone the development of the transport and communication components of regional infrastructure. The painful paradox in the present context is that more resources have been directed to transport and communication in individual Arab countries, particularly to the importation of airplanes, cars, buses, and trucks during the 1970s and 1980s, than ever before, while regional transport links remain largely neglected.

EDUCATION AND THE ACQUISITION OF EFFECTIVE TECHNOLOGY

The last, but by no means the least significant area of activity to discuss in this survey is joint Arab action in the field of education and the acquisition of appropriate and effective technological capability in the region. The expansion of educational facilities and programs continued in the 1980s in virtually every Arab country. However, collective efforts have remained minimal. The Arab League Educational, Cultural, and Scientific Organization (ALECSO) was very active in the 1980s; indeed, it completed the preparation of a number of strategies and programs in the various fields for which it was responsible, including the fight against illiteracy. Still, the gains made in absolute numbers of adults who acquired elementary reading and writing skills were smaller than the absolute numbers of those entering the dark area of illiteracy in several countries of the region.

As in the cases of agriculture and manufacturing industry, ALECSO, too, made remarkable progress in terms of studies, training, seminars, and the formulation of strategies and programs. But, once again, the transmission belt between ALECSO and the ministry or ministries under whose jurisdiction it operates proved defective. The translation of programs and projects into concrete reality by and large was blocked; the only exceptions being training, seminars, the formulation of strategies and programs for the future, and the publication of several valuable studies—areas in which ALECSO was able to execute projects using its own manpower and budgetary resources.

The promotion of the acquisition of advanced technology falls only partially within ALECSO's area of concern. Other bodies are involved as well, directly and indirectly. Perhaps this diffusion of responsibility explains, if only in part, why the drive for the inculcation of greater technological capability has been so slow and its gains so modest. The establishment of a broad, regional base for science and technology has yet to be undertaken seriously. Two major regional programs prepared after extensive consideration during the 1970s remain dormant. The distance between theoretical and applied science in university education remains wide and unbridged. Similarly, the distance between engineering departments, schools, or colleges, and the users of engineering skills, such as the manufacturing industry, transport and communication, agriculture, and construction, remains wide and unbridged, except in a very few cases where trainees move for short periods from formal training to the business sector, to learn how to put their skills to practical use.

It should be stressed that there is still no regional endeavor to explain that the importation of the hardware and software of technology does not amount to the implantation of technological capability in the region. While such importation is thought to be a shortcut to the objective of acquiring the capability in question, it is actually a much longer and less assured conduit to the acquisition presumably sought. Only when such awareness becomes general can the region start the demanding but critical task of building the badly needed but painfully absent science and technology base.

Finally, the acquisition of technological capability need not be attempted in one big jump or in a short span of time. The region could begin by taking small manageable steps. To make this point clear, an Arab scholar experienced in the field estimated that some $5 billion a year was spent on the importation of technological software during the early 1980s. Much of the imported material could have been produced in the region, if the will were there and Arab professional resources were properly mobilized (A.B. Zahlan, quoted in Sayigh 1982, 165; see also ch. 12 below).

Explaining the Record of the 1980s

The discussion thus far must leave the reader with the clear impression that the 1970s witnessed a brisker and more fruitful drive toward integration and complementarity through joint Arab action than did the 1980s. It is necessary now, therefore, to attempt to explore the reasons for the shortfall in integration efforts and results in the 1980s, and to try to explain why the 1970s, in contrast, witnessed markedly better achievement.

As the reader will see, in my search for an explanation, I will have to stray away to a considerable extent from economic explanations and considerations. I realize that I take a risk in trying to find the explanation partly in Arab politics, and partly also in cultural, social, and even psychological factors. I accept that risk because of my conviction that economic factors alone cannot provide a sufficient explanation of important economic processes like integration. Indeed, economic factors acting alone, without any major exception, provide strong justification for the pursuit of integration rather than the opposite. Before I attempt to explain very briefly why the harvest of integration was poor in the 1980s, I should note that the listing of the components of the explanations I venture to make in the following paragraphs does not proceed according to a scale of significance or priority. Clearly, the components interact and supplement each other so closely that it would be most difficult to rank them according to their impact.

THE RETREAT OF INTEGRATION AND JAEA AS MAJOR ARAB CONCERNS

There is an apparent element of circularity in posing this first item as part of the explanation, while it is the phenomenon whose explanation is sought. However, it is worth asking why there is less concern with integration today than in the 1970s; that is, what are the deep causes for the drop in concern. Even the Arab intelligentsia that is highly politicized is less concerned today both with integration and development on the one hand, and with national (that is, regional) security on the other. I believe that the economic prosperity which characterized the 1970s in the oil and non-oil countries, though to different degrees, has generated a drive toward individual opulence at the expense of political and politico-economic desiderata.

This drive toward money-making has also taken hold of the other strata and groups of Arab citizenry—businessmen, professionals, bureaucrats, laborers, and particularly politicians. To the extent that political and politico-economic desiderata relating to the welfare of society as a whole often involve those who uphold them in political (and sometimes physical) risk, there is a discernible shift away from such desiderata toward the pursuit of personal well-being.

INSUFFICIENT AWARENESS OF THE GRAVE DANGER OF ISOLATIONISM

I would contend that awareness by the Arab public, especially by politicized citizens and leaderships in various walks of life, of the benefits that would accrue to the region as a whole and to its constituent parts because of joint economic action and integration, can be clear and strong only if it is preceded by another awareness: that the absence of integration and exaggerated focus on single-country affairs and interests carry with them grave dangers to each of the region's countries. And the dangers mean the distortion and shrinkage of achievement with respect to development, as well as the capability of the region as a whole and its constituent parts to protect its own, and their, security to the extent possible.

There is a two-way relationship between development and security: the former provides a stronger economic base for the latter, and the latter provides a protective shield for the former. Most thinking Arabs are convinced at present that both Arab development and Arab security have been seriously debilitated and eroded, not just since the Gulf crisis and war of 1990–91, but actually since the early 1980s, when the retreat of Arab concern with integration—both economic and political—became marked.

DIVISIVENESS WITHIN INDIVIDUAL ARAB COUNTRIES

The 1980s witnessed greater divisiveness within each of several Arab countries, whether the causes were ideological (political or theological), ethnic, or economic (relating to interest groups, public-vs.-private sector controversies, or labor vs. management). Furthermore, the divisiveness *within* countries had ramifications also *among* countries, although these were less visible. The most serious aspects of divisiveness which went beyond national borders arose from fundamentalist tendencies and loyalties, dichotomy between rich and poor countries, and varying alignments within the world order.

Such a climate of divisiveness will necessarily affect attitudes toward intraregional political and economic relationships. Within this sort of climate, secondary contradictions overshadow basic consensus and shared heritage. Furthermore, the divisiveness has not appeared in a vacuum. It is merely an accentuated tendency that underlines longstanding *qutri* loyalties and tendencies (i.e., those whose focus is their own country rather than the Arab region). It is not certain that a large proportion of Arabs realize that their own *qutri* interests can be better served if they cooperate with the citizens, authorities, and institutions of other countries (*aqtar*) in serving the interests and solving the problems that threaten them, be they economic or political.

The advantages of collective as against individual action are a matter of common knowledge since a group of countries acting as one unit command more energy than the sum of their individual energies. Thus, the case for Arab economic complementarity and joint action is well established with respect to every sector or activity, from food production to manufacturing industry to the establishment of a science and technology base. The pursuit of self-reliance, a difficult objective under the best of circumstances, is hopeless if attempted by Arab countries individually, but possible if attempted collectively (see Sayigh 1991, ch. 4).

DIVORCE BETWEEN THOUGHT AND ACTION IN SOCIETAL CRISES

Here lies a major problem with many Arabs in positions of responsibility, especially in politics. Even when such persons comprehend the nature and dimensions of a social crisis, and realize the criticality and urgency of action to respond to its challenge, they do not put in the planning, determination, and effort to translate their realization into concrete action consistent with their assessment of the crisis. I consider this a kind of separation, if not total divorce, between perception or comprehension, and a consistent response. The inconsistency thus manifested can be seen in our weak and flawed responses to grave matters of a political or security nature as well as to economic matters.

What is baffling here is that the average Arab, faced with a personal crisis, or one relating to family or clan, loses little time in mobilizing his (or her) energy and endowments to face that crisis. He may face it counterproductively, or he may overreact, but he does not show the same slowness or produce the same diluted reaction as in the case of a societal, country-wide, or region-wide crisis. One wonders if matters of personal honor and welfare rank much more highly in our social evaluation than the collective honor of country or society.

Lukewarm reaction to invocations for work and sacrifice in order to achieve development and security through Arab collective action can be understood, though only partly, within the context of the factor I now venture to suggest as an input in the explanation of the sluggishness of the drive for integration. Such reaction is particularly unfathomable because the objective of collective action—integration in the present instance—is not a mere abstraction that eludes the grasp of many people, but rather something that could make a significant and tangible contribution to economic and social development, from which every citizen would benefit.

THE PERSONALIZATION OF AUTHORITY AND POWER

This component of the explanation might also be designated "the excessive centralization of authority and power" in virtually every Arab country. Even where there is political pluralism and a reasonable degree of institutionalization, real power resides in the head of state. In the rare cases where this is not (or has not been) the case, then it resides in some *éminence grise*, a holder of real power behind the titular head of state.

It is a general phenomenon that the more centralized and personalized power is, the more isolated the holder of that power becomes. Consequently, the leader loses touch with currents of thought and mainstream feelings, particularly when these do not harmonize with his own position and wishes. The inner circle of advisers, who usually tell the powerful ruler what they believe he prefers to hear, lose their true function and become simply the echo of whatever they believe the ruler is thinking. Obviously, the popular message for integration or any other process requiring collective Arab action is not very articulate in the Arab region. It would be difficult to hear even if the ruler were not despotic.

In the absence of a well-functioning conveyor belt of ideas, desires, and popular preferences between the people and the center of power, the ruler has only two or three conduits to inform him of what the public wants. These conduits are the advisers, the security services, and the family of the ruler. As these three sources of information usually have an interest in passing the same kind of information on to the ruler, and they mostly represent "intercommunicating compartments," the ruler's isolation becomes complete.

To all this must be added that most rulers are interested in power and how it can be captured and maintained, not in ideas of integration, collective self-reliance, or inner-directed development: these do not seem to the rulers to be direct contributors to their purpose of holding and consolidating power. Most political parties and movements are likewise obsessed with political power, and assign only a marginal part of their attention and platforms to questions such as integration, regional development, and collective self-reliance.

THE STRICT RATIONING OF DEMOCRACY, FREEDOM, AND HUMAN RIGHTS

This factor is organically related to the one immediately preceding it, since excessive centralization and personalization of power are not possible if the population enjoys political participation, freedom of expression and communication, and human rights in general. I believe it is correct to claim that were the exercise of democracy, freedom, and human rights distinctly fuller, the advocates of integration and joint Arab action would have access to the awareness of the people and make their message not only heard but also accepted. In a system where such communication is possible and widespread, public expression of support for intraregional integration and development would become both vocal and communicable to the government through organized political, social, economic, and union groups. From there on the actual pursuit of joint action becomes both feasible and promising.

But democracy, freedom, and human rights are not habitually offered on a silver plate to a people. They have to be struggled for, often wrenched away at a high cost. It is promising to see that most Arab peoples are engaged in an effort, even if still tentative and partial, to reclaim their political, social, and human rights.

The more effective and generalized this effort becomes, the more hope will be generated that socioeconomic objectives like integration will become attainable. Once the hopes materialize sufficiently, the quality of government can be improved. And since governments are at present the tightest bottleneck that blocks the program and projects designed to make integration and regional development a concrete reality, any loosening will permit the flow of ideas into the realm of action and achievement. The process from there on will necessarily be long because durable integration and meaningful development are not easy tasks. The example of the European Community is there to learn from: it took the EC decades to reach its present level of cohesiveness and achievement, both in the political and economic fields.

POLITICAL INTEGRATION AND ECONOMIC INTEGRATION

I have suggested above the imperative of associating political with economic integration. Which should come first is not the basic question here. What is basic is that hesitation in the pursuit of economic integration often derives from the conviction that to be effective, economic integration must be accompanied, sooner or later, by political integration. This is largely true since economic integration involves making major decisions that cannot be made unless there is at least a large measure of policy coordination among the countries seeking integration.

The Arab politicians who express enthusiasm about economic integration but secretly remain at best lukewarm toward it—and these probably represent the majority—are essentially worried that if economic integration were seriously and purposefully sought, it would lead to political integration. And political integration is anathema to them as a class. Here lies one of the main blockages to economic integration.

LIMITATION OF PRIVATE SECTOR PURSUIT OF INTEGRATION

It seems to me plausible that private business people would be in favor of integration once the benefits it could bring them are explained convincingly. Naturally, some would fear the loss of the advantages they now enjoy in their own countries. But even here, compensatory mechanisms could be designed and put to work, and capital could be relocated to help industries that suffer as a result of integration and the competition it might engender.

The real reason for the hesitation of the private sector in the face of arguments for integration is its sensitivity to the hostile climate that governments generate, covertly, if not overtly, vis-à-vis integration. The private sector takes shelter behind the lukewarm official attitude to integration. But it is arguable that a radical change in the official attitude would be met by readiness on the part of the private sector to support integration, once the appropriate compensatory mechanisms have been activated.

THE EXTERNAL FACTOR

So far we have dwelt on internal factors that inhibit the drive toward integration. This is deliberate. But I want to end this enumeration of factors by pointing out that certain Western powers play an influential part in frightening some Arab rulers away from economic integration by stressing the "danger" that political integration would soon follow. The countries most sensitive to this sort of pressure are the oil-producing countries, whose interests are invoked as a central concern of the Western countries exercising the influence. The specter of a rich country vs. poor country confrontation is raised to carry this message to the oil-producing countries. This situation cannot be simply shrugged off as an example of imperialist machination. The non-oil countries are called upon to possess understanding of the concerns of the oil countries and to share with them the overall concern for the whole Arab region.

If the present diagnosis of the causes behind the very limited progress toward economic integration during the 1980s is correct, then why was progress more marked during the 1970s if the explanatory factors suggested have not changed on the whole between the two decades? My only answer is that the 1970s witnessed a unique phenomenon so powerful that it swept aside much of the hesitation hindering the pursuit of economic integration. This phenomenon was the windfall of oil revenues. The unprecedented affluence that these revenues made possible was so reassuring that the oil rulers responded positively to the new situation. Consequently, they showed considerable readiness to encourage, participate in, and finance the widening institutional framework of integration. They also aided needy Arab countries at a rate by far exceeding that of Western aid.

The key to an understanding of the 1970s is therefore both financial and psychological. The relatively vast influx of financial resources created a new mood expressed in joint Arab economic action. But mood is reversible, as we saw in the 1980s and as we can witness today. It will not be brought back to equilibrium until all Arab countries, rich and poor alike, achieve mutual understanding of their common, and also different, endowments, problems, and aspirations.

Endnotes

1. The Report is prepared as a cooperative effort by the Secretariat-General of the League of Arab States, the Arab Monetary Fund, the Arab Fund for Economic and Social

Development, and the Organization of Arab Petroleum Exporting Countries. I will refer to it hereafter as the *Consolidated Report*. Its title in Arabic is *Al-Taqrir al-iqtisadi al-'arabi al-muwahhad*, and the four agencies that prepare it had published a few of the annual issues in English, which uses the word "Joint" instead of "Consolidated." Elsewhere, I have used the term "Unified." See Yusif A. Sayigh, *Elusive Development: From Dependence to Self-Reliance in the Arab Region* (London and New York: Routledge, 1991).

2. A well-informed economist in the Gulf has estimated budget deficits for the years 1983–87 to aggregate about $70 billion for the members of the GCC. See Ali Khalifah al-Kawari, "Comment on Dr. Abdallah al-Quwaiz's Paper on 'Movement of the Co-operation Council in the Field of Investment,'" given at a Symposium held in Dubai, December 12–13, 1989.

3. The total number of GCC joint projects is "said to be" 326. This bit of information most assuredly must be taken with a grain of salt.

4. A much higher estimate of remittances, reaching $6.8 billion at their peak in 1984, is reported in a paper by Abdelatif Y. al-Hamad, "Implications of Oil for Arab Development: Financial and Investment Issues and Options for the Future," given at a seminar on Prospects for Oil and Future Development in the Arab Countries, held in Amman, Jordan, December 1–2, 1987.

5. I am grateful to Professor A. B. Zahlan for making this suggestion.

References

Al-Hamad, Abdelatif Y. "Implications of Oil for Arab Development: Financial and Investment Issues and Options for the Future." Amman, Jordan (seminar on "Prospects for Oil and Future Development in the Arab Countries,") December 1–2, 1987.

Al-Hamad, Abdelatif Y. "The Gulf Cooperation Council: The Experience and Its Lessons" (in Arabic), *Al-Muntada* 3/29 (1988).

Al-Kawari, Ali Khalifah. "Comment on Dr. Abdallah al-Quwaiz's Paper on Movement of the Cooperation Council in the Field of Investment." Dubai (symposium) December 12–13, 1989.

The Consolidated Arab Economic Report, 1983.

The Consolidated Arab Economic Report, 1988.

The Consolidated Arab Economic Report, 1989.

The Consolidated Arab Economic Report, 1990.

Food and Agriculture Organization. *Production Yearbook 1989.* No. 42, . Rome: FAO: 1989.

Ibrahim, Ibrahim, ed. *Arab Resources: The Transformation of A Society.* Washington, DC and London: Center for Contemporary Arab Studies, Georgetown University and Croom Helm, 1983.

Mas'oud, Samih. "Joint Arab Projects: Their Present Status, Importance, Hindrances, and Future" (in Arabic), *Al-Mustaqbal al-'arabi* (September 1987).

Organization of Arab Petroleum Exporting Countries. *Secretary-General's Annual Report AH 1400: AD 1981*. Kuwait: OAPEC, 1981.

Organization of Arab Petroleum Exporting Countries. *Secretary-General's Annual Report AH 1401: AD 1982*. Kuwait: OAPEC, 1982.

Sayigh, Yusif A. *The Arab Economy: Past Performance and Future Prospects*. Oxford: Oxford University Press, 1982.

Sayigh, Yusif A. *Elusive Development: From Dependence to Self-Reliance in the Arab Region*. London and New York: Routledge, 1991.

World Bank. *World Development Report, 1991*. Washington, DC: The World Bank, 1991.

Technology: A Disintegrative Factor in the Arab World

chapter 12

Antoine B. Zahlan

European technological advances since 1498 have contributed greatly to breaking up the integrity, unity, and coherence of the Arab world. The cumulative impact of these advances over many centuries initiated a long process of sociopolitical and economic decline, and to this day the Arab countries find themselves unable to respond to the challenges posed by these advances.

Scientific and technological advances take place constantly everywhere, occurring at different rates in different countries. Invariably, one country achieves superiority in a particular field. Such superiority gives it advantages over others from which it seeks to derive benefits. It is impossible for countries to isolate themselves from the impact of technological disparities, although the response to technological challenges differs from country to country. Some readily adopt new technologies; others are much more reluctant.

Those countries which delay their response to such technological challenges are left with a permanent imprint—a scar—that marks not only their economic life, but even extends to their culture. The rise and fall of civilizations is a testimony to the constant flux of technological change. Failure to make an appropriate response may lead to the demise of an entire culture.

The impact of different technological advances on Third World countries has been multifaceted. The first, and most obvious, impact is that these advances have facilitated colonial (or neocolonial) exploitation of the lagging countries (Headrick 1981). They have posed as well new internal challenges for sociopolitical and economic change. The accumulation of these internal challenges over a long period of time has often become overwhelming; many Third World countries are unable to respond constructively to them.

Vasco da Gama ushered in the process that led to the dismantling of the Arab world when in 1498 he circumnavigated the Cape of Good Hope and reached the waters of the Gulf, thus beginning the long era of European colonization. Over many years, the Arabs fought valiantly to protect their economic system, to prevent occupation, and once occupied, to terminate occupation.

This chapter is in three sections. The first briefly depicts the powerful repercussions of European innovations and inventions in science and technology on the Arab world. It will be shown how, over a period of 500 years, the failure to respond effectively to European technological advances led to the dismantling of the unity, cohesiveness, and socioeconomic structures of the Arab world. The key here has been the inability of the different Arab governments to respond to the challenges: the inability to respond to threatening change is a sure sign of powerlessness, and paves the way for disaster.

The second discusses current patterns of Arab technological behavior. This is based on an examination of contemporary educational and investment programs and policies in the Arab states. The Arab governments have invested 5 to 6 percent of their GNP on education, and 20 to 30 percent of GNP has been devoted to Gross Fixed Capital Formation (GFCF) since independence. The Arab countries now possess considerable professional resources that cannot be put to any useful socioeconomic use because of the underdeveloped state of their national and regional institutions. This underdevelopment is a direct consequence of the strength and stability of the prevailing rent political economy (Beblawi and Luciani 1987).

Massive changes in technology are always accompanied by equally massive political and social changes: witness the effect of the industrial revolution on European countries. In fact, the science and technology aspect of the process is quite simple; the difficult part is effecting required changes in the political culture that underpins the successful utilization of a new technology.

A positive response to Western challenges would require the adoption of a successful program of technology transfer in order to narrow or close the technology gap. Technology transfer takes place over a substantial period of time, and is a cumulative and systemic process. Transfer involves changes in the political culture, the legal system, the economy, social organization, and management. But instead of adopting a program of national development in science and technology, modern Arab governments sought to secure weapons from their erstwhile enemies. This approach deepened technological dependence and accelerated the dismantling of the Arabs' own economic and social systems. These efforts contributed significantly to social and political disintegration (Zahlan and Said Zahlan 1978; Zahlan 1997b).

The practices adopted by the Arab countries toward technology during the past two centuries depended heavily on the use of foreign consulting, contracting, and manufacturing firms; only limited efforts were made to acquire national scientific and technological capabilities. This approach deepened the rent political economy and undermined normal processes of transition to a modern industrial and performance-oriented political economy.

The last section explores future prospects. As a result of the prolonged process of deconstruction, Arab societies have become intensely technologically dependent and appear to have lost the capacity to redress the balance. The Arabs can be said to be suffering from technological anorexia; and they are disheartened because they are powerless. Arab analysts point to a state of paralysis on both the national and regional levels.

Five Centuries of Dismantling

Over the centuries, technological advances have repeatedly enabled foreign powers to interfere with the functioning of the economy and/or to undermine the security of a less-advanced region or country. The dismantling of economic and security structures is a prime consequence of these advances. This section will enumerate some of the main technological events that led to this dismantling process, which continues today.

ARAB COUNTRIES PRIOR TO 1498

Until the sixteenth century, the Arabo-Islamic world was connected by a unique system of trade and transport that unified its large population scattered over vast areas of land and sea. The system sustained the economy of each Arab and Islamic state, underpinned trade with Europe, and fed into the various international trading systems. It is useful to note that at this time the Arab world and Europe were in a state of technological parity.

The Arabs had developed, over some two millennia, a sturdy and effective transnational trading system which reached its apogee in the eighth to sixteenth centuries. It was based on local and national technological inputs: skilled merchants and caravan managers, navigators with an extensive geographic knowledge, efficiently operated ports and trading emporia, scientifically bred camels, seaworthy dhows, and so on. Trust and mutual dependence among closely knit social groups prevailed. The socioeconomic support of the transport and trading system enhanced regional harmony and the stability of local communities.

The system of camel caravans also contributed to social integration between tribes specialized in raising camels on the one hand and city dwellers who managed much of the commercial part of the trading system on the other. Urban areas were the natural markets for goods. The level of specialization was so extensive that the trading system served all areas of the Arabo-Islamic world. The system of low-cost long-distance transport services, once in place, could then easily be extended to include bulk materials such as olive oil, soap, manufactured garments, dates, kema (truffles), sugar, and huge quantities of salt.

The mechanics of the trading system were so flexible that traders could move their business readily from place to place in response to changes in supply and demand, or in order to avoid ruthless rulers or areas of conflict. Since trade brought prosperity and employment, local governments sought to attract traders, and provide security and support facilities to ease the process of trade and the life of the traveler.

The Arab transport system was responsible for the large-scale circulation of people and information. This included the diffusion of agricultural plants, products, inventions, and all types of knowledge. Thus the trade and transport system had a powerful economic, social, and cultural impact. It also integrated the economies of the Arab countries with each other and with those of Asia, the Mediterranean Basin, and Africa. It enabled different regions and producers to exploit their comparative advantages. It brought about the exchange of goods and services between distant regions and engendered prosperity. It was also a multiethnic, multiracial and multinational system. Non-Arabs participated heavily in both the transport system and the trade.

The trading system was fully integrated into the annual haj to Mecca. The pilgrimage temporarily converted hundreds of thousands of pilgrims into traders. The custom was that each pilgrim left his or her country with some products that were traded en route to the Holy City. This converted the pilgrims' caravans into traveling shopping malls. The annual pilgrimage leaving Rabat, for example, would travel overland across Africa (through Niger, Chad, Central Africa, Sudan, and across the Red Sea to Jiddah). These caravans visited towns and villages where the pilgrims undertook commercial transactions with the local markets. Thus the annual pilgrimage contributed to economic activity and to social and cultural transactions; it also contributed to the development and maintenance of social, cultural, and religious bonds between the peoples of the Islamic world.

The first phase of the dismantling of this system was induced by Portuguese technological advances in ship design, navigation, and naval warfare; it began in 1498 when Vasco da Gama entered Gulf waters and initiated a century of Portuguese piracy and warfare. It is well known that the technological accomplishment of the Portuguese was the consequence of a determined effort under the leadership of Prince Henry the Navigator. Prince Henry established what was probably the first dedicated research and development (R & D) institution in the applied sciences. The research work undertaken there rationalized and improved ship design and navigation. The strategic breakthrough was the invention of transoceanic ships. These ships could carry a large number of guns and could navigate the high seas. It was this naval technology that made it possible for the Portuguese and the Spaniards to circumnavigate Africa and to cross the Atlantic to the Americas.

The small but powerful Portuguese fleet interfered violently with trade between the Arab world, Asia, and Africa in the once peaceful waters of the Indian Ocean. Until 1600 the Arab Gulf had been the capital of the Arab world's international trading system and the city of Hormuz was the physical headquarters of this vast global trading empire. The Portuguese used their superior naval force to harass and interfere with shipping, attack coastal towns, loot ships, and pillage coastal towns. The coastal towns of the Gulf and the Indian Ocean suffered considerably from these attacks. The people of the region displayed heroic resistance in the face of superior power. Egyptian naval forces tried to engage the Portuguese in a final naval encounter at Diu (1509) with the support of a Venetian naval force. The attempt failed; the Portuguese won.

Ottoman technical assistance to the cities of the Arabian peninsula ultimately saved the people of the Arab coastal towns from outright massacre by the Portuguese (unlike the native populations of Latin America who had no such a savior). The supreme test occurred in 1517: the superior land forces of the Ottoman army placed their heavy guns at the harbor of Jiddah and saved the Holy Cities of Islam from the possibility of outright occupation by the Portuguese (Guilmartin 1974).

The entry of the Ottomans into the Middle East that year saved the Gulf Arabs from probable decimation at the hands of the Portuguese. For the next three centuries, the forces of the Ottoman Empire protected the region from European devastation. However, the Ottomans themselves were unable to cope with European technological challenges and their empire eventually collapsed.

Although the Portuguese inflicted considerable economic losses on Arab trade in the Gulf, they did not have the resources to destroy it. The Arabs failed to acquire or develop the necessary technological capabilities to match Portuguese naval vessels. There were the usual opportunities to do so. First, industrial espionage was facilitated by the fact that the Portuguese constructed some of their vessels in India; high-level corruption within the Portuguese navy might also have provided opportunities. Second, the very existence of the superior Portuguese vessels should have enabled Arab ship builders to develop similar structures. However, the Arabs—along with other Asians—failed to develop such strategic technologies. The field was left open for further encroachments.

Portugal's naval technology diffused to the European Atlantic states. By the early seventeenth century, the British, the Dutch, and the French had displaced the Portuguese from the Indian Ocean. Between 1620 and 1670 these three countries introduced a new innovation: the East India Company. The English, French and Dutch East India Companies controlled fleets, marketing systems, finances, storage space, and armies.

Arab traders operated on a small scale; the totality of Arab trade depended on the efforts of a very large number of traders, each working on his own. The East India Companies were centrally managed (by the standards of those days) possessing the considerable financial resources necessary to exercise monopolistic behavior. They had the resources to purchase the entire production of spices or goods of an Asian country and thus to control markets.

The trader operating within the Arab system could no longer compete. He could no longer play the role of connecting the various communities and cultures within and on the peripheries of the Islamic world. The East India Companies rapidly eliminated Arab long-distance trade, and by the middle of the seventeenth century, the Arabs had begun to import Asian commodities from European traders.

TRADE AND TRANSPORT SYSTEMS LOST

By the eighteenth century, trade routes throughout North Africa and the Middle East were being reoriented toward coastal towns and European trade and transport. Whereas the Arab international trading system had been heavily land-based and internal, the new system was heavily dependent on European shipping and trade.

This loss was promptly followed by the progressive displacement of internal land-based long-distance travel services (including the haj) by European shipping. No serious Arab competition arose to challenge the rapid development of European Mediterranean shipping firms. At first this shipping attracted pilgrims from the coastal towns of Morocco, Algeria, Tunisia, and Libya. These pilgrims opted for a comfortable sea voyage on board European ships to Alexandria where they joined the haj caravan. But the countries of the interior—Mali, Cameroon, Nigeria, Niger, Chad—still depended on trans-Saharan transportation across central Africa to present-day Port Sudan, and from there to Jiddah by sea. Cities like Djenne and others in central Mali remain living testimonies of that period. Trade and transport to the coastal towns of Algeria, Tunisia, and Libya expanded.

When in 1832 the French occupied Algeria, and later Tunisia and Morocco, they sought to close all trans-Saharan routes which were being used by resistance movements and by "clandestine" trade. Between 1897 and 1912, British forces occupied Nigeria, the French occupied Niger, Chad, and Cameroon, and the Italians occupied Libya.

Thus by the early twentieth century, the complex and rich system of internal trans-Saharan transport had been dismantled. Sub-Saharan Africa has not yet recovered from this mutilation of its sociocultural and economic life. The three imperial powers sought to isolate and dominate these countries: the cultural and economic barriers between the imperial powers and the small African states meant rapid impoverishment and cultural decay. The stoppage of the constant cultural enrichment brought about by the regular flow of pilgrims and traders between these countries could not be replaced by a few scholarships to London, Rome, or Paris.

One of the first objectives of the Algerian revolution in 1962 was to reestablish Algeria's trans-Saharan routes to central Africa (Blin 1987). By 1964, the Algerian government began to plan the construction of desert roads with a view to linking Algiers to Niger and Mali. Plans were completed by the late 1970s. But French and other pressure prevented Niger and Mali from constructing their stretches of the road to link with the Algerian road; they were, however, provided with international assistance to extend their roads to the Atlantic via Nigeria.

Two further technological developments accelerated the dismantling of regional and local trade and transport systems: the construction and operation of railway systems by foreign firms, and the construction of the Suez Canal. By the latter part of the nineteenth century the national system of trade and transport had disintegrated to the level where it was replaced by totally imported systems with very little local participation beyond the commission agents who peddled their political influence to secure concessions (Zahlan and Said Zahlan 1978).

The displacement of camel- and dhow-based transport technology with railway and steamship technologies without the transfer of mechanical and new naval technologies meant that the Arabs lost the employment generated by operating their system of transport. Even today the Arab countries remain unable to acquire the employment derived from operating and maintaining their extensive transport systems.

Several other technological developments during this period contributed to further dismantling and underdevelopment. The first was the successful transplantation of the Yemeni coffee plant to the colonial empires of Britain, France, and Holland. The first to succeed in transplantation on a large commercial scale were the Dutch, who developed modern coffee farming in Brazil. By 1734 non-Yemeni coffee was traded in Salonica, Greece; in 1737 in Cairo and in 1739 in Aleppo. The imported coffee was sold at a quarter of the price of the higher-quality Yemeni coffee. Yemen was able to maintain the volume of its sales (at lower prices) throughout the eighteenth century, but it no longer held a monopoly on coffee production and trade (Raymond 1973). In 1850 Brazil's share of world coffee trade rose to 30 percent and by 1914 it had attained 70 percent. Brazil's coffee production was heavily controlled by British interests (Greenhill 1977).

The Arabs, who had already lost their creative capacities, were unable to acquire, adopt, or develop alternative technologies to contain these technological challenges. These activities gave the kiss of death to the transnational Arab trading system. The forces that bound the Arab communities to each other were thus loosened; the cohesiveness of the Arab and Muslim countries began to weaken. It is of critical importance to appreciate that the strength of the Arab and Muslim worlds was based on a common market and not on political unity; many of the Arab countries were in conflict, but this did not eliminate trade and cultural exchanges between them.

INDUSTRIAL REVOLUTION

The second phase of technology dismantling was induced by the industrial revolution. In the early nineteenth century the main industry in many Arab countries (especially Syria, Egypt, and Iraq) was textile manufacturing. One of the chief byproducts of the industrial revolution was the rapid development of textile industries, which quickly undermined the traditional textile industries which were firmly based in the Arab countries (especially in Syria, Egypt, Iraq, Tunisia, and Morocco) where textile technology was very advanced and self-reliant. By the 1830s these local industries collapsed in the face of European imports. Attempts to acquire new textile technologies are still going on: the Arab countries still lag behind the advanced levels now prevalent in Europe.

The textile revolution was only the beginning. Steam power, machine production, chemical sciences and technology, electrification, petroleum production and refining, communication technologies, radio, electric power and engineering, and countless advances in medical science, construction technologies, city planning, and management systems all had dramatic consequences for the Arab world.

Every technological advance in Europe, and later in the United States, contributed to the continuing decline of inter-Arab cohesiveness. The acquisition of Western military technologies, beginning with the Ottomans and Muhammad Ali, led to the progressive divorce of military institutions from their local environment and to their progressive integration into the military-industrial-intelligence complexes of Western powers.

The introduction of railways into the Arab world via the turnkey mode of contracting pioneered the still-prevailing procedures for trade in technology. During the age of camel caravans and dhows the Arabs were masters of the transport technologies then in use; the new mechanical technologies were imported without any effort being made to acquire them. New technology was imported in a dependent mode and packaged with its consultants, contractors, operators, and financiers. The cost of all of this dependent luxury was enormous; the resulting Egyptian and Ottoman debts had well known economic and political consequences: the occupation of Egypt in 1882, and the collapse of the economy of the Ottoman Empire.

Indigo became a popular dye in Europe during the sixteenth century when it displaced woad. By the eighteenth century European powers began to plant indigo in their colonies. India and Java became main suppliers; Egypt also developed the production of this dye. However, the rapid development of modern chemistry accelerated after 1825 when Faraday discovered benzene, and culminated in the synthesis of indigo in 1890 by Heumann. By 1913, the market for natural indigo collapsed: the industrial production of dyes had taken off.

COLONIZATION AND INDEPENDENCE

The third phase of technology dismantling began with the direct occupation of Arab countries when practically every technical decision of importance was made by the emissaries of the occupying powers. The net result was the further divorce of the elites, the culture, and the economy from technical matters (Zahlan 1997a). The Arabs were not unique in experiencing such colonialist devastation: China did not do much better. Japan benefited from observing China's experience and as a result opted at an early date for closing the technology gap. But the Arabs at that time lacked the ethnic homogeneity and enlightened leadership to pursue a similar strategy. Even the "best" Arab case— Egypt under Muhammad Ali—could not measure up. Muhammad Ali's efforts at industrialization are overrated: he did not appreciate the political and economic implications of the new technologies that he sought to import. Furthermore, he did not identify with Egyptians who were being treated as second-class citizens in their own country.

The fourth phase was ushered in by political independence. When independence was finally achieved, the rulers and elites of the new states who came forward had little knowledge of contemporary developments in science and technology. Foreign control of the political life and economies of the Arab countries was less complete than the foreign control of government operations and of technological activity. Not only did all equipment, industrial supplies, and maintenance services have to be imported but also the Arab countries depended completely on foreign consulting and contracting services when they sought to alter their economic circumstances. As Helie notes after the departure of the French in Algeria and the disorganization of economic life:

> More important is the fact that the colonial machine itself was put back into operation, insofar as possible after independence. It is difficult to believe that [the government] is capable of dealing with the new problems that are arising. Under colonial rule, the administration's objective was to maintain order; its new goal must be to promote economic development (Helie 1973).

A similar observation was made by Charles Debbasch (1975).

The ruling political elites had had no formal or informal training in the requirements and implications of science and technology which had become so central to the industrialized world in the late twentieth century. The modus operandi of the new national governments was that each ministry or parastatal was designed to operate as an independent authority, resulting in the maintenance of the old colonial "referral system." This deepened and promoted the process of dismantling. This system prevails today and its spontaneous formation can be seen taking place in the embryonic Palestinian National Authority.

The new leaders sought to develop their countries through the rapid expansion of educational systems and investment in new industries. Cultural distortions and alienation were intensified by the accelerated programs adopted at this time.

Because they wished to accelerate the process of development, the new national elites who took over from the colonial powers unknowingly adopted methods that ultimately led to even greater technological dependence. Thus they unwittingly established a culture and a political economy that sustained the turnkey approach so well established during the previous centuries. Did they have an alternative? Certainly. Arab elites instead could have adopted a strategy of acquiring and accumulating technology—the course adopted by Western European countries when confronted by the British industrial revolution of the early nineteenth century, and also adopted by Russia and Japan.

The rich oil-producing countries such as Algeria, Iraq, Libya, and the members of the Gulf Cooperation Council had the financial resources to bring the totally dependent technological behavior of the past to new levels of sophistication: the concepts of client-in-hand (GCC, Algeria), "explosive development" (Iraq), "*technologie-de-pointe*" (Algeria), and other such innovations were developed to bizarre levels. Foreign consulting firms conceived and designed enormous projects, foreign accounting and law firms monitored them, and an army of foreign contractors and foreign labor implemented them. In an effort to emulate their richer neighbors, the poorer Arab countries did their best to adopt similar models.

These advanced forms of technological dependence had numerous advantages: they gave decisionmakers the satisfaction of being totally independent of their society and of its underdevelopment; they made decisionmakers feel they had found a magic wand which, when used to sign multi-billion dollar contracts, could transform the work of Bechtel and others into their own science.

Truly wondrous things were built: power and desalination plants, hospitals which could boast the best and latest in medical sciences, irrigation schemes, enormous dams, transport systems, airports, airlines, military installations, radar stations, remote sensing facilities, solar stations, communications systems super-guns, even gold-plated cars and yachts. Liquid Natural Gas technology was brought to Algeria, yet Algerians did not have to contribute to the process. Those who mediated these lavish contracts earned enormous commissions. Well-placed people accumulated multi-billion dollar personal fortunes. They and their progeny now adorn foreign magazines, and their weddings in London, Cannes, or Paris are the talk of the town.

The Arab countries total GFCF, during the past two decades, was in excess of $2,000 billion (in current prices). If this sum were to be converted into 1991 dollars, these investments would probably total between $4,000 and $5,000 billion. The 1993, combined GNP of the Arab countries resulting from this enormous GFCF was barely $380 billion. The gap between the Arab world and industrial countries has continued to grow, and the Arab economies suffer from chronic stagnation and low productivity.

Instruments and Patterns of Technological Development

The major instruments of national technological development have been reasonably well known for at least the past two centuries. The process depends on the availability of qualified professional resources (hence university education); R & D; national consulting and contracting firms; the relevant economic and financial institutions to support technological development; and science policy.

UNIVERSITY EDUCATION

There has been a significant and dramatic expansion of the proportion of Arabs who have completed four or more years of higher education: in 1948, they constituted only 0.06 percent of the population; and by 1990 they had increased to 1.5 percent, and by 1996 to an estimated 2.0 percent. This translates to 8 percent of the economically active population.

In 1984 the Arab countries had a total of 81 universities (ALECSO 1989); these had an enrollment of 1.5 million students. The number of universities increased to 175 in 1995; the Arab governments had also established some 360 two- and three-year post-secondary institutions by 1991. These enrolled some 3.2 million students (Qasem 1998).

The proportion of the 20–24 age group enrolled in post-secondary education in 1991 was 11 percent for the entire Arab world. (By comparison, the EEC average is 14 percent.) In the different countries this proportion was: 27 percent for Jordan; 13–19 percent each in Egypt, Qatar, and Syria; and below 5 percent each in Sudan, the Yemens, Mauritania, and the UAE. Some 35 percent of these students are enrolled in technical and scientific subjects (Qasem 1998).

No accurate and detailed statistics are available on the number of engineers in the Arab world. At a 1989 meeting of the Federation of Arab Engineers in Kuwait, the president of the Federation stated that there were 600,000 Arab engineers in the Arab world. This is a large and significant number: by comparison, there were 1.4 million engineers in the United States in 1986. Arab universities were graduating more than 30,000 engineers annually in the late 1980s, more than graduates from French or British universities. Needless to say, the economies of France and Britain are far larger than that of the entire Arab world.

It is clear from these figures that the Arab states have access to a large and increasing supply of professional manpower, from national as well as foreign universities. Much of the emphasis of Arab foreign education has been in science and engineering: it can be safely assumed that there are substantial numbers of Arabs specialized in every sub-field of science and engineering. In some fields, the number of scientists or engineers may be in the tens of thousands, while in others it may be in the hundreds.

Doctoral-level education is still highly underdeveloped; specialization is pursued abroad. The number of Arab students abroad may be of the order of 250,000. Most of these are working toward advanced degrees in the sciences in leading industrial countries. For example, about 80 percent of Arab students in the United Kingdom are working toward Master of Science or doctorate degrees. The brain drain among Arab students abroad is very high; the brain drain to Organization for Economic Cooperation and Development (OECD) countries is in excess of 500,000 professionals.

R & D

The total number of professors in Arab universities in 1995 was more than 100,000 (63,000 in science and technology; 38,000 in the humanities) compared with 51,000 in 1985. The proportion of faculty members holding a PhD increased from 55 percent in 1985 to 63 percent in 1991 (Qasem 1998).

There were about 250 R & D centers (excluding hospitals, but including research departments and/or programs) in the Arab world in 1984. The universities have 65 centers and/or programs under their umbrella. The centers vary in size, resources, competence and track record. Of the centers outside the universities, 75 percent were established since 1970. Half of the R & D centers were engaged in research in agriculture, nutrition, water and irrigation, marine sciences, and the biological sciences; 14 (6 percent) were in solar energy; 9 (4 percent) in oil and petrochemicals; 11 (4 percent) in ecology; 11 (4 percent) in basic sciences and computer science.

Research activity in the Arab countries is thus highly focused on applied subjects, with a priority in medicine and agriculture: 38 percent in medicine; 20 percent in agriculture; 17 percent in engineering; 17 percent in the basic sciences; and 8 percent in economics and management. The most common research areas are: agronomy, food technology, nutrition, general and internal medicine, general biomedical research, pharmacy, ecology, remote sensing, and water resources. Despite the valiant efforts of a number of scientists, however, basic research is on such a small scale that it is virtually nonexistent (ALECSO 1989, Zahlan 1998).

There were 1.7 researchers outside the university per 10,000 economically active manpower (and 2.7 per 10,000 if the university research workers are included); the equivalent numbers for a select number of countries was: 66 (USA), 99 (Russia), 58 (Japan), 36 (UK), 39 (France). There were 44.6 researchers (with MS and PhD degrees) per million inhabitants, and 0.021 researchers per $1 million of GNP (ALECSO 1989). Expenditure on R & D in the Arab world was $750 million 0.2 percent of GNP in 1995 (Qasem 1998). By comparison, India spent 0.7 percent, Brazil spent 0.6 percent, and industrial countries devoted around 3 percent.

Commitment to R & D can also be compared on the basis of data from the Institute of Scientific Information (USA) on the number of publications in refereed journals. In 1995 the scientific output of various countries (measured as the number of publications per million inhabitants) was: 144 (South Korea), 42 (Brazil), 19 (India), 11 (China), 26 (Arab world), 840 (France), 1,878 (Switzerland), and 1,926 (Israel) (ISI 1996).

The Arab countries are near the top of the Third World level of activity, but far below the levels of industrial countries. Thus, although the output may be comparable, the application of scientific findings is more constrained than in other large Third World countries where there are no political or economic barriers to the circulation of ideas and expertise.

Arab universities have been, and still are, the leading centers for both basic and applied research in science and technology. The number of institutions whose scientists published one or more scientific papers increased from 289 in 1977 to 407 in 1983 and 708 in 1989. The annual growth rate of the number of such institutions was 8 percent. Many of these institutions are hospitals, and are not therefore classified (see above) as R & D centers.

Researchers in the Arab world published a total of 2,612 publications in refereed journals of international standing in 1983, 5,043 in 1989 and 7,139 in 1995. The share of oil-producing countries (Algeria, Bahrain, Iraq, Kuwait, Libya, Qatar, and Saudi Arabia) in total Arab publications increased from 14 percent in 1967 to 19 percent in 1977 to 31 percent in 1983 to 41 percent in 1989 and to 39 in 1995. Most of this output from oil-producing states came from Kuwait and Saudi Arabia. In fact, Kuwait demonstrated a striking capacity to attract and retain Arab scientists: In 1989, the professors at Kuwait University alone published more than all the scientists working in all Iraqi research institutions; in that year, Kuwait University (356) was the second largest producer in the Arab world (Cairo University with 377 publications ranked first). And in 1990 (just before the Iraqi invasion) Kuwait University was the leading publishing institution in the Arab world. In 1995 Kuwait had recovered to 66 percent of its 1990 level of R & D activity (Zahlan 1997b).

R & D organizations play a major role in successful planning, design, and operation of economic installations. However, because the consulting and contracting services utilized in establishing industrial plants are generally imported on a turnkey basis, the demand for local R & D services is still limited. Technological dependence severely constrains the development of the requisite R & D capabilities to support and service the various economic sectors.

Arab science and technology human resources are more than adequate, and could constitute an integrative social factor. But in the absence of rational and appropriate science policies and adequate financial resources, the potential of this human resource is dissipated. As the figures on publications indicate, for every nine Arab science and engineering faculty members, only one publishes a paper annually (60,000 faculty and only 7,139 publications in 1995). The reason for such a low figure is the lack of resources and the absence of demand for services by nationals: both the public and private sectors depend nearly exclusively on foreign firms for technical services. The inappropriate policies now in force promote (albeit not deliberately) the continuing disintegration of Arab society.

CONSULTING, CONTRACTING AND THE MARKET FOR TECHNOLOGY

The Arab world provides a large market for technology products and services. This can be readily seen from the large number of identical contracts that are awarded in a number of technological fields. Contracts for the same technology are awarded repeatedly over short periods of time—often simultaneously—in several Arab countries. Such a market provides excellent opportunities for technology transfer because technology is best acquired as part of the repeated undertaking of similar projects. The absence of adequate financial and insurance services to support national consulting and contracting firms, combined with the absence of adequate technology policies, are the main reasons for the slow pace at which technology trickles into the region (Zahlan 1984).

Contracts with foreign consulting and contracting firms are in agricultural development (terracing, irrigation, drainage, water works), construction (from buildings to public works), transport systems, industry (cement, food, iron and steel, oil production, phosphates, metals), educational technologies, aviation, communication, and so on. (Emery, Graham and Oppenheimer 1986; Zahlan 1981; Ilgen and Pempel 1987; Zahlan 1990, 1991).

Since the national markets of each Arab state for sophisticated technological services are small, any serious effort to transfer technology has to involve substantial Arab economic cooperation. There has been no significant effort to date to implement inter-Arab cooperation in technology.

The subject of technology transfer to the Arab world, in both Western and Arab literature, has become synonymous with trade. In this type of analysis, the Arab is a client of foreign technology and is no longer a participant in a process of technological development. Publications on trade with the Arabs usually focus on the suppliers of technology; the consumers are rarely mentioned. Emphasis is often placed on the competition among the various industrial powers for the lucrative Arab markets; the behavior of the Arab trading parties tends to be of minor interest. This may be because much of the planning and decisionmaking is done by foreign institutions. The leading Arab development institutions (and, of course, Arab governments) utilize foreign consulting firms almost exclusively.

This point is illustrated and reflected in the authoritative United States Office of Technology Assessment (OTA) study entitled *Technology Transfer to the Middle East* (1984). In it, the authors note: "Although Middle East technology trade has increased, OTA's research indicates that technology transfers have been limited. . . . OTA's research shows that technology is much more easily traded internationally than it is absorbed by recipients in developing countries"(5).

Although the 600-page OTA report distinguishes clearly between technology transfer and technology trade, it still regards trade with the Arab world as technology transfer. For example, in chapter 5 on *Petrochemical Technology Transfer* (119–82) less than two of its sixty-three pages are devoted to the subject of "Absorption of petrochemical technologies." But even this has little to do with the topic at hand: "absorption" turns out to mean training technicians to

push the right buttons! The rest of the chapter is devoted to petrochemical production (by plants designed and installed by non-Arab companies), foreign
company participation in the venture, the restructuring of global trade in commodity chemicals expected to result from the investment, implications for U.S.
policy, and so on.

The OTA report goes on to express its views on the manpower constraints
on technology transfer: "In the Middle East a number of factors constrain technology absorption. They all relate to the considerable technological distance
that must be bridged between the suppliers and the recipients. Chief among
them is a disparity between human and financial resources" (5–6).

The OTA report gives the impression that the Arab countries are importing
advanced civilian technologies, while in fact the bulk of the imports consists of
very simple and mundane products. According to *Technology Trade with the
Middle East* the Arabs import far more food, live animals, and tobacco than they
do aircraft! (89–116).

Most of the imports of the Arab world consist of construction services (road
construction, simple houses, airports, bridges, silos, water works, etc. for some
$50 billion annually); equipment (cars, trucks, tractors, forklifts, etc. for some
$35 billion annually); food (milk, meat, cereals, etc. for some $25 billion annually); and so on. Only limited amounts of high technology products are
imported, and these account for barely 10 to 15 percent of total imports.

The construction of petrochemical plants, refineries, and water desalination
plants is well within the capabilities of Arab manpower and organizations
today. Arab firms lack neither the technical expertise, nor the natural, financial,
or human resources to undertake such projects. What is missing is a variety of
other inputs, such as financial, legal and technical support services that Arab
governments, unlike those of the OECD countries, do not make available to
their national organizations.

SCIENCE POLICY

The weakness of the Arab science and technology system and the absence of
effective science policies in the Arab world have made the economic integration
of technological activity very difficult (Zahlan 1980, 1981, 1997b). The inability
to formulate and adopt sensible technology policies has contributed to the continuing disintegration of Arab society and culture.

Of all Arab countries, Egypt has been the most explicit regarding the importance of developing science and technology policies. It has made many
attempts—all unsuccessful—to develop such policies (Zahlan 1980; UNESCWA
1986). The OTA report (469) summarizes seven major recent studies on Egypt
(three by UNESCO, one by USAID, one by UNCTAD and two by an Egyptian

institution in collaboration with U.S. institutions): all find a lack of integrated science and technology policy in Egypt.

Unemployment, alienation, marginalization and the intensification of civil unrest and violence are all direct or indirect indicators of the absence of an integrated science policy and of the impact of that absence on the economic life of the Arab world.

Reflections on the Future

The technological dependence of the Arab countries has enhanced their vulnerability to outside interference and reduced the degree of internal national integration. National integration depends on economic exchanges within society. Dependent technology policies reduce such exchanges. Instead, economic exchanges take place with foreign countries without involving the national population. The extent of forward and backward integration within the national economy of any Arab state is very limited. As a consequence the degree of socioeconomic interdependence within each country is limited and declining. The extent of inter-Arab trade (5 percent of total trade) is insignificant. The counterpart of weak internal cohesiveness is a high degree of dependence on imports. In general the extent of Arab dependence on imports for all necessities of life is striking. The case of Iraq is a dramatic illustration of the depth of dependence.

Since 1970, an increasing number of Arab countries have been entering the fruitless arena of civil unrest, economic paralysis, and civil war. The countries where civil wars have taken place (Lebanon, Sudan, Somalia, Algeria) have not been able to find solutions to their original socioeconomic problems.

The most optimistic view one can adopt is that the Arabs are in a state of transition: they are leaving their dependent phase and entering a self-reliant one. How likely is it that they can effect such a transition?

On the positive side, they possess enormous human, strategic, and natural resources which, if efficiently managed and put to effective use, could arrest further decline and induce a rapid change in fortune. But, in order to do so, they need to adopt a performance-oriented political economy and an appropriate science policy. Is this likely to occur? Is it likely that the highly developed rent political economy which prevails in every Arab country will cede its control under mounting economic pressures?

All countries, including those of the Third World, have immediate access, at low cost, to world-wide knowledge and technological experiences. Furthermore, ongoing technological advances are constantly equalizing industrial and

Third World countries by reducing the importance of carry-over technologies: industrialists in the West must constantly destroy their own obsolete physical assets, along with the corresponding obsolete forms of social organization, in order to replace them with new technologies and organizational forms.

All Third World countries face two major challenges: how to increase the flow of technology and how to develop a niche in the world economy. The systematic pursuit of policies that improve the competitiveness of national labor is of paramount importance. For example, modern information technology is transforming all modes of management and organization, as well as capital goods. All countries have to learn these new technologies. Here industrial countries have the edge, because their populations possess a level of education high enough to facilitate the process of adaptation.

On the negative side, the Arab countries face a number of challenges: population pressure, the dematerialization of the world economy, and declining Arab labor productivity. Mounting population pressure will decrease the resources available for undertaking economic reforms. By the year 2050, an expected increase of some 400 million inhabitants will bring the total population to some 700 million. Half of these will be below the age of 18. This young population could be an important force for positive and creative change if provided with proper education and training. The absence of appropriate technology policies, however, could transform this abundant and youthful population into a disruptive and destabilizing force. The dematerialization of the world economy and the expanding number of gas and oil sources worldwide have combined to reduce Arab income and increase the cost of imports.

Increasing labor productivity in the Newly Industrializing Countries is reducing the attractiveness of the Arab countries for foreign direct investment. Most of the subcontracting to the Arab states now is for low-value-added and low-technology activities.

In other words, internal and external factors are not favorable to promoting technological development. During the past 500 years the Arabs have enjoyed short periods of favorable balances of trade; for example, Egypt enjoyed a low population and an export market for highly lucrative products and services from 1810 to 1870; similarly, several Arab oil-producing countries benefited from the golden period of oil exports during the 1970s and 1980s. In both cases, however, these blessings were squandered. Today, and in the years to come, the Arab countries could bring about prosperity through the elimination of waste and the induction of innovation.

The future of any country is contingent on its capacity to produce the goods and services in demand. The fierce international competition between the industrial countries is all about retaining their capacity to do just that. The major tool in this competition is science and technology. The Arab world has remained outside this competition because it has not sought to acquire the requisite political economy. But no future is foreclosed; a failure to respond to a technological challenge is not synonymous with technological determinism. The Arabs' failure to respond was a consequence of the prevailing political economy. The Arabs retain the capacity to alter their political economy. All countries retain the potential power to shape their own future.

References

ALECSO, Committee for the Development of Science and Technology in the Arab Nation. *A Strategy for the Development of Arab Science and Technology: The General Report and the Sectoral Strategies.* Beirut: Centre for Arab Unity Studies, 1989. In Arabic.

Beblawi, Hazem and Giacomo Luciani eds. *Nation, State and Integration in the Arab World: The Rentier State.* London: Croom Helm, 1987.

Blin, Louis. "Algerie et Route Transsaharienne." *The Maghreb Review*, 12:3–4 (1987), 105–13.

Debbasch, Charles. "Les Elites Maghrebines Devant la Bureaucratie." In Charles Debbasch, ed. *Pouvoir et Administration au Maghreb: Etudes sur les Elites Maghrebines.* Paris: CNRS, 1975, 7–8.

Emery, James J. and Norman A. Graham and Michael F. Oppenheimer. *Technology Trade with the Middle East.* Boulder & London: Westview Press, 1986.

Headrick, Daniel R. *The Tools of Empire: Technology and European Imperialism in the Nineteenth Century.* Oxford: Oxford University Press, 1981.

Helie, Manien. "Industrial Self-management in Algeria." In William Zartman, ed. *Man, State and Society in the Contemporary Maghreb.* London: The Pall Mall Press, 1973, 465 ff, especially 468.

Ilgen, Thomas and T. J. Pempel. *Trading Technology, Europe and Japan in the Middle East.* New York: Praeger, 1987.

Institute of Scientific Information.*Citation Index*, Philadelphia: ISI, 1996.

Greenhill, Robert. "The Brazilian Coffee Trade." In D. C. M. Platt, ed. *Business Imperialism 1840–1930.* Oxford: Oxford University Press, 1977, 198–230.

Guilmartin Jr., John Francis. *Gunpowder and Galleys: Changing Technology and Mediterranean Warfare at Sea in the Sixteenth Century.* London: Cambridge University Press, 1974.

Office of Technology Assessment. *Technology Transfer to the Middle East*, Washington, DC: Congress of the United States, Office of Technology Assessment, 1984.

Qasem, Subhi.*The Higher Education System in the Arab States.* Cairo: UNESCO, 1998.

Raymond, André. *Artisans et Commercants au Caire* Vol.1. Damascus: Institut Français de Damas, 1973, 146–57.

Science and Technology in the Arab World: Progress Without Change. Beirut: Center for Arab Unity Studies, 1998 (in Arabic).

UNESCWA. *Technology Policies in the Arab States.* New York: United Nations, 1986.

Zahlan, A. B. and Rosemarie Said Zahlan, eds. *Technology Transfer and Change in the Arab World.* Oxford: Pergamon Press, 1978.

———. *Science and Science Policy in the Arab World.* London: Croom Helm, 1980.

———. *The Technological Dimension of Arab Unity.* Beirut: Centre for Arab Unity Studies, 1981. In Arabic.

———. *The Arab Construction Industry,* London: Croom Helm, 1984.

———. "The Formation and Employment of Arab Engineers" in Elisabeth Longuenesse, ed. *Batisseurs et Bureaucrates: Ingénieurs et Société au Maghreb et au Moyen-Orient.* Lyons: Maison de L'Orient, 1990.

———. *Acquiring Technological Capacity: A Study of Arab Consulting and Contracting Firms.* London: Macmillan, 1991.

———. "The Integration of Science and Technology into Development Planning." In *Proceedings of the Workshop on Integration of Science and Technology in the Development Planning and Management Process in the ESCWA Region,* New York: United Nations, 1994, 5–34.

———. "The Impact of Technology Change on the Nineteenth Century Arab World," in I. Willam Zartman and Charles E. Butterworth, eds. *State and Islam.* Washington DC: Woodrow Wilson Center, 1997a.

———. "Scientific Communities in Egypt: Emergence and Effectiveness." In Jacques Gaillard, V.V. Krishna, and Roland Waast, eds. *Emergence of Scientific Communities in the Developing Countries.* New Delhi: Sage, 1997b, 81–104.

Labor Migration and Economic Integration in the Middle East

chapter 13

Nemat Shafik

The idea of an economically integrated Arab world has been part of the region's political discourse for decades. While the idea is compelling to many, the Middle East is in some ways one of the least integrated regions in the world, despite decades of attempts to give economic meaning to the notion of Arab unity. The major exception is labor mobility, as intraregional migration flows have been extensive in recent decades. Remittances from migrant labor now exceed the value of regional trade in goods as well as official capital flows.

What are the characteristics of economic integration in the Middle East and why have labor flows been the major channel through which intraregional economic ties have been forged? What are the motives for regional integration, and to what degree is the region integrated—in terms of trade in goods and movement of factors of production? What special role has labor migration played in regional integration in light of the region's endowment and trade policies? The Middle East's pattern of labor-based economic integration is fairly unique. Has it left the region better or worse off? These are the questions that will be analyzed below.

Why Regional Integration?

The appeal of economic integration in the Arab world is based on the circumstances of the region and, increasingly, on the changing characteristics of the world economy. At the regional level there have been two interrelated motives for promoting integration. One was purely political and had its origins in the ideology of Arab nationalism. An economically integrated

Note: The views expressed here are those of the author and do not reflect the views of the World Bank or its affiliated institutions.

Arab world would provide the region with critical support for sustained and meaningful political integration. The second motive was more economic and stemmed from the view that the complementarity of endowments across the region could be the basis for enhanced development. The high-income oil exporters were capital-rich, but poor in labor and productive land. Countries like the Sudan, Egypt, Syria, and Morocco had substantial agricultural potential and low-wage labor, but lacked capital. Lebanon and Jordan had surpluses of skilled labor. The more diversified economies, such as Algeria and Iraq, could also benefit from imports of labor and capital from abroad. Moreover, regional integration would enable all countries to take advantage of economies of scale in production, distribution, and resource use. In the Middle East, there is the added dimension of regional conflict. Many argue that a region that is more economically interdependent and prosperous is less likely to experience political and military conflict. The example of the European Coal and Steel Community formed after World War II is often cited as an example where encouraging economic ties laid the groundwork for peaceful coexistence and eventual integration in the form of the European Union.

The economic motive has become increasingly important as most countries in the region experienced economic stagnation in the late 1980s and the early 1990s. Per capita income growth in the Middle East was respectable from 1960–73, and the period of the oil booms, 1973–81, was one of accelerated growth. With the collapse in oil prices in 1986, most countries in the region experienced negative per capita income growth. Only four countries—Morocco, Turkey, Tunisia, and Yemen—in the region had positive growth rates in the second half of the 1980s. The challenge for the future is even greater because of the region's young, urbanized, and rapidly growing population. The Middle East, along with Sub-Saharan Africa, has the highest rate of population growth in the world. Total population in the Middle East was about 260 million in 1990, 51 percent of whom live in urban areas and 43 percent of whom are under 15 years of age (World Bank 1992). About one-third of the population in the region's developing countries lives in poverty (living on less than $1 per day) (Ravallion, Datt, and Chen 1992). This combination of growing populations and deteriorating living standards has reinforced the imperative for economic development in the region.

Changes in the world economy, and particularly in world trade, have also reinforced the need for integration. Intraregional trade has been growing faster than world trade in recent years. The emergence of three major trading blocks in the world economy—dominated by the United States, Japan, and Europe—has resulted in fears that countries outside such regional arrangements could suffer a fall in exports as the adverse substitution effects of regionalization outweigh the favorable income effects. Such fears have provided a stimulus to renewed attempts at regional trading arrangements all over the world—Latin America, Central America, Africa, and Asia.

The conventional economic view on regional integration is that it is desirable where the trade creation effects are greater than the trade diverting effects. Thus, agreements among countries that would tend to trade with each other anyway would result in greater welfare gains than those that divert trade to higher cost suppliers. This is consistent with the evidence that effective agreements tend to emerge among countries where there is already intense trade. In many cases, the static gains from more efficient resource allocation are overshadowed by the dynamic efficiency gains that result from competition. There is also evidence of the benefits of such agreements. Bigger countries tend to grow faster—lending support to the view that economies of scale and efficiency gains associated with integration result in higher incomes (Lachler 1989).

The numerous attempts to promote economic integration in the Arab world have been analyzed extensively elsewhere (Waterbury and Mallakh 1978; Makdisi 1979; Ghantus 1982). Since the creation of the Arab League in 1945, economic integration has been on the regional agenda. In 1953, Arab countries signed a multilateral trading agreement under the auspices of the Arab League, which exempted Arab agricultural commodities from tariff barriers and reduced tariffs on some industrial goods. The Arab Economic Unity Agreement signed in 1956 sought full economic union among Egypt, Iraq, Jordan, Kuwait, and Syria. The same countries, with the exception of Kuwait in 1964, formed the Arab Common Market that sought the gradual elimination of tariff and nontariff barriers over a ten-year period.

These and numerous other attempts to promote integration failed largely because there was no willingness to subsume national interests to regional ones. Protectionist interests in all countries often secured exemptions to more open trading arrangements that undermined regional integration efforts. Local interest groups also often undermined coordination of other regional policies. The failure of economic integration efforts was not unique to the Middle East. The majority of such efforts failed at promoting integration in virtually every developing region.

The oil boom in the 1970s spurred the growth of institutions to transfer resources from the high-income oil exporters to the poorer states in the region. Kuwait and Abu Dhabi actually set up the national funds (the Kuwait and the Abu Dhabi Fund for Arab Economic Development, respectively) the first oil price increase in 1973, while Saudi Arabia and Iraq created similar funds in 1974. Regional institutions were also established—the Arab Fund for Economic and Social Development (1968), the Islamic Development Bank (1974), the Arab

TABLE 13.1 Intraregional Middle Eastern Exports and Imports as a Share of Total Exports and Imports, 1985–1990

	Exports						Imports					
	1985	1986	1987	1988	1989	1990	1985	1986	1987	1988	1989	1990
Percent distribution												
Industrial countries	60.6	62.9	58.3	56.9	59.0	63.9	68.1	69.3	66.3	66.3	67.4	71.8
Developing countries	31.7	28.9	31.7	33.0	31.5	28.2	26.5	25.7	27.2	28.0	28.3	25.3
Africa	1.8	1.8	1.9	2.1	1.9	1.5	0.8	1.0	0.9	1.0	1.1	1.1
Asia	13.2	11.0	14.0	15.1	15.0	14.6	8.4	8.9	9.7	10.8	10.6	10.9
Europe	6.1	5.5	5.9	5.6	4.7	4.1	7.3	7.3	7.4	7.3	6.7	5.0
Middle East	6.2	6.7	6.3	6.8	6.7	5.0	7.6	6.4	7.3	6.7	7.6	6.1
Western Hemisphere	4.3	4.0	3.6	3.4	3.1	3.1	2.4	2.1	1.9	2.2	2.3	2.2
Former U.S.S.R.	0.8	1.1	1.0	1.0	1.5	1.8	1.2	1.6	1.6	1.4	1.2	1.1
Annual percent change												
World	-12.1	-19.9	12.9	-1.4	22.3	23.9	-17.8	-9.0	1.2	11.5	-0.9	16.9
Industrial countries	-10.8	-18.3	6.5	-3.8	26.8	34.3	-20.7	-7.3	-3.0	11.5	0.6	24.4
Developing Countries	-15.5	-26.8	23.7	2.6	16.5	11.1	-13.0	-11.9	7.4	14.6	–	4.4
Africa	-17.5	-20.2	20.7	11.2	10.0	-2.5	-25.2	18.5	-12.7	24.4	9.4	14.6
Asia	-20.1	-33.4	43.5	6.3	21.4	20.6	-14.8	-4.3	11.1	23.4	-2.8	20.5
Europe	-9.7	-27.9	22.0	-7.1	3.0	7.5	-13.8	-8.8	3.5	10.3	-10.2	-12.6
Middle East	-14.7	-14.1	6.6	6.3	21.0	-8.3	-9.7	-23.9	15.4	2.5	13.2	-6.3
Western Hemisphere	-7.8	-26.0	1.3	-6.3	11.6	21.3	-9.0	-19.8	-9.2	28.9	3.4	11.8
Former U.S.S.R. and selected other countries n.i.e.	18.1	6.4	–	3.7	82.7	48.1	14.6	19.9	-2.8	-1.8	-12.0	1.6

Source: International Monetary Fund (1991)

Bank for Economic Development in Africa (1973), the Arab-African Technical Assistance Fund (1974), the Arab-African Oil Assistance Fund (1974), the Special Fund for Arab Non-Oil-exporting Countries (1974), and the Arab Monetary Fund (1976). Most of these provided balance of payments support or concessional financing for projects. Economic integration increasingly came to mean transfers from rich to poor states, rather than the more solid ties of genuine economic interdependence.

HOW ECONOMICALLY INTEGRATED IS THE MIDDLE EAST?

Economic integration can take many forms. These include free trade areas, customs unions, joint ventures, preferential payments arrangements, favored trading status or common markets. The Arab world has experimented with a variety of mechanisms to promote integration.

The extent of integration in terms of trade in goods and in factor flows that resulted from these experiments will be assessed before considering the special role of labor movements.

Trade. The most striking feature of trade patterns in the Middle East is how little the countries of the region trade with each other. Table 13.1 provides data on Middle Eastern exports and imports in world trade. About two-thirds of all the region's trade is with the industrial countries. Intraregional Middle Eastern trade accounts for only 6–7 percent of total imports and exports. The Middle Eastern countries trade more with Asia and with Eastern Europe and the former Soviet Union than they do with each other.

When intraregional trade is examined by country (table 13.2), the pattern is even more stark. The major share of intraregional trade is dominated by three oil economies: Bahrain, Saudi Arabia, and the United Arab Emirates. This is because the data on trade do not exclude reexports—such as when Saudi Arabia exports oil to Bahrain for refining, which Bahrain then reexports. Such trade involves little value added and the products are not destined ultimately for the regional market. If such reexports were excluded from the data, regional trade would be even less than that reported in tables 13.1 and 13.2.

Some of the explanation for such a low level of intraregional trade must lie in the composition of regional imports and exports. The exports of the Middle East remain dominated by primary products, particularly oil. Petroleum and petroleum products constitute more than 90 percent of total exports for all the Gulf countries, as well as for Algeria and Libya. The Middle East, along with Africa, has the smallest share of world trade in manufactures (World Bank 1992, 17). The region is also a net importer of food. Thus the imports of the region, which consist largely of food, manufactures, and capital goods, are not major exports of the region.

TABLE 13.2 Intraregional Exports and Imports of Middle Eastern Countries, 1985-1990 (US$million)

	Exports						Imports					
	1985	1986	1987	1988	1989	1990	1985	1986	1987	1988	1989	1990
Bahrain	1,224	942	1,189	1,029	1,309	1,390	444	253	258	274	326	351
Egypt	231	197	196	226	230	231	167	131	143	212	271	253
Iran, Islamic	143	152	220	268	372	292	823	327	424	227	292	274
Republic of Iraq	557	483	501	645	824	478	266	337	362	449	529	504
Israel	229	230	140	146	168	5	8	59	27	28	22	7
Jordan	638	479	515	565	497	587	383	329	851	391	465	427
Kuwait	298	322	389	479	588	324	780	605	684	770	843	435
Lebanon	144	100	105	152	253	287	267	251	274	349	261	258
Libya	19	24	13	16	30	40	285	104	143	1	2	4
Oman	43	66	394	472	576	547	28	27	31	38	38	38
Qatar	212	230	111	132	188	187	211	160	158	200	238	226
Saudi Arabia	783	818	634	776	903	903	2,406	1,956	2,084	2,386	2,501	2,527
Syrian Arab Republic	810	281	394	122	152	124	75	128	162	249	512	646
United Arab Emirates	859	961	988	1,071	1,397	1,405	1,216	919	866	1,028	1,190	1,048
Yemen Arab Republic	323	281	130	212	169	176	31	21	34	42	41	43
Yemen P.D. Republic	201	194	226	220	251	264	7	9	15	21	15	16
Middle East not specified	24	19	20	10	23	21	28	31	11	14	15	16

Source: International Monetary Fund (1991)

But the explanation for the composition of trade lies not only in endowment but also in the policies adopted by the governments of the region. Many of the labor surplus economies (such as Egypt, Sudan, and Syria) that could have been meeting the region's demand for food and manufactures have followed import substitution policies for decades. Meanwhile, the capital-surplus economies have tended to have very open trade regimes, which enable them to import from anywhere in the world. The protected production of regional neighbors cannot compete in terms of quality or price with world markets.

The evidence of the enormous divergence in trade policy between the labor surplus and the capital-surplus countries of the region is presented in tables 13.3 to 13.5. Three different measures of openness are reported because there is considerable controversy over which measures are the most appropriate (Pritchett 1991).

The structure adjusted trade intensity ratios in table 13.3 represent the share of imports and exports in gross domestic product (GDP) adjusting for structural characteristics of the economies such as size, per capita income, and oil endowment. Table 13.4 reports average import charges by category, and table 13.5 reports the frequency of non-tariff barriers. The conclusions are consistent across all measures of outward orientation—the capital-surplus oil economies tend to be very open while the labor surplus economies of the region tend to be very closed.

Political alliances have added another dimension to regional trade patterns. The composition of Egypt's trade during the late 1960s and early 1970s and Syria's trade until recently were dominated by the Eastern bloc. Extensive trade with Eastern Europe and the former Soviet Union was a reflection of political alliances, not market incentives. Similarly, the United States has emerged as one of Egypt's major trading partners in the 1980s, not because of comparative advantage, but because American aid is tied to U.S. source restrictions (table 13.5).

Capital Flows. Regional capital flows follow a pattern of movement from the capital-surplus oil exporters to the labor-surplus countries. Because of this pattern, the size of regional capital flows is closely tied to developments in the oil market. The evidence on capital flows, both official aid and private unrequited transfers (largely remittances), is presented in table 13.6. The size of regional capital flows tended to be greatest during the oil boom of the 1970s and fell considerably after the oil price collapse in 1986.

Three economies—Jordan, Yemen, and Egypt—emerge as highly dependent on regional capital flows, as shown in table 13.6. (Lebanon may also be highly dependent on regional capital flows, but the data are too poor to draw any conclusions.) For example, more than two-thirds of Jordan's GDP came from regional transfers in 1979, about half of GDP came from Arab aid and one-fifth of GDP was remittances from Arab countries. In the case of Yemen, remittances

TABLE 13.3 "Structure Adjusted Trade Intensity Ratios, 1985, by Rank: Middle Eastern Countries"

LDCs	Overall		Manufacturing		Agriculture		Resources	
	%	Rank	%	Rank	%	Rank	%	Rank
Bahrain	69.1	4	21.3	6	2.7	26	44.7	
Jordan	27.2	12	11.6	16	2.1	28	9.8	14
Egypt	22.5	17	20.8	7	7.6	11	-6.3	73
Algeria	9.6	25	8.3	23	0.1	37	1.0	26
Morocco	-2.1	40	-0.8	43	-0.9	42	-0.5	33
Sudan	-2.9	41	1.0	32	0.7	33	-4.2	57
Tunisia	-5.0	44	-0.7	42	-6.4	83	3.1	22
Syria, Arab Republic of	-12.4	60	-4.1	56	-0.9	41	-7.4	75
Turkey	-19.2	75	-9.2	72	-6.7	84	-2.1	42
Yemen, Arab Republic of	-21.1	77	-6.7	62	-6.1	81	-7.6	77
United Arab Emirates	-23.0	79	-26.4	92	-2.9	58	7.2	15
Kuwait	-37.7	90	-22.2	87	-1.6	50	-13.1	89
Oman	-43.4	93	-10.8	73	-1.6	49	-31.2	93

Note: The structure adjusted trade intensity ratios are derived from a regression of trade intensity (imports plus exports as a share of GDP) on population, land area, GDP per capita, transportation costs and oil endowment. The resulting residual is an indicator of the openness of the economy taking into account structural characteristics. Rank refers to where a particular country is relative to 93 other countries in the sample.

Source: Adapted from Pritchett (1991)

have been between one-third and one-half of GDP since the 1970s. Egypt, like Jordan, also received substantial Arab aid until the Camp David accords in 1979 when Arab governments isolated Egypt both politically and economically. But private capital flows continued to grow rapidly and remittances emerged as Egypt's major source of foreign exchange in the 1980s and 1990s.

Comprehensive data on other private capital flows, such as Arab investment in other Arab countries, are not available. Data from Egypt on the nationality of private investors under Law 43, the investment promotion legislation, give some indication of the importance of such flows. On average, Arab investors contributed one-half of all foreign investment in both inland and free zone projects under Law 43 between 1977 and 1989 (Isfahani 1990). The remaining foreign investment came from the European Union, the United States, and other

TABLE 13.4 UNCTAD Data on Mean Total Import Charges by Major Aggregate,
In Percent and Rank

LDCs	Overall		Manufacturing		Agriculture		Resources	
	%	Rank	%	Rank	%	Rank	%	Rank
Saudi Arabia	3.7	4	4.1	6	1.4	3	4.4	10
Qatar	4.3	5	4.0	5	5.4	7	4.0	7
United Arab Emirates	4.3	6	4.7	7	1.5	4	5.9	13
Kuwait	6.5	7	3.9	4	2.1	6	23.1	48
Bahrain	7.2	8	7.6	8	7.6	8	5.0	12
Algeria	18.2	21	22.1	27	15.5	20	2.4	5
Syria, Arab Republic of	24.5	34	25.2	33	23.4	33	22.8	47
Jordan	27.1	39	32.2	48	16.3	23	12.4	31
Tunisia	27.5	40	28.0	40	27.8	42	10.7	30
Morocco	34.6	51	35.1	51	29.8	46	37.5	67
Egypt	41.4	62	42.6	61	57.3	68	16.0	37
Turkey	44.8	65	46.9	65	37.3	58	26.7	54
Sudan	47.0	66	49.4	66	54.6	65	25.5	52
Iran	70.1	72	80.4	74	69.2	70	20.4	42

Note: Rank refers to where a particular country is relative to 75 other countries in the sample.

Source: Adapted from Pritchett (1991)

countries. Arab investors were obviously the most important foreign investors in Egypt, but were fairly small compared to Egyptian investors who contributed more than 60 percent of total capital under Law 43 projects between 1977 and 1989. More importantly, the levels of private capital flows from the richer to the poor states in the region are a very small fraction of their total assets held abroad. This reflects the low expected return on regional investments because of risk and the economic policies of the poorer states in the region.

Remittance levels have far exceeded official aid in recent years. In 1987, private unrequited transfers were five times greater than intra-Arab official aid flows. This is largely the result of the reductions in aid after the collapse in oil prices in 1986. Remittances from labor migration are now the largest source of capital flows in the region.

Labor. Labor has been migrating in the Arab world for centuries, but the oil boom of the 1970s triggered a manifold increase in the scale of the phenomenon. In 1975, there were an estimated 1.6 million migrant workers in the labor-

TABLE 13.5 UNCTAD Data on the Frequency of Nontariff Barriers, by Major Aggregate, in Percent and Rank

LDCs	Overall		Manufacturing		Agriculture		Resources	
	Ratio	Rank	Ratio	Rank	Ratio	Rank	Ratio	Rank
United Arab Emirates	0.5	2	0.3	3	1.5	4	0.1	9
Qatar	1.2	3	1.2	4	1.5	5	0.0	1
Bahrain	3.5	4	0.0	1	7.2	10	0.0	3
Oman	4.0	6	5.2	9	1.5	3	0.1	14
Kuwait	7.9	8	7.2	14	15.1	18	0.3	19
Sudan	8.0	9	8.4	16	12.2	14	0.0	7
Saudi Arabia	8.4	11	8.8	18	14.4	17	0.1	11
Libya	9.4	12	10.0	23	14.3	16	0	8
Jordan	16.8	28	7.1	13	66.5	45	0.1	12
Egypt	38.6	40	35.4	42	46.4	37	42.8	35
Morocco	39.7	41	23.0	36	66.6	46	84.4	50
Algeria	68.4	52	60.1	50	86.6	56	87.4	54
Tunisia	77.6	55	71.7	54	84.0	55	94.1	58
Turkey	90.6	59	97.8	60	79.7	50	70.2	40
Iran	98.8	62	98.6	62	94.2	60	100.0	73
Syria, Arab Republic of	100.0	63	100.0	63	100.0	63	100.0	62
Yemen	100.0	71	100.0	71	100.0	71	100.0	70

Note: Rank refers to where a particular country is relative to 75 other countries in the sample.
Source: Adapted from Pritchett (1991)

importing countries of Bahrain, Kuwait, Libya, Oman, Qatar, Saudi Arabia, and the United Arab Emirates. About 1.1 million of those workers were of Arab origin (Serageldin et al. 1983). Projections by Serageldin et al (1983) indicated that the number of migrant workers would double to about 3.5 million by 1985. Subsequent estimates of the actual number of migrants in 1985 are closer to 8 million, implying a fivefold increase since 1975 (Klinov 1991). By the mid-1980s, migrants constituted more than 70 percent of the labor force in the Gulf economies.

It is difficult to assess the scale and composition of labor migration in the 1980s and 1990s because of the absence of comprehensive data. In earlier periods, major studies of migration were conducted by Birks and Sinclair in conjunction with the Economic Commission for West Africa conference on migration in the Arab world in 1981, and later by the World Bank project on

TABLE 13.6 Intraregional Arab Capital Flows—Official and Private, 1973-1987

a. Total official Arab assistance as a percentage of GNP of Arab and recipient countries, 1973–87

	1973	1974	1975	1976	1977	1978	1979	1980	1981	1982	1983	1984	1985	1986	1987	Cumulative
Arab Middle East	3.3	5.3	4.7	5.3	4.7	3.9	6.1	5.6	4.8	3.1	2.7	2.1	1.8	1.7	1.1	3.3
Bahrain	6.1	20.1	20.2	39.6	10.9	7.4	10.1	5.3	4.6	3.4	7.3	7.0	3.6	4.8	-0.1	5.9
Iraq	0.1	0.0	0.2	0.0	0.0	0.1	0.0	0.0	0.0	0.7	0.5	0.1	0.1	0.1	0	0.1
Jordan	13.8	26.8	28.9	32.2	17.3	16.6	47.5	35.5	29.3	20.1	18.4	17.2	12.2	10.5	8.2	20.6
Lebanon	0.1	3.9	0.3	0.5	2.1	5.2	1.9	4.9	9.6	3.1	0.3	0.0	0.6	0.1	0.8	2.5
Oman	3.2	10.7	3.4	6.1	8.3	2.1	6.1	4.9	3.4	1.3	0.6	0.7	0.7	0.9	-0.3	2.2
Syria	8.9	11.0	9.6	6.3	9.8	8.1	16.1	12.1	9.7	5.6	4.6	3.8	3.6	3.5	2.5	6.7
Yemen Arab Republic	3.2	12.8	15.9	17.1	12.8	10.6	6.1	10.4	8.8	5.3	4.5	4.0	3.5	2.6	1.8	6.2
Yemen, P.D.R.	4.3	9.2	15.2	35.6	22.2	9.5	4.6	9.1	3.9	14.1	3.5	5.3	4.9	0.1	4.7	8.1
Arab Africa	2.8	4.6	6.9	4.7	5.0	3.3	1.6	1.5	1.4	0.9	0.7	0.3	0.8	0.3	0.2	1.7
Algeria	0.8	0.1	0.7	0.1	0.9	0.2	0.1	0.1	0.1	-0.5	0.0	-0.1	0.1	0	0	0.1
Egypt	7.4	14.5	22.6	11.9	11.5	9.9	1.2	0.0	-0.1	-0.1	-0.3	-0.1	-0.1	0.2	0.2	3
Mauritania	10.7	17.7	4.7	40.5	21.1	30.1	13.2	22.7	15.4	16.7	10.3	9.9	10.9	8.4	-0.2	14.6
Morocco	0.0	0.2	1.2	1.2	5.3	2.3	1.8	3.8	6.4	4.1	1.1	0.6	4.6	0.6	-0.2	2.4
Somalia	3.0	13.9	14.7	5.4	13.2	10.5	9.2	8.7	3.2	6.9	3.8	0.6	1.3	-0.2	0.1	4.8
Sudan	0.6	6.9	4.6	6.9	3.2	2.2	5.5	4.4	2.4	2.8	5.9	1.3	3.5	2	1.8	3.4
Tunisia	0.2	0.6	1.4	1.6	1.9	0.8	1.6	1.2	0.8	0.6	0.2	0.9	0.5	0	0.7	0.8
Total Aid Recipients	2.9	4.9	6.0	4.9	4.9	3.6	3.5	3.2	2.8	1.9	1.6	1.1	1.2	0.9	0.6	2.3

TABLE 13.6 Intraregional Arab Capital Flows Official and Private, 1973-1987
b. Private unrequited transfers as a percentage of GNP of Arab and recipient countries, 1973–87

	1973	1974	1975	1976	1977	1978	1979	1980	1981	1982	1983	1984	1985	1986	1987	Cumulative
Arab Middle East	3.3	5.3	4.7	5.3	4.7	3.9	6.1	5.6	4.8	3.1	2.7	2.1	1.8	1.7	1.1	3.3
Bahrain	6.1	20.1	20.2	39.6	10.9	7.4	10.1	5.3	4.6	3.4	7.3	7.0	3.6	4.8	-0.1	5.9
Iraq	0.1	0.0	0.2	0.0	0.0	0.1	0.0	0.0	0.0	0.7	0.5	0.1	0.1	0.1	0	0.1
Jordan	13.8	26.8	28.9	32.2	17.3	16.6	47.5	35.5	29.3	20.1	18.4	17.2	12.2	10.5	8.2	20.6
Lebanon	0.1	3.9	0.3	0.5	2.1	5.2	1.9	4.9	9.6	3.1	0.3	0.0	0.6	0.1	0.8	2.5
Oman	3.2	10.7	3.4	6.1	8.3	2.1	6.1	4.9	3.4	1.3	0.6	0.7	0.7	0.9	-0.3	2.2
Syria	8.9	11.0	9.6	6.3	9.8	8.1	16.1	12.1	9.7	5.6	4.6	3.8	3.6	3.5	2.5	6.7
Yemen Arab Republic	3.2	12.8	15.9	17.1	12.8	10.6	6.1	10.4	8.8	5.3	4.5	4.0	3.5	2.6	1.8	6.2
Yemen, P.D.R.	4.3	9.2	15.2	35.6	22.2	9.5	4.6	9.1	3.9	14.1	3.5	5.3	4.9	0.1	4.7	8.1
Arab Africa	2.8	4.6	6.9	4.7	5.0	3.3	1.6	1.5	1.4	0.9	0.7	0.3	0.8	0.3	0.2	1.7
Algeria	0.8	0.1	0.7	0.1	0.9	0.2	0.1	0.1	0.1	-0.5	0.0	-0.1	0.1	0	0	0.1
Egypt	7.4	14.5	22.6	11.9	11.5	9.9	1.2	0.0	-0.1	-0.1	-0.3	-0.1	-0.1	0.2	0.2	3
Mauritania	10.7	17.7	4.7	40.5	21.1	30.1	13.2	22.7	15.4	16.7	10.3	9.9	10.9	8.4	-0.2	14.6
Morocco	0.0	0.2	1.2	1.2	5.3	2.3	1.8	3.8	6.4	4.1	1.1	0.6	4.6	0.6	-0.2	2.4
Somalia	3.0	13.9	14.7	5.4	13.2	10.5	9.2	8.7	3.2	6.9	3.8	0.6	1.3	-0.2	0.1	4.8
Sudan	0.6	6.9	4.6	6.9	3.2	2.2	5.5	4.4	2.4	2.8	5.9	1.3	3.5	2	1.8	3.4
Tunisia	0.2	0.6	1.4	1.6	1.9	0.8	1.6	1.2	0.8	0.6	0.2	0.9	0.5	0	0.7	0.8
Total Aid Recipients	2.9	4.9	6.0	4.9	4.9	3.6	3.5	3.2	2.8	1.9	1.6	1.1	1.2	0.9	0.6	2.3

Manpower and International Labor Migration in the Middle East in 1983. Since then, numerous national studies of emigration have become available, but no comprehensive data for the region is available for the 1980s and 1990s.

A recent survey of the available evidence on migration patterns during the 1980s found that, despite the collapse of oil prices and the recession in the region, aggregate migration levels did not fall, although there was a redistribution of labor across the region (Feiler 1991). Many of the migrant workers were in essential sectors and were retained despite the collapse in oil prices. Remittance levels did not decrease; in many labor-exporting countries they actually increased. The major change in the 1980s was the emergence of Iraq as a major labor importer. With much of its male labor force in uniform during its war with Iran, Iraq became especially important as a destination for Egyptian workers. There were at least 1.25 million Egyptian workers in Iraq alone. This Iraqi demand was particularly timely as the growth of labor demand in the Gulf slowed after the oil price collapse in 1986 and as Asian labor increasingly substituted for Arab labor there. About one in every three Egyptian migrants went to Iraq in the 1980s. There was also some increase in demand for low skilled Egyptian workers from Jordan, which was experiencing a construction boom fueled by the remittances of its own higher-skilled migrants in the Gulf.

Fears that Asian labor would supplant Arab labor during the 1980s appear to have been unwarranted in the aggregate. Although Asian labor is often paid less and is less politically threatening to labor-importing countries, the share of Arab labor has remained fairly stable since 1975 at about 55 percent. The explanation again lies in Iraq, which tended to import mainly Arab labor, particularly Egyptians. This demand from Iraq appears to have offset the rise in the share of Asian labor in the Gulf.

Political reasons as well as wage differentials have played an important role in determining both the level and the composition of labor migration. The level of migrant workers relative to the indigenous workforce has long preoccupied the governments of the labor-importing countries. The proportion of foreigners in the labor force during the 1980s was about 80 percent in Kuwait, 60 percent in Saudi Arabia, 70 percent in the United Arab Emirates, and 80 percent in Bahrain (Feiler 1991). The increasing importance of Asian labor was clearly a response to fears about long-term Arab migrants demanding greater political rights. Moreover, shifting political alliances in the region have affected whether Egyptian, Iranian, Jordanian, or Palestinian workers were welcome in the Gulf, Iraq, or Libya.

The Gulf War has also fundamentally altered migration patterns in the region. As a result of the war, about two million people—including more than two-thirds of Kuwait's citizens and more than a million foreign workers—were displaced from Kuwait, Iraq, and Saudi Arabia (Russell 1992). Particularly hard hit were the Palestinian residents in the Gulf, most of whom fled to Jordan, and the 750,000 Yemeni workers expelled by Saudi Arabia in retaliation for their government's support for Iraq during the war. After the war, migrant workers returned to Kuwait and numbered about 500,000 by early 1992 (Russell 1992). But the composition of migrant labor will change further: Arabs, particularly Palestinians, are likely to be a much smaller proportion of the Kuwaiti work-force as Asians are increasingly favored for jobs that do not require Arabic lan-guage skills. Migrants from countries that supported Iraq during the Gulf war (Palestinians, Jordanians, Yemenis, and Sudanese) are particularly unlikely to be offered job opportunities in the Gulf in the near term. In the case of Iraq, prewar migration levels are unlikely to be restored anytime in the near future, and the Egyptian government has begun to look toward Libya to absorb some of the country's surplus labor.

Why This Pattern of Integration in the Middle East?

The pattern of regional integration that exists in the Middle East is quite unusual. In most parts of the world extensive trade in goods acts as the engine for regional integration. This was certainly the case with the European Union, East Asia, and the North American Free Trade Agreement. The extensive move-ment of goods across borders increases the benefits of coordinated policies on tariffs and non-tariff barriers as well as standards and other policies that gov-ern economic relationships. Labor movement is usually the final, and often the most controversial, feature of regional integration.

In the Middle East, labor flows, and the remittances of capital associated with migration have been the most important feature of regional integration. The explanation lies in the extreme differences in factor endowments across the region and, perhaps more importantly, in the development policies adopted by both the labor-importing and -exporting countries.

The distinction between tradable and nontradable goods and services is cru-cial in explaining the role of factor endowments. Many of the oil-exporting, capital-surplus economies are characterized by structural labor shortages. In the case of tradable goods, these shortages are not problematic because local demand can be met through imports from world markets. In the case of non-tradable goods and services, such as construction, education, health, govern-ment, and domestic services, there is no alternative but to import labor if local demand is to be met. Thus it is not surprising that the vast majority of migrant workers in the oil-exporting countries are employed in the nontradable sectors of the economy.

But why were the oil exporters not importing tradable goods from their neighbors? The explanation lies in the trade orientation of the region's regimes described above. In general, the oil exporters adopted very outward-oriented trade policies in order to meet local demand for tradable goods through the world market. In contrast, the labor-surplus economies that could have been meeting the regional demand for food and manufactures adopted inward-oriented import substitution policies that discouraged the production of tradable goods. Because these import substitution policies tended to favor capital-intensive production (through interest rate subsidies, favorable tariffs on capital goods imports, overvalued exchange rates, and skewed public investment programs), unemployment and underemployment were persistent problems. Thus the migration of labor became a convenient mechanism for labor surplus economies to export their unemployment problems. Remittances were also important for the balance of payments, which was the Achilles heel of import substitution strategies that produced little that would generate foreign exchange from export markets.

Increased regional trade in goods was also undermined by the selective protection policies that made some tradable sectors de facto nontradables. Few regional migrants worked in the tradable sectors, but where they did, there were substantial inefficiencies. The case of Saudi Arabian agriculture, which was highly subsidized through a system of input subsidies and price supports to meet food self-sufficiency goals, provides an example of the disincentives to trade. The incentives provided by the Saudi government ensured that it was more advantageous for landowners to import labor to tend wheatfields in Saudi Arabia than it was to import Egyptian wheat, even though Saudi Arabian wheat cost five times the world market price to produce and that wheat was sold domestically for less than the world price for much of the period. Of course because of the low procurement prices offered to farmers in Egypt, there was no wheat for the country to export. The beneficiaries of Egypt's food pricing policies were urban consumers, who were more likely to threaten the regime than a dispersed and disorganized peasantry. This convoluted set of incentives ensured that Egyptian farmers continued to migrate to produce, often less efficiently, in Saudi Arabia or in Iraq. Those who received rents from the status quo—urban wheat consumers in Egypt and rural landholders in Saudi Arabia—would oppose any moves to achieve a more economically rational distribution of production that might also result in greater regional trade.

In contrast, the obstacles to labor mobility were far fewer than those governing trade in goods. Most of the labor surplus economies in the region actively encouraged migration through a variety of mechanisms. In Egypt, emigration became a constitutional right in 1971, exit visas were abolished in 1973, and a Ministry of Emigrant Affairs was established to address the needs of Egyptians abroad. The officially tolerated "own exchange" market provided a channel through which remittances could enter the country at the parallel exchange rate. The government also exempted migrants from paying taxes on income earned abroad and abolished a law requiring migrants to transfer a minimum of 10 percent of earnings to Egypt at the overvalued official exchange rate (Ibrahim 1982). In Jordan, the government allowed migrants to postpone their military service until the age of 37 if they obtained a work permit from another country (Feiler 1991).

The policies of the labor importers were intended to reduce the long-run dependence on migrant labor, but were generally unsuccessful. A number of policies have been put into place to reduce the dependence on foreign workers, including the use of more capital-intensive technology, expenditures on training, requirements that nationals be in senior positions in all sectors of the economy, and, in some cases, encouraging women to enter the workforce. Despite these efforts, foreigners still constitute the vast majority of the labor force in these economies. Recognizing the limits of indigenous labor substitution, the oil economies also severely restrict the duration of a migrant worker's stay through visas, work contracts, and other policies that prevent foreign workers from becoming permanent residents. These policies also insure that migrants do not become eligible for the benefits, such as housing, education, and health care, associated with nationality.

Labor Migration-Stepping Stone or Substitute for Regional Integration?

Because the obstacles to trade in goods have been greater than the obstacles to labor movements in the Middle East, labor has been the first, and most successful, element of regional economic integration. Labor mobility and its associated capital flows has been the most important mechanism through which the benefits of the oil windfall have been spread to the poorer states of the region. Labor migration has not been a substitute for regional trade where nontradable goods are concerned because there are few alternatives for meeting demand. In the case of tradable goods, sectors in which far fewer migrants are employed, the role of labor migration has been more complex. Those few migrants employed in the tradable sectors could have been more efficient producing at home and exporting to the oil economies. This was especially the case where there are strong externalities associated with domestic production, many of which are not exploited in the oil economies where labor turnover is rapid. But few of the labor-exporting countries were characterized by policy regimes that would have produced such tradable goods, so the migrant workers were generally better off being employed abroad than being unemployed at home.

Is this pattern of integration in the Arab world desirable? It is necessary to distinguish between private and social interests. Migration obviously benefits the individuals involved—migrants earn higher wages and their employers benefit from access to low-cost labor whose training costs they usually do not incur. At the societal level, the assessment is necessarily more complex. Labor-importing countries benefit from the production of migrants but they incur costs in terms of political and social stability as well as questions about the long-run sustainability of their dependence on foreign workers. Labor exporters benefit from less unemployment and from remittances, some of which is invested in the home economy, but often suffer from selective skill shortages and the loss of the external benefits associated with having workers producing domestically. Moreover, the evidence on whether migrants gain new skills abroad that enhance their human capital is mixed and depends very much on the relative skill content of their job at home versus abroad. In some countries, migration has had socially damaging effects—as in Sudan, where much of the scarce human capital of that country is working abroad. But for countries such as Egypt, Jordan, and Yemen, migration was, given the policy regime and the large labor surplus, a benefit to society.

Perhaps the most potentially damaging effect of migration for labor exporters is that it provides a safety valve enabling governments to postpone economic reforms that are more likely to create jobs at home over the long term. Unemployment in Egypt can be blamed in part on an import substitution strategy that failed to produce sufficient gains in labor productivity. In Jordan, which exports skilled labor while simultaneously importing unskilled labor, close integration with regional labor markets has been an effective policy, given the country's endowment of human capital. But Jordan's inability to adequately employ its skilled labor force reflects a low rate of investment, especially in the private sector, which is indicative of an incentive regime that does not promote capital formation. For Yemen, the existence of a high-wage neighbor with a large demand for imported labor has allowed the government to postpone needed reforms to promote labor-intensive growth. In effect, high levels of remittances have resulted in "Dutch disease" effects (whereby a commodity price boom results in a real appreciation of the exchange rate), with losses in competitiveness and disproportionate gains in the nontradable sectors.

Faini and Venturini (1993) have argued that protectionist policies in Europe, especially with respect to agriculture and textiles, will tend to increase migratory flows into Europe to achieve greater factor price equalization. Thus industrial countries cannot hope to succeed at restricting developing countries' access to both their goods and labor markets. In the Middle East, an analogous argument can be made with respect to labor-exporting countries. Protectionist policies in labor-exporting, developing countries will tend to increase out-migration because insufficient jobs tend to be created at home. Since commodity trade and factor mobility are substitutes, Middle Eastern countries with fairly closed trade regimes will tend to have higher out-migration.

In general, labor migration has not been a substitute for greater regional trade because it has been concentrated in nontradable sectors. Given the existing policy regime of economics in the Middle East, immigration has also been somewhat of a stepping stone to greater regional integration by providing a mutually beneficial mechanism for sharing the oil wealth across the region, while taking advantage of underutilized human resources. The evidence on income distribution indicates that, contrary to the popular perception, incomes across the Middle East have become more equal. Figure 13.1 shows Lorenz curves for the region for 1970, 1981, and 1989 indicating that the distribution of income across the Middle East has moved toward the 45 degree line of equality. This tendency toward convergence of per capita incomes has held in years of oil booms (1981) and in periods of low oil prices (1970) and moderate oil prices (1989). The Lorenz curves say nothing about income distribution within countries, about which the data are very poor in the Middle East. Nevertheless, migration has obviously played an important and effective role in spreading the region's wealth across countries.

But migration may not be the most desirable stepping stone toward integration. The macroeconomic policies of the Middle Eastern countries reduced the scope for greater integration of trade and investment flows. Greater trade in goods may be especially important for taking advantage of dynamic gains from greater competition and learning by doing. Migration may also be a weak stepping stone, especially when the political sensitivities of the oil economies as well as the substantial scope for substituting Arab labor with other nationalities are considered. It seems clear that, without efforts to solidify regional economic ties on the basis of efficiency and mutual self-interest, the integration that results from labor migration will remain an anomaly in an otherwise fragmented region.

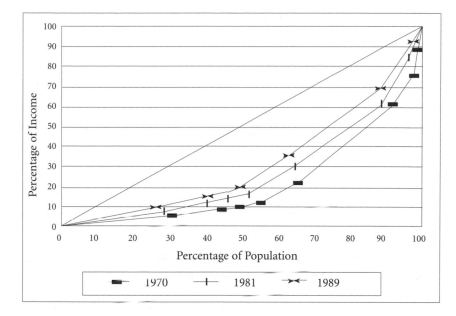

FIGURE 13.1   Income Distribution in MENA Countries
Note: Countries include Kuwait, Libya, Saudi rabia, Iran, Algeria, Tunisia, Syrian Arab Republic, Morocco, and Egypt.

Acknowledgment

An earlier version of this chapter was published in Ismail Sirageldin and Eqbal Al-Rahmani (eds.), *Population and Development Transformations in the Arab World* (London: Jai Press, 1996).

References

Adams, R. "The Economic Uses and Impact of International Remittances in Rural Egypt." *Economic Development and Cultural Change*, 39:4, (July 1991).

Faini, R. and A. Venturini. "Trade, Aid, and Migrations." *European Economic Review*, 37 (1993).

Feiler, G. "Migration and Recession: Arab Labor Mobility in the Middle East, 1982–89." *Population and Development Review*, 17:1 (March 1991).

Ghantus, E. *Arab Industrial Integration: A Strategy for Development*. London: Croom Helm, 1982.

Haseeb, K and S. Makdisi. *Arab Monetary Integration*. London: Croom Helm, 1981.

Ibrahim, S. in M. Kerr and S. El-Yassin, eds. *Rich and Poor States in the Middle East.* Boulder and Cairo: Westview Press and American University of Cairo Press, 1982.

International Monetary Fund. *Direction of Trade Statistics.* Washington, DC: International Monetary Fund, 1991.

Isfahani, H. "The Experience of Foreign Investment in Egypt under Infitah." Faculty Working Paper No. 90–1710. Bureau of Economic and Business Research, University of Illinois, Urbana-Champaign, 1990.

Klinov, R. "Recent Trends in Migration-for-Work from Middle Eastern Countries," paper presented at the Conference on The Economics of Labor Mobility in the Middle East, Kennedy School of Government, Harvard University, Cambridge, Massachusetts, February 7–8, 1992.

Lachler, U. "Regional Integration and Economic Development." Industry and Energy Department Working Paper No. 14. Washington, DC: The World Bank, 1989.

Lucas, R. "On the Mechanics of Economic Development." *Journal of Monetary Economics* 22 (1988).

Makdisi, S. "Arab Economic Cooperation: Implications for the Arab World and World Economies" in R. Albioni, ed. *Arab Industrialization and Economic Integration.* New York: St. Martin's Press, 1979.

Pritchett, L. "Measuring Outward Orientation in Developing Countries: Can it be Done?" PRE Working Paper number 566, Washington, DC: The World Bank, 1991.

Rivera-Batiz, L. and P. Romer. "Economic Integration and Endogenous Growth." *Quarterly Journal of Economics* (May 1991).

Romer, P. "Increasing Returns and Long-Run Growth." *Journal of Political Economy.* 94:5, (1986).

Ravallion, M., S. Chen, and G. Datt. "New Estimates of Poverty in the Developing World," photocopy, Washington, DC: World Bank, 1992.

Russell, S.S. "International Migration in Europe, Central Asia, the Middle East, and North Africa: Issues for the World Bank," photocopy, Washington, DC: World Bank, 1992.

Sayigh, Y. *The Arab Economy: Past Performance and Future Prospects*, Oxford: Oxford University Press, 1982.

Serageldin, I., J. Socknat, S. Birks, B. Li, and C. Sinclair. *Manpower and International Labor Migration in the Middle East and North Africa.* Washington, DC: The World Bank, 1983

van den Boogaerde, P. "The Composition and Distribution of Financial Assistance from Arab Countries and Arab Regional Institutions." Working Paper 90:67, Washington, DC: International Monetary Fund, 1990.

Waterbury, John and Ragaei El Mallakh. *The Middle East in the Coming Decade: From Wellhead to Well-Being?* New York: McGraw-Hill, 1978.

World Bank. *Global Economic Prospects.* Washington, DC: World Bank, 1992.

World Bank. *World Development Report.* Washington, DC: World Bank, 1992.

Prospects for Arab Economic Integration After Oslo

chapter 14

Atif A. Kubursi

In a comparative assessment of the global economy and the capacities of states and societies to adjust to its endemic changes, the American historian Paul Kennedy observes that more than any other developing region the countries of the Middle East and North Africa are afflicted by the debilitating issues of wars and internal disorders as "[v]icious one-man dictatorships glare threateningly at arch-conservative, antidemocratic, feudal sheikdoms" (Kennedy 1994, 209). In Kennedy's assessment, the Arab world remains the least prepared of any region to meet the challenges of the next century.

Equally pessimistic and critical of Arab chances in the next century is a 1995 World Bank study titled *Global Economic Prospects and Developing Countries*, which offers a bleak outlook for economic growth and development in the Middle East and North Africa. During the 1980s, according to this study, the region's economic growth averaged less than 1 percent compared with the world average of over 3 percent. A combination of population growth around 3 percent, falling real oil revenues, dismal export performance, the terrible cost of two Gulf wars, Israel's challenge to the Arab East, civil wars, and an unending wasteful expenditure on military procurement have coalesced to undermine any meaningful future economic prospects for the region.

If indeed the 1980s represented a lost decade for the Arabs and the early 1990s did not augur much improvement, the real question is why has development remained so illusive in the Arab World? What are the basic explanatory factors for this abysmally slow growth? Why have Southeast Asia and other developing regions outperformed the Arabs? What is needed to reverse the negative economic trends? Can a collective Arab development strategy contribute to a brighter economic future for the Arabs? Will peace with Israel bring prosperity or economic domination? Is the Euro-Mediterranean project a viable alternative? Why has Arab economic cooperation been so limited and disappointing? Where should the the Arabs begin?

It is perhaps an understatement to suggest that Arab countries today are wrestling with some of the greatest economic challenges they have ever faced. The future of Arab economies will depend on the choices made today. These choices, however, are being made and will continue to be made under duress with little or no regard for their implications for the future. While there is a critical need to establish broad-based agreements among Arab states on what it takes to succeed in the global economy, there are centrifugal forces throwing them apart and tearing at the fundamental linkages that tie them together.

Each Arab country is taking independent initiatives to deal with its future, and while individual state action is necessary, it is not sufficient in today's globalized economy. This is all the more important in view of Western and Israeli designs for shaping the region's future. These designs are predicated on attracting each Arab country separately into their spheres. The Arabs can no longer escape or postpone choosing their future economic course from among the current alternatives before them. The choices are real and limited. The competition is basically among three contenders: the American-Israeli project, the European (primarily French) Mediterranean project, and a new and invigorated independent Arab collective action. The past record of Arab economic cooperation is dismal, so the question is: Will the severity of the challenges and the new regional projects bring a new life and shape to old Arab aspirations? Or will it add to Arab fragmentation, dependency, and instability?

This chapter begins with a brief examination of old Arab cooperation/integration projects and why they have failed. It considers lessons from other regional cooperation efforts before evaluating the new projects and what they might bode for the Arabs with special emphasis on the Palestinian and Israeli economic agreements as a case study of what other Arab countries can expect from the new Middle East project. The final section ends with some suggestions for an alternative Arab strategy after Oslo.

Lessons from the Past

There is overwhelming international evidence that countries that opted for export promotion and open trade with their partners have achieved higher economic growth rates than those that protected their domestic markets and emphasized import substitution policies. But there is little evidence as to why some countries were successful in exporting in the first place and why others failed to penetrate the world markets despite serious efforts and dogged determination to do so.

Most Arab economies are simply too small to be self-sufficient or self-sustaining. Individually, few of them are of sufficient economic size for rapid industrialization or diversified growth. It follows that Arab regional trade arrangements would be a natural response to these limitations. With cooperation and freer trade would come mutual gains that result from the internal and external economies of larger markets, from augmented bargaining strengths, from the pooling of resources, from inter- and intraindustry specialization, and from freer mobility of resources.

Indeed, the recent history of the Arab world is rife with examples of attempts at Arab economic and/or political cooperation or integration. Unfortunately, most of these attempts were short lived, harvested limited results and were, in general, disappointments. Syria and Lebanon had a full-fledged customs union that operated smoothly throughout the French mandate, but was dissolved in 1950. The British had in effect a less extensive customs union over their mandatory area, which included Palestine, Jordan, and Iraq, that elapsed with the end of British rule in Palestine in 1948. The United Arab Republic (UAR) unified Egypt and Syria for less than three years and was the first such attempt by two independent Arab governments. But it collapsed under the weight of a hostile coup d'état in Syria. The UAR opened the way, however, to many more such attempts. Among them are: the frequent efforts of Muammar al-Qadhafi to unite Libya with Egypt, cooperation efforts with the Sudan and the Maghrib countries; the 1980 formation of the Gulf Cooperation Council; the 1989 Maghrib Cooperation Council, and the 1989 Arab Cooperation Council that included Egypt, Iraq, Jordan, and Yemen. Qadhafi's attempts have failed, the Maghrib Cooperation Council is dormant, and the Arab Cooperation Council is practically dead. Only the Gulf Cooperation Council is still alive, albeit with serious problems and challenges.

More serious and enduring but no more successful perhaps was the project that began in 1953 with the promulgation of the Arab Joint Defense and Economic Cooperation Treaty that gave rise to the Agreement on Arab Economic Unity. It was signed in 1957, came into effect in 1960, and gave birth to the Arab Common Market in 1964. The Agreement, which led to the creation of some sixty pan-Arab or inter-Arab organizations, had otherwise only limited real economic results. Far-reaching economic cooperation or integration remained principally more declaratory than real. Arab leaders and important segments in the Arab state system paid lip-service to the virtues of integration but blocked any real steps toward its realization, preferring instead to shelter their domestic economies and power spheres from any real or perceived "encroachments" by neighbours.

The absence of genuine democracy in most countries of the Arab world has proven to have a real dampening effect on meaningful Arab cooperation. The lack of democratic principles and institutions militated against the ability of those segments of society that believed in and demanded cooperation from being able to exert sufficient pressure on their rulers for accommodating their aspirations. It also meant that whatever agreements were reached remained simply agreements among leaders because they did not involve the direct participation or approval of the people.

With Israel separating physically the Arabs of Africa from those in Western Asia, the effort to link and expand the Arab economic space has suffered yet another setback. But Israel's real negative impact on Arab cooperation came with the 1979 signing of the Camp David Accords which dissociated Egypt from the rest of the Arab cooperative efforts until 1990. The Camp David Accords in turn gave birth to the Oslo Agreements in 1993 and 1995, the Israel-PLO Protocol on Economic Relations signed in Paris in April 1994, and the Peace Treaty between Jordan and Israel in 1994. The Camp David Accords (CDA) created a serious and crucial precedent in the region—an Arab country (a leading one) concluded a separate and secret peace accord with Israel outside all the existing joint Arab treaties and cooperation agreements that precluded this possibility. In this way the CDA paved the way for all the other separate agreements that the Palestinians and Jordanians concluded with Israel. Separately or in combination, these treaties are tearing the Arab World apart, reorienting the Palestinians and Jordanians away from their traditional trading partners and blocking the chances of wider Arab cooperative efforts.

There are, to be sure, also basic economic reasons why Arab economic cooperation efforts have not born the fruits expected. First, many Arab economies are characterized by similar patterns of specialization. This reduced opportunities for avoiding competition among them. Second, most of the projects for wider Arab cooperation were premised on maximizing the effects of "trade diversion" (the shifting of exports and imports away from traditional trade partners to new partners) from the rest of the world with little or no concern for "trade creation." Once the beneficial effects of trade diversion were realized, the benefits from cooperation were exhausted. Not surprisingly, most of these efforts did not last long. Furthermore, Arab efforts toward cooperation were marred by an implicit state agenda for broadening its planning sphere in the economy and for extending the boundaries of production for import substitution. In these circumstances politics inevitably intervened. Partners sometimes avoided the costs of adjustments that these agreements often entailed (Lawrence 1994). They were typically unwilling to risk losing domestic industries and activities to other members of the agreement even if there were supposed to be offsetting gains elsewhere. Allocation and deployment decisions became political decisions that were far removed from market realities and dictates (Langhammer 1992). When one country was given the right to a particular industry or activity, other members demanded compensation, with the result that short-term distributional considerations dominated medium- and long-term efficiency considerations.

Despite many disappointments and failures, a large Arab intellectual constituency remains wedded to the project of wider Arab economic cooperation and collective action . A sample of this literature would include the works of Al-Dajani (1966), Al-Ghandur (1970), Nawfal (1971), and Awwad (1977). The failures of Arab attempts at cooperation or integration are matched only by a flood of literature on the advisability and necessity of Arab collective action. The old emotional appeals are giving in to a more somber literature analyzing failures and pointing to the dangers of individual action in the face of the new challenges posed by new schemes and projects designed for dismantling the region's collective will to work together. One common theme runs across most of the new contributions: the Arabs are better advised to work together and solidify their common interests before they join any new arrangements (see Al-Imam 1994, Al-Khawli 1994, Abd Al-Fadil 1995, and Kubursi 1995).

The dialectics of failures on the ground and high expectations for, and strong emotional commitments to, Arab cooperation are raising doubts about alternative projects that include Israel or wider Mediterranean involvement. This is taking place at precisely the same time that one agreement after another on the ground is being promulgated that set the Arabs away from one another: e.g., the Paris Protocol between Israel and the Palestinians, and North Africa and the European Market. These contradictions are also spawning some highly critical evaluations of old indigenous options and wider realization that the old ways have not worked and that there are some serious economic and political issues that the Arabs need to address at a nonemotional level. The general feeling among Arab economists is that contending alternatives must be evaluated thoroughly and critically against the lessons learned from the experiences and achievements of other regional cooperation projects in the rest of the world, and that regional Arab economic groupings must be retried before investing in Western projects.

Lessons On Regional Cooperation

Preferential trading arrangements (PTAs) do not have a good economic track record (Lawrence 1994). They are typically greeted with justifiable criticisms in developing countries in particular where they failed in the 1950s and 1960s to spur growth and equitable sharing of benefits as it was hoped they would. On the other hand, they have worked very well for the Europeans both in the EEC and in the European Free Trade Area (EFTA). The lesson drawn from this is that these trading arrangements are suitable only for developed countries at the same stage of development and with similar endowments and access to technology. Developing countries, however, are typically at different stages of development, have varying resource endowments and technical skills, and are, therefore, not in a position to benefit much from PTAs (Yamazawa 1992).

There are other opinions, however, as to why these arrangements have failed in developing countries. Lawrence (1994) attributes their failure to the motivation of the participants rather than to differences in resources or stages of development. He argues that the failures arose out of the pursuit of protectionist blocs and from the extension of import substitution policies to the bloc, while success was based on reinforced internal and external liberalization. Lawrence advances the proposition that unless participating countries are willing to allow their economies to be heavily influenced by market forces the arrangements would fail. Amsden (1989), Yamazawa (1992) and others feel that the issue here is not about subordinating the economy to market forces as much as the ability to expand the market, overcome barriers to development, and wider and richer markets. Liberalization seems to work best when an external market exists that allows the exporting country to expand and take advantage of the new economies of scale and scope.

While it is true that developing countries emphasized trade diversion and failed to promote trade creation, whether their failure to create new trade among themselves reflects some developmental barriers rather than resulting from market failures is the subject of controversy. There are many regions within the most advanced economies of the world that rely heavily on market forces and where free mobility of factors of production is assured but where growth remains a problem (e.g., southern Italy, Appalachia, or the Canadian maritime provinces). If subordination to market forces is sufficient, these areas should have no problem.

Equally important is whether the benefits in question are in terms of static or dynamic efficiency. The heart of the problem here is the ability to innovate, to access and adapt new technologies and attract foreign investment. PTAs by themselves cannot spur the entrepreneurial spirit, but neither can liberalization. The issues are more complex. There are new economic models (e.g., Endogenous Growth Theory, Chaos Theory) that emphasize different factors from those invoked by free traders and import substitutionists. The EEC countries and Mercosur (involving Argentina, Brazil, Paraguay, and Uruguay) instituted liberalized trade policies among members, but they had achieved a level of efficiency, maturity, and specialization before liberalization which allowed them to capitalize on that liberalization. When and at what level of development does one start a liberalization process? When and at what stage of development will the dynamic processes governing a country's growth kick in? And at what stage would self-reinforcing forces count more in shaping development, growth, benefits from trade, etc., than static efficiency conditions? There are no clear cut answers to these questions, but, increasingly, economists are skeptical about the undue emphasis some put on static market conditions and their neglect of the importance of dynamic forces in determining success in world markets.

One of the most distinctive features of the EEC has been the dynamic gains from internal trade liberalization. With it came rapid and extensive intra-industry trade where industries specialized in well-defined niches and increased trade within the same industry. Thus, European economic integration was built on specialization within industries rather than on movement of resources from import competing to export industries. (Sapir 1992). The key to their success was trade creation that superseded trade diversion (although this was itself important and substantial) and the freeing of the mobility of resources. What started as a simple sectoral agreement in coal and steel was expanded into a free trade area with a common tariff against the rest of the world, then a common market where factors of production moved freely from one country to the other. They are steadily but slowly moving into full economic integration and harmonization of currencies, and fiscal and monetary policies.

There are many lessons to learn from their experience. First, they began with sectoral agreements among a small subset of countries. Second, they moved very quickly to liberalize trade among themselves and to free resource mobility. Third, they gradually expanded the geographical and industrial scope of the agreement. Fourth, they erected an elaborate institutional structure to promote and cushion the adjustment processes of harmonization. Fifth, the initial interest of the United States in the success of the common market was instrumental in protecting the fledgling organization through its formative years. Sixth, the intersection of the political interests of the two principal members—Germany and France—in the success of the project coupled economic interest with a strong political will to succeed.

The North American Free Trade Agreement (NAFTA) is a less ambitious project than the EEC. The United States aimed at enhancing its competitive position in world trade by extending its resource base to include resource-rich Canada and energy-rich Mexico and by associating its high cost industries with low-cost supplies from Mexico (Brown, Deardorff and Stern, 1992a and b). Mounting U.S. concerns about many illegal Mexicans in the U.S. Southwest played a major role in prompting the U.S. to woo Mexico into its free trade area (FTA) with Canada. There are many problems, however, with NAFTA. It does not have any compensation mechanism to smooth the adjustment process which is borne unevenly by Mexico and Canada. It proceeded quickly with little preparation time, especially for Mexico. Canada had an Auto Pact with the U.S. for fifteen years before the FTA between them came about. The jury is still out on NAFTA's success. There are many complications that are difficult to untangle in order to assess the impacts of NAFTA in isolation of the other forces. Ironically, it is the experience of NAFTA that is most relevant to the evaluation of the proposed regional arrangements for the Middle East. This follows from the fact that a developing country like Mexico joined two more economically advanced countries. The Asia-Pacific arrangements have also some strong relevance to this issue as they involve clear sharing and patterns of industrial deployment among the constituent members.

The Association of Southeast Asian Nations (ASEAN) and other Asia-Pacific regional economic projects are far less formal than either EEC or even NAFTA. Yamazawa (1992) argued that East Asia has not been particularly enthusiastic about formal economic integration of the EEC type. There is nothing like a Rome Treaty or a free trade area. The main mechanism underlying their cooperation is the deliberate transfer of manufacturing industry from early starters to late comers, from Japan to the newly industrialized countries (NICs) of Asia and from the Asian NICs to ASEAN countries. This pattern has been dubbed as the "flying geese pattern" in industrial development.

In summary, the lessons drawn from the experiences of several regional economic cooperation projects world wide are clear. PTAs work best when they proceed slowly and cumulatively, preferably with sectoral arrangements preceding overall agreements and among a symmetrical grouping of countries that can expand its membership. They work when trade creation objectives go hand in hand with trade diversion, when they establish compensation mechanisms to smooth the adjustment processes in the weaker economies, and when they arise out of a free democratic process and with wide participation of the population. PTAs function best when efficiency considerations do not subordinate equity considerations since membership is likely to expand and solidify when member countries feel that they are treated fairly; when investment liberalization forms

an important plank of trade liberalization; when there are chances for redeployment of industry and wide-range intra-industry trade and specialization;
when external forces are accommodating, and when a principal member(s) has
a strong political commitment for its success.

The New Middle East

Suppose you are in Europe in 1940 imagining the Europe of 1970, or a Japanese
in 1940 imagining the Japan of 1970. How far would you dare imagine? In 1970,
the Israeli Association of Peace asked why the people of the Middle East could
not resolve their conflicts in the same way the Europeans and Japanese did; why
the frontiers of the national states of the area could not be open for trade and
why cooperation should not replace conflict. Why should the problems and
conflicts in the Middle East today be assumed to be more intransigent than the
conflicts among Europeans a few decades ago? Peres's "New Middle East" (1993)
raises the same questions. Put in this framework, the Middle East conflict is
reduced to a conflict over frontiers and a simple power struggle among neighbors. Israel is assumed to be as Middle Eastern as Germany is European. Peace
is touted as holding benefits for the Palestinians in particular and for the Arabs
in general. The Arab "peace dividends" envisioned are presumed to derive from
an increase in external aid, from the rebuilding of indigenous institutional
capacities to guide economic and reconstruction efforts, from greater and more
guaranteed access to the Israeli and possibly other Western markets, from an
increased Palestinian command over domestic natural resources, from
expected tourism increases, from the decrease in military spending, and from
the reduction in political instability and general uncertainty that has worked
against foreign investment in the region. The Israeli benefits are less discussed,
but these, I fear, are far larger and more certain than Arab benefits. Under peace,
Israel appears to be guaranteed all the benefits it derived from the Palestinians
under occupation, the opening of new trade vistas with countries that never
before traded with it, the possibility of reducing its defense expenditures, the
dismantling of the costly Arab Boycott, the increased likelihood of attracting
foreign investment and the ability to attract large flows of international tourists.

The alleged peace benefits for Arabs and Palestinians rest on some strong
claims that must be examined against the experience of the Palestinians under
occupation and traditional economic analysis of evaluating opportunity costs
and alternatives. What is unfolding in the Occupied Territories is seen as a test
case and as a precedent of what is likely to await the Arab economy at large. The

more realistic, credible, and visible the benefits of peace are, the less skeptical neighbors will be.

The economic conditions and problems the Palestinians endured under occupation should provide a background and a yardstick for judging the promises and achievements of peace and the new regional plans. Israeli occupation of the West Bank and Gaza was very costly for the Palestinians and other Arabs. These costs manifested themselves in a loss of control over water, loss of prime agricultural land, severance from traditional markets, constrained industrial growth, disarticulated and precarious education, inadequate and insufficient investment in physical infrastructure, loss of the indigenous public sector that can protect and guide the process of development, subjugation of the Palestinian population to the occupiers' tax and import regimes, transfer of Palestinian social surplus to Israel, the export of the local producers to either Israel or the Gulf, and political disruption and violence as people rebelled against the humiliating tyranny of repression.

While the occupation has not been a zero-sum game, Israel has derived enormous gains from it. These gains included Palestinian water, a captive export market, a cheap labor pool, prime agricultural land and skimming all the free rents derived from it, tax revenues far in excess of occupation costs, and the large foreign exchange flows from Palestinian remittances from the Gulf and elsewhere. It is natural to expect that under peace most of these factors will be eliminated, some gains will be realized, and the Palestinians will be compensated for their losses and suffering.

Under occupation the West Bank and Gaza were forced into an economic union with Israel, not much different from the vision of the New Middle East. A small, fragmented, disarticulated, poor, and labor-intensive economy was confronted with a relatively rich, advanced, capital-intensive, strategic, and highly centralized economy. This confrontation took place at a time when the Palestinians were denied their most vital resource (water), when access to the Israeli markets was blocked, and ties to traditional Arab markets were severed. It is small wonder that agriculture, the pre-occupation economic mainstay, faltered.

Displaced from agriculture with no alternative employment in industry, labor from the territories moved to work in Israel at generally higher pay than in the territories but at the bottom of the Israeli wage scale. Although Palestinian workers represented no more than eight percent of total employment in Israel, they constituted the majority of workers in construction and a large share of agricultural labor. On the other hand, they represented more than one-third of all employed residents in the Occupied Territories. Their earnings were about one-quarter of the GNP of the West Bank and 40 percent of Gaza's.

This export of labor and the rise in labor costs in the Occupied Territories destroyed any possibility of developing domestic manufacturing. Earnings in Israeli shekels went ultimately to buy Israeli goods. Israeli net exports to the territories were more than $500 million per year before the intifada (Kleiman 1995).

Israeli manufacturing could have taken advantage of cheap, unemployed and uprooted labor by locating in the territories. This did not happen. Some limited subcontracting of clothing and textile subactivities occurred, but their magnitude was limited and restricted to minor assembly generally performed by women. Some have even argued that the security situation in the Occupied Territories and the general uncertainty about the future of the areas scared investment away (Kleiman 1995). The insecurity during the intifada and the uncertainty about the future fate of the Territories may explain the lack of investment in the late 1980s, but what about the lack of investment between 1967 and 1987?

The collective pauperization of the Palestinians cannot be dismissed as a pure accident of history nor as an unintended and incidental effect of the occupation. Rather, it is part of a long-standing Israeli denial of the existence of the Palestinians as a people and a community capable of leading an independent national existence. Improvement in Palestinian economic prospects then requires their reconstitution as an independent national community. No amount of international aid can make up for the loss of land and water. In a primarily agrarian economy, water is the most critical economic factor upon which the Palestinian economy can be reconstructed, at least in the initial stages.

The financial requirements for development and reconstruction of the Palestinian economy are finite but massive. The list of urgent needs for sewers, roads, schools, hospitals, ports, airports, etc., is long. But finance without real resources will perpetuate the state of dependency on outside help and on the Israeli economy. Any large investments made now will go through the Israeli economy and would most likely not be sustainable. All current Palestinian trade goes through Israel. The Palestinians do not have control over their borders and do not have an independent port or airport.

This pessimistic view is based on a review of the Arab economy in the 1980s where its GDP rate of growth fell far below other regions, including sub-Saharan Africa. Collectively the Middle East and North Africa grew at less than .5 percent per year between 1980 and 1990, whereas the Third World grew at an average rate of 3.4 percent per year during the same period.

Many underlying structural weaknesses in the Arab economy hamper its ability to adjust to global change and meet the challenges of "peace" while protecting itself from adverse changes in the international economic environment. Throughout the 1970s and 1980s Arab economic success masked many structural problems that are now becoming more critical to future economic performance. The Arabs will have to deal with these structural difficulties before contemplating regional associations with more advanced and vibrant economies.

The most fundamental problem afflicting the Arab economy is its heavy (if not exclusive) direct and indirect dependence on rent from natural resources—namely, oil, which has propagated the "Arab Disease." This disease has raised the exchange values of most currencies in the region to the detriment of effective manufacturing exports, inflated the costs of production and undermined local industry and agriculture, flooded domestic markets with cheap imports that ultimately compromised the balance of payments of even the richest states, and engendered unsustainably high consumption patterns that are divorced from high production costs. It has encouraged investments in large projects that were often unnecessary and unproductive and ultimately saddled the economy with large maintenance costs, bloated domestic bureaucracies with overlapping rings of rent seekers, divorced income from production, and exposed domestic economies to the wide fluctuations of the world oil market over which the Arabs had little control.

It may be convenient to argue that the Arab economic difficulties in the 1980s can be explained totally by falling oil prices, but the truth is more complex. The fact that oil prices so adversely affect all economic indicators of performance is itself revealing. In this respect the heavy dependence on oil rents is symptomatic of general economic failure.

The Arab economy today remains almost as undiversified as it was in the 1970s: oil exports are still the exclusive economic engine of the region. Rentierism is a widespread phenomenon and is not restricted to the oil-rich countries. There is now a "secondary dependence" on oil revenues throughout the region. Exports of manufactured renewable commodities and services contribute only modestly to the external sources of finance of all Arab countries.

Non-oil producing Arab countries have exported labor to the Gulf and have enjoyed the convenience of remittances while neglecting the development of domestic exports. Manufacturing activity outside oil is limited, disarticulated, traditional, inward-looking, and technologically dependent on outside sources. Little or no technological capabilities have been developed within the region. There is strong preference for turnkey projects. Expenditures on research and development have been modest if not totally inconspicuous. Regional cooperation is a political slogan without any real economic transactions (until today, exclusive of oil, Arab regional trade is only 4 percent of their total international trade). Most Arab countries are linking to non-Arab economic centers with little or no concern for their Arab neighbors. External indebtedness is massive and is beginning to sap the energies of the region. The Arab region is still gambling on "sunset" industries and old Fordist and smokestack manufacturing activities. There is little evidence of the new economy in the industrial structures of most Arab economies. Domestic savings are inadequate; they rarely finance investment. High and unproductive consumption habits have been staunchly ingrained in the operating systems of most Arab societies. Illiteracy is still excessively high. Mean years of schooling have increased but remain far below other successful developing countries. Industrial policies are often too stringent or absent and there is a tendency to adopt IMF-peddled "policy fads" that are inappropriate for Arab development and values.

In short, dependency on the rent from oil has reduced Arab incentives to diversify their economies, develop alternative manufacturing capacities, promote export-oriented industries, encourage domestic savings, and anchor income on solid productivity grounds. Traditional economic activities and structures are maintained. Dependence on external sources of finance has deepened and economic performance has slipped. Although large oil revenues brought about significant improvements in health, education, and infrastructure throughout the Arab world, they diminished the incentive to capitalize on these achievements. Arab economic performance in the 1980s is symptomatic of the "Arab Disease" that is more fundamentally damaging than the "Dutch Disease" that afflicted Holland in the 1940s following the discovery and commercialization of natural gas. But Holland had fertile land, abundant water, a highly skilled labor force, and a European infrastructure and market.

For the Palestinians, the need for external sources of finance is urgent, but must be balanced against the negative and disastrous dependency on precarious international charity. They should avoid repeating the Arab experience in the 1970s and 1980s.

While water issues are still to be negotiated, all the agreements with Israel concluded so far do not augur for reasonable Palestinian control over this vital resource. There is a lot of discussion about "unitizing" the management of this "common" resource. Indeed, there are efficiencies in jointly managing this resource, but before any procedures are put in place it is critical that "property rights" be established. Agreement (Oslo I) after agreement (Paris Protocol and Oslo II) still treat Palestinian water as Israeli charity to the Palestinians.[1] Israel raises the share of the Palestinian allotment by a modest amount, presupposing Israeli exclusive control and management of the water. Peace will be credible and visible to the extent the Palestinians are able to reclaim their lost land and water. Even under Oslo II and in the last phase of the Agreement, the Palestinians will have authority over only one-third of their land and less than one-fifth of their water.

Dismantling the occupation should allow the Palestinians to manage their economic affairs as they choose and to protect and guide their economy in the manner they see as best serving their interests. The Paris Protocol makes sure that this shall not be the case. The Palestinian economy is put under the Israeli import and tax regimes. Fearing that the Palestinian economy may be used to smuggle duty-free goods into Israel or may act as a tax haven, Israel moved very quickly to impose its own tariff regime (the same tariffs on all foreign goods in both Palestine Authority territory and Israel). Few exceptions are allowed as an afterthought to provide some latitude for the Palestinians over goods imported from countries that do not trade with Israel. The rule is the Palestinians must impose the same tariffs on imports as the Israelis. These tariffs have evolved to protect and promote the Israeli economy, and are not consistent with the interest of a fledgling economy with limited productive capacity. The Palestinians received promises for smoother access to the Israeli market. But for now, quotas are imposed on Palestinian poultry, eggs, potatoes, cucumbers, tomatoes, and melons entering the Israeli market. Although the quotas in principle apply to exports from either side to the other, with the exception of melons these restrictions apply only to the Palestinians.

The price of these Protocols is even greater integration with the Israeli economy. What the Palestinians have worked out is a sort of a mix between a Customs Union and a Common Market with the Israelis. Any such arrangement generally involves "trade creation" and "trade diversion." One wonders whether giving the Israelis full and unimpeded access to the Palestinian market is good for their long-term prospects in building a diversified and productive economy. For all practical purposes, this agreement perpetuates and legitimates the economic structures that emerged under occupation. Accepting the "trade diversion" implications of the Agreement simply means that Palestinian Authority has preferred to tie its economic fortune to Israel rather than the Arabs. Did the Palestinian negotiators concluding this Agreement carefully think through all of its implications? I suspect not. It does not appear to be consistent with their interest in accessing the wider and less competitive Arab markets.

Defenders of the agreements often quote the many advantages that economic theory generally predicts will follow from freer trade. The general belief is that smaller and poorer countries are supposed to gain most from access to the market of richer partners. Missing from this argument are many factors and conditions upon which the theory is built that are present in the

Palestinian reality. Economists tend to exaggerate the spread effects of free trade and underrepresent its "backwash effects" and adjustment costs (Kubursi 1997).

Actually, bargaining theory is perhaps more clear and more realistic about the outcomes of negotiations among unequal partners. It predicts that the party with most options is likely to dictate its interests on the party with little or no options. It does not stretch the imagination much to suggest that all the agreements concluded so far between the Israelis and Palestinians have been concluded between grossly unequal partners.

We are told that Palestinian gains will be from the dynamics of foreign investment, large tourism flows, and higher productivity that springs from competing with more advanced competitors. But it is precisely in these areas that the Arabs will lose most. There is the expectation that foreign investment will be attracted to the region and that peace will encourage a larger flow and a more certain attraction. That indeed is likely to be the case. But much, if not all, of this investment will likely go to the Israelis. Much of the foreign investment that is taking place today is of the tariff-jumping kind. The more custom unions the Israelis succeed in drawing in the region and the more clauses they eliminate from the Arab Boycott, the more foreign investment will be attracted to Israel.

The Arab Boycott was very costly for the Israelis. Some estimates put the cost at $40 billion over the past four decades. I believe it may have been even higher if one were to include the amount of foreign investment that Israel could have attracted and if one were to adopt a real present value approach.

The Israelis have increasingly become concerned about the nature of their dependence on foreign aid from the United States. As pressures mount to balance the monumental U.S. federal budget, foreign aid will most likely be on the chopping block, and Israel currently claims the lion's share of foreign aid. Peace will give Israel some breathing space; it will postpone the cutting but not the cut. Foreign investment of the order of $3 to $4 billion will be the only reliable alternative. Israel has not been very successful in attracting foreign investment in the past ($200 million per year on average). An end to the Arab Boycott and a few customs unions ensuring unimpeded access to Arab markets will change Israel's picture dramatically. It is already changing. In 1996 Israel was successful in raising more than $1.7 billion in foreign investment. Motorola, Volkswagen, Cable and Wireless, Intel, and many other high-tech firms have plans to locate in Israel. And Israel's gain here could easily be the Arabs' loss (see, e.g., *The New York Times*, August 19, 1995).

Foreign investment in the Arab region has drastically declined from the high levels of the 1950s. The share of the region in total world foreign investment is now less than 3 percent (Page 1995). Access to world markets, new technology, advanced management systems, and large investments are almost the exclusive preserve of the multinational corporations. The Palestinians will be ill advised not to take advantage of the current favorable international climate to host and attract foreign investment. There are abundant examples, however, of multinationals that exploit the local market, wrestle concessions that far outweigh their positive contributions, and provide little or no transfer of technology. It is invariably the case that positive net benefits from foreign investment were derived by enlightened governments that obstinately negotiated favorable terms from multinationals that included product mandates, home base operations, and systematic technology transfer. In the absence of a representative national government and wider Arab cooperation, the Palestinians are in a weak position to negotiate favorable terms. Besides, their chances of getting a respectable share of foreign investment could depend critically on their guaranteed access to the wider Arab market. The more the Palestinians tie their economic fortunes to the Israelis, the less likely that they will be able to derive concessions from their Arab brethren in this regard.

Greece, which is an hour's flying time from Palestine, attracts 12 million international tourists a year. Israel attracts no more than 2 million. With peace, international tourism is likely to increase rapidly. The Arab region is not well prepared for this influx. Tourism infrastructure in the Arab world is limited and international linkages are almost absent. Lebanon used to have a competitive tourism infrastructure but that was destroyed in the civil war. Today it is not even sufficient to meet the demand of returning Lebanese visitors. Egypt is the only Arab country with the capacity to benefit from the increased flow, but its share of the total is not certain.

The bottom line in tourism is length of stay. The longer tourists stay in a country the more they spend and the larger the benefits from tourism to the host country. Under the prevailing circumstances, even under peace, without sufficient planning and preparation, the rewards of this tourism bonanza will be lost by the Arabs who may even lose existing tourism as Israel may succeed in diverting tourists away from traditional Arab tourist centers (e.g., tourists from Gulf states may visit Israel instead of Lebanon or Egypt.)

The potential rewards from increased tourism are there and would be more certain with proactive preparation and planning. A concerted Arab tourism strategy is required to mount joint marketing and advertising campaigns and to connect tourism flows. In the absence of proactive planning, Israel will be the only beneficiary of increased numbers of tourists and will determine how long they stay, how much they spend, and where they spend their dollars. The Arabs will get at most daytrippers or safari-like visits where foreign tourists will simply pass by Arab areas. The Jordanians are already experiencing some of these negative effects.

For every dollar spent on education in the Arab world $166 is spent on defense. If peace were to be just and enduring, there could be substantial savings in wasteful military expenditures. The Middle East has the dubious distinction of having the highest military expenditures shares to GDP than any other region in the world. Of the ten largest military spenders, seven countries are in the Middle East. Israel has already reduced defense expenditures from 22 percent of GNP before the Camp David Agreement to the current 10 percent. Israel will benefit far more than the Arabs from the reallocation of resources away from the military given the high differential average productivity of the resources in the military in Israel and in the Arab world (Kubursi 1981).

Israeli exports correspond very closely to Arab imports. My own calculation of the concordance indices (indices of structural similarity of trade composition by commodity) shows that the degree of Israeli concordance with Saudi, Iraqi, Syrian, etc., trade is twice as large as the corresponding indices with Europe or the U.S. My estimates suggest a doubling of Israeli exports under peace.

In the past two years Israel has experienced trade surpluses due to increased trade with China, India, and Japan—countries that would not have dared to do business with Israel before the new arrangements with the Palestinians were in place.

Conclusion

Israel's "peace dividend potential" is massive while Palestinian and Arab gains are conditional, precarious, and highly illusive. The peace agreements concluded so far not only guarantee Israel all the economic benefits it derived under occupation, but also open new trade vistas, allow for reduced defense expenditures, dismantle the Arab boycott, and attract new foreign investment and increased international tourism.

There is no level playing field between the Palestinians or the Arabs and the Israelis. The agreements reflect the vertical organization of power in existence. What is concluded under duress cannot last. The interest of peace calls for immediate and unconditional independence of the Palestinians and an Arab cooperation strategy. It is only then that the Palestinians can be expected to conclude meaningful, symmetrical, and lasting agreements. Arabs who are watching both the Israelis and the Palestinians are not encouraged. Israel is using its superior bargaining power to wrestle enormous concessions from the Palestinians and now from the Jordanians. This is to be expected from dis-jointed Arab bargaining. Unfortunately, the only way to correct the situation will be to start over. This is admittedly difficult. But the Arabs must make the painful economic adjustments and true reforms (stemming from the ingrained rentierism from the operating systems of their economy and society by balancing production and consumption, increasing the share of the new economy, improving productivity and efficiency of enterprises, relying on market determined exchange rates, harmonizing tariffs and fiscal/monetary policies with their neighbors and opening their economies to international trade) that their dependence on oil have allowed them to postpone before they contemplate joining any regional arrangement with more advanced economies.

First among the pressing needs is the formation of more meaningful regional economic groupings among the Arabs (Fertile Crescent countries, Maghrib countries, etc.) that can create true dynamic gains in productivity and export performance. Drawing on the many lessons of regional economic coop-eration programs around the world, Arab economic integration programs will work best when they proceed slowly and cumulatively, preferably starting with sectoral arrangements among a symmetrical and contiguous grouping of coun-tries. These arrangements also require that trade creation objectives supersede or go hand in hand with trade diversion, a compensation mechanism to smoothe the adjustment processes in the weaker economies, and a democratic process that involves the wide participation of the population at large in its sup-port. They will be sustainable when efficiency considerations do not subordi-nate equity concerns since membership is likely to expand and solidify when member countries feel that they are treated fairly; when investment liberaliza-tion is an important plank of trade liberalization; when there are chances for redeployment of industry and wide-range intra-industry trade and specializa-tion; when external forces are accommodating, and when a principal mem-ber(s) has a strong political commitment to its success.

Once the Arabs succeed in restructuring and rebalancing their economies they will be ready for joining the world wide movement toward trade and investment liberalization be it within the framework of multilateral agreements or regional ones. The Euro-Mediterranean project suffers from the same diffi-culties and weaknesses that characterize the New Middle East project. The fact that there is more than one project from which to choose should give the Arabs room to maneuver. At present the only strategic option for them is to avoid being dragged away from each other.

Endnotes

1. The Paris Protocol is formally "Protocol on Economic Relations Between Israel and the PLO as Representing the Palestinian People." It is incorporated as Annex IV in the Cairo Agreement signed on May 4, 1994.

References

The Association of Peace. *The Middle East in the Year 2000.* Tel Aviv, 1970.

Abd Al-Fadil, Mahmoud. "The Middle Eastern Free Trade Area: A Sceptical Note." in L. Blin and Ph. Fargue, eds. *The Economy of Peace in the Middle East.* vol. 1. Paris: Maisonneuve et Larouse, CEDEJ, 1995.

Al-Dajani, Burhan. "Economic Relations Among the Arab Countries." Cairo: Institute of Arab Research and Studies, The Arab League, 1966, 63.

Al-Ghandur, Ahmad. "Arab Economic Integration." Cairo: Institute of Research and Studies, The Arab League, 1970, 157.

Al-Imam, Muhammad. "A Hebrew Bazaar for the Middle East: Collapse of the Foundations." *Awraq al-sharq al-awsat* 12 (July 1994), 38–58.

Al-Khawli, Lutfi. "Arabs, Yes: and Middle Eastern Also!" Cairo: Al-Ahram Centre for Translation and Publication, 1994, 192.

Amsden, Alice, *Asia's Next Giant: South Korea and Late Industrialization.* New York: Oxford University Press, 1989.

Arnon, A., and J. Weinblatt. "Trade Potential Between Israel, the Palestinians and Jordan." *Discussion Paper* 10.94 (In Hebrew). Jerusalem: Bank of Israel, July 1994.

Avineri, S. "Sidestepping Dependancy." *Foreign Affairs* (July-August 1994).

Awwad, Fuad Hashim. "The Use of Arab Oil Revenues Until the End of the 1970's." Cairo: Institute of Arab Research and Studies, 1977, 214.

Balassa, Bela and Ardy Stout J. Sdijk. "Economic Integration Among Developing Countries." *Journal of Common Market Studies* 14 (September 1975).

Ben Chaim, M. "Potential Trade Between Israel and Its Arab Neighbours." Tel Aviv: The Armand Hammer Fund for Economic Cooperation in the Middle East, Tel Aviv University, 1993.

Brown, D.K., A. V. Deardorff and R. M. Stern. "A North American Free Trade Agreement: Analytical Issues and a Computational Assessment." *The World Economy* 15 (1992a).

Brown, D.K., A. V. Deardorff and R. M. Stern. "North American Integration." *The Economic Journal* 102 (November 1992b).

Diwan, I., and M. Walton. "The Economy of the West Bank and Gaza: From Dependent to Autonomous Growth." *Finance and Development*, September 1994.

Fishlow, A. and S. Haggard. *The United States and Regionalisation of the World Economy.* Paris: Organization for Economic Cooperation and Development, 1992.

Fukasaku, K. *Economic Regionalisation and Intra-Industry Trade: Pacific-Asian Perspectives.* Paris: OECD Development Centre, 1992.

Halevi, N. *Trade Relations Between Israel and Jordan: Considerations and Prospects.* Tel Aviv: The Pinhas Sapir Center for Development and the Armand Hammer Fund for Economic Cooperation in the Middle East, 1994.

Halevi, N. and E. Kleiman. "Israeli-Jordanian Trade Relations: Alternatives and Recommendations." Tel Aviv: Pinhas Saphir Center for Development and the Armand Hammer Fund for Economic Cooperation in the Middle East, 1994.

Hirsh, Seev. "Trade Regimes in the Middle East" in G. Fishelson, ed., *Economic Cooperation in the Middle East.* Boulder, CO: Westview Press, 1989.

Hirsh, S., I. Ayal and G. Fishelson. "The Arab-Israeli Trade Potential: Methodological Considerations and Examples." Working Paper 7.95. Tel Aviv: The Israel Institute of Business Research, Tel Aviv University, March 1995.

Institute for Social and Economic Policy in the Middle East. *NEEP1: Near East Economic Progress Report.* Cambridge, MA, March 1994(a).

Institute for Social and Economic Policy in the Middle East. *NEEP1: Near East Economic Progress Report.* Cambridge, MA, September 1994(b).

Institute for Social and Economic Policy in the Middle East. *Securing Peace in the Middle East: Project on Economic Transition*, Cambridge, MA, 1993.

Kennedy, Paul. *Preparing for the Twenty-First Century.* New York: Harper Collins, 1994.

Kleiman, Ephraim. "Geography, Culture and Religion, and Middle East Trade Patterns." Working Paper 262. Jerusalem: Hebrew University, June 1992.

———. "Israeli Challange and Arab Response." ESCWA Working Paper, 1995.

"The Economic Provisions of the Agreement Between Israel and the PLO." Working Paper 300. Jerusalem: Hebrew University, February 1995.

Kubursi, Atif. *The Economic Consequences of the Camp David Agreements*, Beirut: Institute for Palestine Studies; Kuwait City: Kuwait Chamber of Commerce and Industry, 1981.

———. "Israeli Challange and Arab Response." ESCWA Working Paper, 1995.

———. "Economic Exchange Under Asymmetrical Options: The Challenge of Peace with Israel." Economic and Social Commission for West Asia, June 1997.

Langhammer, R.J. " The Developing Countries and Regionalism." *Journal of Common Market Studies*, 30:2 (1992), 212.

Lawrence, Robert Z. "Regionalism: An Overview." *Journal of the Japanese and International Economies* 8 (1994).

Nawfal, Said. "Joint Arab Activity in the International Field." Cairo: Institute of Arab Research and Studies, The Arab League, 1971, 283.

Page, John, "Economic Prospects and the Role of Foreign Development Finance Institutions." in *Regional Economic Development in the Middle East: Opportunities and Risks.* Washington, DC: The Center for Policy Analysis on Palestine, 1995, 5–17.

Peres, Shimon and Arye Naor. *The New Middle East.* New York: Henry Holt & Company, 1993.

Shafik, Nemat . "Learning from Doers: Lessons on Regional Integration for the Middle

East." World Bank. Paper presented at a Conference on Economic Cooperation in the Middle East: Prospects and Challenges, Cairo, May 14–16, 1994.

Sapir, Andre. "Regional Integration in Europe." *The Economic Journal* 102 (November 1992).

Yamazawa, Ippei. "On Pacific Economic Integration." *The Economic Journal* 102 (November 1992).

Index